InterActive Marketing

How to use integrated offer-driven advertising, database marketing and sales promotion to create maximum action

To my parents, my wife Jenny, our son Jamie, and the memory of my friend Matt Stogdon, killed in Bosnia on 30 September 1993, while serving with Scottish European Aid.

InterActive Marketing

How to use integrated offer-driven advertising, database marketing and sales promotion to create maximum action

Martin Williams FCIM, FAIM, FAMI, DIP M

PRENTICE HALL

• Sydney • Melbourne • New York • London • Singapore •
• Auckland • Mexico City • Amsterdam • Toronto •

Acquisitions Editor: Pat Evans
Production Editor: Fiona Marcar
Typeset by: Vantage Graphics, Chippendale NSW

Printed in Australia by Star Printery, Erskineville, NSW
1 2 3 4 5 98 97 96 95 94

National Library of Australia
Cataloguing-in-Publication Data

Williams, Martin
InterActive Marketing

Includes index.
ISBN 0 7248 1094 3.

1. Sales promotion. 2. Selling. 3. Marketing. I. Title.
658.82

Prentice Hall, Inc., *Englewood Cliffs, New Jersey*
Prentice Hall Canada, Inc., *Toronto*
Prentice Hall Hispanoamericana, SA, *Mexico*
Prentice Hall of India Private Ltd, *New Delhi*
Prentice Hall International, Inc., *London*
Prentice Hall of Japan, Inc., *Tokyo*
Prentice Hall of Southeast Asia Pty Ltd, *Singapore*
Editora Prentice Hall do Brasil Ltda, *Rio de Janeiro*

Prentice Hall
A division of Simon & Schuster

This book is based on the belief that interactive marketing incorporating an offer is the way to achieve the highest sales levels in the 1990s. The market circumstances of your product—its pricing, competition, distribution and positioning in the market—will dictate the value of the offer and hence the levels of expenditure needed to generate above-average interest and response. Your target market will always consider a really good offer if its perceived value outweighs the effort and trouble that has to be expended to take advantage of it.

Foreword

Every year it seems to get tougher and tougher for marketers.

There's less time to think, less money to achieve results—yet those results are expected to improve every year.

The luxury of experiment is fast vanishing. Today you are expected to get the answer right first time, every time.

That is why a book like this is so valuable. It gives you the answers. Try an experiment. Turn at random to any page—as I did. You are pretty certain to find some advice, a checklist or a relevant example. Stuff you can put to work immediately.

So I cordially recommend this book. Not least because, in addition to the practical virtues I have mentioned, it's well written and remarkably free of meaningless jargon and marketing mumbo jumbo.

Drayton Bird
Managing Director, Drayton Bird Direct
Author of *Commonsense Direct Marketing*
London, September 1993.

About the Series

The Competitive Edge Management Series is a joint publishing venture between the Australian Institute of Management NSW Training Centre and Prentice Hall Australia Pty Ltd. Books published in the Series will provide today's practical managers with the skills and insights they need to achieve a competitive edge in the marketplace. The Series will enable Australian authors and their scholarship to be published to appropriate markets by using the resources of these two organisations. Enquiries about books in this Series or information regarding the submission of manuscripts should be directed to either partners in this venture.

Other books in the Series

Telephone Skill Builder for Sales and Service Professionals
by Geoff Clynes
Reglomania: The Curse of Organisational Reform and How to Cure it
by Roy Gilbert
How to Write Your Business Plan: Workbook and Tapes
by Don Vogelaar
Know Your Customers: Using Practical Market Research for Profit
by Don Vogelaar
Crystal Clear Communication: Skills for Understanding and Being Understood
by Kris Cole
Making it Happen: Managing Performance at Work
by Murray Ainsworth & Neville Smith
Good Service is Good Business: 7 Simple Strategies for Success
by Catherine DeVrye
Down-to-Earth Strategic Planning
by Neville Smith

Contents

Preface

Never before have marketers gazed out upon such a changing scene. The mass market is breaking up into small, hard-to-reach groups. National TV is losing its magic and its audiences. Late night and 24-hour shopping are revolutionising consumer buying patterns. Scanning and retailer information systems are giving retailers more control than manufacturers over stock levels and displays—while more and more shelf space is going to private label house brands.

Many manufacturers are trying to respond with heavy price cutting that is eroding brand values and returning few benefits. Attempting to reach a mass market through traditional media is becoming more expensive and less effective. And in the near future, it will be even more so—when new technology creates a proliferation of channels, far greater audience fragmentation and interactive media with all its two-way communication potential. Those developments will forever change consumers from passive recipients of advertising messages to controllers who choose the nature and time of the message they receive.

Adding value to the product

As these changes render old ways obsolete, what can marketers do to regain the initiative?

'Nationally advertised brands have got to find new ways to add value to the product without adding materially to the production cost, cut waste in advertising and promotion and improve communication with prime prospects and wavering customers,' say Tom Collins and Stan Rapp in their book *The Great Marketing Turnaround.*[1]

Adding value to the product through what I call *interactive* or *offer-driven marketing* is, I believe, the first step. The product or service is only one part of a satisfying solution to a consumer need. People will respond to an offer that, together with the product or service, represents total value beyond their expectations.

The second step is to take full advantage of modern databases. Their rapidly growing capacities are leading us into an age of almost one-to-one communication—and opening up mindblowing marketing possibilities in the process.

The third step is to recognise that the age of what we might call 'biblical' marketing—the left hand not knowing what the right hand was doing—are over. Back in the 1970s, as diagram 1 suggests[2], advertising, PR, sales promotion, direct mail and so on all tended to happen in separate boxes. There was little or no joint planning or even a search for a common creative theme.

Point of Sale	**Merchandising**	**Telephone Sales**	**Sales Motivation**
Research + New Product Development	**Advertising**	**Public Relations**	**Salesforce**
Mail Order	**Sales Promotion**	**Events Marketing**	**Sponsorship**

Diagram 1 1970s separate boxes 'pigeon-holed' marketing

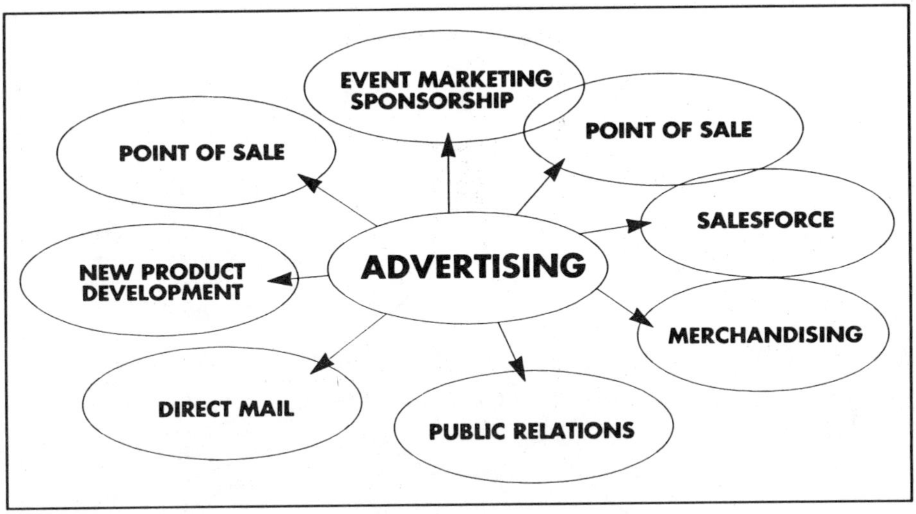

Diagram 2 1980s marketing—from isolation towards integration

In the 1980s, this pigeon-hole approach started to break down. Inventive marketers experimented with some overlapping of techniques as shown in diagram 2. Many found that the further they went in this direction, the better results they achieved.

The way ahead

Their pioneering efforts opened up what I believe is the way ahead in the 1990s. Interactive Marketing—a seamless, fully integrated blend of marketing techniques, including sales promotion and direct marketing, all built around one big idea, and using the latest technology to deliver the message and receive a response (diagram 3).

The 'Big Idea' will form the basis of the integrated strategy, which will be offer-driven, database-empowered and expressed appropriately through every medium and marketing technique.

Achieving that integration will not be easy for all companies. It sometimes flies in the face of corporate culture, structures and operational procedures. But it will have to be done—or the company will fall into step with the other non-adaptable dinosaurs that perished before it.

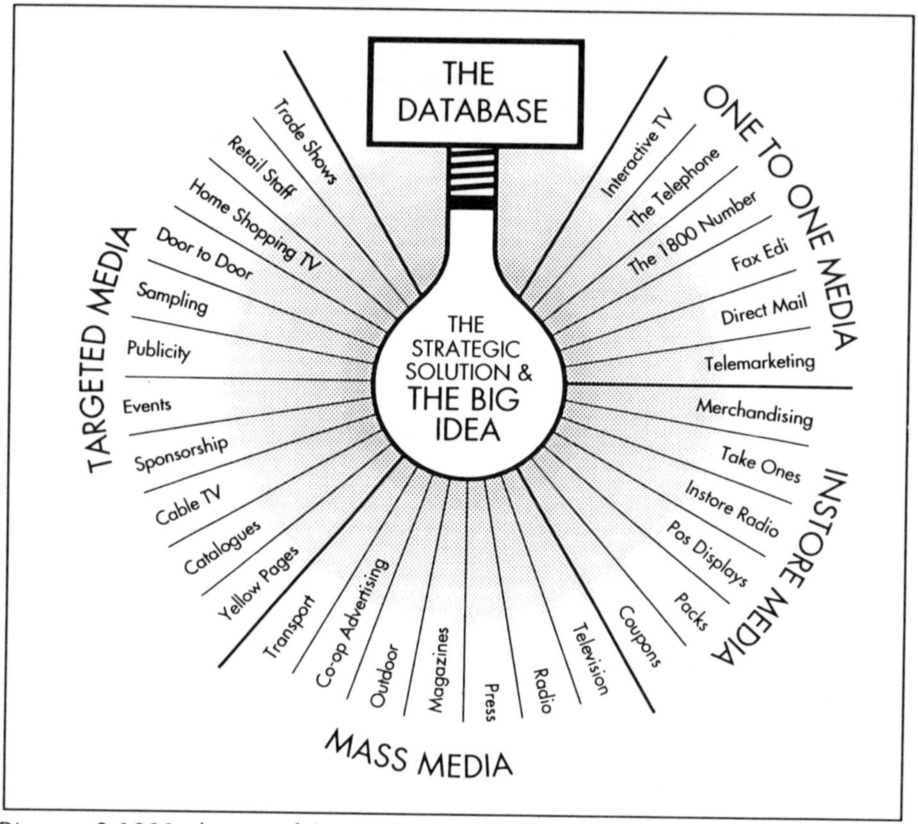

Diagram 3 1990s the age of the database and 'seamless' integrated communications

Sales promotion the hero

In this new integrated, interactive environment, sales promotion may well prove to be the most important strand of all. It's the sales promotion offer that inserts a 'don't-miss-this-opportunity' note of urgency into the sale. Above all, it's offer-driven sales promotion that provides a real reason to buy product A instead of product B, when the two share similar features and attributes.

There's considerable evidence that the importance of sales promotion is becoming increasingly recognised. More and more companies, organisations, retailers and even government utilities are using offer-driven strategies, to achieve goals ranging from sales increases to faster collection of rates.

The growing significance of offer-driven sales promotion is underlined by a remarkable change in the make-up of marketing budgets. As recently as the mid-1980s, the typical marketing budget was 90% advertising and 10% promotion. Today it's much more likely to be a 50%–50% split, if not 60%–40% in favour of sales promotional expenditure. In fact, *Advertising Age* estimates 65% of all marketing dollars in the USA are now spent on 'non-traditional' media.[3]

A shift like that in such a short time represents a quantum leap in marketing attitudes. And it's happening here in Australia, as well as in the USA and in Europe, for one simple reason. Sales promotion offers work. In product category after product category, they are delivering solid, measurable, bottom-line results of a kind and to a degree that traditional advertising can rarely match. Sales promotion techniques are being used on their own to achieve marketing goals. They are being brought into media advertising campaigns to increase the advertising's effectiveness and accountability. They are being blended with direct marketing activities to add extra impact and immediacy. They are creating traffic at point of sale, maximising awareness there and stimulating impulse purchases. In a host of different ways and situations, sales promotion is breaking new ground and getting very impressive results.

Groping after a definition

What exactly, you may ask, do we mean by 'sales promotion'? That's a good question. As the discipline grows rapidly in popularity and usage, several practitioners have attempted a definition. Interestingly, although they certainly know what sales promotion can do, few appear to agree on precisely what it is—a dilemma also faced, I've noticed, by direct marketers.

Most leading sales promotion practitioners in Australia, the UK, Europe and the USA belong to the Council of Sales Promotion Agencies (CSPA). CSPA members have spent innumerable hours in an effort to define their profession better. No doubt because of their committee process, they finally came up with a definition that, to me, reads more like a mission statement. It is:

'The act of influencing customer/consumer perception and behaviour to build market share and sales which reinforces brand image.'[4]

Obviously, one of their intentions was to overcome the idea that sales promotions are nothing but short-term sales support programmes. Today, as we'll see in this book, they can be much more than that. But one of the clear weaknesses in the CSPA definition is that it could equally apply to media advertising, direct marketing or virtually any other sales-building activity. It contains no dimension that is exclusive to sales promotion alone.

A step further

In his book *Sales Promotion in Action*, the late Christian Petersen went a step further and, I think, supplied that exclusive dimension.[5] Rather than defining sales promotion exactly, he preferred to put forward elements that should be incorporated in a definition. These, he wrote, were:

- a featured offer;
- tangible advantage(s) not inherent in a product or service;
- the achievement of marketing objectives.

He emphasised the points that the offer has to be tangible (as against the intangible advantages frequently offered in advertising), and that it must not be inherent in the product or service. A simple example would be '10% off—this week only!' That's a tangible offer, but not a benefit that the product or service offers automatically as part of its nature.

Even Petersen's contribution, however, doesn't give us a wide enough definition. Sales promotion is more than a technique to persuade customers to buy. It can also be a way to motivate the trade to increase stocks and to drive the sales force to sell more vigorously.

A still broader definition, then, would include these aspects:

- *As a featured offer:* Sales promotion presents *tangible advantages* not inherent in the product or service, and which are designed to achieve specific marketing objectives.
- *As a motivation:* Sales promotion is *a way to achieve greater sales*, and to motivate others to sell more, mount displays, increase stocks or learn more about a product or service.

- *As a communication:* Sales promotion is *a means by which marketers draw attention* to a product or service, for a specified period.

That, I suppose, could be wrapped up in one definition, as follows:

Sales promotion is any marketing activity that creates a benefit over and above a product's or service's normal features and conditions of sale, which achieves an immediate sales increase or motivates the sales force, retailers or other interested parties to sell more, mount displays, increase stocks or learn more about the product or service.

That is, I know, a very long and clumsy sentence. In their comprehensive book *Sales Promotion Management*, Don E. Schultz and William A. Robinson boil the definition down to this:

> 'Sales promotion is a direct inducement or incentive to the sales force, the distributor or the consumer, with the primary objective of creating an immediate sale.'[6]

An old boss of mine, Alan Toop (whose penetrating ideas we'll meet again in this book), deliberately avoids definition-creating altogether. In his book *European Sales Promotion—Great Campaigns in Action*, he simply says that sales promotion covers a very broad spectrum of marketing activities.[7] He adds that general statements about sales promotion are difficult to make with accuracy and precision—and to be valid, they are best assessed pragmatically! Well, maybe so. But I still think a definition is possible and desirable. For the record, here's mine:

> 'Sales promotion is an offer-driven marketing activity that creates a benefit over and above the intrinsic value of the normal conditions of sale of a product or service, and which induces an immediate effect on sales.'

To me, at any rate, that sums up as pithily as I can just what the exciting, frustrating, challenging, demanding—and potentially highly rewarding—profession of sales promotion is all about, within a total interactive marketing environment.

The differences

Our understanding of the discipline will probably be strengthened even further if we take a moment to consider the differences between sales promotion and other marketing tools.

Direct marketing, for instance, has been well defined by Drayton Bird in his excellent book *Commonsense Direct Marketing*. He calls it 'any advertising activity which creates and exploits a direct relationship between you and your prospect or customer as an individual'.[8] When you think of sales promotion as basically an offer-driven affair—a marketing activity focused on a specific offer that's not an intrinsic product benefit—the difference is clear. Another distinction is that, while sales promotion can be directed very specifically to individuals (as it is when linked with direct marketing programmes), it is less likely than direct marketing to be totally personalised. Nor, in most cases, does it go on as direct marketing does to build a personal relationship with individual customers.

Its difference from other communication tools is even more marked. Media advertising, for instance, speaks to people en masse and not as individuals. Its purpose is to predispose people towards a particular product before they reach the point of purchase. PR has a different purpose again—to create a favourable climate of opinion around a product or service, by obtaining free media time or space through techniques such as press releases, press kits, media conferences and product launches.

The job of sales promotion, on the other hand, is to produce an immediate effect on sales by communicating the offer—the 'big idea' that's not intrinsic to the product and motivates people to buy promptly or more frequently. Sometimes, the sales promotion idea is so strong that it does become a permanent part of the brand proposition. Ronald McDonald House, for instance, started as a sales promotion and has now become an essential component of the product offering. This phenomenon happens when consumers virtually demand it in return for their continued custom.

Of course, it's one thing to ponder the nature of sales promotion and to work out a definition of it. Turning the definition into action is quite another. Combining sales promotion with other techniques to create an integrated interactive marketing package is something else again. But there are many proven ways of achieving both those aims. An offer, or a series of offers, is at the heart of them all. And this book explains how to use them to the best—and most profitable—effect.

Who should read this book?

If you're a marketing student, you'll find this book of great value. It will introduce you to the subject of interactive marketing, which includes sales promotion, offer-driven advertising and direct marketing—a total concept as yet inadequately covered by text books. Furthermore, if you join a marketing or sales department, you're likely to cut your marketing teeth on interactive marketing activities—and if you know how to maximise their potential in all media and communication channels, you'll have a tremendous opportunity to make a pretty massive mark at a very early stage of your career.

However, this book is not just for students. Far from it. It's equally as relevant to everybody now engaged in any aspect of selling goods and services. People in marketing and sales. People in advertising agencies, sales promotion agencies and the media. People in the expanding fields of direct marketing, database marketing and telemarketing. People engaged in the printing and supply of sales promotion material and literature. Even those people working behind the scenes in marketing systems, data processing and fulfilment—because they need to know how their work can help build their organisations' sales and profits.

In short, this book is for everyone who believes 'the customer is king'.

How this book can help you

In the 22 chapters ahead, we'll take a detailed look at just about every known interactive marketing and sales promotion technique. We'll see when and when not to use each one, based on what it can and can't do. We'll examine many case histories that demonstrate each technique's potential. We'll look at the pitfalls as well as the possibilities of each. We'll see how imagination and a 'big idea' can make every technique vastly more effective—and how, if the idea is big enough, it can travel the world with very little modification.

First, in our **Introduction**, we look at an overview of the whole subject. Then we start our journey proper in **Chapter 1**, where we assess the current retail scene—and learn that, while some special factors affect the Australian situation, the basic pressures for change are much the same the world over.

Chapter 2 takes us right into the store—to point of sale. This is the crucial place where the sale is lost or won. Here we look at different ways of creating impact, attracting attention and maximising the selling opportunity—and of tapping the huge potential of impulse sales.

The most popular weapon in the sales promotion armoury—sweepstakes—occupies us in **Chapters 3** and **4**. Sweepstakes may be the most widely used sales promotion technique of all, but it's possible to make them even more productive. These chapters show you how.

In **Chapter 5**, cartoon characters and super heroes take centre stage. We look at character licensing, and how to use it for best results.

Of all the rewards sales promotion can give a consumer, money is the most welcomed. **Chapter 6** probes the ins and outs of cashbacks and shareouts, and explains how to balance a high response rate with cost-effective sales.

Chapter 7 examines one of the most powerful media at your disposal—your pack. The chapter not only considers what has been and is being done, but encourages you to think how it could be done better.

In **Chapters 8** and **9**, we look at the use of premiums as a reward for purchase. We assess the value of the various varieties—free in-pack, on-pack, near-pack and self-liquidating. The technique can be a very profitable one—but as we see, it's fraught with minefields you need to know about. And avoid.

Coupons are one of the oldest sales promotion techniques around. Now, however, the latest database technology is giving them stunning new possibilities—especially in the retail field, where sales promotion and direct marketing methods are merging. We examine the new roles of 'smart' and 'dumb' coupons and clubs in **Chapter 10**.

Without doubt, the most effective way to get trial of your product is to put a sample in your customer's hands. Sampling is now a highly targeted exercise that can pin-point households with minimum waste. **Chapter 11** tells you how to go about it.

Chapter 12 is a composite—a collection of nine miscellaneous sales-boosting techniques that don't fit into any other categories, yet aren't quite detailed enough to warrant chapters of their own. Gathered together, they make this a chapter that will repay careful reading.

In the Middle Ages, the patronage of wealthy individuals enabled penniless but brilliant artists and composers to produce masterpieces, and add lustre to their patrons' names. The same principle applies today—only now we call it 'sponsorship'. How to use sporting, artistic and even scientific sponsorships most profitably is the subject of **Chapter 13**.

In **Chapter 14**, we go into an area of great profit potential—using the media to extend your brand proposition. This can involve event creation and management, PR, media-backed contests, advertising—even tie-ins with the story lines of TV soapies. We also cover interactive media techniques, interactive TV and home shopping. The possibilities for ground-breaking offer-driven creativity and big sales boosts with these techniques are almost endless.

Everyone likes the warm inner glow that comes from supporting a worthwhile cause. **Chapter 15** explains how cause-related marketing can give people that happy experience—and sell a lot of product for you as well.

We tackle a very big subject in **Chapter 16**. Sales incentive programmes are sales promotion events in themselves, targeted at the sales force and motivating them through compelling offers to new heights of effort. The chapter gives many examples of successful sales incentive operations, plus guidelines on how to construct them.

Business gifts and customer incentives are the first cousins of sales incentive programmes. In **Chapter 17**, we look at how they can be employed to best effect—and how to choose the ones that tie-in most effectively with your brand, yet deliver maximum satisfaction and incentive to your customer.

Chapter 18 covers one of the fastest-developing selling concepts of our time—relationship marketing. We look at the beginnings of an integration between direct marketing and sales promotion. We see how databases are helping both to work together to win customers and build their loyalty. We examine the concept of a customer's 'lifetime value'. We also probe the workings of frequent buyer clubs, as they strive to keep consumers committed to a brand for long periods of time.

Keeping track of your customers' preferences is a vital part of relationship marketing. It's also the way to success in the 1990s for companies as diverse as retailers and financial institutions. **Chapter 19** looks at ways of using the latest technologies to give your customers what they want. It also examines cost-effective direct marketing techniques that will help you find new customers.

The new centrality of databases in marketing comes to the fore again in **Chapter 20**. Here it's linked with the telephone, which is now becoming this century's most potent marketing device. Together, databases and telephones can make sales forces more productive than ever before—and keep customers happier too. This chapter explains how it can be done.

Experience is perhaps the greatest teacher of all. Research enables you to learn from each promotion and make the next one even better. It's a vital yet much under-used key to sales promotion effectiveness. How to go about it in an offer-driven context is the theme of **Chapter 21**.

Finally, **Chapter 22** explores a vital subject—briefing your advertising, direct marketing or sales promotion agency, and evaluating their work. We see that, by following a distinct briefing sequence, you can get much better-than-average results from them. That in turn ensures you get maximum selling power from every dollar in your budget.

This book, then, is a comprehensive guide to all major interactive marketing techniques. It forms the basis for understanding successful offer-driven advertising, direct marketing and sales promotion strategies. Whether you're active in the industry or a student, it will give you ideas and insights you can't afford to be without—because in the next few years, interactive marketing will form an increasingly important part of your professional marketing life.

Notes

1. Stan Rapp and Tom Collins, *The Great Marketing Turnaround*, Prentice Hall, Inc., 1990, Englewood Cliffs, New Jersey.
2. This diagram has been developed from an idea of Alan Kuszinski's in an article in *Marketing Magazine*, June 1992, entitled *Beyond Advertising Towards Integration*, 1992, by Michael Kiely.
3. Editorial, *Advertising Age*, January 1993.
4. CSPA Minutes, Chicago Convention, 1992.

5. Christian Petersen, *Sales Promotion in Action*, Associated Business Press, 1979, London.
6. Don E. Shultz and William A. Robinson, *Sales Promotion Management*, Crain Books, 1982, Chicago.
7. Alan Toop, *European Sales Promotion—Great Campaigns in Action*, Kogan Page Ltd, 1992, London.
8. Drayton Bird, *Commonsense Direct Marketing (What is Direct Marketing?)*, p28. Kogan Page Ltd, 1989, London.

Acknowledgments

Many people contributed to this book—in some cases, unconsciously—over a long period of time.

Among them are some of my mentors and colleagues of the past. Without their influence, I would never have been in a position to write it. So, first of all, I want to thank James Hann, CBE, FCIM, who introduced me to the world of marketing; Alan Toop, FCIM, of the Sales Machine International, author of many books including *European Sales Promotion – Great Campaigns in Action*; Bob Bayley of Option One Integrated Communications, London; and David Sherbon of Sherbon Greenlaw Advertising, with whom I created my first promotional campaigns in Australia.

I'd also like to thank some others for what you might call general inspiration. These include Henry 'Pete' Hoke of Hoke Publications, whose magazine *Direct Marketing* provides constantly high quality news and information, and the educators quoted in this book—particularly Stan Rapp, James Rosenfield, Murray Raphel and Ernan Roman. I have benefited from attending some of their seminars in Australia, Switzerland and the USA.

To those more directly involved with the book, my thanks first of all to Drayton Bird for the Foreword. Many other people helped by reading part or all of the manuscript and commenting, correcting, suggesting and guiding. My thanks for this to Paul Blanket of The Blanket Partnership, and Visiting Fellow, Macquarie University and the University of New South Wales; Dieter Garbade of Roche Vitamins (who re-learned English in the process!); Gerry Grace of Grace Communications and a director of McDonald's; Tony Thirlwell, marketing director of the New South Wales Tourist Commission; Trish Berendson of Westpac Direct Marketing; Trish Manners of Rapp & Collins/DDB Needham; Tony Whiting, Marketing Director of J. B. Fairfax Pty Ltd; Max Hunt, Global Director of Seagrams Duty Free; Richard Flood; and Stephen Biss, whose retail input was invaluable. And my thanks must also go to those marketers who have allowed their more successful campaigns to be featured in this book.

My appreciation is also extended to the staff and clients of my company, Cartwright Williams Pty Ltd, whose work provided many of the case histories in this book. I'm particularly grateful to my partner Andrew Edwards, who willingly (apparently so, anyway) shouldered extra loads while the book preoccupied me.

Kate Baker, Christina Browne and Maree Kennedy keyed the early drafts and last minute revisions. My thanks to them, to Mike Chittenden, for the photographs and to Kevin Cosgrove for the front cover design.

A special word of thanks to Margaret Lynn, who spent night after long night keying the entire book. Her speed and skill advanced the publication date by weeks, if not months. Thanks, too, to my good friend and colleague Ross Meillon for considerable editorial help.

As well, I am indebted to those friends and colleagues who gave me encouragement, help and ideas. In particular, I would like to thank Jeff Brooks of Logos for supplying lists, Pat Evans, Julia King, Robyn Holt, Sharon Goldie, Vicki Hogan, Liz Courtney, Chris Adams, John Taylor, David Wylie, David Simmons, Hans Aigner, Phil Fagan, Mike Jagard, Michael Kiely, Geof Minter and Tony Anisimoff for his guidance on legal requirements.

My gratitude also goes to the many marketers and their legal counsels from all over the world who spent time sourcing and arranging approvals of their campaigns illustrated in this book.

Introduction

In the Preface, we noted that the sales promotion offer is probably the most important single strand of 1990s-style interactive marketing. Then we used up a page or two on the question of just what sales promotion is. After ploughing through a few definitions, we decided that the distinguishing feature of a sales promotion is that it offers a tangible reward over and above the normal benefits of a product or service.

That tangible offer-driven benefit within your advertising, direct marketing or sales promotion communication could take one of many forms. It might be a cashback, a price-off, extra product free, free valuable information, a chance to win an attractive prize, the satisfaction of helping a good cause or any of the many other techniques we'll examine in this book. It takes skill, insight and experience to choose the right technique for a particular product at a particular time—and to communicate the offer to the target market in the most cost-effective and compelling way.

Hopefully, by the time you finish this book, you'll have gone far towards acquiring the necessary skills and insights. The experience, unfortunately, is something you'll have to pick up for yourself.

Today, the supermarket. Tomorrow . . .

Sales promotion as we know it now really began at point of sale in supermarkets. Its earliest practitioners learnt how it works as they sought to move more fast-moving consumer goods off the shelves into shopping trolleys. In the last 25 years, however, sales promotion has widened its horizons immensely. While it's still very visible at point of sale—where it often takes over the role of the old-time salesperson—sales promotion is now found in all distribution methods and all media, selling every imaginable kind of product.

We see it associated with packaged goods, household appliances, consumer durables, transport, tourism, travel, the hospitality industry and many more. Increasingly, sales promotion is being used in the fiercely competitive fields of banking, insurance, financial services, housing and property. It enlists the selling support of children through devices like Kellogg's® in-pack toy models and Mickey Mouse soaps and toothbrushes. Governments are using it to persuade people to consume less and conserve energy. And the media themselves employ it widely to boost radio and TV audiences, and press and magazine circulations.

The enhancer

A sales promotion offer bobs up today in many campaigns that embrace a wide range of marketing tactics. In event marketing, it is often used to draw attention to the event, particularly in media extensions. In licensed character marketing, it can make the character more relevant to the product. In sponsorships, it can dramatise the connection between the product and the sponsorship activity. In sales incentive schemes, it provides the essential motivation that makes the schemes work. In direct marketing, the sales promotion offer brings the prospect closer to the sale. And in offer-driven press and magazine advertisements, it adds interest, prolongs the time the reader spends in considering the proposition and generates a higher level of immediate response. In many ways, the sales promotion offer can be used to enhance and strengthen other marketing tactics, and increase both their short- and long-term impact.

® Registered Trademark Kellogg (Aust) Pty Ltd, Authorised User

The missing link

One of sales promotion's most effective arenas is still the one where it all began—at point of sale. There, sales promotion can form the missing link between product and consumer. It can heighten product interest, maximise awareness and direct store traffic to your display. It can create impulse purchase from brand loyalists and infrequent buyers alike. It can stimulate trial and repeat purchase, encourage customers to move up to larger sizes, persuade them to buy more profitable products and motivate brand switching. It can also be used tactically, to cut across competitors' efforts to increase their brand share.

Most importantly, the sales promotion offer can help win your brand a strong shelf presence at the right eye height and in sufficient volume to obtain shelf facings and additional in-store displays. By encouraging the trade to buy, it can substantially increase stocking and widen distribution.

Sales promotion can achieve these and many other marketing goals, using a variety of reward techniques from couponing to sweepstakes to plastic cards. What's more, it can do so measurably and very cost-efficiently.

Blurring the boundaries

It's perhaps ironic that, just when sales promotion is growing so rapidly, the boundaries between it and other marketing disciplines are becoming blurred. In particular, the previous distinctions between sales promotion and direct marketing are becoming less marked. The main reason for this is the advent of databases and the continuing decline in the costs of storing detailed customer information. More and more marketers are tracking their customers and working towards relationship-building goals, over relatively long time spans. Most pursue this aim through direct marketing techniques—and in the process, many have made a very important discovery.

Adding a sales promotion offer to their communication creates extra interest and attention, increases involvement, stimulates interaction between the marketer and the customer or prospect and boosts responses and sales. In fact, it's true to say that the best of today's highly targeted lead and order generation strategies are strengthened by a sales promotion offer. That fairly sweeping statement applies to all media, including direct mail, direct response advertising in print, radio and TV, telemarketing, faxes and even electronic mail, computer disks and interactive TV.

One result of this has been a fundamental change in our understanding of sales promotion. The technique used to be regarded as a short-term, quick-fix type of activity you resorted to when sales slowed down—and which was usually left to the marketing department's most junior people to devise and run. Now, future-oriented marketers are seeing sales promotion offers as an essential element of any carefully planned, long-term interactive marketing and advertising strategy. Personally, I believe that a large-scale marketing programme without database-linked interactive marketing dimensions will fail utterly to meet the challenges of the mid-1990s and beyond. And I am certain that the planning and inclusion of those dimensions should be the responsibility of the most senior and most experienced marketing personnel the company possesses.

Back to the corner grocer

As these very senior people integrate direct marketing and sales promotion into their marketing plans, they will take full advantage of modern databases' mindboggling capabilities. They will use the database not only to analyse frequency and weight of purchase, but to cross-sell products and create sales force leads. They will use it to track individual customers' responses for years on end. They will use it, as some say, to replicate 'the memory and mind of the corner grocer', to recapture a little of the personal touch of pre-mass-market selling.

In those long-vanished days, the corner grocer knew each of his customers personally. He was well aware of their individual wants, needs and preferences, and did everything possible to meet them. Now, in an incredibly advanced leap back into the past, databases enable the largest marketers to do the same. Harvard University's Tom Jones, the co-founder of Epsilon, sums up our new ability to treat customers as individuals in these words:

> 'What's going to happen is that we're going to be able to communicate with people directly at the point of sale, or at a relevant point in the decision-making process, or in their homes at the key times when they want to talk, and that's going to have a critical impact on our business.'[1]

Mr Jones is especially thinking here of the new interactive media about to come on line—two-way TV and the like. With these devices, which will change the way we currently buy things forever, consumers will have the power to invite retailers and marketers into their homes at whatever times they feel like buying. And thanks to their databases, the sellers will be ready with goods and services targeted precisely to each consumer's known wants and needs.

Databases and Direct Marketing

Databases are also the reason why offer-driven direct marketing has moved to the forefront of promotional techniques in just a few years. Because of databases, direct marketing can now contribute much more to your selling efforts than mass marketing and advertising alone. Here are 10 good reasons for using direct marketing methods, sent to me by Freeman Gosden Jnr, and used by his agency, now part of the FCB network. I've modified them slightly in a few places.

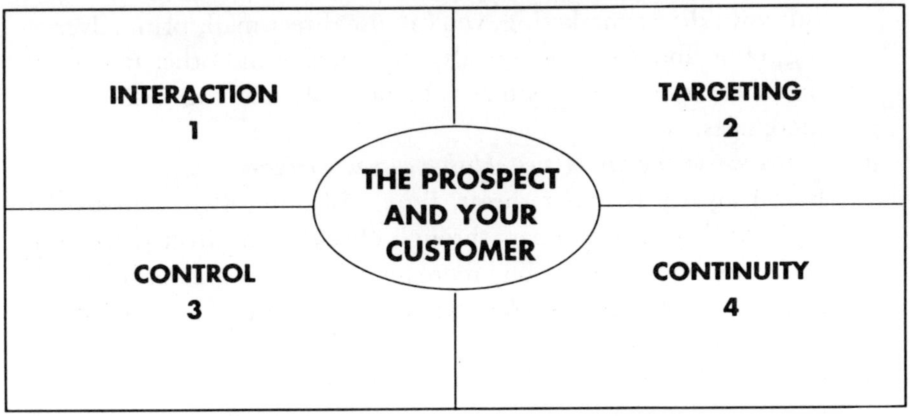

These four cornerstones of direct marketing are the keys to the future of successful selling and continued profitability

1. *Direct marketing reduces the high cost of personal sales calls.*
   Personal selling is expensive—as much as several hundred dollars a call. By using direct response advertising to generate leads, your sales force can identify better prospects and make more cost-efficient sales calls.
   In addition, you can pre-sell by mail and other direct response media to soften sales resistance and increase people's willingness to buy. A sales lead is an invitation that erases the apprehension of a cold call.
2. *Direct marketing can increase your sales with targeted promotions.*
   Using a database, you can target your audience with direct marketing, then employ print, broadcast media, direct mail, telemarketing, fax or a combination to go where the selling is best. For direct mail, many mailing lists are available to you. Through computer-controlled selection and subselection, you can pinpoint and zero in on your best markets.
3. *Direct marketing can reduce your inventory and increase turnover.*
   One central mail order warehouse needs only a fraction of the inventory a retail operation demands. This eliminates overstocking headaches and gives you an easier-to-control, shorter lead time for reordering. It all adds up to faster turnover and more profit.
4. *Direct marketing helps you reach your customers more often.*
   You can't control how many times a customer will come to you. But with direct marketing, you can use direct mail, print advertising, radio and TV commercials, infomercials and other interactive media to 'enter' your customer's home as often as you wish. Result: more sales.
5. *Direct marketing can help establish a customer relationship.*
   Brand loyalty is under threat. By establishing a continuous dialogue with your customers through offer-driven direct marketing, you can induce them to buy more regularly or in greater quantities and at higher margins. You can also exclude competitors' incursions more easily.
6. *Direct marketing offers at-home shopping convenience.*
   In-store shopping is no longer enjoyable for most people. With so many husbands and wives both working, family activity time is

precious. Direct marketing enables families to shop by mail or phone at their convenience, 24 hours a day, seven days a week. Manufacturers, wholesalers, bankers and other retailers are using direct marketing to find out what their customers want, so they can open new markets and enjoy additional sales.

7. *Direct marketing turns buying impulses into sales.*
   The extensive use of toll-free 1 800 numbers and credit cards means customers can purchase goods and services instantly via mail or phone. A customer can act the instant he or she is enthused about the product. Direct marketing eliminates the 'time delay factor' that can increase buyer resistance and lose sales.
8. *Direct marketing gives buyers a wider choice.*
   Some merchandise never finds its way onto retail shelves or is hidden from view. But it can be attractively displayed and more fully described in newspaper and magazine advertisements, in specialty catalogues and brochures, or even on computer networks. A few examples are hard-to-find tools, specialty clothing and unusual services.
9. *Direct marketing gives you the space you need to tell your whole story.*
   To move merchandise or services, you must first move people. Direct marketing gives you the room to tell prospects everything they need to know about your product. And direct marketing is versatile. Your mail package can be large or small—whatever size you need to do a complete job of telling . . . and selling.
10. *Direct marketing picks up where mass marketing and mass merchandising fail.*
    You don't have to trust your sales success to retail sales people who may not know all the benefits your product offers. As a marketer, *you* know your product best. Because direct marketing is a one-to-one communication between you and your customer or prospect, it gives you the opportunity to tell *everything* you want him or her to know—and to tell it the way *you* want to. It also allows your customers to decide how they want to buy.

As well as all that, databases enhance one of the most important features of sales promotion and direct marketing—their accountability. Even before databases, the dollars spent in sales promotion could be pretty well equated with dollars earned—which, incidentally, showed that sales promotion was often a lot more cost-effective than advertising in achieving marketing objectives. For decades, companies like Proctor and Gamble, Unilever and Kraft General Foods all swung money into sales promotions, and had a very good idea of the efficiency of their investment.

Combining the techniques

In this book, we'll look at just about every known interactive marketing approach, including many direct marketing strategies that include sales promotion offers. Of necessity, we'll consider them separately, to avoid becoming hopelessly confused. But at this early stage, I'd like to emphasise that many of the most successful selling campaigns in recent years have been interactive in nature, because they have included a combination of two or even more techniques to improve response from and dialogue with the consumer. And when this integration has been extended to include the product's media advertising theme and its corporate image, some truly massive sales increases have occurred.

Integrated marketing, in short, is one of those activities where the whole can be considerably greater than the sum of the parts.

We'll meet many of these multi-technique strategies as we move through the book. For instance, we'll see how CSR combined cause-related marketing, direct marketing, free premiums and tailor-made joint promotion activity to gain a response and reverse a decline in sugar sales. We'll look at a very successful Toohey's effort that linked sports sponsorship, a sweepstake and a 'Limited Edition' approach. And we'll examine a joint promotion between Coles Supermarkets and Apple Computers that took on a cause-related dimension.

Many other examples abound, including a recent Cadbury's venture that coupled a free product offer (an extra Crunchie bar) with licensed characters (the Super Mario Brothers) and a sweepstake. Also becoming popular are combined approaches that offer a sweepstake prize opportunity for one proof of purchase, or a free gift in return for multiple proofs. Such promotions can meet two objectives—immediate trial of the product, plus the building up of a more habitual purchase pattern and loyalty. An increasing number meet even more through their creative blending of sales promotion, direct marketing and database strategies.

Crossing the categories

Another integrated type of promotion is the one whose execution spills across several promotional categories. Pizza Hut is currently running such a programme in Australia, called 'Book It'. Based on an American prototype, it's an ambitious venture, designed to help increase reading levels and literacy skills in school children from Kindergarten to Year 6. If the children read at least five books a month for four months, they are rewarded with a certificate, a badge—and a Pizza Hut pizza. If the whole class reaches the goal, they and their teacher get a free Pizza Hut party.

Now, what promotional category does that fall into? Relationship-building? Yes, certainly. Sampling? That too. Direct marketing? Most definitely. Cause-related marketing? Undeniably—especially in light of a 1993 Commonwealth Government report that said that 10%–20% of children finish primary school with literacy problems, and that early intervention is the key to solving the problem.

While very aware of its long-term value to Pizza Hut, senior company personnel see the programme as a genuine attempt to help the community. Managing director David Chapman said, 'We believe it is important for business to support programmes such as Book It that put something back into the local community and provide an investment in the future for our children.' Marketing manager Kevin Jurd added that the children were given pizzas because parents and teachers had recommended they receive a 'tangible reward' for their achievement.

In 1992, over 40 000 primary school children and 14 800 teachers from 1700 schools took part in Book It. While small compared with the 14 million children sponsored to date in the long-running US programme, those figures are significant in the Australian context. Research from the programme has shown a 50% increase in the number of books read by participating children in four months. It has also shown that 70% of the children improved their ability and enjoyment, while 61% improved scholastically during the programme.[2]

Results like that point to long-term benefits for Australia through the promotion, as well as for Pizza Hut.

Creating these very imaginative combined techniques and multi-category promotions demands skills most often found in people who adopt an offer-driven attitude to marketing strategy. Such people tend to surface in client marketing divisions, sales promotion houses and some good direct marketing companies. And the best offer-driven thinking comes when they sit down and plan together. At the moment, anyway, it rarely comes from traditional advertising agencies, where the emphasis is more on creating 'image' than on giving consumers real reasons to buy.

The creative process

As we look at the case histories in the chapters ahead, we'll see that one point is common to the world's most successful interactive marketing ventures, whether they use one, two or half a dozen techniques. That common point is a big idea.

In this respect, interactive marketing has much in common with media advertising. A big idea is the basis of outstanding success in both. And in sales promotional strategy, the idea—which is basically the offer itself, plus the way it's communicated—has to be strong enough to drag the target audience away from what they were thinking about. It has to catch their imagination and interest them in an offer they hadn't previously considered. And ideally, it has to reflect both your company image and your main advertising message—because these are the mental keys by which people recognise you.

Now, of course, we've come to the core of integrated marketing. This is the concept that everything you do—from advertising to PR to direct marketing to sales promotion to bus sides to point of sale—has to say the same thing in the same way. It has to convey the same central message and image. That means all your communications in all these different media have to be built around one central idea. If they can't be, then the idea itself is at fault.

The days have gone when you dreamed up an advertising idea, then tried to adapt it for other media as an afterthought. Today, when your central theme is being planned, the creative people can't simply confine their thinking to TV, print and PR. They have to consider just as carefully how the theme will work in all sales promotion and direct marketing channels—because today, they're every bit as important, if not more so. They also have to develop an understanding of all the communication possibilities offered up by the latest technology. If your creative people can't stretch their thinking that far, you need a new creative team. A 1960s approach to advertising and marketing creativity will leave you floundering in the 1990s. Single-minded communication through all media is the only way to maximise a company's resources, marketing expenditure, livery and people.

The tyranny of tininess

Of course, in many sales promotion situations, that ideal is more easily expounded than carried out. The problem of communicating image as well as offer is extremely difficult in the tiny space of a pack flash, a headcard, a small leaflet or even the inside of the pack.

Difficult, but not impossible.

The secret is to make the offer the hero, and incorporate image associations through devices like a typeface, a theme line or an illustration (or even part of one). It can be done, but it demands at least as much creativity as the most expensive TV commercial. That's why the creative people who work on your sales promotions and direct marketing have to be the best around.

Amaze your prospects

In most cases, your prospect is being wooed very briefly or from afar—across the road, across a supermarket aisle, on the radio, in a newspaper or by a few seconds tagged onto a TV commercial. So your message must be readable, dynamic and meaningful. Your prospects must be surprised, amazed or even delighted at the idea of obtaining such a benefit over and above the product's normal attributes. Your offer must be a triumph of the unexpected! Above all, it must be strong enough to draw an immediate response. If your prospect doesn't act immediately, he or she is most unlikely to do so later on—in which case your campaign will be unsuccessful.

Use four (and three) letter words

To cut through the clutter and involve your prospect, sales promotion offers have to:

1. Attract attention (loudly).
2. State the benefit (clearly).
3. Dramatise the benefit (excitingly).
4. Tell the prospect what to do (compellingly).
5. Provide a call to action (immediately).

Experience shows that a number of key words are most likely to get these results. They include:

NEW! WIN! SAVE! ONLY $XX! FREE! MORE FOR LESS!
TRIAL OFFER! PRICE OFF! SALE! 10% OFF!

All these are proven attention-getters and interest-creators. Use them as big, loudly and clearly as your media and space permit. As well, always include the closing date of the offer. In my experience, this helps to speed up the customer's action. It also avoids the negative reaction towards you that follows if he or she responds to a promotion that has already closed.

Think in pictures, too

If you have room for pictures in your sales promotion communication, they're just as important as the words. Often, in fact, the words in sales promotions are formed into pictures—word pictures. The words have to stand out as they would on a book jacket, a fair ground carousel header board or a cinema poster. Achieving that calls for graphic design skills of a very high order. Unnecessary words like prepositions must be ruthlessly eliminated. The words most likely to gain attention and get action must be emphasised. And the pictures and words must work together to enhance the communication and maximise the impact.

At this point, it's worth looking at a brief checklist Drayton Bird provides in *Commonsense Direct Marketing*.[3] He's devised it for broadcast media, but I think it applies equally well to sales promotions. Where necessary, I've refocused it on sales promotions by means of the words in brackets.

- What's the idea? Is it really a big idea?
- Is the technique stronger than the content? Are you relying upon

the dancing and singing rather than the strengths of the concept? (In sales promotion too, puffery is no substitute for substance.)

- If you switched the sound off (if you cut out the words), would the pictures communicate the idea? And vice versa? (This is not an essential point, Drayton says, but it helps.)
- Are you using supers—words over the screen (promotional messages on your pictures)—to help communicate the benefits (offer)? These can be very powerful.
- Do the scenes (words) flow logically one after another? If they don't, you're in trouble.

The hand that decides

Part of the challenge in any interactive marketing communication is to hold the prospect's attention long enough for him or her to decide. One way to do that is to design a response device that requires prospects to use their hands a little more than usual. This may sound a little odd at first, but experience confirms the ploy's effectiveness.

Of course, virtually any response procedure involves the prospect's hands—perhaps in dropping the product into a shopping trolley, signing a cheque, posting a response, picking up a telephone and calling a number, sending in an order or cutting out a coupon. But if that hand involvement can be increased, better results will very often follow.

James Rosenfield, the prolific direct marketing writer and pundit, wrote of the hand's importance in a recent Hoke Publications *Direct Marketing* article. He made these points:[4]

- Getting the hand involved prolongs the time spent with the purchase. The prolongation is meaningful.
- A good involvement device will triple, quadruple, even quintuple the time the prospect spends with our solicitations.

I agree. Most of our best work has featured a device that engages consumers and leaves an imprint on their memories.

'As post literacy takes a hold, the visually iconic nature of involvement devices becomes even more important,'[5] Rosenfield went on in his article. He pointed to the personally tactile nature of modern technology, adding that people control their lives through their hands when they operate home alarm systems, PCs, touch tone telephones, TV remote controls and so on. All these demand a high degree of hand action. He stated that the hand equals control, and staying in control is the main theme for the 1990s, because of its increasing digitisation.

In that environment, he concluded, 'tactile devices become the more important'.[6] While Rosenfield was talking primarily about direct marketing, I believe his point is just as valid for sales promotion. With their use of 'yes' and 'no' stickers, response emblems that you slip into 'yes' and 'no' slots and so on, Readers Digest have been employing tactile devices for decades—and with great success.

The involvement medium

While they may not automatically be 'tactile' in its true sense, sales promotion offers are certainly 'involvement devices'. They provide an extended 'window' into your consumers' minds, by giving you more time to present your case. Their interest and promise of an immediate benefit can hold consumers long enough to consider your promise in greater depth.

That's vital, when you think of that nanosecond of time when the consumer (who from psychographic research is indicated to be brand loyal) stands before a supermarket shelf—then extends a hand and moves it a fraction. At that very moment, all original purchase intentions vanish. It's this important 'moment of truth' that preoccupies many of today's marketers. What happens to make that change?

Many believe that consumers have a repertoire of brands to which they are brand loyal—in the 1990s, loyalty simply extends over more than one brand. If this is so, and if each brand satisfies consumer needs adequately, the marketer's task is clear. It is provide the added interest, excitement and call to action which will, in that critical nanosecond, attract the wavering hand to their brand. In fast-moving consumer products marketing, I believe that purchase trigger is most likely to be a compelling point-of-sale device or an arresting feature on the pack.

The biggest barrier to communication, conviction and buying action is casual consideration—the skimmed and quickly turned page, the ignored TV commercial, the glanced-at and thrown away direct mail letter. Sales promotion offers can deliver the precious extra moments we need to gain attention and lock in our selling proposition. They can do this in a whole host of different and intriguing ways. We'll explore almost all of them in the chapters ahead. But as background, let's first consider the radical changes now happening in two areas absolutely crucial to your sales success.

Retailing and distribution.

Notes

1. Tom Jones quoted by Howard Draft, *Dateline*, DMA, January 1993, Volume 8, Number 1, in an article entitled *The Destiny of Direct*.
2. 'Pizza Hut in Reading Row', by Karen Davey, *The Sun Herald*, 8 August 1993.
3. Drayton Bird, *Commonsense Direct Marketing*, Kogan Page, 1982, 1989, London.
4. James Rosenfield's article 'In the Mail', in *Direct Marketing*, Hoke Communications, February 1993.
5. Ibid.
6. Ibid.

1

CHAPTER

Retailing and Distribution Today

Once upon a time, marketing was a pretty straightforward business. You created a product. You put a price on it. Your sales team sold it into stores. Your advertising agency ran advertisements for it. Your customers bought it.

And you sat back and grew rich.

It was all nice and uncomplicated and predictable. But then, I suppose, so was life for the dodo colonies on Mauritius before the first sailors came ashore. The radical changes that followed proved too much for the sleepy, well-fed birds. Today, their sad fate is being replayed over and over—as company after company, unable to adapt to a radically changed marketing environment, slides into a bewildered extinction.

Presumably, you don't want to follow the way of the dodo. Nor do you have to. The key to survival is realising that the world is changing rapidly, and that the successful marketing techniques of the early 1980s don't necessarily work today. Regis McKenna, the author of *Relationship Marketing*, sums it up this way:

> 'The decline of mass marketing and continued refinement of submarkets, the customisation of services and products, intense global competition and the use of new technology tools in business all have led to a re-evaluation of marketing.'[1]

By and large, however, that re-evaluation has been positive. New marketing tools for a new age have emerged and older ones have been adapted to serve in the new situation. The current upheaval may be creating big problems, but it's also opening up unprecedented opportunities. Marketers who understand that are the 'sunrise people'. They'll ride out the changes. They may even pioneer some changes of their own—and prosper in the process.

When you finish this book, I hope you'll have the insights to be among them.

So let's start our dodo-dodging by looking at a fundamental marketing area—the retail arena where products vie for consumer attention, and the distribution channels that take them there. Even in this sphere, huge changes are occurring. Every consumer goods manufacturer needs to understand them, and grasp their significance. If we can get our heads around what's happening at the retail level, we've taken a vital step to marketing success in the 'nervous '90s'.

An $88 billion industry

Retailing in Australia is a major economic activity. Employing 13% of the country's labour force, the industry turned over some $88.4 billion in 1990–1991. In 1989, it represented 40% of private consumption and 23% of GDP.

The Australian retail market is one of the world's most concentrated. Coles-Myer has a 17.1% market share, while two Adelaide Steamship subsidiaries (Woolworths with 8.6% and David Jones with 1.6%) have a further 10.2%. This means that just two companies control nearly 30% of the market. Coles-Myer, in fact, has the highest sale per head of population of any retailer in the world. Franklins, the next chain in size after Woolworths, has just 2.6% of the market.[2]

Channels of distribution

Working out the most cost-efficient way to get products from manufacturer to customer—usually, via a retailer—is an important aspect of successful marketing. A variety of options is open to you, and it pays to consider them carefully.

Growing numbers of manufacturers are sending their products directly to retailers through their own delivery system, but the majority still get them into the stores through a wholesaler. People often wonder why this extra level of cost and activity is introduced into the distribution channel. There's a simple answer. The advantages of using a wholesaler actually make it a much more cost-efficient route for most manufacturers than direct delivery.

Wholesalers: a multi-level service

This is because wholesalers do much more for manufacturers than simply deliver their products. Their sales forces can reach many small stores far more economically than the manufacturers could. They cut the manufacturer's inventory costs and risks by holding goods in warehouses. They help finance manufacturers by ordering early and paying promptly. They even absorb risks, by carrying the cost of theft, damage and spoilage. And their transportation network is the fastest and cheapest way of getting more products into more stores.

On many levels, wholesalers have a great deal going for them. But there is a downside: rising costs, especially in the real estate they need for their warehouses and transport depots, are making their services more expensive. While they're still more cost-effective than the do-it-yourself route, the gap is narrowing—and narrowing quickly.

Brokers: the substitute sales force

If a manufacturer is too small to have a substantial sales force and can't afford a wholesaler distribution, a broker is a very good alternative. Brokers are quite different from wholesalers, in that they probably never touch or see the goods at any time. Brokers assume no risk, carry no inventory and don't get involved in financing. Acting purely as go-betweens, they sell the goods into the stores and organise shelf space, displays and so on. When using brokers, manufacturers usually deliver their products to retailers themselves. Manufacturers' agents do a similar job to brokers, but normally on a longer-term basis.

Both groups can do a good job for smaller manufacturers with limited sales resources. However, rising costs are making an impact here too—as is the whole ferment of change in retailing, which we'll look at more closely in a moment.

Bypassing the retailer

Retail outlets are where the vast majority of products find their way into consumers' hands. But there are other routes that bypass the retailers altogether—and of these, one in particular is currently displaying quite extraordinary growth in Australia. It may, in fact, be the country's fastest growing retail technique.

I refer to direct selling, or moving products purely by word of mouth.

Direct selling involves local distributors—mainly but by no means only women—who work from home on a part- or full-time basis. They sell a product range to neighbours, friends, acquaintances and other locals through personal contacts, referrals, church and community groups, stalls at fetes and any other way they can think of. The products are mostly home-oriented, like cosmetics, kitchenware, household cleaners, purified water, nutritional supplements, toys, jewellery, clothing and books.

The technique is very appealing to customers, because the distributor brings the range to their home and gives them the in-depth demonstration and personal attention they don't get in retail stores. Cyndi Kaplan, author of *The Beauty of Business*, the definitive book on direct selling, writes, 'Consumers are becoming more conscious of quality products and value of services. Most direct selling companies produce or distribute a superior quality product and provide personalised service. This is sadly lacking in the market-place today.'[3]

The customers' appreciation is usually expressed in a substantial level of sales per visit. This has carried some brands that are only available through direct selling, such as Amway and Rawleighs, to spectacular heights throughout the world. Indeed, Amway, the biggest direct seller of them all, has recently gone beyond its own-brand products. It now offers Coca-Cola, men's suits, other clothing items and even cars through its distributors—all by word of mouth.

On a smaller scale, real success is being enjoyed by many other brands exploring the direct selling route. This is certainly one reason why the technique is growing so quickly. John Fulton, executive director of the Direct Selling Association of Australia, puts its present Australian growth rate at about 20% per annum.

Good people

The other factor pushing it ahead is the number and quality of people who are becoming distributors. In a time of high unemployment, many women have correctly identified direct selling as a way not only to supplement the family income, but to build their own business—one, moreover, they can juggle happily with the demands of home-making and child-raising. In addition, some extremely bright retailing people have seen the potential of direct selling, and decided that their future lies there rather than in a traditional retail store.

It's not a hard industry to enter, either. The companies provide training at little or no cost to the distributors. Start-up expenses, too, are minimal. Joining fees are small, and most starter product kits are priced under $200.

As I write, some 400 000 Australians are engaged in direct selling. They are generating annual sales in the area of $1 billion. Clearly, direct selling is a route worth watching—especially if you're a manufacturer with home-oriented products.

Or someone seeking your own independent niche in the retail industry.

Variations on the theme: not for everyone

Two variations on the direct selling theme are party plans and door-to-door selling. Both work very well for a handful of products. Tupperware and Nutri-Metics have built their prosperity on party plans. And your friendly Avon Lady is following in the profitable footsteps of America's ubiquitous Fuller Brush Man, who pioneered large-scale door-to-door selling decades ago.

While highly successful for those select products, party plans and widespread door-knocking are difficult routes to develop. It can be a long, slow and costly slog to get them off the ground. And more importantly, there's only room on each route for a few contenders.

How many product parties would you be prepared to attend in a month?

The failed revolution

Another non-retail route that can't be totally ignored, I suppose, even in a survey as brief as this, is automatic vending machines.

Hailed back in the 1940s as a revolution in retailing, they have largely failed to live up to their initial promise. Early on, a spectacular vending machine company crash cost investors a fortune, and tarnished the machines' image for a generation. Even today, their small capacity and difficult locations (like city railway platforms) make them costly to service. They can never be any more than a minor supplement to the main retail outlets.

Anyway, I've mentioned them.

Direct marketing: the way of the future

That brings me to the last major distribution channel in common use—one that was in the Cinderella category until quite recently, and whose recent advances are, I believe, only a hint of the future that lies before it.

I refer to direct marketing and mail order—both in their manufacturer-to-customer and business-to-business applications. In my view, the direct supply of products from manufacturer to customer will certainly grow. The rising cost of traditional distribution methods, the whirlwinds of change in retailing and the rapidly widening capabilities of databases will inevitably see to that.

Alert retailers will also benefit from the coming direct marketing boom. Peter Wilkinson, Coles-Myer chief operations officer retail,

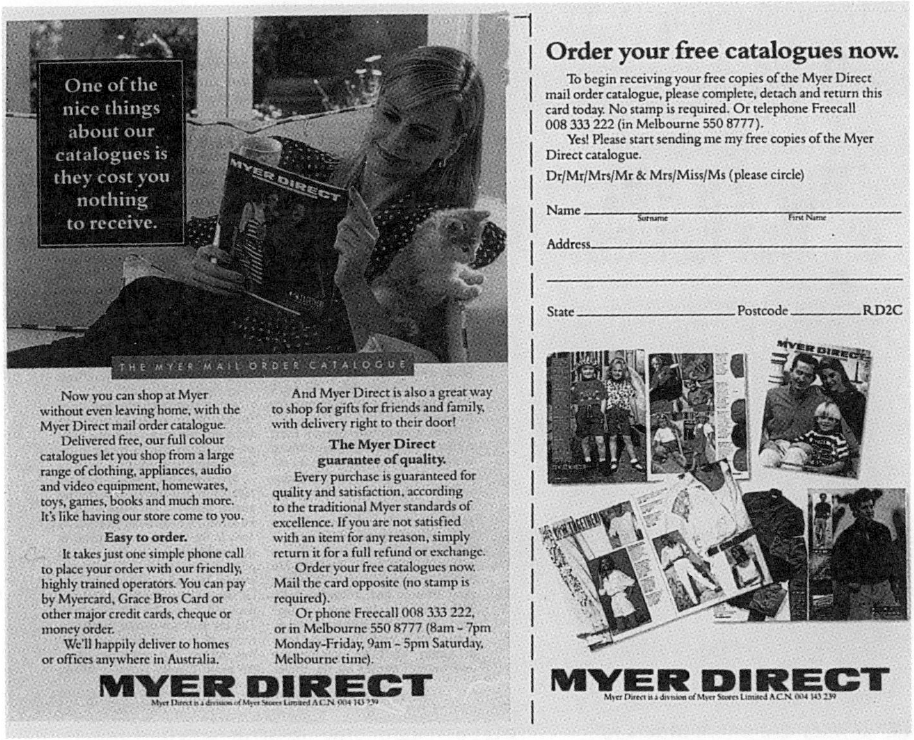

Myer establishes a segmented database of customers, and markets to them individually. Sales are expected to soar.
Courtesy of Myer Stores Limited

predicts that Myer Direct annual sales will soar from their current level of $70 million to about $300 million.[4] This is an indication of the power of one-to-one communication. Most of the sales will come from the 10 catalogues Myer sends each year to its 500 000 known customers. They form the basis of its direct marketing efforts.

Retailers threatened

While retailers can certainly use direct marketing to their own advantage, a variation of the technique could well pose a threat to many of them.

It's called Home Shopping by TV. And it's already up and running successfully in the USA.

Home Shopping by TV could well be the easiest way to buy yet devised. It enables a 'virtual' company to offer top quality, well-known brand names to customers sitting at home in front of their TVs. When you see something you want, you simply lift the phone and order it. If you've bought from the company before, they already have your address and (if it's clothing) your size. All you need to tell them is the colour you want—and your order will be rushed to you immediately.

TV viewers are encouraged to watch the Home Shopping Club by attractive offers and cash inducements featured in the press and on other TV channels.
Courtesy The Home Shopping Club

The process will only get easier in the years ahead, as TVs, PCs, phones, faxes and remotes become one compact contact point with the outside world.

It's easy to see why Home Shopping by TV is a threat to retailers who have massive areas of space tied up by high-margin items. Not only does it give customers an easier way to buy—in most cases, it will probably offer them a price advantage too. Some manufacturers, however, can welcome Home Shopping by TV as an ally. Because the technique works best with top brand names, it may give their manufacturers a new opportunity to go directly to their customers and cut out the retailer altogether.

$2 billion turnover

Writing in *Direct Marketing* magazine, July 1993, Harvey D. Braun, a national partner of Deloitte and Touche (USA), underlined the technique's potential. Braun reported that Barry Diller, the founder of Fox TV, had invested a considerable sum in a home shopping network called QVC. Diller, he stated, is enthusiastic about what is shaping up as a $2 billion turnover industry. And no wonder!

The QVC network can handle 20 000 calls a minute. So its customers will rarely have to put up with frustrating phone delays. Recently, for instance, the network happily coped with sales of Diane von Furstenberg dresses and silk separates worth $1.2 million in less than two hours.

There's no doubt, according to Braun, that Home Shopping by TV threatens catalogue mail order marketers as well as up-market retailers—especially as his research shows that TV buyers in the USA aren't all that different from the average in-store shopper. Catalogues face another technically-based threat, too. It seems they could, in time, disappear completely, because they'll be available on one of the multi-channels coming directly into the home via the interactive TV/PC. Alternatively, they'll come on diskette or CD Rom, with all the advantages of providing a 'live action' demonstration of each product.[5]

The everyday application of those developments is not far down the line. In late September 1993, Optus announced a joint venture to deliver Home Shopping by TV in Australia. They will push ahead with their plans to broadcast between 12 a.m. and 6 p.m. Manufacturers and retailers need to think about Home Shopping by TV now—to work out how to use it and guard against it respectively.

A 1990s winner: multi-channel distribution

There is one further development that is just gathering pace—and it may well prove to be the major advance of the 1990s. This is multi-channel distribution. It happens when a single manufacturer sets up two or more marketing channels to reach different market segments, or even different markets.

Black & Decker, for instance, is now selling its electrical products through department stores, hardware stores, mail order and mass merchandisers. It may streamline its product range to get maximum benefit from doing so. IBM, Unisys and Digital Equipment Corporation have carved up their markets, and sell their personal computers through dealer networks, value-added retailers, department stores and electrical discounters. Apple does the same. These and other manufacturers have also added speciality computer retailers to this mix, as well as marketing directly to the consumer.

Digital was the first in the computer field to go for multi-channel distribution. As well as selling through retailers and specialist consultants and their own sales force, they went directly to consumers through off-the-page advertising featuring a response 1 800 number. Others are now following their lead.
Courtesy of Digital Equipment Corporation

A huge shake-up

For most products today, however, supermarkets and stores are still by far the most important outlets. Yet as I've hinted a few times, those retailers are currently involved in a huge shake-up. What we're about to see in Australia is already happening in the USA. Retailer R. H. Macy recently announced the creation of 'TV Macy's', a 24-hour TV home shopping channel to roll out in the autumn of 1994 on Cablevision and other systems around the USA. The channel is expected to generate sales outside the existing customer base on the east and west coasts, by offering much of the merchandise found in the 110 Macy's and Bullock's department stores, including apparel, accessories, jewellery and home goods. The channel is also expected to promote store traffic in markets where the stores are located.

By the end of the century, retailing in Australia will have a very different face. The marketers who understand what's happening now—and who shape their marketing and distribution plans accordingly—will have a head start over those who just react to events as they occur.

No population growth

Basically, the changes confronting retailing are being generated from three sources. The first, of course, is mind-boggling technological change. The second is the result of plunging birthrates and a reduction in immigration. Australia's slow but steady population growth has all but ground to a halt. Consequently, the retail stores' customer pool is now virtually static. No longer can the stores expect growing market shares fuelled purely by population expansion. Today, the only way they can increase market share is to steal customers from each other. And for the last few years, they've gone all out to do just that.

Coles triggers a check-out price war

By SUE MITCHELL

Coles Myer Ltd's supermarket division has triggered a price war among grocery retailers by announcing a nationwide price reduction campaign in what seems a last-ditch attempt to boost sales and regain lost market share.

Coles closed most of its 383 supermarkets across Australia yesterday to cut the prices of about 75 to 85 per cent of grocery items as part of a permanent move to a cheaper pricing policy.

The company declined to reveal the size of the cuts, saying they would vary from State to State, depending on the wants of consumers.

However, Coles' competitors said they would immediately adjust their own prices, and said Coles had started a price war that would have no overall benefits for retailers but would provide a boon to consumers hit by the recession.

The price war is likely to put downward pressure on the Consumer Price Index, about 18 per cent of which reflects grocery prices.

"I can assure you we're not going to let them steal back share they have lost," said Mr Paul Simons, the chairman of Woolworths Ltd.

"Within 48 hours, Coles will have no advantage in price."

Continued page 2

Do consumers really believe that price cuts are passed on?
Australian Financial Review, Tuesday, 20 August 1991

The weapon they've used is the price cut. Australia's big supermarket chains—Woolworths, Franklins and Coles-Myer—have clashed in a savage and costly price war that has to date gained them little or nothing. After the first few years of battle, all three combatants have found themselves pretty much where they were before in terms of market share.

Meanwhile, a third source of change—an even more profound one—has begun to shake the industry.

The shrinking middle class

The worst recession in 60 years has had a polarising effect on the Australian community. A few middle class people have moved upwards into a small affluent group, but many more have been forced downwards into a newly underprivileged sector. The middle class itself—once the very basis of Australian society—has shrunk considerably. The purchasing power of hundreds of thousands of people has been drastically reduced.

Joe Cappo, senior vice president of Crain Communications, USA, has identified yet another trend. He noted it in the American context, but I believe it applies equally strongly to Australian retailing. At the National Infomercial Marketing Association meeting in New York City, Cappo said:

> 'Women in the work force are also a major factor. They have different shopping habits than our mothers. They make 70% of their purchasing decisions on impulse. That's why more money is going into sales promotion. The supermarket is a new medium unto itself. Possibly the most important reason for the shift in consumer habits is the declining demand for products. People no longer have the Depression mentality, no pent-up demand. Young people today are not as interested in possessions, but rather a better environment, health and ethics.'[6]

The retail stores have to adapt quickly to these new realities—ones that look like being fixtures on the Australian scene for a long time to come.

Fewer, better stores

Over the longer term, their response will probably be fewer stores (to cut their high and growing rental overheads) with improved levels of service. We can look forward to longer opening hours, with 24-hour operation becoming the norm. Trends to larger premises away from normal shopping malls will continue. Ikea and Freedom Furniture, who both offer modern, high quality, design-oriented yet economical products, are also going this route. Another is BBC Hardware, which plans to build ever larger home depot stores of 185 000 square feet with 80 000 under one roof.

Only by choosing locations outside ordinary high-rent shopping areas can these very large stores be viable. These sites will also give them ease of access for hefty displays, room to store large quantities of merchandise, and space to show things like well-displayed household goods, trade building materials, and garden equipment and plants. The large stores will want to open seven days a week too, which they still can't do in some shopping malls.

Significantly, it looks as though the growth of retail food barns will also increase. A percentage of consumers will always buy on price and find these bulk buy barns and warehouses attractive.

The 'Main Street Programme'

Meanwhile, what of small stores in suburban shopping strips and rural towns? Will current and coming changes leave them high and dry—doomed relics of a past age?

Not necessarily.

True, numbers of them have lost out very seriously to larger shopping developments and shifts in the population's shopping habits. But a programme originally begun by the NSW Government and now managed by my friend Lee Anderson and her colleague Libby Ozinga has brought new hope to many.

Called the 'Main Street Programme' and based on a Canadian model of the same name, the venture involves the whole community in a five-point plan to revitalise their suburb or town centre. Urban design, organisation, business development, promotion and heritage conservation are all employed. Street beautification is carried out where needed. Events are staged to create excitement and bring people back into the area. Workshops are conducted to help retailers improve their competitiveness and marketing skills. All kinds of strategies to build customer traffic are hammered out and adopted.

The programme has been extremely successful in communities ranging from sleepy country towns to Sydney's bustling inner-city Paddington. It shows that small retailers in stagnating areas can have a bright future—if they can draw local government and residents into an enthusiastic partnership for local renewal.

The 'Main Street Programme' shows them how to do it.

Return of the dinosaurs

'There are those who say department stores are dinosaurs—doomed by a fast changing environment,' Ed Meyer, chairman and CEO of Grey

Advertising Inc., wrote in Hoke Communications' *Direct Marketing* magazine in May 1990. Pundits say they're too bulky, too unfocused and too slow-moving to compete successfully with a mall full of agile niche marketers running speciality stores.

However, mall sprawl may be creating a real opportunity for traditional department stores. Meyer explained:

> 'Over the last 30 years, malls have become more and more proficient at satisfying consumers' cravings for novelty and abundance. Obviously, with their many ambitions and responsibilities, today's consumers do require a wide variety of goods and services. Yet they also demand that variety in a simplified, convenient environment. For that reason, as the 1990s progress, department stores may turn out to be exactly what today's overburdened consumers are looking for in terms of an "ideal shopping experience".'[7]

Not enough time

That prediction presupposes a fundamental attitude shift on the part of consumers—and that's exactly what emerged from a recent survey by Grey Advertising Inc. in the USA. Entitled 'American Households of the 1990s', it asked several questions. How do today's consumers differ from those of the past? What do today's consumers really care about? How do they spend their time? What do they want from life? How do they expect to get it?

The study revealed that 74% of consumers don't have enough time to accomplish all they need and want to do. And it emphasised that not having enough time is the single greatest source of stress in today's consumers' lives. A large segment of the population, the survey found, is engaged in a losing battle to accomplish infinite goals within the very finite boundaries of a 24-hour day. Once, people's lives had clearly defined, central roles. As Ed Meyer went on to say, 'Dad was the breadwinner. Mum was the homemaker. Today, one person may live out many roles. And each of those roles seems to come with its own laundry list of things to do.'[8]

Leaving fun behind

At the moment, this trend is most apparent among baby boomers. Now that they're entering middle age, they've added marriage, parenthood, home ownership and other 'heavy' activities to their previous agenda of career fulfilment and fun.

In their effort to do more and more, today's hyperactive consumers are discovering that it pays to streamline their lives. In light of all this, shopping is not considered an enjoyable pastime. That finding agrees with other recent surveys. For example, the *Wall Street Journal's* 1989 survey, 'The American Way of Buying', found that one out of three consumers actively hates going shopping. They hate to go browsing. They don't even want to window shop. One in three would rather do housework than go shopping.

Meyer expostulated that the main reason for this animosity towards shopping was simply that it takes too much time. 'About two out of three consumers in the survey said shopping was extremely stressful—because they felt they were using time inefficiently while engaged in it.'[9]

The vanishing commodity: service

'Adding to consumers' unhappiness was an impression that service is vanishing. The biggest problem consumers perceive in their area today is not a shortage of high-touch contact, but rather an excess of disinterested, undertrained salespeople, out-of-stock merchandise and slow-moving lines,' Meyer said.[10]

Australian research seems to indicate a similar state of affairs here. The March 1991 edition of *The Mackay Report* carried a heading, 'The Impersonal System'. Under that, Hugh Mackay wrote, 'consumers characterise the contemporary retail environment as one which is largely lacking in personal service'. The retail environment, he added, 'has almost removed the sense of a personal relationship between customer and shopkeeper'.[11]

HOW YOU CAN WIN 50 COMPACT DISCS FOR CHRISTMAS

EXTRA

SCIENCE AND EDUCATION

Doubt over Alzheimer's-aluminium link

As from today ALL the following

FRANKLINS No Frills

DISCOUNT SUPERMARKETS WILL

OPEN EVERY SUNDAY

10am-4pm

Franklins BigFresh THE HUGE NEW FRESH FOOD AND DISCOUNT GROCERY SUPER-STORE AT MARKETOWN LEICHHARDT ALSO OPENS 10AM-4PM SUNDAYS

LONGER HOURS MAKE SHOPPING EASIER IN ALL THESE FRANKLINS STORES

MON-FRI open till 9pm

MON-FRI open till 10pm

FRANKLINS No Frills PRICES NOW AVAILABLE EVERY DAY

Retailers' initiatives are profoundly changing the face of retailing in Australia. Larger outlets, longer trading hours, Sunday trading and a growing emphasis on house-branded products are just some of the current trends.
Courtesy of Franklins Limited

Sales and promotions the key

The retail business has always been heavily involved in the politics of price. Traditionally, sales and promotion have outweighed image in most retail marketing plans. At this time of great financial turmoil, the emphasis on sales and promotions seems likely to grow even stronger.

The retailer must now become an innovator of convenience—finding ways to satisfy consumers' urgent need for a shopping experience that's not only pleasant and rewarding, but timesaving too. As well, retailers must now respond to consumers' growing demand for quality—offering them *quality* merchandise and *quality* shopping experiences.

But all these changes I've outlined can't be achieved overnight. The crisis is upon the stores now. They have to move quickly to meet the urgent imperative of a static market, with less money to spend. And perhaps even a very different, more frugal, attitude to spending it.

Cheaper products—but how?

Clearly, cheaper products must be the mainstay of the stores' immediate reaction. And that raises the question—how can they get them?

There are two ways. They can force manufacturers to lower their prices on existing items. Or the retailers themselves can take the initiative and launch their own product ranges, at prices significantly under those of branded products. Both avenues are being pursued vigorously by Australia's retailers as I write—and they affect manufacturers in two quite serious ways.

To start with, manufacturers are being forced into discount situations they don't necessarily want. True, price cuts have always been an important sales promotion technique—but only at a time and to an extent of the manufacturers' own choosing. To have price cuts forced upon them at any old time by retailers is a very different thing.

Secondly, the rapid rise of low-priced generics poses a real threat. In Britain, 40% of all products in Sainsbury, Tesco and Waitrose stores are now generics. The figure in Australia is 15%–30% in most stores, and it's growing—for products priced right for the new less-than-affluent consumer, and projecting just the austere, no-waste image that echoes most people's feelings today.

Losing control

The real result of these two factors is that manufacturers are losing control. Until recently, they created the products and set their prices. Now, in Australia—and in many other Western countries as well—the initiative has passed into the retailers' hands. They're the ones creating, pricing and controlling their own new product ranges. They're the ones setting the prices on branded products. They're also the ones who give their generic products more and more of the available shelf space and display opportunities.

Nor are their actions carried out arbitrarily. The instant data from scanning tools and computerised registers gives them a clear picture of consumer preferences and buying trends long before the information reaches manufacturers. As a result, many retail chains are leaving manufacturers flat-footed in getting new products onto the market. They're responding far more quickly to consumer needs not only with house brands but with their own lookalike versions of top-selling branded products. National Foods' Fruche dairy dessert and Arnott's Tiny Teddy biscuits are just two that have been very successfully imitated in recent times.

In short, retailers can now give consumers what they want, quickly and at generally lower prices. No wonder they're increasingly calling the tune.

The Wall Street Journal saw the power shift beginning as long ago as 1980. On August 29 that year, it commented:

> 'Manufacturers once held the upper hand because of the tremendous advertising and promotional budgets they deployed to pull consumers into the stores. Supermarkets

> deferred to suppliers' merchandising suggestions and relied on their data to determine which products to stock . . . But retailers aren't willing to continue as silent conduits between manufacturers and consumers. Lenn Daykin, director of merchandising for Foote Cone and Belding advertising agency, said, "In a battle between giants like Proctor and Gamble and Safeway five years ago, P & G would have prevailed. Now Safeway can call the tune".'[12]

A more recent sign of the times is the fact that Wal-Mart stores in the USA now don't pay manufacturers for their products until they've actually been bought by the consumer. Writing in *Retail and Distribution Management* in 1987, Penelope Ody stated, 'Those with an understanding of both industries (retailing and manufacturing) and how they interact sense that private label threatens to change the old order for ever.'[13]

Retailers' sophistication

Another way retailers are calling the tune today is through the increasing sophistication of their store layouts. In supermarkets and more and more in department stores, the layout is designed to present 100% of the goods to the maximum number of shoppers. Supermarket retailers are particularly geared to giving their customers the maximum opportunity to part with their money. They place the top-selling lines in the best positions—but locate them in such a way that customers have to pass a great many other things to reach them. And as they do, their opportunities to see and buy are increased.

Note, however, the key to this process. It's the retailer who decides which products are performing best and gives them the top places. If your product isn't a big seller, your chances of getting above-average display space are growing steadily dimmer.

Apollo pulls the winners

A hi-tech system called Apollo is being used by many retailers to help them pick the front-runners. Apollo measures the shelf-facings' profitability of brands in terms of price, margin and off-take, as against the facing and space allocated. This system is normally owned and operated by the brand leader, who advises the retailer on space/face allocations. However, store management is now attempting to embrace the technology and prevent brand leaders from dictating which brands will enjoy the best positioning. Today, most key account managers are assisted by an Apollo expert. This is lifting the stocking and buying decision to a much more scientific level.

Practices such as these will dictate which brands survive and which brands die. Manufacturers will find it harder and harder to get new products onto shelves. The competition with house brands for space will intensify. New branded products will have less time to establish consumer appeal. Only those that quickly provide faster sales turnover or a higher margin will get favoured treatment from the retailer. This in turn will lead inevitably to a restriction in brand offerings to the consumer.

And massive sales losses to the companies whose products fail to sell.

Partnerships in profit

In light of all this, how can manufacturers fight back? One way is to see the retailer not as a usurper but a partner—and go all out to make the partnership work. It's an approach that has everything going for it. Indeed, the Wal-Mart case study (where manufacturers are paid for the goods only when the customer has purchased them) suggests that, to ensure longevity and success in manufacturing, a closer tie with the retailer is not only desirable but inevitable. The fortunes of both are becoming more and more closely linked.

The manufacturer needs the retailers to be successful, to retain a selling channel to consumers. The retailer needs the manufacturer to be successful to ensure a consistent supply of dependable, high quality consumer products. The manufacturer also needs to gain as much consumer knowledge as possible, to cater more adequately for changing consumer needs. To obtain this, the manufacturer has to form close retailer ties. But you can't do that just by supplying them with products. You have to give their customers real satisfaction—and be able to prove it.

Replication

A further change manufacturers have to confront is the fact that products are becoming more similar. Most cars in certain price bands such as \$20 000–\$25 000, \$26 000–\$30 000 and \$30 000–\$40 000 are, within their types, becoming less easy to distinguish. Even with very sophisticated computers, the differences are disappearing. Machines using MS DOS can now replicate the user friendliness of an Apple. Each brand varies little in its engineering—while clones which perform similar tasks, but are not as accepted, proliferate in an already overcrowded market-place.

What's more, the consumer knows this. He or she confidently orders this sophisticated technology today by mail from the manufacturer or even from a computer superstore, without the need for a dealer or distributor. One result is that the manufacturer can, as we have seen, supply this very complex machinery at less cost directly to the consumer.

In this situation, the manufacturer must take on responsibilities originally held by the reseller or distributor. One reason for the change is that these machines are becoming more and more reliable. There are less roles for a distributor or reseller to play—a development brought about by advances in miniaturisation. These have changed the face of the computer industry, as it has found out to its cost.

Many computer companies have already changed their patterns of distribution and sale. They now offer a variety of ways for the consumer to buy, including direct mail, telephone, fax, resellers and distributors, their own sales forces and value-added resellers.

Today in most industries, product innovations by the manufacturer can be replicated not in a matter of months but a matter of weeks. This is having repercussions the world over. No manufacturer is now safe from the threat of a competitor matching a product, yet not infringing original patents.

Has advertising done its job?

It can be argued that advertising in the 1990s is failing in its most important task—persuading people to change their existing purchasing behaviour. There is also evidence to suggest that advertising is no longer as effective in building brands, to give them solid and indestructible marketing foundations. Simply, advertising has become too expensive, the media much too fragmented and peoples' opportunities to see very much less predictable. Most advertising budgets are just not large enough to reach the 1990s' highly mobile and sophisticated consumer.

Consequently, advertising's role in creating brand loyalty with the maximum possible efficiency is also in question. Advertising is increasingly performing the peripheral task of announcing availability, instead of being used to build lasting values. Perhaps this is why so much emphasis is now being given to promotion and to promotional expenditure. The answer must be that these other methods are more successful today in achieving sales and customer loyalty. In their book, *The Great Marketing Turnaround*, Stan Rapp and Tom Collins make this point:

> '... the old true and tried methods of making sales via advertising, promotion and marketing are just not going to get the job done. Bombarding the mass market no longer makes sense ... Both consumer markets and business to business markets are splintering into smaller and smaller niches, each demanding its own customised treatment.'[14]

This development demands a complete rethink of the way we go to market. Increasing numbers of marketers are taking up the challenge of getting closer to their customers. They're employing more strategic sales promotion and direct marketing practices to build sales by fostering longer-term relationships and lasting loyalty. I believe that, in many cases, these techniques will become the only effective way to tell one product from another.

The following chapters tell you which interactive marketing tools are available to you. They explain how offer-driven strategies can make sales, improve profits and help you thrive within our rapidly altering marketing and selling environments.

Fighting back

The changes I've outlined are only going to intensify. But the marketer has some good weapons with which to meet them. If properly used, those weapons can put the marketer back in control in the retail situation. They can convince the consumer not only that branded products are better value, but that the manufacturer is right in touch with his or her needs, and cares about the sale and the consumer. What's more, they can actually convince the retailer that the branded product is still the best profit source, and bring him back on side as an ally.

The name of these tide-turning weapons? Integrated offer-driven sales promotion, database-driven direct marketing and response advertising techniques—the dynamic trio that come together as interactive marketing.

And this book tells you how to use them.

Notes

1. Regis McKenna, *Relationship Marketing*, Addison-Wesley Publishing Company, Inc., Reading, Massachusetts, USA, 1991.
2. Stephen Biss, Research for MBA thesis, 1991.
3. Cyndi Kaplan, *The Beauty of Business*, Godiva Press, Sydney, Australia, 1993.
4. 'Shops of the Future', Neil Shoebridge, *BRW*, 23 July 1993.
5. 'Guess Who's Watching', Harvey D. Braun, *Direct Marketing*, Hoke Communications, July 1993.
6. 'As Consumers Change, So Does Advertising', Joe Cappo, *Direct Marketing*, Hoke Communications, July 1993.
7. 'Retail on the Rebound', Ed Meyer, *Direct Marketing*, Hoke Communications, May 1990.
8. Ibid.
9. Ibid.
10. Ibid.
11. Hugh Mackay, *The Mackay Report*, March 1991.
12. Lenn Daykin, *Wall Street Journal*, 29 August 1980.
13. Penelope Ody, *Retail and Distribution Management* Magazine, 1987.
14. Stan Rapp and Tom Collins, *The Great Marketing Turnaround*, Prentice Hall, Inc., Englewood Cliffs, New Jersey, USA, 1990.

2

CHAPTER

Point of Sale—Where Buying Begins

You can bombard your customers with costly TV commercials, lure them with high-impact press advertisements and grab their ears with creative radio spots. But you haven't sold them a thing—until that magic moment when they pick up your product, rather than your competitor's, at point of sale.

To underline that bit of homespun philosophy, here are a couple of thought-provoking statistics. Only 40% of brand purchasing decisions are made before a shopper enters a supermarket. The other 60% are totally governed by what the shopper sees in the store. And of the shoppers who use lists, an overwhelming 80%–90% identify product categories, not brands—which leaves them completely open to promotional influences when they reach the supermarket aisles.

That influence can utterly overcome the impact of media advertising, according to Anne Yeoman, general manager of the Sales Advantage, DDB Needham's sales promotional arm in Australia.

In a special *B&T* magazine feature on retail marketing, Ms Yeoman pointed out that a very good TV commercial could drive a customer into a store to buy that product. But on arriving in the supermarket, the customer might run into a stack of appealing lures for opposition products—perhaps a demonstrator sampling one, a price-off offer, an on-pack sweepstake and in-store radio.

'We know from US research that consumers will change their minds 60% of the time if confronted with a demonstrator. In the case of snack foods, that can go as high as 80%–90% in brand switch.'[1]

As Ms Yeoman rightly stressed, it would be rare indeed for consumers' previously-made brand choices to survive all those pressures. 'The poor old TV advertiser hasn't got a hope by the time they make their decisions,' she concluded.

Consider all that for a moment, and the crucial importance of a strong selling presence at point of sale becomes obvious. In fact, if your product is sold through any kind of retail outlet, I'm certain point of sale is your most important marketing arena. This is where the actual purchase decision is made. This is where all your above-the-line advertising efforts ultimately come to fruition.

Or wither and die.

Start with POS

The importance of point of sale (POS) is now becoming far more widely recognised. Point of Purchase, a company whose research supplied the shopping list statistics above, reports that many US marketers today are planning their in-store programme before their general marketing. They regard positioning and shelf presence as their top priorities, and make retailing and distribution their primary focus.

John Cann, Point of Purchase's managing director, gives a recent example. The Quaker Group put the bulk of Granola Bar's advertising budget into POS. They used ad trolleys, card and shelf advertising, sampling, price discounts and coupons—and lifted Granola Bar sales by up to 326%. True, there's not much scope for shelf advertising in Australia, and we don't yet have coupons—but as this chapter will show, a wealth of other POS techniques is at our disposal.

Clearly, too, the Quaker Group is not the only US marketer reaping rich rewards from POS promotions. According to figures from the Point of Purchase Advertising Institute in New Jersey, POS advertising expenditure in the USA trebled between 1981 and 1991—from $5.1 billion to $15.2 billion.

I'm certain this trend will continue. In my view, point of sale is so vital that I believe all your advertising and marketing planning should begin there. What offer, what message, what contest, what selling point will have maximum impact at point of sale? What POS media will present it most effectively? How much will the POS displays cost? Once you answer those questions, you can work back to distribution and then into media. And you'll know precisely how much money is left for above-the-line promotional activities.

I realise this procedure is the exact opposite of that usually followed. Traditionally, marketers get their advertising agencies to prepare a media advertising campaign. If any of the budget remains, the campaign is then adapted (sometimes) for such 'fringe' activities as point of sale. But instead of treating POS as an optional extra to be looked at if the budget allows, I'm saying it should be the primary focus of your planning, as it has become for so many US marketers. Already, here in Australia I've seen this back-to-front (by traditional thinking) approach gain spectacular sales results not only for grocery brands but for financial and other retail products as well.

Begin at POS and you'll minimise the risk of misspending your budget. You'll put your promotional efforts into a strategy context instead of a one-off quick fix. You'll achieve something I'll be hammering throughout this book—the complete integration of your advertising theme and brand image in everything you do. And you'll bring a new discipline into your budget-setting process— because you'll force yourself to allocate adequate dollars to the key POS area.

The area where the sales rubber finally hits the road.

POS as media

Another way of looking at it is to regard POS as one of your biggest media opportunities. When you think of 'media', you probably think of TV, radio, press, magazines, outdoor, direct mail and maybe PR. I'm arguing that POS is a medium just like any of these—and that it's the vital one you should plan and budget for first, before turning your mind to the others.

True, your opportunities to exploit the POS media depend to a large extent on the nature of the outlet. Packaged goods manufacturers, for instance, obviously have far wider POS media scope in grocery stores than in route trade outlets like milk bars, corner shops and school canteens. In route trade outlets, you're basically limited to company-owned shelving and maybe a poster or two. But even here, you can make good use of one of the most potent POS media of all.

Your pack itself.

Put enough stock weight on the floor, and you create a medium of your own.
Courtesy of Allied Lyons Carlsberg-Tetley Brewing Limited

Your power-packed pack

As we'll see in Chapter 7, your pack is far and away the strongest and most cost-effective medium for publicising promotions like sweepstakes, premium offers and cashbacks. That makes it an extremely valuable selling tool, no matter what sort of outlet it's in—because sweepstakes, premiums, cashbacks and other promotional techniques can bring you many benefits beyond a short-term sales boost. If properly planned, they can add to your product's perceived value on a long-term basis. They can enhance your brand image and positioning. They can raise consumer awareness of your brand. And the prizes and premiums they offer can be matched to—and underline—your product's attributes.

Now, do you notice anything about that list of capabilities? They're exactly the kind of things you hope to achieve through media advertising. So if you can achieve them through the creative use of your pack, that certainly qualifies it to be regarded as a major advertising and communication medium.

The other POS media

Heading the media available to you at point of sale, then, are your pack and the almost limitless promotional possibilities you can feature on it. But there are a host of other POS media as well. The most familiar are display pieces in a wide variety of shapes, sizes and positions. They include:

- *Gondola ends and freestanding display stands.* Like all good media, these give your product extra exposure. The higher and wider your product stack, the better. And the lower the cost you can negotiate, the more efficient your 'media' buy.
- *Dumpbins in high traffic areas.* A tried and proven way to attract passing shoppers and increase impulse sales.
- *Shelf talkers, wobblers and price cut screamers.* If the store lets you put up these temporary items, you'll get extra attention as a result.
- *Posters, header cards, leaflets (the 'please take one' variety) and leaflet dispensers.* Such media do a dual job. They increase consumer awareness of your product and extend the space the store gives to it.
- *Shopping trolley advertisements.* The only mobile in-store display media, they're a good way to keep your product before consumers as they wander the aisles.
- *Floor stickers or footprints.* This somewhat zany idea can be quite effective in leading people straight to your product, especially when you have a promotion going.

A near relative of these display media is your product's outer packaging. With in-store stacking in food barns and the common practice of storing outers above the retail shelves, your outer packaging is frequently visible to shoppers. In those cases, it gives you extra space to promote your product and any offer you may be making. These are extra 'opportunities to see' that shouldn't be ignored.

Given in exchange for multiple proofs of purchase, 3M's $9 'action cash back' was designed to give the brand an unmatched price advantage over its rivals.
Courtesy of 3M Australia Pty Ltd

The spoken word

A good way to strengthen your in-store marketing is to add an audio dimension. In-store radio is becoming an increasingly used medium, as results demonstrate its effectiveness. Advertising agencies are now treating it very seriously, and creating messages specifically for it. A. C. Nielsen research has reported sales gains of 15.3% for products using Superradio, the in-store radio for Woolworths, Tuckerbag and Safeway Supermarkets in New South Wales, the Australian Capital Territory, Victoria and Queensland.[2]

Even the humble loudspeaker can give your in-store efforts a boost. Especially if you're having a contest or promotion, a vocal element can provide extra urgency and excitement, and capture consumers' attention from all over the store.

Another very effective, if more expensive, way to use the spoken word is to give it a body—in the form of a 'mystery shopper' who approaches shoppers as they reach the checkouts. The mystery shopper asks them whether a particular product is in their trolleys. If it is, they win attractive prizes. This technique began in the 1960s in the USA and Europe, where it was widely employed by Proctor & Gamble and Unilever. Originally, the mystery shoppers called on homes in selected suburbs. Now, as most women work and homes are empty during the day, the technique has moved into shopping centres. A variation of it is often used in department stores, where sales staff are available to influence the sale. With the permission of store management, the sales staff are urged to recommend participating brands. If their recommendation leads to sales, both they and the purchaser receive a reward.

The sweet smell of success

So far, we've talked about grabbing shoppers' attention through the senses of sight and sound. My wife, Jennifer McKay Williams, an aromatherapist by profession, has reminded me of another sense—one that could be even more effective than vivid visual images and arresting aural impacts in inducing sales.

The sense of smell.

She's right, of course (and not just because she's my wife!). Close your eyes for a moment and imagine you're in a baker's shop. Can't you just smell the fresh bread, the pies, the cakes? Tempting, isn't it? In recent years, some supermarket chains have included a bakery as an integral part of their product offering. Their success is one pointer to the power of aromas in the selling process.

But there are many others. As early as 1908, Freud recognised a strong link between odours and emotions. In fact, he claimed that the most powerful impact on the emotions comes through the sense of smell—and that a vivid memory of a smell is often associated with a positive mood. Do you, for instance, remember the smell of a new car, the tang of leather in a Jaguar, the clean, antiseptic aroma of a pharmacy?

I'll bet you do—especially if you have pleasant memories associated with them.

It's not surprising, then, to read a statement by Dr Alan R. Hirsh, neurological director of the Chicago-based Smell and Taste Treatment and Research Foundation, in the *International Journal of Aromatherapy*.[3]

Back to childhood

Dr Hirsh maintains that the impact of certain smells on the emotions can have 'quite profound effects' for marketers. He states that evoked memories of smells in childhood usually generate positive emotions—which can then be transferred to the store and the products that triggered them. Already, Dr Hirsh points out, the makers of certain oriental perfumes take advantage of the effect by adding the smell of baby powder to their formulas. Why? Because that smell is associated in our adult minds with 'a clean, safe environment'.

In 1991, Dr Hirsh interviewed about 1000 people in a Chicago shopping mall. He based his research on the fact that the olfactory nerves—those associated with smelling—send messages directly to the brain's limbic system, which is linked to the nervous system and emotions. In other words, olfactory substances stimulate our bodies, our psyches and our minds. This, by the way, is the basis of aromatherapy—a type of therapy that uses olfactory substances to promote healing.

Blasts from the past

Dr Hirsh found that over 85% of the people he tested displayed what he termed 'olfactory-evoked recall'. In those people, particular smells called up childhood memories and the overall level of happiness associated with them. Nostalgia in those born in and after the 1930s was most often induced by food odours. Those born before the 1930s were more likely to experience nostalgia from the smells of pine, sea air and meadows.

'Through odours, nostalgia may be induced with the greatest ease,' Dr Hirsh summed up.[4] One might well speculate that nostalgia desires will increase in the next decade, because the more we feel dissatisfied with the present, the more we idealise the past. So in the hard times still to come, nostalgia may well prove a powerful selling tool.

And it seems that nothing evokes it like aromas.

Purpose-created aromas

Scientists at Warwick University have taken the research of Dr Hirsh and others a step further. They have actually created special odours for a variety of purposes. These include purifying work environments, reducing stress, impregnating company stationery with a corporate aroma (I know of successful direct marketing campaigns employing aroma-impregnated mail pieces)—and influencing buying behaviour in shops.

Putting this developmental work to commercial use, a company called Marketing Aromatics offers companies tailor-made smells designed to have a positive influence on staff or customers. Other research has shown the potential of such activity. During a 48-hour test in a Las Vegas casino, a smell dispersed through a bank of slot machines led players to pump in an average of 45% more money. It was estimated that, if the aromatic lure were introduced permanently, it could increase Nevada's slot machine revenue by $750 million a year!

There's a lot of evidence, in short, that aromas can evoke powerful and positive emotions—at least as powerful as those created by our sight and sound senses, if not more so. Consequently, while the science is in its infancy, alert marketers have a huge opportunity to be among the first to use aromas creatively at point of sale—in the product, its packaging and promotional material.

It would seem that (and I've tried to resist writing this, but have failed) heeding Dr Hirsh would make a great deal of scents.

Two-way communication

A fairly new innovation—and a very powerful one—allows shoppers to phone and hear the day's specials. You can arrange this by a 0055 number, and let the customer pay for the call while you pocket the Telecom rebate. Or you can organise a 1 800 or 13 number, and foot the bill yourself. Either way, you can expect excellent results.

You can also use your dedicated phone number as a POS response device, to work alongside couponed leaflets and packs. To enter a contest, request a premium or obtain more product information, consumers simply dial the number. In a rapidly growing related technique, they lodge requests or entries through a computer keyboard incorporated in a display unit.

Whether you employ a dedicated phone number or a computer, you'll find these sophisticated response devices work spectacularly well. They greatly increase response rates because they make it so much easier and quicker for the consumer to reply. Pencils, stamps and envelopes are eliminated, fulfilment costs are halved and database information collection for store and manufacturer alike is enormously simplified.

The next technological step will make things easier still. To enter contests or order premiums, the consumer will simply pass a frequent shopper card or credit card through a barcode reader machine. Technologies are in development which will allow each of us to carry a miniaturised mobile phone about the size of a hearing aid. But that's a little way off yet. Meanwhile, do your best to find creative ways of using phone or computer response devices. They'll vastly improve your response rate and add an extra dimension of immediacy to your promotion. Above all, they'll bring you one step closer to marketing's ultimate goal: a one-to-one relationship between the marketer and every individual consumer.

More new ideas

One reason why interactive response devices work so brilliantly is that they're not only easier but much more fun than filling out coupons. If you can find ways of injecting fun into shopping trips, you'll be amazed at the results you achieve.

Many such opportunities are now available to you, courtesy of the electronic revolution. Most are quite mind boggling, yet surprisingly inexpensive. But perhaps the most startling thing about them all is how little they are being used. Writing recently in *B&T* magazine, John Wassner put it this way: 'Electronic sophistication means that a veritable treasure of promotional opportunities has emerged—at an affordable price. Yet how many promotions take advantage of the advances?'[5]

These remarkable new electronic POS media come in many forms. Among the most practical are:

- *Smart posters*: a device in these intriguing items detects the presence of a passing shopper and activates a pre-recorded and changeable sales message. Although small enough to be fitted into header cards, shelf strips or pack replicas, 'smart' posters are still rare in Australian supermarkets.
- *Two-way videos*: imagine the impact of a video that stops shoppers in the aisles, flags a product, provides information and answers questions on the spot. It's certain to get your customer's undivided attention.
- *Talking necktags*: just like any other necktag, these sit around the neck of a bottle—but unlike the others, they provide product

Traffic to your product on shelf will be enhanced by this Speakstakes™ card which can be attached to packs or tipped into a press advertisement. Take it to your favourite store and you can listen to hear if you've won when you slide your card into this shelf talker display.
Speakstakes™ Courtesy Data Display NY

information verbally or play a jingle when opened. This is a novel and memorable way to add interest to your product.

- *'Pop-out' shelf facings*: these give your product display the extra appeal of motion. A small hidden motor moves product packs on the shelf—an eye-catching effect that passers-by can't help noticing.
- *Holography*: an increasingly common but always stunning technique, holography makes three-dimensional POS material possible. The cost factor usually confines it to permanent displays, but experience suggests it's a worthwhile investment.
- *Video games*: as a visit to any video parlour will indicate, com-puter-generated animation and three-dimensional effects have reached extremely high levels of sophistication. You can use the same technology in-store to demonstrate and sell products, highlight special offers or give further information at the touch of a button.

- *Robots:* not a new idea, but still one with a touch of science fiction magic. When a robot bowls up to people and hands them a leaflet, few, if any, will refuse to take it.

Tomorrow's World

An in-store system that can deliver coupons and collect purchasing data at the supermarket till? Yes, it exists now.

Called Vision Value Network, it has been developed by Advanced Promotion Technologies of Deerfield Beach, Florida. Successful trials have been completed at over 100 US supermarkets, *Precision Marketing* reported following the DMA's (Direct Marketing Association of America) annual 1993 conference.

Shoppers are alerted by shelf promotions and money-off offers. At the checkout, the promotional coupon is printed out directly. It can be backed by live action video or audio messages and interactive offers activated by a touchscreen.

The system can also instantly deduct money from shoppers' bills as orders are processed. Data capture and targeted promotions can be added to the system if shoppers have a Vision Value Network smart card. These store demographic and lifestyle data on individual customers and can be used to trigger information-specific promotions.

At the same time, data on an individual's purchasing habits is added so that a complete pattern of their buying habits is established.

Big US brand operations like HJ Heinz, RJ Reynolds and Procter & Gamble have already tested the system in 52 million separate transactions.

APT describes Vision Value Network as a 'one-stop, in-store system that delivers virtually any imaginable marketing programme—targeted coupons, personalised letters, sweepstakes, games, recipes, discounts and video messages instantly'.

Pictures and sound

Another idea just emerged is the Kodak Photo CD System. This integrates photo CD capability and 'one bit' audio technology to produce outstanding picture quality and sound reproduction. With easy control mechanisms, consumers can select individual information and pictures together with a voice soundtrack. Coupled with advances in big screen technology, touch screen controls, movement and information access at POS, this system will open up new possibilities for interaction between customer and product.

These 'gee-whiz' gadgets are just some of the coming wave of hi-tech POS media. Whether you use the ones I've outlined or adapt other electronic possibilities, this is a great way to add excitement to your POS presence. But don't overlook the older POS media, either.

Warren Gilmer of Southdown Press said in *Australian Professional Marketing*: 'Marketing support for magazine titles is critical and point of sale promotion, in particular, has become a lot more competitive and professionally run, particularly in newsagents.' He goes on to say, 'All publishers are recognising the power of point of sale in newsagencies and sub-agencies, so it's not just a matter of posters now. It's specially designed display bins, streamers, balloons, professionally designed counter display units and header boards. Everything that moves and whistles can be put into a newsagency these days. Promotion at point of sale shifts a lot of product which illustrates the point that POS is important in any retail situation.'[6]

What you want is the most powerful media combination possible at point of sale. Exactly how you obtain it will depend on your product, your product positioning, your brand image, your budget and your promotional activities. My point is that your advertising plan should begin at point of sale—and that POS should never be dismissed as a 'nice if we can afford it but not essential' afterthought.

What store management wants

Obviously, it's no good spending money on brilliant POS displays if the stores won't let you put them up. So how can you ensure that store management will be as enthusiastic about them as you are?

Start by making sure your display communicates a clear benefit and looks good. If you do, says Woolworths' Alan Holroyd, 'there's a good chance of it being placed on show for a period of time'.

'We also appreciate the value of good in-store material. We want to convey the feeling of business and freshness and a good ambience.'[7]

However, for consistent placement, you have to go beyond good communication and design. Put yourself in the store manager's shoes. He or she has one basic aim—to move stock out the door. At any given time, there will be perhaps 6000–8000 products in a fair-sized store. The marketers of hundreds of them will be clamouring for special display space. However, because more and more space is being devoted to house brands, only 50 or so will get it. Which ones will they be? Clearly, the ones that store management believes will perform best at the checkout. That decision will be based not just on past performance or the creativity of the proposed display—although both factors will certainly be considered. To a great extent, the decision will be based on the sales representative concerned, and how far his or her judgement is trusted by store management.

The importance of trust

Trust, then, is a vitally important part of the POS display process. And to earn it, your representatives have to prove themselves to store management. They have to demonstrate a concern for total store sales as well as their own. They have to show a flair for erecting displays that make shopping at that store more interesting and eventful. In short,

The Kiwi Shoe Care Centre not only offers a full range of shoe care products, but helps you choose the right one for you. Information like this at point-of-sale can be a powerful sales generator.
Courtesy of ASDA Stores Ltd

The Melitta Coffee Shop gives shoppers a little excitement. It breaks up the monotony of a shopping trip with a trial and purchase opportunity.
Courtesy of Melitta House of Coffee Pty Ltd

they have to convince store management that they can help them attract more customers and move more stock.

Building up such trust is not an overnight job, but it has to be a top priority if you're going to seize the huge selling opportunities POS offers. Many—if not most—manufacturers miss the opportunity. I believe this is why POS promotion has become one of modern marketing's most underrated sales techniques. Used properly and with imagination, however, it can be enormously impactful, most effective strategically and very economical.

'Who offers fun wins'

John David of Davids Holdings said in the *Retail Grocer* way back in 1984, 'Let's get back to some of that old fashioned gimmickry and fun and excitement in our stores to help diffuse the price emphasis.'[8]

Tom Peters at a seminar in Sydney in 1993 quoted the hugely successful grocery retailer Stew Leonard: 'I'm doing my job if I can get the customer when in store to say, "Wow!".'[9] Few, I believe, have begun to scratch the Wow! (Action now) surface. The most notable exception here is Paul Simon's 'Woolworths—The Fresh Food People'.

The 'fun' and 'Wow!' emphases are in full flight in some of Australia's progressive supermarkets. These include Franklins' Big Fresh and Western Australia's Advantage Rockinghams. In these stores, Anne Yeoman told *B&T*, 'the whole supermarket environment is fun, alive. There's a huge assortment of groceries available, a fish market, a bakery,

CSR's long running cause-related strategy reversed a slump in sugar sales. It convinced many that making cakes, desserts and jams was indeed a 'natural part of life'. CSR sugar also gather a number of brands essential to cooking with sugar under their promotional banner to create an event instore.
Courtesy of CSR Refined Sugars

games for the kids to play and demonstrations and samplings of all sorts of products. It makes shopping more interesting. That's where the trend will be.'[10]

The P. T. Barnum of shoe selling

In some American specialist stores known as 'category killers', the fun trend is already sharing top billing with deep price cuts. In 1993, a 39-store chain called Shoe Carnival sold Rockports, Reeboks and Hush Puppies worth $127 million. That's an average of $3.4 million per store, and $278 per square foot—64% more sales than the US shoe store average. In 1992, the company's profits were $45 million, or 83¢ a share.

How do they do it? *Business Review Weekly*, reporting a *Forbes* magazine case study,[11] commented that shopping at Shoe Carnival was 'a little like going to the circus, without paying admission'. It traced the visit of one woman, who brought her sister to share the experience.

Forty minutes after arriving, the woman had bought five pairs of shoes. She had also:

- won a T-shirt for having the most keys (15) on her key-ring;
- entered the Big Toe contest—the shopper with the longest toe gets a chance to grab for cash and coupons being blown around inside a glass booth (she didn't win that);
- watched her son win a T-shirt for scoring at the basketball machine;
- been handed $1 cash by a tuxedo-ed employee, who had been

> calling the bargains like a carnival barker. The $1 was hers if she bought a pair of Dr Scholl's walking shoes. She bought two pairs for $17.88 each, instead of the normal $24.97.

In short, she bought a lot of shoes—and she had a wonderful time. The two are obviously interrelated.

Shoe Carnival's proprietor, David Russell, follows the same basic philosophy as other current winners like Toys'R'Us and Bed Bath & Beyond. He aims to dominate the market by offering shoes more cheaply than anyone else. But he also recognises that shoppers want to have fun.

'Russell is the P. T. Barnum of the shoe industry,' says his partner. 'People love to buy new shoes because it makes them feel good,' adds Russell himself. 'We're just making it fun.'

The lesson for marketers

It's true that, in all the 'fun' exhortations and examples I've just quoted, the initiative has come from the retailers. But there's a lesson here for marketers too. When you plan your POS promotion, see if you can work a fun dimension into it. If you can make the whole thing a fun event or contest, so much the better.

The more fun it is, the better it's likely to work—and the happier the stores will be to give it space and time.

A 'category killer' retailer ideally placed to offer in-store fun is Toys'R'Us, who see a wide-open market in Australia. Our penetration in toys here is much lower than that of the USA or Europe—and so is our motivation to add excitement at POS. This retailer will provide the excitement for all ages because product and point of sale together will create the Wow! to make the sale. Other retailers watch out!

Setting your budget

As with any medium, good POS planning begins with sound budgeting. Basically, that means estimating the number of stores that will take your display (not all will), and determining production costs for the necessary display pieces, promotional packs, outer packaging, header cards, gondola ends, electronic devices or whatever.

The big point here, I believe, is to cost all these items from the one marketing budget and not from budgets that have been departmentalised into separate sales force or key account budgets. Only then will they get the priority and the resources they deserve.

Creating the material

The first thing to stress about the actual creation of your POS material is the need to start it early. We've always found that the biggest problem is getting it all done in time. And running late with it, in our experience, can lead to acrimony between sales and marketing of fairly awesome dimensions.

Consider, for instance, a back-to-school display scheduled to break on 16 January. You'd need to allow around six weeks for design and development, four weeks for artwork and six weeks for printing, trimming, cutting and packing. Then you'd need to get it into the holding store before Christmas, in the kind of clearly marked packaging that will save it from sinking without trace for distribution and siting early in the New Year. In all, you're looking at a total cycle of 20 weeks. It sounds a long time, but allow any less than that, and you'll find yourself cutting corners—and effectiveness—somewhere along the way.

Go for great design

I never cease to be amazed at the top marketers who spend vast sums on TV, radio, press and magazines—only to settle for truly awful graphics and doubtful consumer offers at point of sale. It's just as vital to invest in the best creative and design talent at POS as it is in any other medium, if not more so. You can't afford anything less than material that's well-thought-out, highly creative and totally in line with brand values, brand positioning and above-the-line advertising themes. If you can build in a seasonal flavour, that helps too. And if you can include a store theme as well, the store manager will be more inclined to view your display with a favourable eye.

Besides being brilliant, however, all POS design has to be practical as well. To start with, the material has to break down to fit in salespeople's

As the school holidays end, Smiths use point-of-sale impact to awaken repurchase habits among shoppers with school age children.
Courtesy of The Smiths Snack Food Company

cars. And it has to be simple and easy to erect. I remember standing for an hour with a salesperson, trying to assemble a rocket-shaped display. Such a struggle only frustrates the salesperson, and kills his or her enthusiasm.

Ten tips for success

In his book *Only £3.95?!*, Alan Toop cites nine key sales promotion principles which apply with equal force to point of sale.[12] Take all nine into consideration, and you'll create some very potent POS displays.

1. *Link displays closely with the brand.* Both in words and visual presentation, make certain your display is clearly linked with your brand. Be sure it's strong on brand values, positioning and themes.
2. *Urge the consumer to immediate action.* Leave the consumer in no doubt as to the immediate action you want. 'Get XXX free!' 'Collect just 3 wrappers!' 'Enter now and win!' Make your appeal in the form of a direct command, which is always stronger than a polite suggestion.
3. *Be honest and credible.* Tell the truth without exaggeration. Make your claims believable. Never resort to dishonesty—if you feel your offer isn't strong enough, go back to the drawing board and create one that is.
4. *Give consumers what they want.* Be alert to the market's needs and meet them.
5. *Be highly visible.* Ensure that your packs, leaflets, display units and so on stand out. Be unusual, imaginative and surprising. Above all, make your offer exciting and generous.

6. *Be clear.* Is your offer obvious at a glance? Can people take it up with the minimum of effort and obstacles? If not, think again.
7. *Benefit everyone concerned.* As well as benefiting the consumer and yourself, your offer should also benefit everyone else along the way. Don't, for instance, rob the store of a sale by offering an article they sell as a free premium.
8. *Be legal.* You need to abide very strictly by both the letter and the spirit of the law.
9. *Make sure the promotion can be implemented efficiently.* Your POS promotion involves a lot of people—your advertising or sales promotion agency, printers, distributors, sales representatives, merchandisers and others. The effective co-ordination of these people is one of the most important POS elements. Fail here, and you're likely to fail everywhere.

   Those are Alan's nine points. Now I'd like to add another.
10. *Give the customer solid, factual, reason-to-buy information.* Woolworths' national advertising manager Alan Holroyd says:

    'Customers want more information than ever before. We're much more analytical. Our basic level of education has risen and schools are teaching people to ask 'why' more often. Marketers who can explain why they should buy their products, with the right amount of information, will see the results.'[13]

I believe him. In this information society, much business-to-business sales talk is about transferring knowledge and information from one person to another. I'm certain the same principle applies to shoppers in stores. Wise marketers will take careful note of Alan Holroyd's observations.

Keep your display sparkling

If your display has a life of more than a few days, be sure to keep it in tip-top condition. I remember one case of a display that was well maintained in one store and neglected in another. In the first store, sales fell by an expected 30% in the second week. In the second store, second-week sales plunged by an incredible 512%.

So good housekeeping pays off—but, of course, only up to a point.

Once a display has run its planned course, remove it promptly. There's nothing worse or more costly than letting a tired old display struggle on long after it should have been gracefully retired.

Use the store's resources

In some instances, the store itself has resources that can help you strengthen your display. My agency was involved in launching one of the most effective of these yet seen in Australia—Retail Ticket System's magnetic price tickets.

Based on the humble fridge magnet, this simple system has provided the answer to the bane of store management's lives—pricing. Now retailers can alter prices instantly, just by changing magnetic figures. No more crude hand-written signs, or throwing out recently printed signs because of late price changes from head office. Reusable magnetic numbers cut costs and give a pleasing uniform appearance throughout the store.

Before...

After...

Meat counters were transformed when butchers and consumers were taught new ways to think about meat as part of a balanced diet.
Courtesy of Australian Meat and Livestock Corporation

That's the story we sold to the retail trade—and for which we gained wide acceptance. BBC Hardware has saved $250 000 a year in printed price tickets and even more in manpower. The new system has helped to boost sales, because it makes prices clear and easy to understand. It has also greatly improved the stores' appearance. If the magnetic tickets are available in your product outlets, they could help you design better-looking and more economical displays.

Improving the environment

Perhaps the biggest single point of sale revolution in Australia happened when the Australian Meat and Livestock Corporation (AMLC) transformed butchers' shops across the nation.

Back in 1984, butchers' shops were viewed as 'high street morgues with uninspiring red meat and price tags'.[14] Butchers themselves were seen purely as macho fellows who waved choppers around. Their customers wanted meal suggestions—but the butchers could give them nothing but meat. The AMLC changed all that with a brilliant marketing campaign. Conceived and produced by the Campaign Palace, Sydney, it involved advertising, education to help butchers display their meat more attractively, a dramatically increased meat product range—and a very heavy emphasis not only on point of sale promotion but a complete revamp of the sales outlets themselves.

Chris Adams of Chris Adams Research said in *B&T* magazine:

> 'The campaign was supported at point of sale. Free recipe cards, placed in all butchers and supermarkets, provided consumers with direct access to Short Cut meals. The convenience benefit was underscored by ensuring the preparation time rarely went beyond 20 minutes and the meal ingredients were accessible and affordable. The cards were constantly updated to maintain consumer interest.
>
> 'Point of sale was transformed. Pristine tiles replaced sawdust-covered floors. Merchandising material festooned walls and counters, recalling Short Cuts advertising and underpinning red meat with nutritional information. Butchers' display win dows metamorphasised into an exhilarating feast of options,

> seducing consumers with a tempting variety of meat products and relieving women of the pressure to come up with meal ideas. Butchers began to learn the art of salesmanship, paying heed to customer questions and suggestions, innovating with new product concepts and marketing tactics.'[15]

Through this campaign, red meat took its own shortcut to success. The entire venture has come to be a case study in imaginative and innovative marketing.

The School Bus Spectacular

Frito-Lay, formerly Arnott's Snack Foods, is one major marketer that has learnt to exploit point of sale very successfully. Their spectacular and creative displays are designed to make the most of seasonal opportunities, and to generate a high level of impulse sales.

Typical for impact and imagination was their 'School Bus Spectacular' display. From its commanding in-store position, it urged parents to put chips in their children's lunch boxes after the long summer holidays. As a further inducement, and to speed the pull-through of Ruffles and Thins, the display also offered a free movie ticket with every pack purchased. It was a great success.

Another top performer was Arnott's 'Big Grab' POS promotion in

Frito-Lay impact consumers with outstanding graphics. Communicated via posters, TV and instore media, their promise offered 50 grams at a 25 gram price.
Courtesy of Frito-Lay Australia

Big instore events can stir enthusiasm among the salesforce and consumers alike, and create huge display and sales opportunities.
Courtesy of Frito-Lay Australia

route trade outlets, offering more product for the same price. The display was celloglazed for durability, and just went on stimulating sales throughout its long in-store life.

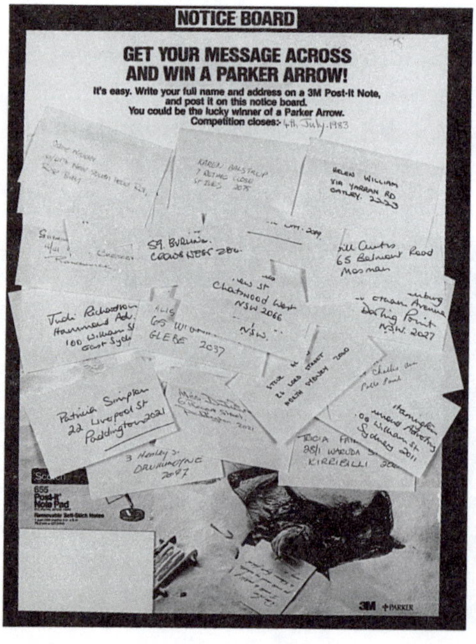

3M Post It Notes cleverly employ their product as an entry device which demonstrates its use and builds three dimensional interest. Such point-of-sale intrigue promotes involvement, understanding of the product and 'bucks' buying.
Courtesy of 3M Australia Pty Ltd

Grand Final glamour

Continuing the company's seasonal concept are special displays timed to coincide with the football Grand Finals in Sydney and Melbourne. Their design gives the salespeople plenty of opportunity to drape the displays with

Coppertone use a dial-your-own-skin-type sundial to underpin their sun factor (SPF) range proposition and create interest and involvement at point of sale.
Courtesy of Wella Australia

local team colours—which consumers even have a chance to win. Tieing in with football final fever in this way has enhanced the company's popular image, and given impulse buying a substantial boost.

Dial your skin type

Coppertone, a long-established suntan lotion brand, designed a very involving 94-product off-shelf display. It featured the brand's famous small-girl-and-dog motif, plus a sundial device that invited shoppers to dial their skin type and SPF factor. It helped the brand to achieve a 144% sales increase in 1991 over the previous year.

Welcome to the Green and Gold

BP now employ an elaborate and distinctive livery on their forecourts worldwide. Probably, there is no better example of the positive effect at point of sale that good, clean, well-thought-out design can have on a company's corporate image. BP's green and gold colours and the unique facia design with its rounded corners and modern signage demonstrate to us that BP is environmentally aware. The combination of colours, typestyle and design makes for a look that suggests efficiency, cleanliness and an attitude and service not obtainable elsewhere. Importantly, the design and colours are not incompatible with BP's product range extension into forecourt shops.

This uniformity and attention to detail are reinforced every time you pass a BP station. The image says 'it's worthwhile missing a few other

BP's livery reinforces brand perception. It is distinctive, clean and uniform worldwide.
Courtesy of BP Australia Limited

stations for this!'. The pride of appearance, both externally and internally, rubs off on BP, their franchisees and their staff. The whole image is designed to give consumers a feeling of uniformity, a common standard of excellence of service and a warm 'welcome'—a classic case of the book being better than its cover.

BP's promotions stand out a mile against this attractive background.

On the scent of sales

In the cosmetics industry, POS gets a bigger share of the budget than advertising or PR. Free-standing displays spearhead the selling effort in hotels, airports and department stores. They're at least as important as the consultant in making the sale—and with every new marketing year comes the challenge to create still more effective selling pieces. The cosmetics industry in general would rather impact customers at the counter than spend money on bringing them into the stores.

Seagrams Global Duty Free mirror the success of the fragrance houses in the design of their point of sale and their 'high touch' personal service. This further enhances their brands' premium price and images. As well, they reinforce customer relationships through their Premier Club.
Courtesy Seagrams Global Duty Free

Some cosmetic companies, however, go even further. They include coupons in advertisements and inserts in upmarket magazines, which consumers can redeem for free gifts or discounts at point of sale. This brings in new prospects and increases store traffic, to the benefit of the brand and the delight of the retailer. With such activity bringing in more customers, how can any retailer refuse to stock the brand?

Robyn Holt, general manager of Yves Saint Laurent in Australia, suggests an even more integrated approach. She says, 'We place a great deal of importance on our merchandising and point of sale material and therefore as with advertising, we have a concentrated dollar spend in this area'. Robyn goes on to explain:

> 'Yves Saint Laurent creates theatre with his fashion, and his fragrances and beauty are the accessories. All over the world, the images and theatre of Yves Saint Laurent are re-invented in department stores via display and merchandising material to entrance the consumers as they escape into the world of Yves Saint Laurent. In our corner of the busy cosmetic and fragrance department, we must create an atmosphere where our customer can escape. Where she can be whisked off to Paris with the scent of fresh roses and scenes of the Eiffel Tower or take in the heady notes of Opium and the Far East. To create such an atmosphere we must make extensive use of point of sale material such as cafe chairs and tables to create a Rive Gauche scene of Jazz musicians with trumpets blaing to

herald the sweet smell of Jazz. The customer wants to feel beautiful, invigorated and be given a special feeling of confidence—this our consultants offer and also make available sweet smelling spray cards and samples as a reminder of our customers' brief interlude with another time, another place.'[16]

I believe the thinking underlining the cosmetic industry's approach, could well be copied by other product manufacturers as it has by Max Hunt and his team at Seagrams. From experience, I'm convinced POS can at least equal, if not outstrip, advertising as a contributor to brand profits.

Beyond doubt, in my view, point of sale is one of the most potentially rewarding—and most overlooked—areas in the whole armoury of modern marketing and promotion.

The point of purchase communications mix

Ten recommendations for better management at the point of sale and purchase.

This list of recommendations was made available by my partner,

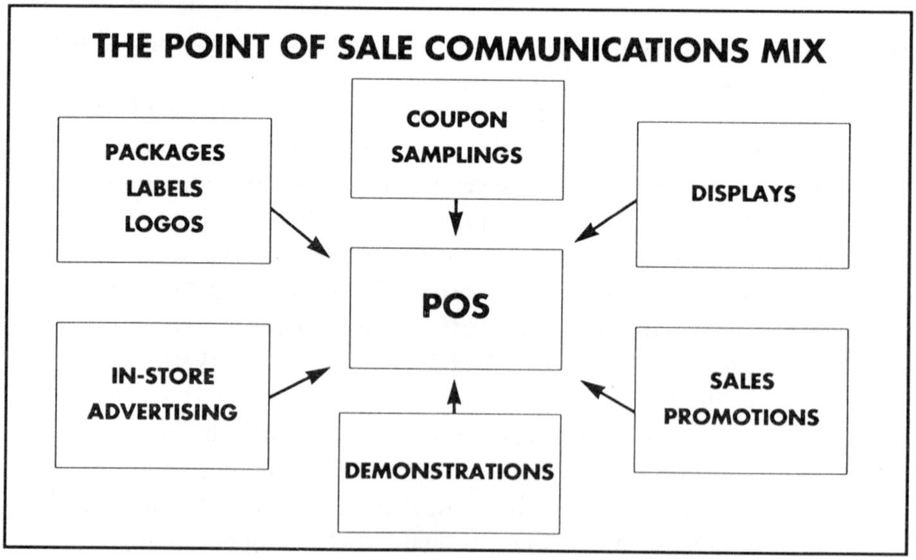

Andrew Edwards. While it is most appropriate to mass merchandisers, it is also relevant to all retail point of purchase thinking.

1. Develop POS programmes, not POS materials.
2. Develop POS programmes that are consistent with consumer behaviour and add value for the consumer.
3. Integrate POS programmes within the communications mix.
4. Co-ordinate POS programmes across the product line.
5. Develop POS programmes that are:
   - creative;
   - flexible;
   - easy to understand;
   - easy to implement.
6. Carefully plan the implementation of POS programmes and compensate fairly those who implement them.
7. Develop POS programmes that make money for the trade by:
   - increasing store traffic;
   - increasing the average dollar sale;
   - cross selling other products;
   - fitting with store decors, merchandising themes and strategies;
   - tailoring POS programmes by class of trade and by account.
8. Develop POS programmes as part of an integrated customer service programme for trade accounts.
9. Test alternatives, monitor performance and play the customer.
10. Think about point of sale programmes *strategically* as well as tactically.

Notes

1. Anne Yeoman, *B&T magazine*, special report, Retail Marketing by Sally Rawlings, 2 July 1993.
2. *B&T magazine*, special report, Retail Marketing by Sally Rawlings, 2 July 1993.
3. Dr Alan Hirsh, 'The Therapy of Smell', *International Journal of Aromatherapy*, June 1993.

4. Article entitled 'Market Facts', *International Journal of Aromatherapy*, July 1993.
5. *B&T magazine*, 'Point of Sale', by John Wassner, in special feature on sales promotion, July 1991.
6. Warren Gilmer, quoted in article by Chris Pearson, in *Australian Professional Marketing*, Thompson Publications, June 1993.
7. *B&T magazine*, special report, Retail Marketing by Sally Rawlings, 2 July, 1993.
8. *Retail Grocer*, May 1984.
9. Tom Peter's seminar, Darling Harbour, May 1993.
10. *B&T magazine*, special report, Retail Marketing by Sally Rawlings, 2 July, 1993.
11. 'These shoes are made for hawking', by Darron Darlia, quoted from *Forbes magazine* in *BRW*, July 1993.
12. Alan Toop, *Only £3.95?!*, The Sales Machine Ltd, London, 1978.
13. *B&T magazine*, special report, Retail Marketing by Sally Rawlings, 2 July 1993.
14. Reg Bryson, The AMLC Case Study by Chris Pearson, *B&T magazine*, May 1985.
15. Chris Adams, The AMLC Case Study by Chris Pearson, *B&T magazine*, May 1985.
16. Robyn Holt, general manager of Yves St Laurent, in a letter to M. Williams, 1993.

3

CHAPTER

Sweepstakes' Winning Ways

Like a familiar face in a crowded street, one sales promotion technique among today's horde of options is well known to us all. In fact, I'll wager we've all responded to it ourselves at one time or another. I refer to the most popular and most widely used sales promotion technique around: the sweepstake and its close relatives—prize draws, instant win games and competitions. Why is the sweepstake Number 1 in the sales promotion popularity stakes? Several obvious reasons leap to mind.

No other technique gives consumers a chance to win enticing prizes for little or no outlay and no effort beyond completing and returning an entry coupon. No other technique creates such an air of excitement and occasion. And from the promoter's viewpoint, no other technique is as quick and easy to put into practice. All that's usually needed is a little legal input on rules and regulations, and permit numbers for each state.

The lure of the lottery

The lure of big prizes for a minimal outlay has made lotteries the world's most widely entered form of contest. As sweepstakes are basically lotteries, it's easy to see why consumers around the globe respond so enthusiastically to them.

This ready response is even more understandable in Australia. After all, we're a nation of gamblers. We put money on everything from poker machines to horses to dogs to two flies climbing up the wall. The mere fact that we lose most of the time doesn't deter us in the least. In such a cultural climate, it's hardly surprising that sweepstakes and their relatives flourish—and deliver huge numbers of entries and (even more importantly) increased sales to alert marketers.

Relaxing the laws

The worldwide popularity of the technique can be traced back to a relaxing of US laws in the early 1960s. Those laws had been put in place in the 1930s and 1940s. Draconian in their effect and intent, they had virtually eliminated 'games of chance' from commercial promotions. Definite elements of skill and judgement had to be included in all competitions. But early in the 1960s, the US laws were eased. The rest of the world swiftly followed suit, and sweepstakes soared to a level of popularity they have maintained ever since.

Strengths and weaknesses

However, before you rush off and splash your budget into a sweepstakes spectacular, let me issue a word of caution.

Sweepstakes are not a cure-all for every marketing problem. They have definite strengths, true—but they also have definite weaknesses. As with every other sales promotion technique, the key to success with sweepstakes lies in knowing what they can and cannot do.

First, their strengths. They're very good at building an air of excitement around your product. Moreover, that excitement is infectious among customers, your sales force and the trade in general. Usually it spreads to the retailers too—because they can see the merits of an event that brings prize-hunting people into their stores. People who are likely to buy not only your product but also other products while they're there.

Joint promotions create bigger events and better offers. Extensive media coverage made this joint promotion an attractive one for British Airways, the Ritz and ITT Sheraton Hotels and Resorts Pacific. They were happy to add their endorsement and participation. *Courtesy of Unifoods: a Division of Unilever Australia*

Sweepstakes attract more entries than any other sales promotion technique. They can build your product image and strengthen your brand identity and positioning. They can reinforce your advertising theme. And they can be highly effective in expanding your share of in-store shelf and aisle space.

Now, their weaknesses—of which the first, it must be admitted, is a fairly major one.

A temporary blip

Sweepstakes as traditionally run are not all that effective in developing long-term sales. Certainly, one based on a solid, well-thought-out strategy should at least get you a decent blip on the sales curve—but as most contestants are only there for the prizes, the blip is very likely to be a temporary one.

Nor do traditional sweepstakes have a good track record in obtaining large-scale product sampling. Their power to motivate substantial brand switching remains in doubt, too. A Kellogg's® Corn Flakes on-pack sweepstake recently drew 300 000 entries. By any standards, that's a massive result. It probably represented 10% of all the promotional packs in the market-place. But the question is: how many of those entries came from people who don't normally buy the brand?

Instant prize promises, so near at hand as buying hands waver around the supermarket shelves. The idea that the prize could be as near as inside these cans helped guide consumers unerringly to Copper Kettle and Pedigree Chum.
The label illustrations appearing on pages 56 and 72 are reproduced with the permission of copyright owner, Uncle Ben's of Australia. Copper Kettle appears courtesy of Cottees.

Accentuate the positive

However, please don't let that litany of gloom turn you off sweepstakes as a technique. The strengths I listed above are all very worthwhile objectives. What's more, the weaknesses are by no means chipped in stone. The proof-of-purchase approach, for instance, is being increasingly used to generate immediate sales from sweepstakes. People have to buy the product at least once before they can enter the draw for the goodies.

You may have noticed that I put the word 'traditional' before 'sweepstakes' when I outlined their weaknesses. We have found recently that some 'untraditional' thinking can turn the weaknesses into quite spectacular strengths. I'll expand that point in a moment. But before I do, let's consider another question of more than passing interest to sweepstake promoters—what kind of people enter sweepstakes?

Who enters sweepstakes?

The short but not very helpful answer is just about everybody. Most people will tell you they never enter contests or sweepstakes. When you hear such claims, smile politely but don't believe them. The evidence shows that almost everyone tries their luck in a sweepstake, sooner or later.

Now, let me attempt a more specific and learned-sounding answer to the question. All sweepstakes attract a hard core of what we might call sweepstakes junkies—people who enter every contest in sight that offers halfway decent prizes. And there are plenty of folk in that category. In fact, our research suggests that over 25% of Australian households enter sweepstakes every year, purely with an eye on the potential rewards. What's more, a fair percentage of them enter virtually every promotion they see. The trouble is, of course, that such undiscriminating contestants are less likely to become long-term converts to your brand.

Beyond that core of professional contest-enterers, sweepstake entrants tend to come from across the board. But here's the good news. There's a discernible skew towards people who are the product's market. Women, for instance, are the main buyers of grocery items—and in grocery-item-based sweepstakes, the majority of entrants tend to be women.

That's not all the good news, either. It's possible to increase the percentage of entrants who are potential long-term buyers, and reduce the percentage of those who aren't. I'll keep you in suspense by saying again, 'more on that shortly'.

Prizes the key

Perhaps unsurprisingly, the key to cutting through the clutter and achieving success in any sweepstakes promotion is to offer the right prizes. That sounds easy if you say it quickly. But in practice, choosing the 'right' prizes is a difficult business indeed.

Over the years, sweepstake promoters have offered the most incredible array of attractions—thousands of dollars, lire, pounds and marks; bars of gold; precious gems; cars; boats; homes; exotic holiday destinations. A veritable Aladdin's Cave of glittering prizes, all designed to seize our imaginations, make us feel good about the brand and gain our response.

Kellogg's® Corn Flakes reflect their simple no-nonsense advertising proposition with spectacular prizes that would certainly 'make life a lot simpler' for lucky families.
Courtesy of Kellogg (Aust) Pty Ltd. Registered trademark of Kellogg (Aust) Pty Ltd

In such company, the legendary offer of 'a block of flats—plus Tasmania' doesn't sound too far removed from reality.

Perhaps the most out-of-this-world (literally) prize yet to be offered was put up by Pan Am back in the 1960s. I remember it well. I was 14 years old, and an American Apollo spacecraft was orbiting the moon. My friend Christopher Munro told me he would soon be going to the moon too, courtesy of Pan Am. When I expressed polite but firm scepticism, he took me into the nearest Pan Am office. There I learnt that, for a payment of some £10, Pan Am travellers would have a chance to win a free seat on the first commercial flight to the moon. Christopher's parents were frequent travellers. He persuaded them to switch to Pan Am, and put the moon ticket in his name. I don't know whether he still has the ticket, but the prize certainly caught the imagination then. It still does now. And at least one confirmed instance of brand switching can definitely be attributed to the promotion.

Match the mood of the moment

Meanwhile, back on earth, what kind of prizes should you offer to get the best possible response?

A good way to start is to consider the economic mood of the moment. When times are tough, which they are as I write, people aren't so interested in 'lifestyle' prizes. It's not much use winning a big gas-guzzling car if you can't afford to run it. But what will appeal strongly to people

The 'Choice' brand name was well reflected by a choice of prizes that appealed to the target market and echoed the brand image.
Courtesy of Unifoods: a Division of Unilever Australia

are security-type prizes like money and mortgage relief. In difficult days, such prizes are realistic. They address people's immediate needs, and they tell them that the marketer is more aware of their situation than most others and wants to help.

Which isn't a bad sort of image to be building up in the community.

As times improve and people regain their confidence, the emphasis will swing back onto lifestyle prizes—the kind of merchandise and travel opportunities that everyone dreams of but few ever get to enjoy.

The big hook isn't everything

Most sweepstake promoters start by planning the 'big hook'—the major prize that will look stunning in advertising and lead, they hope, to a flood of entries. I agree with that approach—up to a point. The big hook certainly is important. It's also a highly creative challenge to select one that's not only irresistible to the entrants but affordable for the promoter. But the big hook isn't everything. Even more important, in my experience, is a good range of supporting prizes—appealing but less expensive items that give a much wider circle of people a chance to be a winner. If you offer only a few prizes, you will attract, on the average, comparatively fewer entries. But if you spread the winning chances around by offering more prizes, the number of entries you get is likely to be much higher.

In short, then, don't compromise on the major prize—the big hook—but don't rely on it alone. If your budget makes it possible, have a pyramid of attractive prizes under the big one—with the lowest level perhaps being prizes of your product itself, if that's appropriate.

A fortune—or french fries

McDonald's do this regularly and very successfully. Not long ago in the USA, they ran a promotion that offered prizes ranging from tens of thousands of dollars down to menu items. It was called the '$1.5 Million Touchdown Game'. Customers received a 'game card' with every meal they bought. If it were a winner, they'd pick up a fortune on the spot. But if not, they could stick the card in a game booklet they could obtain from the counter. When the booklet was filled with cards, it could be entered for a second chance at the big prizes.

It's interesting to see the 'odds charts' calculated for these promotions. This chart shows the odds against winning a big prize are usually very long. However, this doesn't seem to deter McDonald's customers, who enter their competitions in droves. I believe it is the lure of the big prizes that attracts them—while picking up the supporting menu item prizes keeps them coming back for another try. If the chain only offered big prizes, I think the number of entrants—and meals sold—would be significantly smaller.

A relatively low cost prize dressed up to offer value and a 'big prize' feel. Comparatively economical prizes can be featured creatively to offer value, if they synergise with the brand and its product positioning.
Courtesy of H J Heinz Company Australia Ltd

Sometimes, small is beautiful

There's another reason for

thinking beyond blockbuster prizes, too. Sometimes, smaller ones can actually be more appealing to particular groups of people. This is where I think many marketers err. They pin their hopes on a few big prizes, gained perhaps through 'contra' (which I'll discuss later in this chapter). But that's the easy way out. The harder—and potentially more effective—way is to think through the possibilities of unusual and original smaller prizes. Such items would not only give more people a chance to win. They could also be far more appropriate to the brand, and to the target audience's real needs and desires.

In fact, travelling that less-crowded route is the way, I believe, to turn sweepstakes' weaknesses into strengths. There are basically two things I'm convinced you should do. First, take the time and trouble to select prizes that enhance the brand's creative positioning. Second, theme the promotion to underline the product's attributes. Our experience suggests you'll then get more than just excitement and heightened brand awareness from your sweepstake.

You'll get impressive sales results as well.

Don't waste a creative opportunity!

My friend and partner, Andrew Edwards, has long argued for this approach. He maintains that to offer a prize—however attractive—that doesn't relate to the brand's values is a cardinal error. It wastes a creative opportunity to underpin what the brand means to the consumer. Similarly, he asserts that if the brand's advertising is correct and has promotional potential, the publicity for the sweepstakes should always endorse the creative proposition contained in the advertising. Nor are Andrew's views mere theory. Results have underlined their soundness time and time again.

For instance, his client Westons Biscuits embraced them for the Chocolate Wheaton brand, Australia's Number 2 chocolate biscuit in terms of sales. Resisting the temptation to offer glittering sweepstakes prizes, Westons went instead for some that reflected the brand's 'full of wholesome country goodness' positioning. They offered a range of down-on-the-farm country holidays. These were promoted on-pack and on point of sale displays, which used a scene from a TV commercial to help endorse the brand's values.

The response to the sweepstake was well down on those of others he'd run—but the promotion gained the extra leverage wanted at point of sale. The result? Sales of Chocolate Wheatons rocketed up 80% over the previous year's figures. The conventional wisdom that sweepstakes don't markedly increase sales was dramatically overthrown. A weakness became a strength—because marketer and agency took the time to match sweepstake prizes to the brand's personality and advertising positioning, and so gained maximum leverage from the brand's advertising proposition.

That demands a lot more effort (and sometimes courage!) than just selecting the biggest prize your budget can afford. But if building sales is more important to you than a mountain of entries, I am certain it's the way to go.

Point of Sale and on-pack promotion work together. First, point of sale creates impact and offtake. Then the on-pack message helps to create repeat purchase, often after expensive off-shelf display has finished. The use of a 0055 number as an alternative to the mail increases response, because it makes it easier to enter. As well, the multiple choice element of the promotion gives more chances to win and should lead to repeat purchasing over a longer time period.
Courtesy of Westons Baked Foods: a Division of George Weston Foods Limited

A golden reward

Unusual and imaginative prizes can draw a big response, too. In the UK, Coca-Cola offered a totally unique one—their distinctively designed original Coca-Cola bottle, cast in pure 18 carat gold. And that wasn't all. To add even more value, they threw in the opportunity to auction this unique trophy at Christies' auction rooms in New York. This let the winners turn their golden prize into a huge amount of cash. Coca-Cola also stressed the fact that the golden bottle was the 'one and only'—which echoed the brand's above-the-line positioning theme at the time.

The sweepstake was a shattering success in the number of entries received, and the reinforcement it gave to Coke's advertising theme line.

What do your customers really want?

Almost every sweepstake offers the chance for highly creative prize selection. Besides taking your brand's characteristics and positioning into account, think carefully about your target audience's needs and desires. What 18-year-old macho youth could resist the chance of winning a Harley Davidson? What young family with children would pass up an opportunity to pay $12 000 off their mortgage? These prize selection points can be summarised as an equation:

Unusual prizes linked to the target group + a tie-in with product values and positioning = above-average entries + higher subsequent sales.

So sit down with your agency and think the possibilities through. You'll find they're almost endless.

The great dictator: the budget

Naturally, your final choice of prizes will be dictated not only by your product's values and your consumers' tastes, but by the toughest arbiter of them all—your budget.

How much money should you allocate to prizes, to make your sweepstake as attractive as possible? That, of course, is a classic 'how long is a piece of string' kind of question. The answer depends on your company, your product, your market, your place within it and your financial situation. You have to consider how much it will cost to gain consumer and trade awareness through leaflets, on-pack communication, point of sale displays and media advertising.

Just to depress you while you're pondering that, a typical large-scale sweepstake promotion in the USA would have a good pyramid of prizes valued at around $750 000. That might include a $250 000 superprize, three grand prizes of $100 000, various quantities of fourth, fifth and sixth prizes, and a myriad of $5 consolation ones. Apart from retailer promotions like those of McDonald's, such a budget is almost unheard-of in Australia. We simply don't have the population or distribution to justify it. But it does underline the importance of allocating enough money to get the right prizes—because they're the major factor in determining the effectiveness of your promotion.

A realistic budget

What, then, is a realistic figure for the Australian situation? Our clients' research suggests there's a prize value threshold, under which entries lag. Some set this threshold as low as $10 000. Our experience points to $25 000 as a more realistic, if not always achievable, figure. I feel that if you can't get at least somewhere near that amount with prizes appropriate to your target market, you should give sweepstakes a miss. You should try another sales promotion technique—especially if you want an immediate lift in sales.

How to stretch your budget

Having said that, I can offer words of comfort and cheer. There are several ways to stretch your budget, and make each dollar work harder for you.

To start with, whatever size your budget is, you don't have to blow it in one hit. Even the US mega-budgets of $100 000–$200 000 or more are commonly stretched over, say, 10 weeks. They might offer weekly prizes worth around $15 000 plus smaller cash prizes, to keep the excitement growing—and give people more chances to buy—as the major prize draws come nearer. You can do the same, even if your budget is vastly smaller. In fact, it's a good idea to do so. Our research suggests that, unless people are regular buyers of a brand, it's very unusual for them to enter a sweepstake more than once. Dividing your prize pool into separate segments can lead them to make multiple purchases of your product, because it gives them more opportunities to win.

Cadbury's did this in 1991, when they ran a 'stretched' sweepstake from May to October, divided into 10 fortnightly games. Contestants could enter as many games as they liked, by forwarding five wrappers from any Cadbury's chocolate bar for each one. There was a Toyota Seca to be won every fortnight, plus holidays in Hawaii, Sharp home entertainment centres, Repco mountain bikes and much more.

If you do stretch your sweepstakes in this way, be sure to specify exactly what can be won in each segment. Honesty and integrity are just as important in your promotions as they are in your product and your advertising.

Amortise your costs

Another way to stretch your budget is to involve several brands in the one sweepstakes promotion. S. C. Johnson did this very successfully with their 'Johnson Wax Spring Clean Sweep-stakes', which also recognised a seasonal opportunity. This promotion featured six complementary brands—Pledge, Johnson Floor Polish, Toilet Duck, Glory Carpet Shampoo, Freedom Dry Spray and Wettex Sponge Cloths. They not only blended together logically from the consumer's viewpoint, at the right time of the year, but amortised the promotion's cost for S. C. Johnson.

An extra thought: if you go this multi-brand route, consider including an own-label product as well—preferably one that complements your product. That will greatly enhance your standing with the retailer, and open doors to extra product and display placement at point of sale—doors that might otherwise have stayed firmly shut.

Get other people to pay

Finally, a most effective way to make a medium to large budget go further is to persuade someone else to pick up the tab—which, in sweepstakes parlance, means getting your prizes via 'contra'.

There are certainly big opportunities for promoters and prize providers alike in the contra approach. But I have some reservations about it. Contra can be a substitute for thinking—an instinctive grab after a big and glittering prize, when the hard slog of selecting less expensive but more appropriate prizes could work much better for you.

Even when contra is the way to go, there are many pitfalls along the road. Your potential contra partners will be just as keen as you are to get maximum benefit from the deal. And if you're not careful, you could find yourself giving up too much of your valuable exposure to someone else—just to clinch a deal that looked great on paper but works rather less well for you in reality. Anyone involved in contra deals quickly learns the truth behind two hoary old cliches—'there's no such thing as a free lunch' and 'you only get what you pay for'.

Here's the reality: it takes great skill, considerable experience and a lot of time to negotiate sweepstake prizes successfully on contra. In fact, I think contra prizes are only worth considering if at least one of three conditions applies:

1. You have a larger-than-average budget and never a small one.
2. The product you're after has a natural link with your product or your market.
3. The sweepstake's media component is big enough to give everyone a fair share of the consumer action.

I'm inclined to add a fourth condition, too. Consider contra only if you have access to a skilled and experienced adviser who can handle the negotiations for you. Otherwise, you could finish up in a severely disadvantaged situation—even if the three conditions I've listed above do apply.

How many hoops are too many?

Earlier, I said the right prizes were a major factor in determining the attractiveness of your sweepstakes. There's another major factor, too—how easy your contest is to enter. Or, to quote some skilled sweepstakes practitioners, how many 'hoops' do your potential entrants have to jump through?

One such practitioner, whose name even rhymes with 'hoop', is my old boss and mentor Alan Toop of The Sales Machine International. Alan

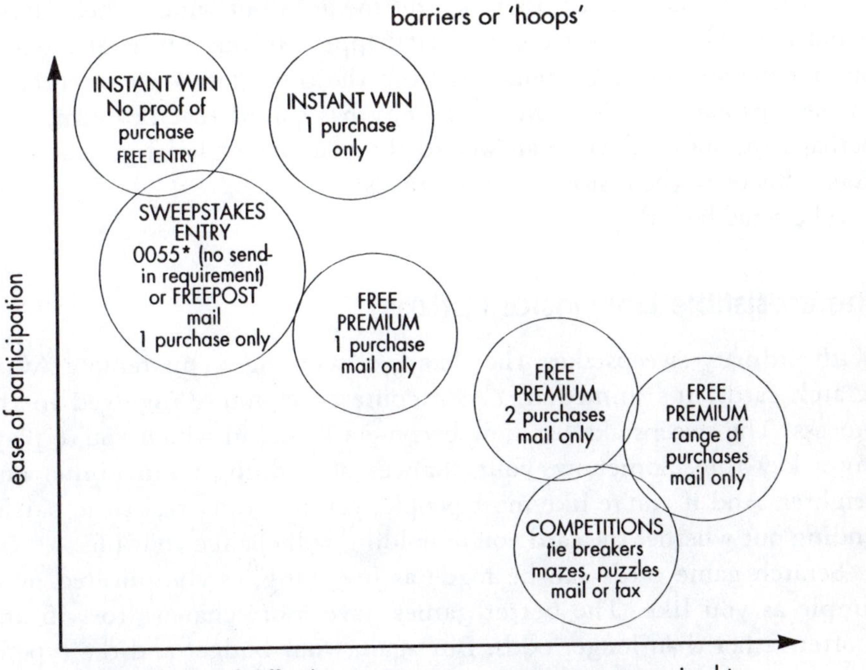

The degree of difficulty increases as consumers are required to provide more proofs of purchase and their efforts and involvement get more demanding. The greater the difficulty, the fewer the entries you're likely to receive.

always maintained that the more things entrants had to do, the fewer entries you would get. 'Hoops are for dogs to go through—not housewives!', he would say (and I would add—'nor for anybody else!'). And he set out his points in the diagram above (which we still call 'Toop's hoops').

You'll notice proofs of purchase are regarded as negatives. Alan didn't mean we shouldn't ask for them. He meant we should recognise the thresholds of effort people are prepared to pass to enter a promotion—and the more proofs of purchase we demand, especially across multiple products, the more hoops we are setting up. A good rule of thumb in judging your hoop level is to ask yourself—would I be prepared to do all that? Ask your friends and colleagues also. If you and they would find the number of hoops a little off-putting, chances are your potential entrants will too.

There's one hoop Alan Toop doesn't mention but which I believe is a major one. That's the prize draw that happens in the future, at a never-never time and place far removed from the contestant's act of entering the sweepstake. But modern technology has solved that problem, with perhaps the most effective answer to the negative or lethargic effects of Toop's hoops in the history of sweepstakes.

The scratch card.

The irresistible bait: instant prizes

With ordinary sweepstakes, the chance of winning seems remote. With scratch cards, it's immediate. As a contestant, you're involved in the process. The sweepstake has now become a game, in which you're playing a key role. Somehow, your chances of winning seem higher and brighter. And if you're like most people, you just can't resist the bait of finding out whether the card you're holding will change your life.

Scratch game cards can be made as involving, as complicated or as simple as you like. The better games have more chances to win and shorter rather than longer odds. But again, your budget and the type of product you're marketing will determine these criteria and the scale of prizes you can offer.

Scratch card promotions have been used very successfully by marketers ranging from Sunday newspapers to retailers to grocery brands to McDonald's restaurants. To increase customer loyalty and maintain circulation, the Sydney *Sun-Herald* ran what was virtually a bingo contest (it couldn't be called such for legal reasons). The promotion offered weekly instant win games, plus one that ran for eight consecutive Sundays—and, by doing so, effectively broke down the multiple-proof-of-purchase hoop.

McDonald's added an extra dimension to theirs, by making it a Trivial Pursuit exercise. Diners received a scratch card with every burger. The card posed a question, and contestants had to scratch one of several alternative answers. Here again, the aim was to boost customer loyalty and prompt more return visits to the restaurants. And it worked. The lure of the scratch card and the fun of the challenge kept people coming back for another try, week after week.

The Channel 9 Big Winners Game attracted viewers to Channel 9 News, by introducing the competition through inserts in newspapers. Winning combinations were announced on TV. Non-stop excitement was guaranteed by attractive prizes and rub-off Instant Win opportunities that were created by watching Channel 9 News.
Courtesy of Channel 9. © Dynamic Marketing and Printing Pty Ltd

These and other scratch card sweepstakes can certainly claim enormous numbers of entries. What's more, they can really increase sales during their course. Our own experience leads me to say that scratch cards can double a promotion's impact—which they need to do, because they're much more expensive to produce than common or garden sweepstakes entry leaflets.

Scratch cards have another advantage for marketers—a sting in the tail that increases their customer appeal. This is the second chance prize draw. Every non-winning ticket can be entered into a further sweepstakes, with a chance to win the unclaimed prizes. So contestants know that if they don't win the first time, they still have a chance to pick up a very attractive item. This adds an extra dimension of interest and excitement to the whole promotion.

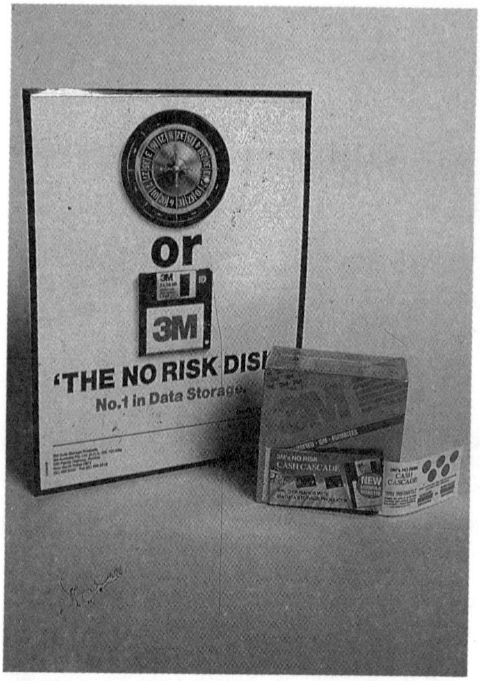

Instant WIN scratch off techniques enhance customer involvement with immediacy and excitement. Using on-pack media, they can be the deciding factor in purchase choice. Integration with outdoor poster and press media increases 3M recognition.
Courtesy of 3M Australia Pty Ltd

Since their introduction, scratch cards have demonstrated their ability to gain impressive numbers of entries. There's only one question mark hovering over them, in my opinion. Will their long-term benefits in regard to increased sales and heightened brand awareness be worth their quite considerable cost?

McDonald's believe so, and have run the Trivial Pursuit game in various similar formats over a three-year period. Time will tell whether other users of the technique will be as successful.

What about you?

Well—we've probed and prodded our way around sweepstakes at some length. Now comes the most important question of all. Is a sweepstake promotion right for you? That's a question that only you and your strategy can ultimately answer. But let me offer a few thoughts that may help you decide, and guide you along the way.

First, think carefully through the technique's strengths and weaknesses. I'm struck by the number of clients whose only promotions, before they came to us, have been sweepstakes—and who can offer no real reason why that is so. Nor are they unique in this respect. There's quite a bit of evidence to suggest that too many marketers go into sweepstakes with only the haziest expectations of results. True, sweepstakes are probably the least measurable of sales promotion techniques. But their cost alone surely demands that more thought be given to their likely outcome, to the reasons for choosing them—and to alternative ways of achieving marketing objectives, if sweepstake's weaknesses appear, in that situation, to outweigh their strengths.

Sometimes, you get the distinct feeling that people opt for a sweepstake because they can't afford a free mail-in or a sampling campaign or a demonstration effort—or even more frequently, because they have no experience of other techniques. But in these tight times, it's just not good enough to say, in effect, 'we can't really think of anything else to do, so we'll have a sweepstake to be seen to be doing something'.

There are so many other techniques to choose from.

Media and POS: the twin pillars

Let's assume, though, that you've decided compelling reasons do exist for you to run a sweepstake. Next question: can you give it a budget that not only allows for imaginative prizes linked to your product, your positioning and your customers' tastes—but lets you put considerable media exposure and point of sale display weight behind it?

Both those latter aspects are, in my experience, equally important. Sweepstakes with heavy media promotion tend to attract a greater number of entries. We have found that if you combine a solid media schedule with good presence at point of sale, you'll do even better—and that if you neglect the POS dimension, media weight alone won't get you optimal sales results.

Furthermore, good POS can win you a very valuable bonus indeed—greater store space both on shelves and aisles. If you can achieve that, the sweepstake will more than justify itself with increased sales. In fact, if your promotion is designed to lift sales through increased stock weight, you could probably run it without asking for a proof of purchase—and so boost the sales promotion's effectiveness even further, by removing an unnecessary 'hoop' and giving your product an even friendlier image.

More buyers, less deadwood

It would obviously be good to encourage more potential buyers to enter

Entries in this Whiskas promotion were valid only for a variety of purchases. Trial across the Whiskas cat food range was created as a result.

The label illustration appearing on pages 56 and 72 are reproduced with the permission of copyright owner, Uncle Ben's of Australia.

your competition, and discourage non-target-audience folk who are merely after the prizes. And as I inferred several pages back, this apparently Utopian state of affairs can in fact be engineered. You can manage it in several ways, including that of linking your prizes closely to your target market's desires.

We did it once for a youth-oriented hair care product, by suggesting that anyone over 18 was ineligible to enter the sweepstakes. This gave young people a great feeling of 'belonging' towards the brand, and attracted a swag of entries from them. Many, no doubt, came from people pretty close to the borderline, but we received many more than we'd normally expect from our target group. We may have annoyed those who were outside it, but the consequent sales results more than justified the risk we took.

Another way to target potential buyers is to combine techniques. For instance, we have linked proof-of-purchase sweepstakes to promotions that also offered attractive free gifts or cash-backs for three or four proofs of purchase.

Such a blend of techniques opens up the promotion to a wider audience and increases its sales-boosting potential. It also focuses on potential purchasers rather than prize-hunters, because it combines a powerful reason to try the product with an offer that encourages repeat purchases—the first step towards building long-term brand loyalty.

Make them think

A third way to control your entrants and make them work harder is to turn your sweepstake into a game of skill—one where entrants have to make choices based on knowledge and judgement. They may have to answer questions about your brand, rank its attributes in what they feel are their order of importance, or finish a rhyme or sentence about the product. Obviously, the number of 'hoops' here is vast indeed. And each entry has to be judged individually on its merits, which is time-consuming for the promoter and hence a more costly exercise.

For those reasons, plus the fact that skill is not a legal requirement of entry here when proof of purchase is requested, the skill competition is seldom used in Australia. But you may have a cerebral market with a deep professional interest in your product, or you may want to teach them more about its attributes. In these cases, the skill competition can be a good way to go. We've seen it used successfully with doctors and dentists, for instance—although even here there's a caveat. Our research suggests that it is very often the doctor's assistant who takes it on herself to fill out and return the competition forms. However, if the doctor has been sufficiently motivated too, the promotion's impact has probably not been totally lost.

Other ways of engaging consumers and creating additional product involvement include challenges such as solving a riddle or finding the way through a maze. Some fascinating mazes can take hours, days or even weeks to crack, and work very well in certain direct mail situations.

Place an X to win

'Spot the ball', 'spot the sun' and 'spot the difference' techniques are tried and proven ways of capturing interest and providing a game of involvement. With a little thought, they can often be used creatively to endorse product values. 'Spot the ball' has always been very popular in places and at times when any form of lottery is forbidden if a proof of purchase is required. It can still work very well in countries where cricket, football or basketball are national priorities.

Consider PR after the event

Some time ago, we ran a sweepstake for Cinzano called, 'Mix with the Stars and Win a Part in Dallas'. Not surprisingly, it received a good deal of PR exposure. Yet when my colleague Andrew Edwards rang the winner with the good news, the phone went dead. In fact, Andrew had to make the call three times before the winner would believe he'd won!

This suggests one of two things. Either we'd created a promotion with an unbelievable prize, or consumers don't really believe anybody wins competitions at all. So the lesson is that we have to run promotions with the utmost integrity. Furthermore, good PR after the event is well worth considering.

In this case, our prize winner, who was soon to be married, was interviewed in *The Australian Women's Weekly* and on several radio and TV stations. His enthusiasm after appearing in 'Dallas' and meeting J.R. Ewing and the whole cast gave further valuable publicity to Cinzano. But such post-event PR should be kept to a moderate level. You must protect your winner from the kind of pressures and demands for handouts that lottery winners have been known to experience.

The disappointment factor

I believe the main thing to watch in sweepstakes is that you don't abuse the customers' trust by demanding too many proofs of purchase. If you do, they'll simply vote with their feet and not enter in large numbers. What I don't think you should worry about is what is sometimes called the 'disappointment' factor.

I've heard some marketers dismiss sweepstakes rather scornfully as 'chance to lose' rather than 'chance to win' events. Their point is that the entrant is considerably more likely to lose than win, and the result must

Compare this Nestlé Polo promotion with Pedigree Chum and Copper Kettle on p. 56. Nestlé are able to add fun and excitement to their promotion by changing the product itself into a winning game piece.
Reproduced with the permission of Societe des Produits Nestlé SA, Vevey, Switzerland, the owners of the registered trade marks Smarties, Polo, Lifesavers and Nescafé

be a lot of disappointed people out there, thinking baleful thoughts about your product. To me, this concern is totally misplaced. I think most, if not all, entrants realise their chances of winning are slim—even if your promotion appears to give them a better-than-average chance to win, as it should. Further, I believe the fun involved in entering, plus a chance to win, however remote, are ample compensation to most people for the slight effort involved. The evidence for that, I feel, comes from one simple and unarguable fact. Vast numbers of people keep entering sweepstakes!

The real winner

Sweepstakes, then, can do an excellent job for you in building your product image, in reinforcing your advertising themes, in strengthening your positioning and in raising your brand awareness. And if you're prepared to take the time and trouble, you can select prizes that work towards those goals, instead of prizes that merely glitter. Furthermore, you can do a lot to increase the percentage of entrants who are real prospects for buying your product. Play your cards right, in other words, and you'll have a lot of people seeking the prizes you offer.

But the real winner will be you.

Your sweepstakes checklist

To help you decide whether, in your case, sweepstakes' strengths outweigh their weaknesses, see how many 'yes' answers you get from this checklist.

1. Do your current marketing goals call for increased brand and product awareness?
2. Are you looking for POS input and increased stock weight?
3. Are you looking for trial?
4. Have you carefully thought through the alternatives to a sweepstake?
5. Can you afford a sweepstake prize budget of at least $25 000?
6. Can you afford significant media and point-of-sale components in your programme?
7. Are you prepared to take the extra time and effort involved in selecting prizes that not only enhance your product's attributes but reflect your consumer's needs and wants?
8. Can you echo your advertising theme and positioning statement in your sweepstakes promotion?
9. Can you structure your competition to attract a higher percentage of potential long-term buyers in your entrants?
10. Can you keep the entry 'hoops' to a minimum?

If the 'yesses' have it, a sweepstake could be a good way for you to build your brand awareness and market share among people who'll stay with your product.

And not just use you as a possible stepping-stone to riches.

® Registered Trademark Kellogg (Aust) Pty Ltd, Authorised User

4

CHAPTER

The Creative Elements of Sweepstakes

In the last chapter, we looked at sweepstakes on a broad canvas. Now we'll move in closer, take out our magnifying glasses and study some of the details.

In any sweepstakes, there are three essential elements: your target audience, your product and its brand image, and your idea. If you can create a promotion that relates all three elements to each other in a strong and logical way, you're very likely to have a winner on your hands.

Let's start by thinking about your target audience, and the kind of prize that will appeal to them. I touched on prize selection in the previous chapter. Now I want to consider it briefly from your target audience's viewpoint. Clearly, before you can select prizes that will catch their imaginations, you need to know a great deal about them.

And the road to that goal starts—as such roads so often do—with a series of questions.

What level of income do they have? Where do they live? Where do they go on holidays? What are their aspirations? What are their needs, as opposed to their wants? What do they drive? What kind of food do they eat? Which restaurants do they go to? And so on. When these and similar questions are answered, you'll have a pretty good profile of your target audience. That in turn will help you answer the biggest (in this context) question of all—what kind of sweepstakes prizes will appeal to them most?

Over their heads

Getting answers to those questions is, admittedly, a time-consuming exercise. But I still maintain it's vital. The easiest thing of all in this business is to choose a prize that sounds good to you but would go straight over your audience's collective heads. Obviously, you'd never offer patent absurdities like jet skis for a pensioner market or crochet kits for teenage boys. But you might well offer help with mortgage repayments (if you didn't know that 80% of your target audience have paid off their homes) or a trip to Las Vegas (if you hadn't learned that 75% of your audience are conservative people who strongly disapprove of gambling). It's worth a little time and money to avoid financially disastrous prize selections like those.

Two audiences

Sometimes, you'll be in a position where you're talking to two audiences at once. Snack foods are a classic example. The people who eat them most avidly are kids aged 8–16. Many brands target that group with advertising designed to appeal to independent, rebellious, aspirational youth. Yet most snack food is bought not by kids but for kids—by their parents. Both advertising and sales promotion have to recognise that basic fact of snack food marketing life.

Smith's Crisps does so brilliantly by building its advertising around a universally appealing character: the gobbledock. And while the brand's sales promotion is youth-oriented, involving outdoor events like surf carnivals and surf spectaculars, its in-store and on-pack sweepstakes are aimed much more widely. 'Win the Smith's Classic Car' appeals to parents as much as it does to car-crazy teenagers.

So when you put your audience under the microscope, bear in mind that you may really have two of them: one that consumes your product, and one that buys it. Your sweepstakes prize may have to appeal to both.

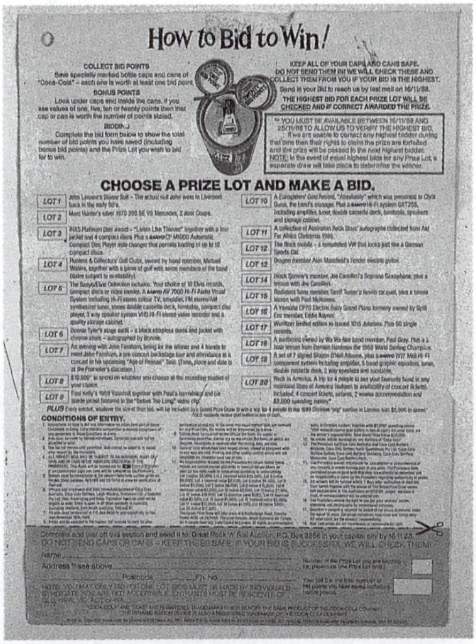

'Coca-Cola'® appeals to its target groups with a relevant promotion that offers multi levels of 'Rock Star' prizes. Repeat purchase migration is promoted across light, medium and heavy buyers. Multiple proofs of purchase act as auction bids to open the door to a huge choice of prizes of escalating value. The more proofs sent in, the greater the chance of winning each prize.
Reproduced with the permission of the Coca-Cola Company, owner of the registered trademarks 'Coca-Cola' and 'Coke'

Support your branding

The second essential in the sweepstakes mix is your product, and its inseparable companion—its brand image.

In the previous chapter, I stated my conviction that strengthening your product's brand image should be a major objective of your sweepstakes—or for that matter, of any other sales promotion technique you may use. I want to underline that point again. I believe it is crucial. If it didn't sink in the first time, please take it on board permanently now.

Let me repeat this, too. There are basically two things you can do to strengthen your brand image through a sweepstake. You can offer prizes that echo the brand's creative positioning (as Chocolate Wheaton echoed their 'full of wholesome country goodness' theme by offering country farm holidays). And you can restate your above-the-line advertising theme in your promotion.

Look for the big idea

Some would argue that our third essential—the idea—is the most essential of them all. I would agree—just as long as it strongly supports your product's branding and doesn't become a big idea that's totally irrelevant to your advertising, positioning and brand image.

Perhaps the biggest idea ever was the now-famous British Airways promotion that was launched on 27 March 1991. Immodestly (but accurately) entitled 'The World's Biggest Offer', it echoed BA's advertising theme of 'The World's Favourite Airline'. It was designed to kick-start the world back into international travel after the Gulf War—by offering no fewer than 50 000 free return trips to London, for entrants outside the UK, or free return trips anywhere in the world for UK residents. At current retail values, that was a total prize pool of something like $100 million. Of course, it really cost British Airways a mere fraction of that, because the winners were just plunked into seats that would otherwise have been empty. But the response, predictably, was vast.

The contest was advertised in newspapers in all BA's far-flung destinations. The press campaign was backed by literature and even special additions to the livery on the aircraft. Two weeks later, a staggering 5 million entries had been received. Australia contributed 200 000 of them and New Zealand 100 000—a per capita response rate three times that of Australia! To enter 'The World's Biggest Offer', all you had to do was write out your name and address and send them in. While the competition's primary objective was to lure the world back to international travel, it had three other vital aims—to raise awareness of British Airways, to get the airline and its offer talked about all over the world, and to predispose millions of people to fly BA on their next trip.

In passing, it also collected a 5-million-strong mailing list that BA will use to the full in future cut-price offers and in canvassing prospects.

British Airways' post Gulf War promotion created massive awareness by its sheer size and audacity. The clever use of TV and press media, working in concert with PR, ensured enormous awareness and participation.
Courtesy of British Airways

Smaller big ideas

You are, I imagine, hardly in a position to offer prizes of such mind-boggling magnitude to the whole world. But that doesn't stop you having a big idea that strengthens your product positioning and your advertising theme.

Brand image from television commercial (TVC) to pack attracts consumers with a variety of techniques in the one promotion—a sweepstakes prize, a FREE premium and a cause-related donation. The presence of the TV campaign's Iron Man Hero provides the essential element of integration. *Courtesy of Kellogg Australia Pty Ltd*

Marlboro did it with their 'Big Country' promotion. This venture strengthened the brand identity by restating the above-the-line advertising theme. It also offered a choice of attractive prizes all linked with outdoor activity—which supported the central brand proposition simply but effectively.

Another excellent use of a big idea that supported branding was a Kellogg's® Nutri-Grain promotion. It brought Grant Kenny, the former Iron Man turned Olympic athlete who featured in the advertising, onto the pack in a creatively relevant way. And it gave away two free trips to the Olympic Games—plus Grant's *Fit for Gold* training book free in exchange for three proofs of purchase. As well, there was the satisfaction of knowing that, by buying the product, you were helping Kellogg® to donate $20 000 to the Olympic Fund.

All of which was very much in line with the target audience's needs, interests and aspirations.

Nestlé's Chocolates are, of course, a Swiss company. So how would you design a sweepstake to strengthen their brand identity, offer an extremely appealing prize and home right in on their target audience without spending a fortune? If you answered 'make the prize a family holiday in Switzerland, with, let's say, $4000 spending money', go to the top of the class. That's just what they did, with excellent results. I particularly liked their theme line, which was 'Win a Taste of Switzerland'.

I thought that said it all.

Making good prizes sound better

The first step in creating the big sweepstakes idea is, of course, to set your prize budget. Once you've done that, you (or your agency) have to start thinking—and when you do, there are some tricks you can use to maximise your prizes' appeal.

A discovery we have made applies equally to sweepstakes and to direct marketing. It is the intriguing fact that, up to a point, round figures sound like better value and get a bigger response than non-round figures—even if they are, in fact, slightly smaller. For instance, consumers perceive $10 000 as better value than $11 000; $20 000 sounds better to them than $23 000; $25 000 outpulls $26 000. But the phenomenon works only up to a point—$50 000 sounds much better than $45 000. It works in reverse, too—$20 000 sounds more than $1000 better than $19 000. And if your budget indicates a maximum prize value of $23 000, dig into all the hollow logs you can find to boost your prize pool to $25 000. It will be one of the best $2000 you'll ever spend.

Osborne Mavor a.k.a. James Bridie, my great uncle, wrote, perhaps perceptively, in his book, *One Way of Living,* published in 1939:

> 'Five is a gallant number, with its swelling paunch and its little flag. It is the finest of all the multiplying numbers except seven. Any number multiplied by five gains an added grace and so do objects so enumerated.
> Five pounds.
> Ten virgins.
> Fifteen men on a dead man's chest.
> Twenty sonnets.
> Forty days and forty nights.
> Forty-five guardsmen.
> A hundred rounds.

A thousand chariots.
Fifty thousand copies.
A million anything.
Five million red corpuscles.'[1]

He postulated too that life moves, if it moves at all, in five-year cycles. But, back to the subject in hand.

Why are some smaller amounts more appealing than larger ones? We don't really know, but the research leaves little doubt as to the fact. One possible clue is that the more zeros in the figure, the better the prize looks. That could explain why \$10 000 seems better than \$11 000, and \$20 000 better than \$23 000.

Herschell Gordon Lewis, one of direct marketing's greatest copywriter teachers, has written a book called *Copywriting Secrets and Tactics*. In a chapter entitled 'Power Communication with Numbers and Punctuation Marks', he writes:

> 'In sweepstakes copy, use as many zeros as you can. Zeros add the impression of size. So \$1 000 000 is more money than \$1 million. For that matter, \$1 000 000.00 is more money than \$1 000 000. Primitive psychology is at work here. Let's have it help us whip up a head of steam. The lower the number, the more valuable zeros become. So using them for \$200–\$200.00 is more significant than using them for \$1 000 000. Why? Because the million dollars has six zeros. We're adding one-third more. \$200 has two zeros. We're doubling the number.'[2]

This recommendation, Lewis points out, is for direct marketing sweepstakes copy. High-fashion and top-of-the-line appeals should drop the zeros. At the very top, it's 'one million dollars', not '\$1 000 000' or '\$1 million'.

Dressing up the prize

The perceived value of your prizes depends not only on their dollar value but on what you're actually offering. Let's say that, after probing every hollow log in your corporate forest, you can scrape up only a measly \$12 000. 'Win \$12 000', while not to be sneezed at, is not exactly a breathtaking come-on. But what if you dressed it up in a creative garb, and made one of these offers:

Win a $12 000 trip around the world.
Win $12 000 worth of home improvements.
Take $12 000 off your mortgage.
Win a $12 000 shopping spree.
Win a wish to the value of $12 000.
Win a year of luxuries worth $12 000.
Win $1000 every month of the year.
Win $12 000 to take your family and friends on holiday.
Win $12 000 to spend as you like.
Win a $12 000 second honeymoon.
Win a trip on the Orient Express worth $12 000.
Win $12 000 to spend in a day.

Which of those offers the best value in your eyes? Probably not the one that appeals most to me. Or to your secretary. Or to the guy next door. We're all different, with different needs, wants and priorities. That's why, as I said earlier, you have to know your products and your target audience well before you can design sweepstakes prizes that will effectively link your product's positioning with your customers' needs.

With an upmarket product, for instance, you might offer something with very attractive associations—which could range from a trip on the Orient Express to perfume or even a box of prestige chocolates. On the other hand, a household product might do better with a '$12 000 off your mortgage' prize—while 'Win a $12 000 second honeymoon' is the sort of thing you'd offer to an older rather than a younger target audience.

Often, the age of your target audience is a valuable clue to prize selection. Over the years, we have found this list a helpful guide (but by no means an infallible one, as so many other factors are involved):

- 10 years: games, bicycles, hi-fi/electrical equipment, sports equipment.
- 20 years: rock party, motorbike, sports trip, utility wagon.
- 25 years: sports car, shopping spree, electrical, cash.
- 30 years: income for life, dream home, kitchen, family travel.
- 40 years: Disneyland (for the children), cars, cash, travel.
- 50 years: cash, second honeymoon, cruise, travel in general.

Variations on a theme

Now, back for a moment to another point I made in the last chapter—namely, that giving many people a chance to win smaller prizes gets better results than offering one big prize. So when you've determined the total value of your prize pool, you have to decide how you're going to divide it up. There's plenty of opportunity for creativity in that exercise.

Say, for instance, you have $100 000 available for prizes. There are a lot of possible variations on that theme. You could (but you shouldn't) put all your eggs in the big prize basket and say 'Win $100 000!'. You could say 'Win $50 000—plus $5000 a week for 10 weeks' (which not only widens the prize winners' circle but stretches your budget over a more comfortable period). You could say 'Win $25 000—plus a second chance draw for unclaimed prizes worth $75 000' or '$100 000 to be won—5 prizes of $10 000, plus 10 prizes of $5000'. And so on. Which one would work best? That would vary from time to time and case to case, depending on the product, its brand image, the target audience, the current market situation and a dozen other factors.

With so many possibilities and variables, you can see why so many people get it wrong so much of the time. And why seeking expert guidance is a wise investment indeed.

The magic of rhyme and rhythm

One creative element that should never be underestimated is the power of words. There's no doubt that consumers will respond better to your offer if a catchy turn of phrase embeds it in their minds.

One way of doing that is to use the magic of rhyme and rhythm. There's a lot of evidence to suggest that the most memorable themes, slogans and headlines are those that scan. 'Beats as it Sweeps as it Cleans' for Hoover was a classic example. And a simple rhyme—like 'The Pacific Prize Surprise'—can be a burr that tunnels its way into people's minds and sticks there.

We had evidence of that a few years ago with one of our CSR Sugar 'Jampot Jamboree' promotions. As I spell out in the chapter on cause-related marketing (Chapter 15), the idea of this promotion was for families to help Scout groups raise money, by making jam for them to sell.

And one year, we tried a bit of rhyme and rhythm on the sugar pack. We used the headline 'CSR Jampot Jamboree Cookbook Free!', followed by these lines of verse (Tennyson, eat your heart out):

'Be prepared to join us in our Jampot Jamboree.
There's ($)50 000 for the Scouts and cookbooks which are free.
Make marmalade and strawberry jam and other good things too.
Send in your money symbols and we'll send the book to you.'

The Poet Laureate wouldn't approve? Maybe not—but the customers did. We increased our response by almost double over the previous promotion—because this one had factors that caught the imagination, seized the memory and were easy to follow.

In passing, I think it's worth noting that consumers are becoming less literate as time goes on. Furthermore, in both the USA and Australia, there is a high percentage of people for whom English is not their first language. These facts suggest that our communication has to become easier to understand and more digestible. Rhythm and rhyme can be valuable allies in that endeavour.

Alliteration achieves a lot

Another technique that can add memorability, distinctiveness and impact to your promotion is alliteration. Used creatively, alliteration can provide the essential hook that fastens your message in your prospect's mind, and doesn't let go until he or she does something about it.

Consequently, if you were running a cashback for Redhead Firelighters, you might call it 'Redhead's Roaring Refund—$3 free!' The alliteration would worm itself into the memory—while the phrase itself might suggest both a roaring fire and the velocity of the cashback you get free by buying Redhead products. Many other examples come to mind, such as 'Hoseasons Super Savers', 'Curry's Cash Cascade' and 'Win a Hoover on the House'.

Then there was the time we produced a promotion (see how effortlessly it keeps flowing from the pen?) for Lipton's Tea. When you want alliteration, you obviously look for the dominant letter or syllable. In this case, it was the 't' of 'tons' and 'tea'. After some pondering, we came up with an alliterative twist on a cash prize: 'We'll pay your tax for two years!'. Coming a close second in our thinking was 'Win a year away from work!'. However, we felt that the alliteration of 't', echoing the product name as it did, was more relevant than a repeated 'w'.

Next time you plan a promotion, try for alliteration and see how you go. If you can build in rhythm or rhyme too, so much the better. In fact, just rhythm or rhyme alone can give you an extremely memorable headline or slogan. 'Beats as it Sweeps as it Cleans' scans beautifully and served Hoover for decades. So if you can get alliteration, rhythm and rhyme into one phrase, you could really be on a winner. For client recall, aim for all!

Try your skill

By this stage, hopefully, you have a pretty good idea of the attributes a successful sweepstake needs. So the time has come for a little test of your newly-acquired skills. I list below the main themes of 13 major sweepstakes that have been run in recent years. Which ones do you think:

(a) best support the product's branding and image;
(b) offer prizes to a wide circle of potential winners;
(c) feature a big idea?

Choose your answers carefully—because if you're right, you'll win a valuable prize.

1. Enter the $1 000 000 sweepstakes at Woolworths.
2. Name the cocktail competition from Schweppes.
   $50 000 in prizes to be won!
3. Pacific Prize Surprise (Pacific Film).
   A Pacific holiday for two worth $5000 to be won.
4. Lipton English Breakfast Tea.
   Win a 21-piece Royal Albert Tea Set when you buy Royal Albert Tableware.
5. Bailey's Irish Cream.
   A gift for mothers and lovers. 100 diamond rings to be won.
6. Crack the Cadbury's Creme Egg mystery.
   Discover 12 real gold eggs worth $10 000 each.
7. Win a holiday for four in Switzerland with Nestlé's Chocolates.
8. You and a friend can share in the Cadbury's $250 000 reward.

9. Bushell's Tea Cup Bags.
   Money Bags $100 000 instant win game.
10. Jiggle 'n' Win Sweepstakes.
    Thousands of instant jiggle fun prizes to be won from Lipton's Tea.
11. Cinzano—Mix with the Stars and Win a part in 'Dallas'.
12. Melitta Coffee.
    Have a coffee with the parents of a well-known English lady and holiday on us for two weeks (take coffee with Lady Di's parents!).
13. Kit Kat—have a Kool break.
    Win holiday breaks to LA and Hawaii, plus over 6000 other prizes.

Personally, I think numbers 2, 3, 4, 5, 7, 9, 10, 11, 12 and 13 score well in category (a), numbers 1, 2, 5, 6, 10 and 13 in category (b) and numbers 1, 5, 6, 7, 8, 11 and 12 in category (c). But you're not necessarily wrong if you disagree with me. You could well be right even if your list differs quite markedly from mine—because what we don't have here is all the other factors such as target audience profiles, media weight, POS effectiveness and so on that affect the promotion's success. So let's assume that you're 100% right. And your prize?

You've already received it—the understanding and insights you need to run a highly profitable sweepstake of your own.

Rules

One of the most difficult aspects of running sweepstakes is the daunting number of rules you're usually required to print as part of the promotion. Sometimes, this factor will actually stop you running a sweepstake at all, as you just can't fit the rules and conditions of entry on packs or even in advertising.

Generally, however, the rules and conditions can be written concisely. Tony Anisimoff, of Anisimoff Davenport in Sydney, has them down to a fine art. We both warn, though, that every promotion you ever run should be checked through lawyers familiar with the relevant legislation. You must also apply for permit numbers where they are required, well in advance of the promotion itself.

Here are some typical words often used for rules and conditions in various instant win and sweepstake promotions.

Instant win with second chance draw—rules and conditions

BASIC RULES

1. Information on prizes and how to enter forms part of these rules and conditions.
2. Entry open to all residents of ______________ except employees and their immediate families of the promoter, and its agencies and companies associated with this promotion.
3. Instant win prize claims and second chance draw entries close last mail received __/__/__.
4. Instant win prizes are _____________. Total value of prizes is $________. Any unclaimed instant win prizes will be awarded in the second chance draw scheduled in _________ on __/__/__. Prizes are not transferable or exchangeable and are offered as is.
5. All winners in the draw will be notified by mail and announced in the public notices section of the ____________ on __/__/__.
6. Unless otherwise due to fraud or ineligibility under these terms and conditions, all prize claims in excess of the advertised prize pool will be honoured.
7. No responsibility accepted for lost, late or misdirected mail. Judges' decision is final. No correspondence will be entered into. Only complete and original prize panels are eligible. Prize panels stolen, unlawfully obtained, forged, altered, defaced, mutilated or tampered with in any way are automatically void. Printing or other quality control errors will not invalidate an otherwise valid prize claim. Prize panels are subject to security and verification check at the absolute discretion of the promoter.
8. The promoter is ______________, ___________________, ___, _________.

NSW Permit No. TC__/____.
Raffles and Bingo Permit Board No. __/____ issued on __/__/__.
ACT permit No. __/_____ issued under the Lotteries Ordinance, 1964.
NT ____/__.

SUPPLEMENTARY RULES (AS REQUIRED)

1. Queensland winners must take any cash prize valued under $100 as a retail voucher to be redeemed at a store nominated by the promoter, or any cash prize valued at $100 and over as gold bullion to the nearest value at the absolute discretion of the promoter.
2. Residents of South Australia may obtain one only free randomly selected instant win card by sending their name, address and a hand drawn facsimile of the promoter's logo to Freepost XXX. Only one entry per person permitted by this method in South Australia.
3. Travel prize is for __ people and includes return ___________ airfares, __ nights accommodation and $_____ spending money. Trip must be taken by __/__/__, is subject to availability and departs from _________. Transfers to and from point of departure, passports, travel insurance, meals and all other ancillary costs are the responsibility of the winner.
4. Not more than $250 000 in prizes will be won in NSW.
5. Unless otherwise due to fraud or ineligibility under these terms and conditions, all prize claims in excess of the advertised prize pool will not be honoured.

Sweepstake draw—rules and conditions

BASIC RULES

1. Information on prizes and how to enter forms part of these rules and conditions.
2. Entry is open to all residents of ___________ except employees and their immediate families of the promoter, and its agencies and companies associated with this promotion.
3. Offer closes last mail received __/__/__ or while stocks last and the draw is scheduled in ____________ on __/__/__.
4. Prizes are ____________. Total value of prize is $_______. Prizes are not transferable or exchangeable and are offered as is.
5. All winners in the draw will be notified by mail and announced in the public notices section of the ____________ on __/__/__.

6. There is no limit to the number of entries but each entry must be on the official entry form and be accompanied by __________. One entry only per envelope. No responsibility accepted for lost, late or misdirected mail. Judges' decision is final. No correspondence will be entered into.
7. The promoter is ____________, ______________, ___, ______.

NSW Permit No. TC__/____.
Raffles and Bingo Permit Board No. __/____ issued on __/__/__.
ACT Permit No. __/_____ issued under the Lotteries Ordinance, 1964.
NT ____/__.

SUPPLEMENTARY RULES (AS REQUIRED)

1. Residents of South Australia may obtain one only free entry into the draw by sending their name, address and a hand drawn facsimile of the promoter's logo to the nominated address. Only one entry per person permitted by this method in South Australia.
   OR
2. No purchase necessary in South Australia whose residents may obtain __ free entry forms per person, address on application to FREEPOST ___, _________, ____, _____. No stamp necessary on freepost applications. Only __ entry/ies per ___________ permitted by this method.
   OR
3. No purchase necessary in South Australia whose residents may enter by sending a stamped, self-addressed envelope to __________, ____________, ___, _______. Only __ free entry/ies per ___________ permitted by this method.
4. Travel prize is for __ people and includes return ___________ airfares, __ nights accommodation and $_____ spending money. Trip must be taken by __/__/__, is subject to availability and departs from __________. Transfers to and from point of departure, passports, travel insurance, meals and all other ancillary costs are the responsibility of the winner. Queensland winner must take spending money as gold bullion to the nearest value.
5. Not more than $250 000 in prizes will be won in NSW.

As you can see, the rules are complex and extensive. Tony Anisimoff advises that they can be shortened. You can, for instance, say that the full rules and conditions can be obtained by sending a self-addressed envelope to the competition or sweepstakes address. Similarly, we have had success in having rules and conditions available on a 0055 number, 008 number, or 13 number where the entrant can call and listen to the full list. This has helped us devote maximum space to the sweepstakes communication.

Through the sheer amount of space given to them on leaflets, packs, mailpacks and in advertisements, rules can deter people from entering. Many promoters make them seem complicated or threatening because of the type, weight or space given to them. They will receive fewer entries. Print the rules in the smallest possible typeface—6/7-point will do in most cases. Don't mix the rules and conditions with the method of entry. Consider Tony Anisimoff's suggestions for divorcing them entirely from the contest promotion.

Fortunately, free promotions where a premium gift is guaranteed don't need lengthy rules, because there is no element of chance. This gives you maximum space for the promotional message. Promotion sweepstakes or prize draws run by radio stations and the media themselves don't require rules either, as they are open to public scrutiny. However, all other commercial companies mounting a lottery must have permits. That includes political parties running sweepstakes at their fund raising events!

Try to relegate rules to smaller spaces or the inside of packs or the backs of brochures. Entrants seldom give them anything but a cursory glance. Give more space to the promotion, and you'll attract more people and more entries with larger typefaces and more eye-catching graphics. On a rub-off spot card, the rules have to be condensed to fit on an area much the size of a business card. You don't really want to give any more space to rules and conditions than the space equivalent to two business cards in any promotion you run. Doing this will not harm your promotional results—in fact, it will improve them. Nobody thinks the lesser of you if you put the rules in relatively small type. Consumers know the rules are mandatory and that the legislation is there to protect their interests. They also know you have to print the rules in their interests and that of government legislation and that it's a necessary evil. Your consumers' prime motivation is to get into the promotion. In most instances, they only want to know what the exclusions are, particularly the closing dates, before they enter with the intention to win.

Consumers appreciate promotions that are simple and straightforward. The more complicated the rules, the lesser the interest. Here, as everywhere else in sales promotion, the KISS principal (keep it simple, stupid) applies in full measure. There's just one possible exception to this rule—if your promotion is aimed at retirees and there are factors in the rules they need to know (like closing dates), then you may need to print the rules in an easier-to-read size.

Notes

1. James Bridie, *One Way of Living*, Collins, Glasgow, 1939.
2. Herschell Gordon Lewis, *Copywriting Secrets and Tactics*, Dartnell Publishing, Chicago, Illinois, USA, 1992.

5

CHAPTER

The Heroes and Villains of Character Licensing

On the face of it, pinning one's financial hopes on a mouse, a turtle, a robot or a henpecked Viking chieftain may seem a bizarre way to run a business. Yet as many astute marketers can testify, linking your product with the likes of Mickey Mouse, the Teenage Mutant Ninja Turtles, R2D2, Hagar the Horrible or the Super Mario Bros from Nintendo can be a very shrewd move indeed.

The whole subject of licensing—using well-known characters as sales promotion tools—is quite fascinating from a psychological viewpoint. Its roots go far back into history and touch deep chords in all our subconscious minds. The phenomenon probably began when the ancient Greeks created the first superheroes—a splendid pantheon of gods, backed by spectacular mortals such as Hercules, Jason and the Argonauts, Hector, Theseus and others of similarly intrepid ilk.

To gain impact and sales, Cadbury used a three-technique combination—an extra bar in this 5 bar multi-pack, 5 sweepstakes prizes and an endorsement from the popular Super Mario Bros.
Courtesy of Cadbury. © Nintendo and The Marketing Triangle Ltd

A lingering influence

These heroes, in fact, had only one failing. They were around much too early to cash in on the modern hero licensing boom. But their influence is still with us—because their larger-than-life courage, tenacity and general derring-do have helped shape the personalities of their modern successors. A glance at the prowess of Superman, Batman, Spiderman and their confrères makes that abundantly clear.

But it's interesting to observe that, if their feats are to tower above those of ordinary folk, heroes need anti-heroes. Superman has Lex Luthor, Batman has the Joker, Dick Tracey has Scarface, Luke Skywalker has Darth Vader. Sometimes, in a perverse sort of way, these anti-heroes generate a following of their own. Their main function, however, is to prevail temporarily and then be overthrown—because in the process, they raise our heroes above run-of-the-mill heroic status. They turn them into the superheroes in whom our deepest—and most secret—fantasies of self-realisation take form and substance.

This brings us to the very core of the licensed character—its reason for being. A successful hero's attitudes and behaviour reflect morals and ethics that society widely accepts. They represent the age-old battle of good against evil—and they lead always to the inevitable triumph of good. As long as those elements are present, the character's fringe attributes are not really important. The Teenage Mutant Ninja Turtles may come from the sewers, be reared by a rat and eat pizza—but

Michelangelo, Donatello, Raphaello and Leonardo are out to save the world. That excuses everything else.

Battlers and nice guys

However, soul-stirring heroes are only one kind of character. Another very successful breed is the 'battler': the average guy who struggles through life, keeps his head above water—just—and survives outrageous fortune's slings and arrows with wry good humour. We like that, because it mirrors our own experience. Most of us can identify with battlers like Dagwood, Dog (in Footrot Flats), Hagar the Horrible, Snake and Fred Flintstone.

Then there are characters who are not really heroes, not really battlers, not really anything except just plain likeable. Names such as Mickey Mouse, Fred Basset and Snoopy leap to mind. True, some in this category may be a little sly (like Yogi Bear) or even, on occasions, downright cantankerous (like Garfield or Donald Duck). And yet, you simply can't help liking them. Why? Because here again, we see in them a glimpse of the kind of personalities we ourselves would like to be.

Picking the winners

So now, perhaps, we have unearthed some guidelines for selecting *marketable* characters—those who could carry your product to the stars, as opposed to those who might hoist it shakily onto their shoulders, only to stagger and drop it (and you) in the mud.

Experience suggests that character licensing is most successful when the characters are larger than life and invite hero worship—or at the very least, arouse a strong sense of identification and wish-fulfilment. If they are symbols of universally admired traits like courage, strength and invincibility—and if something of a cult following has developed around them—so much the better. Symbolism and the need to belong both go deep into our psyches.

Longevity is a vital factor, too. In fact, it's absolutely critical—when you consider that your return on investment for a character promotion can be two years down the line, following a year's development work and another year of test-marketing. Investing money

McCain co-opt the Ninja Turtles to increase impact at point-of-sale and build sales.
Courtesy of McCains Foods Australia Pty Ltd

in licensing fees, product development and advertising campaigns is not much use if the character sinks without trace before the promotion breaks.

Long-term exposure

How can you judge a character's potential longevity? One clue is to consider the amount of long-term exposure it is likely to get. It may be born in a one-off blockbuster movie—but if the movie is the sum total of the character's career, it will very probably die there too. Look instead for characters who may indeed begin life as movie stars, but who then progress through into longer-lived media—a TV series, newspaper and magazine comic strips, comic books, or even soft toys (like the Care Bears, who were worth $22 million a year in Australia at their peak).

Alternatively, watch for those who appear in a series of smash hit movies over a period of years, with all the rumour, news stories, previews and general hype that surface in between.

A classic example of the second kind is the spectacularly successful characters from Star Wars. And typifying the first kind are a string of characters whose longevity has been quite remarkable—Mickey Mouse, Snoopy, Popeye, Superman and Batman, to name a few.

A handful of masters

Many of the long-lived characters come from a handful of creators and licensees who are past masters in the long-term exposure business.

George Lucas and Stephen Spielberg are perhaps the most successful character creators of recent times. Luke Skywalker, Princess Leia, Hans Solo, Chewbacca, R2D2, C3PO, Darth Vader and Indiana Jones are known around the world. And the exposure-building skill of major licensing companies can be seen in the longevity of their characters—Snoopy, Charlie Brown, Linus and company (now 40 years old), Super

Heroes from United Features Syndicate, Popeye and Hagar (King Features Syndicate), the Pink Panther (United Artists), Superman, Loony Tunes and Dick Tracey (Warner Brothers) and the Muppets (Henson Associates).

Of course, coming from one of those stables doesn't necessarily guarantee merchandising success. ET (Stephen Spielberg) was a box-office phenomenon but a merchandising flop. Why? Possibly because he appeared in just one marvellous movie. And possibly, because he lacked the superhero qualities we pondered earlier. But it's easy to be wise after the event...

What do the kids think?

Now we come to the most important question of all. Will your proposed character appeal to children? And as an immediate corollary: will parents and grandparents approve of it?

These questions are crucial for one simple reason. Most successful licensed character promotions are directed at children—*Jurassic Park,* for example. That makes sense when you think about it, because most characters are designed to appeal to children as their primary audience. Adults may enjoy Superman and Star Wars movies, but it's the kids who want the merchandise that flows from them.

However, they won't get it if the parents disapprove. Parental acceptance may be wholehearted (ideally) or given somewhat grudgingly (as tends to happen with the Turtles and Bart Simpson). But the promotion certainly won't work if the character alienates the parents. They, after all, are the ones who have to fork out the purchase dollar.

Reckon on 10%, up front

Speaking of dollars leads to another unavoidable question. How much will the character cost? Asking that is rather like enquiring about the length of the proverbial piece of string. Quite obviously, it depends on the character, the level of demand for it, the duration and type of licence

Win 'Masters of the Universe' toys by collecting a combination of labels from both impulse and take home packs. This licensed character promotion was designed to beat off the head-to-head competition from Transformers 'Snack Attacks'. It also encouraged purchase of the larger, more expensive take home multipack.
Courtesy of Frito-Lay Australia and 'Masters of the Universe' © Mattel

you want, and a dozen other factors. An obscure comic strip character will be yours far more cheaply than a TV series hero who enjoys 20% of the children's audience over a 20-week, 100-episode series.

But of course, you get what you pay for. The TV series character will probably be a far better buy long-term, because he, she or it will have those essential factors of long-term exposure and proven appeal to children. In fact, hot properties like that are eagerly sought after and contested by astute marketers—many of whom trek annually to the world's international toy fairs, to register their claims as early as possible.

So it's impossible to generalise on price. However, as a ball park guide, a typical licence fee for a successful character might be around 10% of the wholesale value of your production run. And be prepared, in most cases, to pay it all up front.

Don't mess around with Garfield

Be prepared, too, for strict conditions governing the use of your character. For instance, Garfield's owners, United Features Syndicate, place stringent guidelines not just on things like the cynical feline's colour and expression, but on the kinds of merchandise they will accept. It must, in their view, be appropriate both to Garfield himself and to his well-defined audience.

Such caution is not really surprising. To protect the character's image—and its all-important longevity—licensees must ensure that the merchandise associated with their character is of a high standard, socially desirable and in line with the character's audience, nature and personality. Only if they believe your product meets those criteria will they approve your licence.

Both tooth brush and toothpaste marketers compete for the attention of children. The more the children brush, the more sales the manufacturers will make—especially if brand loyalty can be established at an early age.
Courtesy Oral B, Unilever and The Boots Company. Sesame Street copyright, Children's Television Network, Mickey Mouse copyright the Walt Disney Company, Tom and Jerry copyright Turner Broadcasting

The big bucks beckon

If your licence is approved—and if you've chosen the right character—you could be on the way to a huge sales success. The amount of money earned each year by shrewd character merchandising is staggering—for marketers, licensees and creators alike. Much of Stephen Spielberg's vast wealth, for example, has come not only from his films but from the merchandising and licensing of his carefully contrived characters. They translate easily into posters, toys and T-shirts because they were designed from the outset to do so.

In a different area, the Hard Rock Cafés around the world make at least as much money from merchandise as from food. The Rolling Stones and other pop groups earn very large sums on tour from merchandise, books, programmes, T-shirts, photographs and posters. The pop group field, however, can be a risky one for marketers. Pop stars are not wholly controllable fantasy characters. They are alive and totally unpredictable—with a penchant for doing unexpected and embarrassing things or even dying inconveniently. The other side of that coin, though, is that some dead pop stars like Elvis Presley, Buddy Holly and John Lennon still have great merchandising potential. Elvis, in fact, is bigger in this regard now than when he was alive!

But naturally enough, you're not too interested in what licensees, creators and originators earn. You're far more concerned about the earning potential that awaits you. To judge the possibilities of that, simply take a look at the food, confectionery, clothing, soap and toothbrush shelves in any supermarket. See how much space is taken up by licensed character merchandise. Walk around a department store. Note the dominance of characters in the toy and clothing sections. There are a lot of manufacturers out there making a lot of money from character merchandising. And there's no reason whatsoever why you can't be among them.

Think kids, think characters

That's especially true if you're selling to teenagers or children—or to adults who buy for them. And while characters have performed splendidly in almost all market categories, they have notched up exceptional results in youth-oriented clothes (particularly T-shirts), food, breakfast cereals, fast food outlets, confectionery (from bubble gum to ice cream) and bathroom products (from shampoo to toothbrushes). If you're in one of those fields, character marketing could be an extremely viable option for you. Others have ridden to fame and fortune on the broad shoulders of Batman or Superman, or arrived there clutching the coat-tails of Yogi Bear.

Out there somewhere is a character who can do the same for you.

Getting the most from your character

Let's suppose, then, that you've chosen a character who seems to meet all our criteria for success, and you've hammered out a satisfactory deal with the licensee. How should you use your character to get the best results?

The number of possible ways is limited only by your imagination. But over the years, the following routes have consistently proved the most reliable:

1. Personality endorsement—the licensed character endorses the product just like a real-life celebrity does. A classic example is the Smurfs, who have become synonymous with BP.
2. The licensed character actually 'becomes' the product, as in the case of Mickey Mouse Soap or Teenage Mutant Ninja Turtles

Lemonade. A somewhat bizarre recent example was Mullo's Cereal, a breakfast cereal bearing the name and likeness of Doug Mulray, a Sydney breakfast radio announcer.

3. The licensed character is used as a premium attached to the product—of which more in a moment.
4. The licensed character is used in a short-term promotion associated with the product—as when the pizza-eating Teenage Mutant Ninja Turtles put their weight behind McCain's Pizzas and Pies.

Many very successful promotions have been built around example 2. In those cases, the product exists simply on the appeal of the character, and develops no real image of its own—although, naturally, its shape, taste and colour have to meet the market's expectations.

The great skill in following this path lies in making the licensed character and the product appear as one concept. It isn't easy, as anyone in the new product department of a snack food, ice cream or confectionery company will testify. Many long days, weeks and even months of research and development are needed. But if it all comes together, the rewards can be very great.

Bridging the credibility gap

Sometimes, it doesn't come together—or it clearly won't, right from the start. The product simply doesn't project the character's nature and personality. For instance, it is doubtful whether a green and purple ice-lolly could really be seen, even in a child's vivid imagination, as the Incredible Hulk. Despite the picture on the wrapper, and the brand manager's most fervent hopes, the credibility gap is just too wide to be bridged.

This critical factor is too often missed by marketers. But if it's foreseen, all is by no means lost. A sales promotion programme can carry out the necessary bridge-building work—and turn a potential disaster into a resounding success. Take the Incredible Hulk dilemma as an example. Instead of trying to turn a lolly into the multi-hued monster himself, you'd be far better off to put a free Hulk picture card into the wrapper. Then you'd follow it up throughout the selling season with a collectable series of hero cards.

And your product would suddenly have a powerful new appeal to its target market.

Could your product be a character?

So far, we've looked at using a licensed character to promote your product. But just possibly, the reverse could be the case. Your product could itself become a character you could license out to others. Fantasy? Not always.

Vegemite is certainly one of Australia's best-known brand names. Back in the early 1980s, its marketer, Kraft Foods, moved to exploit its popularity in a radical new way. With the guidance of its advertising agency, Kraft licensed the Vegemite name, jar and logo for use on non-food products. As a result, the Vegemite identity began to appear on a wide range of products—including doona covers, T-shirts, windcheaters, beach towels, children's raincoats, schoolbags, shoelaces and aprons. It made money for the manufacturers who used it. And—very importantly—the Vegemite name gained vast amounts of additional exposure.

Exposure that not only cost Kraft nothing, but actually generated extra income for them. Whichever way you look at it, that has to be good business.

Your character promotion checklist

In all probability, however, your product is in the position of needing a character rather than being one. In that case, use the following checklist as a guide to the results you can expect from a character promotion—and the likely effectiveness of the character or characters you have in mind.

1. At which target group is your product aimed:
   (a) the buyers (e.g. parents, grandparents)?
   (b) the users (e.g. children, teenagers)?
   (c) the key influencers (e.g. peer groups)?
2. Does your target group have a favourable perception of your proposed character or characters?
3. Does the character's personality blend with your product's image?

4. Is there a logical link between your product, your character and your target audiences?
5. Will the time you'll need to develop, evaluate, manufacture and market the product exceed the likely longevity of the character (if, for example, it's appearing in a film and nowhere else)?
6. What is the likely return on investment (ROI) on the product if you don't use a character?
7. What is the likely ROI on the product if you do—taking into account the cost of the licence versus faster rates of sale, repeat purchases and so on?
8. Will using the character allow you to charge a higher price, and gain you better distribution and retail stocking, as against competitive products?
9. Will you need a promotional device (such as a picture card) to bridge the gap between the image of the character and the reality of your product?
10. What levels of support will the licensor put behind the character—in advertising, PR, sales promotion and so on?
11. What are other licensees likely to spend in their promotions? (The more they spend on the character, the more you benefit.)
12. Are they in areas that will really strengthen the character—exceptional toys, for instance, or 'walking billboards' like T-shirts and other clothing?
13. The amount of exposure your character will receive during your promotional period is vital to its effectiveness. Rate its exposure level on this star rating system:
    (a) Is the character appearing in a TV series?
    Yes ☐ No ☐
    (b) If yes, will the series run throughout the time you're licensing the character?
    Yes ☐ No ☐
    (c) Is your character:
    (i) very familiar, like Mickey Mouse?
    Yes ☐ No ☐
    (ii) appearing in:
    - comic books? Yes ☐ No ☐

- comic strips? Yes ☐ No ☐
- videos? Yes ☐ No ☐
- video games, like Pacman? Yes ☐ No ☐
- music? Yes ☐ No ☐
- books? Yes ☐ No ☐
- toys or soft toys? Yes ☐ No ☐

Give your character two stars for a 'yes' in question (a), and one star for every 'yes' in questions (b) and (c). If the character scores six stars or above, you have every reason to expect a successful promotion.

It's instructive, if you have the information, to do this star rating exercise on previous promotions that used hit characters like Mickey Mouse, the Star Wars team, Care Bears, Superman, the Smurfs, the Turtles, the Muppets and Snoopy, as well as less successful characters like Dick Tracey and ET. That will help you to pinpoint the vital factors that can make the difference between success and failure for your product or service.

6
CHAPTER

Cashbacks and Shareouts—Free Money

Some years ago, during an Australian Federal Election campaign, one party's advertisement featured a hand offering the reader a lot of money. Dubbed the 'Fistful of Dollars' approach, the ploy apparently worked. The party using it won the election. How much the advertisement really contributed to the victory may be debatable. But beyond doubt, people will sit up and take notice if you offer them money—cash in the hand in return for their vote. Or their brand loyalty.

This is why the cashback technique is such a popular variation on the free premium theme. Your customers may or may not like the free premium you chose so carefully for them, but they certainly will like your offer of free money.

The word *free*, incidentally, is the most important four-letter word in the sales and marketing vocabulary. No other four-letter word comes near it. *Save*, for instance, is not nearly as powerful.

The claim, however, must of course be absolutely true. And the integrity of the word 'FREE' must be kept in your graphic design. Don't let your art director dress it up, integrate it into the design or give it a

Bosch's powerful cashback offer was promoted via a full colour insert. This could be used at point of sale and as an insert into the media.
Bosch power their sales with a cash back or factory rebate offer—the best price wherever you buy, plus a sizeable reward when you send in evidence of purchase. The benefit of purchasing Bosch is passed on to the purchaser and is not absorbed by the retailer. A little extra $ reward can help to get additional customer information to build a database to use for future offers.
Courtesy of Robert Bosch Australia Pty Ltd

fancy feel. Keep it clear of all encumbrances. It will work best for you when it's big and bold and stands out from everything else in the layout. If you can genuinely make a free offer of something your customers would like, the word FREE should be the most dominant part of your communication.

Many use the word *bonus* when they could quite legitimately use *free*. They do themselves a great injustice. Sometimes, it's a case of weakening the marketing effort to please the legal eagles. Push hard to get *free* past them if at all possible. The rewards in sales and profits are too good to miss.

But I digress.

Cashbacks—free money—are one of the most effective ways to create an inducement to buy. They're simple, straightforward, easy to understand and aim straight at the hip pocket. They're different from price-offs, because they don't offer an immediate discount. Instead, people have to buy the product at full normal price first. Then, they send in one or more proofs of purchase to claim whatever amount of money is being offered—which is usually quite a lot more than would be given through a price-off.

So cashbacks are a true reward for purchase. In a situation of product and pricing parity, they give people a real reason to buy your product—and to go on buying it, if multiple proofs of purchase are needed to claim the reward. Naturally, people have to trust you to honour your promise of money. This is why cashbacks work best when the manufacturer is well-known and trusted.

Multiple purchases

Cashbacks are most often used to gain multiple purchases of a product, usually in the grocery area. They normally do this by requiring three or four proofs of purchase—and sometimes more—before the reward is paid. It's a proven and effective technique. And as we'll see later, it probably won't cost you as much as you might expect.

However, multi-proof cashbacks need not be confined to a single product. They can be very successful in boosting the sales of a product range, by requiring proofs of purchase from several products. They can even be used in the same way across seemingly unrelated brands.

In the latter instance, a popular product can carry lesser-known brands to success. Back in 1974, for example, a UK 'Persil Pay Packet' promotion offered consumers £10 if they bought the required quantities of eight well-known grocery brand items featured on the Persil pack. The offer was made on the Persil pack itself. It was an attractive one, because £10 was not to be sneezed at in those days. And as this (at the time) huge reward seemed to come with the compliments of Persil, it was excellent PR for that very well-known and much-bought brand. In fact, of course, the participating brands—most of which came from the

As an incentive to switch airlines, Qantas offers travellers to the USA value over and above a competitive fare. The benefit for flying Qantas is passed onto the purchaser and not absorbed by the travel agent.
Courtesy of Qantas Airways Limited

Unilever stable anyway—funded the whole promotion. They could afford to do so, as it brought them increased penetration and repeat sales. It was a well-thought-out exercise, in which all participants benefited.

Including the consumers.

Look for the fast movers

In my experience, cashbacks which require multiple proofs of purchase to claim them are particularly suited to products that have a high use-up rate and are bought regularly. Products that sit around the home for months, such as Dettol and Band-Aids, and others that make the shopping list only occasionally, aren't repeat purchase candidates. So they aren't cashback material. Consumers will only pantry-stock products they know will be used up quickly, or ones that have a long shelf-life. With slow-turnover products, the gap between purchases is so long that a multi-proof cashback offer lacks credibility. The reward is just too far in the future to be attractive.

Other grocery products that do extremely well with cashbacks include pet foods of all kinds, and baby food. This suggests to me that consumers are particularly attracted by the prospect of getting money back on items they don't necessarily consume themselves—especially when those items are very similar to their competitors.

From cat food to cars

While cashbacks are particularly associated with fast-turnover grocery lines, they are by no means confined to them. They can work just as well with more expensive items, where the cashback is, of course, much larger. New cars, for instance, are one of the most expensive consumer items of all, and cashbacks are widely employed to help move them off the lot. Usually called 'factory bonuses' in this context, they can amount to $2000 or more, on an average family car price of $20 000. But the principle is exactly the same as with a can of cat food. The purchaser pays the full price and sends the proof of purchase not to the retailer (or dealer) in this case, but directly to the manufacturer—who responds with an eagerly-awaited cheque.

Why people use cashbacks

At first glance, the question 'why do people use cashbacks?' may seem absurdly simple. 'To increase sales' would appear to be the obvious answer. But as with so much else in life, the obvious is not always the full

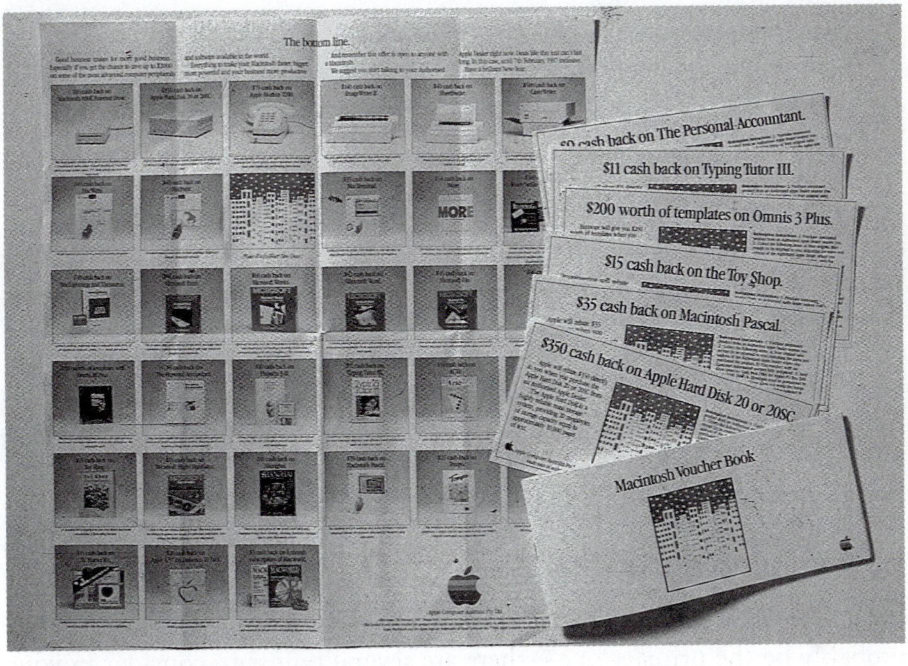

Buyers of Apple equipment and Apple computer software could gain generous incentives to purchase add-ons from this joint promotion between Apple and software manufacturers, who paid for the big dollar rewards.
Courtesy of Apple Computer Australia Pty Limited

story. For example, cashbacks are sometimes employed not so much to increase sales as to exclude other brands from the market. True, a sales increase will usually accompany that manoeuvre, but it's not the primary aim.

There are several other reasons why cashbacks might be employed. They can be used to promote impulse purchases, or to reward regular customers. Or the aim might be to gain trial of a new product—in which case, a relatively lower reward is usually offered in line with low proof of purchase requirements.

Recently, we ran a survey of several marketers, to find out the motive behind their cashbacks. The results, which follow, were interesting:

Encourage repeat purchase	65%
Sample new users	48%
Induce dealers to stock	43%
Give sales force talking point to sell more	41%
Increase goodwill amongst existing customers	34%
Increase incidence of off-shelf floor display	31%
Gain attention on-shelf	29%
Build interest in advertising	26%
Dramatise the display feature	15%

As you can see, increased purchases are certainly the main goal. But other reasons can play a significant part in the decision to go the cashback route.

There are other good reasons for selecting a cashback. One is to ensure your money-off offer gets passed on to the purchaser and is not absorbed by the trade. Another is to attract buyers who will benefit because the purchase is actually being made by another party. The rebate for purchase, however, is sent subsequently to the original 'buyer' of the product.

How to run a cashback

Whatever your motives for having a cashback—and increased sales will probably be the primary one—there are several points to consider in your planning.

The skill in running cashbacks comes in knowing how much to reward purchasers without over-rewarding them—and in the case of

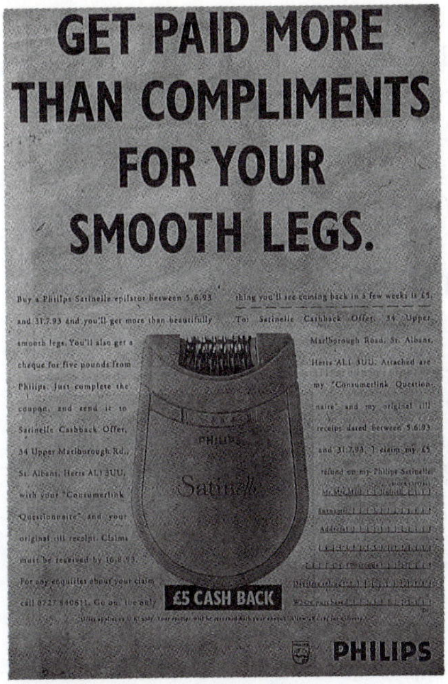

Philips turn a cash-back proposition into a thematic advertisement and collect names to build a database.
Courtesy of Philips UK

multi-proof cashbacks, knowing how many purchases you can demand before giving a reward.

I'm afraid the 'correct' figures differ from product to product, and you'll discover them for yours only through experience. But as a rough rule of thumb, I'd suggest that a minimum of 20% of the purchase price should be set for the reward. And I'd think three to five proofs of purchase would get you a good sales return without pushing the customer too far.

Of course, there are many exceptions to these sweeping generalisations. I've known cashbacks that offered a 100% return on the purchase price, when the aim was something other than increased sales. I also remember a successful 1982 cashback for Uncle Ben's dog food that asked for 60 proofs of purchase to get back $3 (although I wouldn't try that now!). But unless there are special reasons to choose other figures, I would run a trial cashback on those suggested above.

Analyse the value

One thing you have to do, especially with single proof-of-purchase cashbacks, is to look at the value of the reward through your customer's eyes. When you go through that exercise, you realise that even 20% of the purchase price may not be high enough in some circumstances—because of a phenomenon I call the 'threshold of effort'.

Let me illustrate. If your product sells for $2.50 and you want to achieve four repeat sales over a 12-week promotional period, the 20%

rule would suggest a cashback offer of $2. But bear this in mind. When customers come to buy, their response depends on the 'threshold of effort' they need to put in to get the reward, compared to the perceived value of it. They won't respond if the actual cash value of the reward seems too little for the effort required.

The 20% level, then, only applies if your offer reaches or exceeds the 'threshold of effort'. In 1990, in our experience, the lowest reward that met this threshold was $3 free. Anything less than that tended to be bypassed, even if it did represent 20% or more of the purchase price.

When you look at it through your customer's eyes, you can see why. A $1 cashback for one purchase of a $5 product—a 20% offer—may seem generous to you. But look at the 'threshold of effort' involved. The customer has to buy the product, tear off the label, fill in the details, buy a 45¢ stamp, find an envelope, put the whole thing together and mail it—all to receive $1. In fact, when you deduct the cost of the stamp and envelope, they're getting less than 50¢.

Would you go to all that trouble for such a measly reward? No? Then how many of your customers would be attracted by the offer? You're right. Not too many.

More purchases, more reward

This is another reason why multi-proof cashbacks are most marketers' preferred option. They not only have more impact on sales. They allow you to offer a larger reward—perhaps $5 free for five sales, instead of $1 free for one. And that's starting to be large enough to make the claim

Brush regularly to receive a reward. A clever way to motivate parents to buy the brand for their young families.
Courtesy of SmithKline Beecham

rigmarole worthwhile. It's above the 'threshold of effort' needed to achieve success.

Once you've settled on the reward value, the next issue to be decided is equally crucial. It's the length of time the promotion should run. And it's here that many an unwary marketer has come to grief.

The perils of miscalculation

The basic principle is to give consumers enough time to collect however many proofs of purchase you're requesting. To do that, you have to calculate the average use-up time of your product, because you can't rely on people stockpiling it. You also need to estimate the number of people likely to make the required number of purchases and send in for the cashback.

If you don't allow people sufficient time to collect their proofs of purchase, you'll create a host of enemies. You'll do likewise if you underestimate their numbers—because there won't be enough specially printed packs in the stores for them to claim their rewards.

To avoid arguments later on, it's very advisable to print the closing date in large and prominent type on the pack. That can have a positive effect—people will often speed up their normal purchase cycle in response. But you should also honour all claims that reach you for up to six weeks after the closing date. This will allow for a complete run-out of your promotional packs.

And the 'get-around-to-it-tomorrow' attitude of many of your customers.

Money is an emotive issue. If people think you've tried to trick them with impossible time frames or conditions, the consequences could haunt you for years.

The security problem

Your customers won't be happy, either, if their cashback disappears en route to them. If you send cheques or money orders, the problem won't arise: but your costs and general hassles will increase. If you send cash, however, fairly stringent security measures are needed to ensure its safe

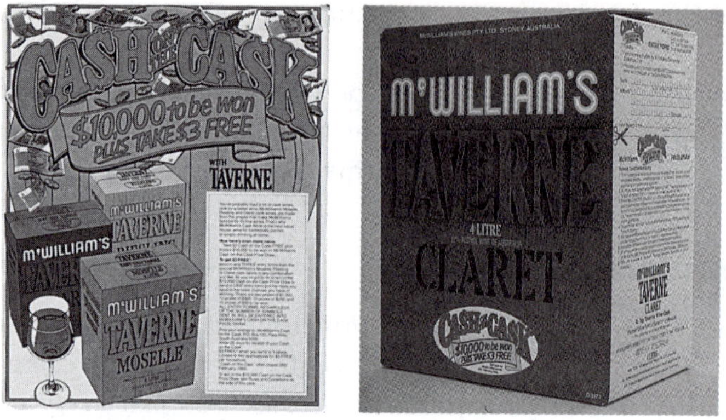

A two-tiered promotion, designed to gain trial from a $10 000 sweepstake, plus on-going buying motivated by a guarantee of FREE cash for buying two more packs. *Courtesy of McWilliam's Wines Pty Ltd*

arrival. We have devised some, which have worked well for our clients. To keep the crims guessing, I won't divulge them here—but be assured, the problem can be solved.

On-pack plugs the best

If your budget runs to it, you may wish to advertise your cashback in the media. But whether you do so or not, you still have to plug it strongly at point of sale. And here—for grocery items anyway—the promotion should always be made on the actual pack. Promoting it on a bottle collar or a nearby leaflet almost never works. Experience is quite clear on that point.

Why? That's not so easy to answer. My guess is that promotion elsewhere than on the pack is just too far removed from the product to motivate the consumer and make the connection between incentive and action. I may or may not be right in that, but there's no doubt about the fact itself. So for a successful cashback, you can't escape the need to print a special section on the pack. Keep it short and simple—'Buy 5, get $5 free! Hurry—offer ends (date)', followed by details of how to claim, is all you require.

The 'slippage' factor

Earlier in the chapter, I observed that your cashback offer might not cost as much as you expect. This is due to what is known as the 'slippage' factor. There'll be many consumers who'll respond to your offer and start buying. But instead of buying the whole five (or whatever) packs they need to qualify, they'll stop after three or four. Or they may indeed buy all five, but never get around to sending in for their reward. So you've achieved a swag of extra sales—and you don't have to outlay a bean in return.

Now on the face of it, that's a highly satisfactory result for you. But what you have to guard against is the temptation to engineer it deliberately—either by setting too short a promotional period or demanding too many proofs of purchase. It's morally wrong and naive to promise an attractive reward but make it too hard to earn. You'll only annoy the consumer and damage your product or service. As a marketer, you're in a position of trust. You must live up to what you're promising. You must be true to your word.

Legitimate limitation

That said, however, it's quite legitimate—in fact, vital—to guard yourself against over-response. It's a good idea, for example, to limit larger offers to one per household. This guards you against multiple redemptions from hotels or clubs, where your product may be bought in bulk. And if you promote the cashback only on specially printed packs, you'll stop people claiming refunds on products they bought before the promotion began.

As I said, you have to be fair to your customers. But that doesn't mean you have to let unscrupulous people take you to the cleaners.

Let 'slippage' be a bonus

There's a high probability that you'll benefit from the 'slippage' factor. But you shouldn't strive to make it happen—and you shouldn't budget on the assumption that it will. Yours might just be one of the occasional promotions that gets an above-average response. It's safer to budget for a response around the 10% mark. If you get less than that, consider it a bonus.

Even so, don't regard 'slippage' as an unqualified blessing. If your response is under 5%, the most likely reason is that you've set your reward too low or your proofs of purchase too high. There could be lessons to be learnt there before you try the technique again.

Calculating cashbacks

Another lesson to learn is that circumstances will change redemption or response rates quite dramatically. Wide distribution of a product carrying an offer will also reduce the number of people who can take up your proposition. Stock which is more thinly spread can quickly run out if, due to the offer, purchasing velocity is faster. Conversely, a higher stock weight, in limited distribution, gives the consumer opportunity to collect more packs and fulfil the offer over relatively shorter periods more easily.

Competitive activity can also change response rates significantly—for instance, if your competition is running a more attractive offer. Competitor stock weight or a competitor's deep cut promotion which offers more value to the consumer can also affect the outcome of your promotional activity.

It's always wise to plan on *maximum* response, in planning any free mail-in or cashback promotion. It's also wise to base these scenarios on experience, to ensure you aren't being too generous. The critical issue is to motivate people enough without giving too much away!

The workings in the table opposite demonstrate how the generosity of the reward and subsequent response rate increases can radically affect the budget available. In example A versus B, the costs of B could be almost half A, yet there is only a relatively minor reduction in budgeted sales volume. My advice is 'hasten slowly' and test or go to a practitioner who can demonstrate the effect of such a promotion. This is critical, especially where relatively larger volumes of packs are in the market-place.

As you can see, we have been able to reduce the budget from a potential $150 000 to $85 000 by reducing the reward by 50¢, which in turn has changed the volume sale as well as the response. The reality of this scenario will best be established by testing. This illustration demonstrates that reducing the reward could save the budget and the brand substantial amounts, without reducing the volume and profit expectation.

EXAMPLE A: A 12-week on-pack cashback promotion on Brand X which has a retail selling price of $3.50 per standard unit of sale. Our promotion demands four proofs of purchase for $4 *free*.

Response Estimates	*Sales Units*
Total number of on-pack promoted promotional units available worth $3.50 RSP each, including, say, 20% volume increase over a 12-week promotional period.	1 500 000
Total possible redemptions on an offer requiring four proofs of purchase, ÷ 4.	375 000
Forecast total guesstimated maximum redemptions (based on experience) @ 7.5%.	28 125
Cost Estimates	*$*
Total cost of cashback @ $4 each x 28 125	112 500
Receipt, handling, postage @ $1.10 each x 28 125	30 937
Compliments/coin note card @ $0.15 each x 28 125	4 218
Envelope @ $0.10 x 28 125	2 812
Total cost	*$150 467*

EXAMPLE B: Alternatively, this promotion is based on a $3.50 reward on Brand X. It is in effect a 'Buy four, get one free' proposition. Brand X retails at $3.50 per standard unit of sale.

Response Estimates	*Sales Units*
Total number of on-pack promoted units available worth $3.50 RSP each, including, say, 15% volume increase over a 12-week promotional period.	1 400 000
Total possible redemptions on an offer requiring four proofs of purchase, ÷ 4.	350 000
Forecast total guesstimated maximum redemption (based on experience) @ 5%.	17 500
Cost Estimates	*$*
Total cost of cashback @ $3.50 each x 17 500	61 250
Receipt handling and postage @ $1.10 each x 17 500	19 250
Compliments/coin note card @ $0.20 each x 17 500	3 500
Envelope @ $0.10 x 1750	1 750
Total cost	*$85 750*

While there is a limit to the number of people who will respond to any one promotion, cashback (and free premium) promotions are open-ended. Redemptions, as a result, could theoretically be limited only by the number of promotional packages in the market-place. Previous experience may not be duplicated by future outcomes. Most people who get into serious trouble do so by offering too much money with too little proof of purchase or by not placing enough 'hoops' between the customer and the offer. Equally, efforts can fail if, in the consumer's mind, the reward does not exceed the effort involved in claiming it.

The dynamics of the take-up and response are complicated and apply to any cashback or free premium promotion. Response can be lowered or dramatically increased by many factors, as follows:

- The start date of promotion versus closing date.
- Asking for proofs of purchase in excess of anticipated purchase patterns.
- Normal use-up rate of the product versus promotional take up.
- A deep price cut plus the cashback reward on top.
- Size of household/consumer or institution buying and responding.
- Size of reward/adequacy of incentive.
- Out of stock/current in-stock position versus competition.
- The retail trade knowledge and scheduling.
- Your sales force programming and scheduling.
- Packing out too little product/no product/too much product.
- Your closing date—too short, or perhaps even too long.
- The number of pay days your promotion embraces.
- On-shelf and off-shelf locations.

With any promotion, it is imperative to inform everyone. Be sure to brief every department in the chain of production, including distribution and sales in the company as well as merchandisers, right through to the retailer. The ease with which the consumer can enter the promotion will also affect response rates quite apart from the generosity of your offer. Consider the following:

- How the promotion is communicated and the opportunities to see and buy the product.
- Part payment for return postage of reward.

- Freepost address facility.
- Entry coupon, if any, and its size and clarity.
- Numbers of proofs of purchase required.

Clever cashbacks

When you plan your cashback, let your thinking travel a bit beyond the straight 'Buy 5, get $5 free' approach. A little imagination could increase not only your response, but your sales. For example, you might try:

- an escalating cashback, where you offer (say) $2 *free* for three purchases, $3 *free* for five and $5 *free* for six. That way, you give the consumer an incentive to buy more, while still offering a reward for smaller purchases. You could add further creativity by making the reply form look like a cheque—and inviting the consumer to 'Write your own refund'.
- a cashback-plus-sweepstake promotion, that might offer a $5 cash refund for five proofs of purchase, plus the chance to multiply your money 1000 times—and win $5000.
- a product range cashback that asks consumers to buy different products within a range, for an attractive total refund.
- a cross-brand cashback, such as one that invites consumers to buy 'a' brand bread and 'b' brand butter, or perhaps 'a' brand bread and 'c' brand jam, to get their reward. In this case, the refund would probably be promoted on the brand with the highest market penetration.

A bingo cashback

There are many other ways of handling cashbacks creatively. Pine-O-Clean liquid cleaner did it with a cashback that worked like a bingo game.

A bingo token with a value of $1, $2 or $3 was placed inside each Pine-O-Clean bottle. It could be seen, but its value could only be discovered by removing it from the bottle—a device that hastened the use-up rate and led to faster repeat sales. The idea was that the consumer had to collect the tokens and match them according to their value. Three $1 tokens earned a refund of $3, and so on. So the refund after purchasing three bottles was at least $3 and possibly as high as $9. This format encouraged consumers to try for higher refunds by buying more than three bottles, and introduced a real element of fun into the whole promotion.

The Cash Call

Black & Decker, frequent users of cashbacks, developed one with an impressive prize fund that gave it unusual appeal.

When consumers bought a Black & Decker product, they could then make a 0055 Cash Call to find out the size of their refund. Every caller won a prize, which could vary from $25 up to the big payout of $1000. It was necessary, of course, to make the lowest level large enough to head off consumer disappointment at not being a major prize winner. Basically, this promotion was a $25 cashback offer—but the larger bonuses available at random gave it considerable impact. Both Black & Decker and Pine-O-Clean reported higher-than-expected response and sales from their creative use of cashbacks.

A little extra thought put into your cashback could well reap similar results for you.

Shareouts

A variation on the cashback theme is called a shareout. And while shareouts are generally less attractive both to marketers and consumers, they do have their place—especially with products where sharing actually occurs, such as chocolates and boxes of sweets.

In that sort of product category, they can be very effective in getting you extra displays at point of sale. This is because they share out a relatively larger sum of money than a cashback—say $20 000—among all the entrants. And a poster that says '$20 000 to be shared' has considerable POS impact—because a promise involving that kind of money will certainly grab attention. Of course, no-one gets the $20 000, or anything like it. What happens is that consumers earn a share of the $20 000, in proportion to the number of proofs of purchase they return. So they take a punt on the amount they'll receive. Obviously, the more people who enter, the less each one gets.

To avoid massive disappointment, you need to consider the number of likely entrants very carefully, to make sure each one doesn't receive too little money for too much effort expended. To guard against that possibility—and to insure yourself against customer ill-will—it's wise somewhere in the rules to stipulate a minimum payment reward. This should be much in line with what customers would expect to get from an average cashback.

A shareout does simplify your budgeting, because you know from the start the exact amount of money you'll have to refund. But personally, I'd consider a cashback before a shareout every time. With a cashback, the consumers know (in most cases) the exact amount of money they'll get. And they get it earlier than they do with a shareout, in which nobody gets a cent until the whole promotion is finished.

So in almost every instance, a cashback is more appealing to the consumer than a shareout. And I'd always rather make the consumer happy than simplify my own budgeting.

Wouldn't you?

7

CHAPTER

Clever Tricks with Packs

If you're marketing an insurance company or a bank, give this chapter a miss. It's mainly for packaged goods manufacturers—people whose product reaches the consumer in a pack, via a supermarket shelf.

If you're in that category, you have a definite advantage over those who push intangible things like most services. Your pack, or even your transport's livery, is not just a container that delivers your product to a purchaser. It's a powerful communication medium in its own right, as British Airways demonstrated when they promoted 'The World's Biggest Offer' on all their 747s. 'On-pack' communication is a highly cost-efficient alternative medium for selling a promotion to your customers.

Why on-pack promotions perform

In fact, I'd go as far as to say that the pack is the most cost-efficient vehicle of all for carrying a promotional message. That's particularly true in the case of fast-moving consumer goods. Basically, the only real expense involved is a few printing plate changes, and the cost of those is usually minimal.

This imaginative trade and consumer campaign distinguishes Redheads from other brands. It adds life and personality and a reason for buying.
Courtesy of Bryant & May

But an on-pack promotion not only communicates itself economically. It can also be among the most effective promotions of all—especially if it supports your product's branding and image in a powerful way and ties in with its advertising proposition. If it meets those criteria, experience shows it can give you high point of sale impact and set you apart dramatically from your competitors on the shelf. And those achievements are frequently followed by one you want even more—increased sales, usually involving a pleasing degree of brand switching.

Virtually any kind of promotion can be run on-pack. The technique is ideal for self-liquidating offers, sweepstakes, premiums and almost anything else you like to name. Naturally, the particular type of promotion you choose will depend on your marketing objectives. A sweepstake, for instance, won't get you the same results as a free mail-in premium, while a self-liquidating premium will deliver a different set of responses again. Always bear in mind that the pack is simply a very cost-efficient communication medium. You have to decide how its power can best be harnessed to meet your current marketing needs.

Innovative use of the pack plus the 'Redhead brand' characters created a unique promotion.
Courtesy of Bryant & May

Don't let the packs outlive the promotion!

A good way to lose friends and annoy people is to close the promotion while the special packs are still in the store or in the cupboard at home. Arousing people's interest, only to squash it with a 'contest closes' date that's already past, is not calculated to endear you to them.

Because of that, most on-pack promotions run for about 12–14 weeks, depending on brand volumes. You have to ensure that the specially printed-packs will run out in the stores well before the competition's closing date. A slip-up there will not only antagonise and disappoint many of your customers. It could also lead the stores to demand that you withdraw all stocks featuring the out-of-date promotion. Either consequence is one you can well do without.

How to set your closing date

So if you do run an on-pack promotion, you'll have to judge your sales rate very carefully. You'll need to consider the period over which the promotion is running, work out your average sales for that length of time, and allow for the extra sales the promotion will (hopefully) generate. That should give you a rough idea of when the special packs will clear the stores (and, incidentally, tell you how many you should budget for and produce). Then, make sure you allow sufficient time for the packs to be produced, filled, distributed and placed on shelf. You'll also need to leave the consumer enough use-up time as well.

When all that's been worked out, you can set your contest closing date. Experience suggests it ought to be at least two or three weeks after the promotional packs should have disappeared. Complicated? Yes—but it can be done. And the results should make it well worth your while.

More of the mechanics

Before we leave the boring (but vital) topic of mechanics, let's dispose of a few more. With on-pack promotions that carry closing dates, you have to:

- make sure the promotional packs reach the stores well before the promotion begins—especially if you have media support;

- be certain you can control the packs from marketing to production to distribution to retail warehouse, and then to point of sale;
- be careful that your creative presentation of the promotion on-pack does not detract from brand values;
- consider alternative methods of customising the pack, such as stickers, if you can't change it—perhaps because your product is imported ready-packed. If you can't do that with enough impact, an on-pack promotion is not for you.

When on-pack becomes inside-pack

By definition, on-pack promotions are presented and described in detail on the outside of the pack. Or rather, most of them are.

Clever use of the cup's rollover lip heightens the excitement and fun of winning—an effective way to promote 'Coke' and boost sales.
Reproduced with the permission of The Coca-Cola Company, owner of the registered trademarks 'Coca-Cola' and 'Coke'.

The product's stick is used to create a popular yearly promotion for both Streets and Peters ice cream. The deciding factor for purchase is: who can be the most creative in delivering prizes and excitement?
Courtesy of Peters Ice Cream

Not too many marketers have an area as big as the back of a Kellogg's® Corn Flakes pack on which to tell their story. What if you want to try an on-pack promotion, but you only have a small can or a little pack?

You try a little lateral thinking. And put at least some of your message on the inside.

Cadbury's did this successfully with a recent sweepstake (see Chapter 3 for details). There's not a lot of room for a detailed story on the outside of a chocolate wrapper. So they flashed the news of the promotion on the outside—and told the whole story on the wrapper's normally blank inside.

In some instances, sophisticated printing processes allow the inside of the pack to reveal a message or competition clue, in much the same way as a scratch card. Or an enclosed game piece can be found when a consumer opens the pack.

Coca-Cola and Schweppes follow this revelatory route in a slightly different way. Several times, they've announced a promotion on the outside of the can—and then imprinted a vital clue or code number on the bottom, inside. This, of course, can only be read when the can is empty. So you have to drink the product to enter the competition. In a related ploy, they've often had winning competition numbers printed under the rolled lips of Coke paper cups. When a cup's contents have been drunk, the contestant just presses a prepared tab and rolls the lip over to see if he or she is a winner.

Both techniques deliver the added dividend of quick product turnover and repeat sales.

Adding to the pack

The other way to solve the lack-of-space problem also involves lateral thinking. If there's not enough space on the pack for your message, you can just go ahead and create more space—by using Avery Labels' unique Fix-a-Form system.

Basically, this consists of a tiny multi-page leaflet with a self-adhesive label for a back cover. The front cover carries an eye-catching message, the pages provide all the competition details and the back cover fastens

Tip Top use clever printing techniques on the inside and outside of the packaging to add excitement and involvement. Only when the bread is taken from the pack can the winning combination be discovered, by looking through the 'window' in the wrapper.
Courtesy of Tip Top bakeries, a division of George Weston Foods

the whole thing onto the pack. To make life even easier, Fix-a-Forms are supplied in reels. They can be applied to any product automatically, using standard label applicators.

A variation of Fix-a-Form is the Auto-Collar. This is another mini-booklet, in the form of a neck tag for bottles. What's more, it can be applied to them at high speed, either on the production line or as a separate process. So it avoids the slow manual application of normal neck tags, and eliminates the production back-logs and high labour costs they often cause.

A complicated story and a small pack, then, needn't stop you having an on-pack promotion. There are many creative ways to break the space barrier and communicate your message.

The English experience

On a recent trip to England, I became a heavy purchaser of just about all the cereal brands on Sainsbury's shelves, apart from the own-labels. It was an eye-opening experience. Virtually every Kellogg's®, Nabisco and Weetabix pack carried a promotion of some kind. It seemed they could maintain brand share and fend off the own-labels in no other way. And I believe it's a positive development for them, because each promotion should not only contribute to brand volume, but strengthen the penetration of the whole breakfast food market.

A typical range of branded cereals fighting for attention in a UK supermarket. Although the retailer's 'house' label products don't appear here, they too feature offers of similar value to those shown.
Which motivates the most, the brand or the offer? A glance at a supermarket shelf shows a bewildering range of FREE classic prints, FREE Matchbox cars, FREE Dennis the Menace gifts, FREE 'super spookers', FREE glitter sticker, FREE Corgi model cars, FREE wildlife transfers kit, FREE body care range, FREE touring maps, FREE alarm clocks, FREE glow in the dark cosmic stickers, FREE illustrated dictionary, FREE Rice Crispies 'super-hero' personal radio and FREE Basildon Bond Stationery. To name some!
Courtesy of Kellogg Australia Pty Ltd, Weetabix and Nabisco

Extra product FREE and unmistakably from Mr Heinz.
Courtesy of H J Heinz Company Australia Ltd

'Good News' makes you smile. Then when you're feeling good about the brand, the 10% extra product FREE looks like even better value.
Courtesy of Mars Confectionery

Of course, it does mean that the promotion is often as important a choice factor as the brand itself! It's hard for a purchaser to decide which pack offers the best taste and value while the children are screaming, 'We want the one with the Ninja Turtles inside!'.

Bonus packs: more product, same price

Your pack, then, can deliver a sales-boosting promotional message in a very effective and cost-efficient way. But in many cases, it can be more than just a brilliant promotional medium. It can actually be the promotion itself.

Bonus packs are an excellent example. These are specially produced packs that contain 10%–25% more product than standard packs, yet sell for the same price. They're particularly popular with the manufacturers of larger volume products like soap powders and breakfast cereals. The pack sizes can be altered fairly easily, without radical changes to the on-shelf dimensions. This usually means extending the pack vertically, while keeping the normal shelf facing size. Manufacturers with smaller packs, however, can still use the technique. Chocolate bars with a temporary 20% or so extension appear fairly regularly and do well. In fact, bonus packs large or small are generally so successful that, apart from discounting, they're probably sales promotion's most widely used in-store mechanism.

Their appeal to the consumer is obvious. More product at the same price equals more value. But the technique has real appeal to the manufacturer, too. Bonus packs can be arranged fairly easily within the company, and are therefore quite economical. Furthermore, as the value of the product is normally less than a significant price cut, bonus packs normally cost you less than price reductions.

Who are you rewarding?

One proviso on the bonus pack technique: recent direct marketing tracking studies suggest that brands offering such bonuses may be rewarding their existing users very heavily. In fact, they may be subsidising them to an unacceptable degree.

So while bonus packs normally gain large sales increases, most of the extra sales may be coming from brand loyalists stocking up on the product. Now that's not necessarily a negative thing—rewarding brand loyalists, we have discovered, is one of the best ways to keep them loyal. But if your main aim is to attract new users, you may need to consider other techniques.

Get off the shelf if you can

However, let me immediately qualify that. If you can negotiate large gondola ends or other off-shelf locations for your bonus packs, you can look forward to quite spectacular results—including a significant percentage of new users. My work for Unilever has demonstrated this, time and again.

Of course, it can be argued that any pack will do better in an off-shelf display. That may be so—but in my experience, the bonus pack outperforms all others in this situation. After all, off-shelf displays virtually guarantee that your product will be noticed. And getting noticed while you're offering extra value is an extraordinarily potent selling formula.

Usually, it's not too difficult to organise off-shelf displays for bonus packs. Many stores like them, regarding them as certain sellers and almost as new lines. Occasionally, however, you'll strike store management who claim that, by selling more product for the same price, they're missing out on volume sales. They may want to discuss with you ways in which they can defray this perceived loss of income.

You can't please all the people all the time ...

Banded packs

Another way of offering some of your product free is the banded pack—two packs joined together by Scotch tape or shrink-wrap.

This alternative has some attractive aspects. It gives you twice the selling face to communicate a sales message. It also gives you more flexibility in creating your offer. Two packs can mean even greater savings for your customers than two single bonus packs or a single price-off pack. If you want to gain product trial or block a new competitive product, you can even offer the two packs for the price of one—an almost irresistible 50% saving.

But the other good point is this. Not only do two packs mean you're moving more product—your price reduction can actually cost you less. Two packs at a 20% reduction is really a 10% cut per pack. That's a lot better for you than offering one pack at 20% off. What's more, your turnover per sale is greater. Your factory throughput is also attractive on a cost per unit basis. And to top it off, the trade is pretty well disposed towards banded packs too. Of course, the technique doesn't work physically with some items. You'd have a job, for instance, to band two round tins together. But others, such as rectangular toothpaste packs, are made to order for it.

An instant reward

Colgate Dental Cream has used the technique many times over the years with considerable success. The company recognised long ago that if packs were wrapped strongly with Scotch tape, they couldn't be cut apart and sold separately—a now thankfully rare problem that used to dog some manufacturers.

Some years back, Colgate also hit on a novel way of offering a saving with banded packs of their mint toothpaste. And not only did it give consumers an instant reward—it saved Colgate some money in the process. Their innovative approach was to use heavy duty Scotch tape to bind a bright, shiny, newly minted 20¢ coin onto the packs. At the time, this represented about a 15% saving on the purchase price of two packs. So Colgate saved 5% on the usual discount, which is 20%—while consumers were attracted by the novelty value and the immediate tangible reward of a bright, shiny, brand new 20¢ coin.

Some stores worried initially that the coin might attract pilferers as readily as it did consumers. However, the Scotch tape's extra strength won the day, and the banded, coin-equipped packs sold very well indeed. The promotion helped strengthen the mint toothpaste's selling proposition, too, with its theme line 'Newly minted 20¢ coin *free*'.

Trial across the range

Today, banded packs are often used by hair care and cosmetics manufacturers to create trial across their ranges. They do so by banding trial samples of various products, often in smaller trial sizes, to normal packs of their best sellers. All sorts of interesting combinations can be put together in this way. Loyal purchasers appreciate the opportunity to sample other products from a brand they like—and it's cost-effective for manufacturers to use their own products as a vehicle for presenting new lines.

Trial-sized packs

In Chapter 11, we'll see how effective trial-sized packs are in sampling promotions generally. What's more, they have a much wider application in the grocery field than is generally realised.

Normally, the trial pack is specially produced by the manufacturer. It can, if required, be tailored to a particular store. And the whole trick with it is to ensure that consumers see it as real value for money. That means doing a juggling act when you set the price. It has to be low enough to be extremely attractive to the consumer—yet high enough to allow the retailer a worthwhile margin.

Trial packs are a good place to run an on-pack promotion, too. In their case, it should take the form of an incentive offer, such as a cash-back, to persuade the purchasers to return and buy the full-size product.

My personal favourite trial pack added a sense of timing and humour to the technique. I have not seen its equal since. It concerned Carnation Go Cat cat food, a trial-sized pack offered in grocery stores near us, and our very discriminating moggie Muffy. For the full story, turn to Chapter 11.

Multipacks

Our probing of pack possibilities ends with what I call the 'love child' of banded packs—the multipack. This is a large pack, containing several small snack-packs of potato chips, chocolates, confectionery or whatever. The small packs are just the right size for family snacks, school lunches and so on. The multiple pack offers them at a price single-serve packs can't match. So the consumer saves money, and the manufacturer moves more product with every sale.

This explains why multipacks are proliferating. If you have a confectionery-type product that can be sold in snack-size lots, a multipack is well worth thinking about.

All in all, a lot of very clever selling tricks can be performed by the humble, all-too-familiar pack. So the next time you pick up one of yours, look at it with new respect. It's one of the best promotional tools you have.

® Registered Trademark Kellogg (Aust) Pty Ltd, Authorised User

8 CHAPTER

Free Offers that Push Sales Further

Picture yourself for a moment as a Roman centurion, in the halcyon days of the Empire. Vast crowds cheer as you and your soldiers march through Rome, bringing home the booty from a successful campaign. You reach the Forum—and more cheering breaks out as beaming toga-clad senators heap further rewards upon you.

Why the Ben Hur imagery? Because this chapter is all about premiums—a word that comes from the Latin *praemium*, meaning booty or reward. And when you consider the profit potential of premiums today, perhaps the Roman mind-pictures are not too far removed from modern reality.

Premiums are basically gifts given in return for purchase. Ranging in style from trite to very imaginative, they perform many different marketing tasks for a wide variety of products. They're sent away for. They're fastened to, positioned near, put inside and even replace packs. And they're despatched to their target audiences to pave the way for selling efforts that will come after them.

This FREE fluffy toy dog (in the window) personality beckons investors to consider the competitive loan interest rates of SGIO. This unlikely offer helped SGIO win customers over in droves.
Courtesy of SGIO Building Society 1983 (now Suncorp)

Seven spheres of service

Because premiums reward a customer for buying a product, they add extra perceived value—and extra sales appeal—to your goods and services. They can be offered in many different ways, of which these seven are the most common:

1. *Mail-in or accumulator premiums*, where the customer mails the required number of proofs of purchase, and gets the article through the mail in return.
2. *With-pack premiums*, an immediate-reward technique that attaches the premium article to the actual pack.
3. *Near-pack premiums*, a variation where the premium is located near the pack on the shelf.
4. *Display premiums*, articles specially chosen to give the product a very high profile at point of sale.
5. *In-pack premiums*, which locate the premium inside the pack.
6. *Reusable containers*, a situation where the pack actually becomes the premium.
7. *Trial premiums*, which are sent out before a sale is made, to act as purchase bait.

Mail-ins the most popular

Of these, free mail-in premiums are the most widely used. They allow for a much wider choice of premiums, because you're not limited to

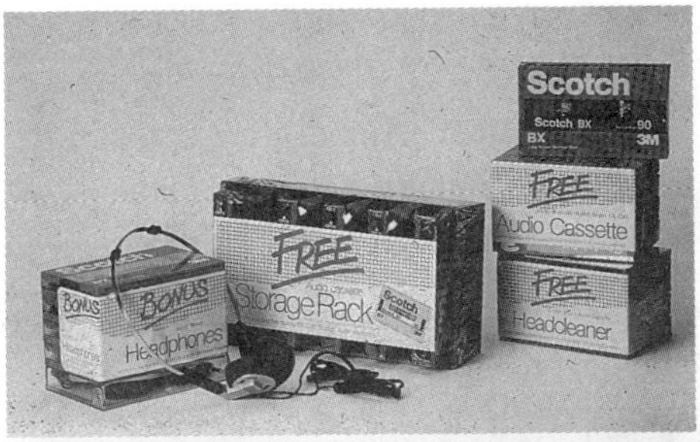

3M attach sought-after premiums to complement their range, add value and differentiate the brand.
Courtesy of 3M Australia Pty Ltd

Aquafresh add in-pack value with offers to attract trial from double pack purchases. That's enough toothpaste to go beyond trial, establish a liking in the family and encourage habit-forming repeat purchase patterns.
Courtesy of SmithKline Beecham

A product feature or a promotional add-on? Whichever it is, it underpins Duracell's 'power' positioning and concern for the consumer at point of sale.
Courtesy of Duracell

something that can fit on, in or near the pack. This in turn gives full rein to the creativity you need to maximise the technique's potential.

Equally importantly, mail-in premiums can motivate the customer to buy not once or twice, but several times. All the other premium types listed above can achieve only one sale per premium. But if mail-in premiums are tempting enough, you can ask for three or even more proofs of purchase before you send them—especially if the magic word *free* is there to add to their appeal.

The cashback link

Mail-in premiums have a great deal in common with cashbacks (see

A highly creative way of attracting attention and delivering a colourful FREE offer from Kodak, redeemable at video shops. The promotion also gave the video shops the extra traffic they wanted.
Courtesy of Kodak Limited

Chapter 6). In fact, the only difference is that you're offering an attractive article instead of cash. The mechanics are the same—people send in so many proofs of purchase and receive the reward through the mail. The proofs can be labels, barcodes, or supermarket till roll receipts with the purchase price circled.

Another point of similarity between the techniques is the reason for choosing them. Like cashbacks, mail-in premiums are particularly effective with products that are bought regularly, because such products minimise the gap between purchase and reward. If yours is one, and you want to increase sales, speed up cashflow and reduce brand switching among regular purchasers, a mail-in premium could be the way to go. It can also perform most effectively in the role of 'dealer loader'. If it's sufficiently appealing and of some value, you can give it away to the trade to strengthen relationships, get better displays or boost your efforts to increase stock levels.

Mail-in premiums, however, are not the best way to launch a new product. Nor are they the best approach for impulse sales items. Neither situation lends itself to the multi-sale commitment people have to make to earn their reward.

An on-pack promotion

When applied to supermarket lines, free mail-in premiums are usually promoted on-pack. In that case, all the on-pack promotion points made in Chapter 7 should be considered when planning them. They can, however, be successfully promoted through on-pack or near-pack leaflets, or even through the media, as long as there's a strong reminder on the pack to link promotion with product.

A future reward

With both cashbacks and free mail-in premiums, the customer's reward is not immediate, as it is with price discounts, reusable containers and pack-related premiums. He or she has to make the necessary number of purchases, send in the proofs and then wait for the premium to arrive in the mail. To pull customers into what can be quite a lengthy process, the reward obviously has to be very attractive. Cash fills that bill, as we saw in Chapter 6. But for an article to do the job, it clearly has to be something appealing, imaginative and useful to the customer—something that offers excellent value and is difficult or impossible to obtain elsewhere.

A tall order? Well, yes and no. Certainly, many marketers fail to come up with the right item, and are left up to their ears in a stack of mundane merchandise. But lots of others have created exactly the right thing, and laughed about it all the way to the bank.

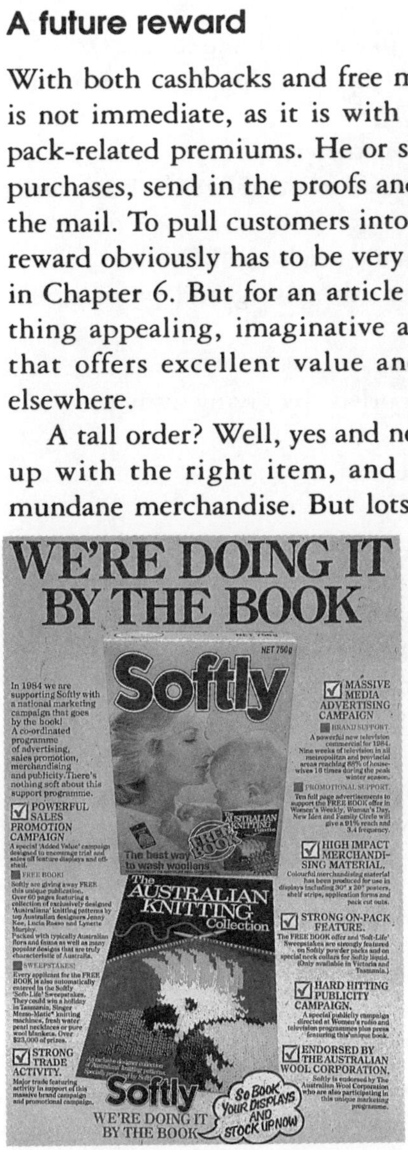

Softly's FREE knitting book helps the target audience demonstrate their innate skills under top designer and knitting colourist Jenny Kee's direction. The promotion carried the added authority of The Wool Corporation's endorsement.
Permission of L & K: Rexona Pty Ltd., a division of Unilever

Creating the right premium

I can tell you the parameters within which your mail-in premium should be designed. But for its actual creation, I'm afraid you're on your own—or in the company of your advertising or sales promotion agency. No matter how well the parameters are understood, imagination, innovation and experience are the vital extras most likely to produce a top-class premium.

However, here are the parameters you need to frame your thinking. Your mail-in premium should:

- be naturally linked to your product (like a cake knife to cakes);
- ideally, help to increase its usage (like a recipe book with food products);
- be useful to the customer, not a dust-gatherer;
- underline brand values (like a home first aid reference book with pharmaceutical lines);
- be appropriate to your customers' wants, needs and lifestyles;
- be capable of integrating with your advertising and promotional themes;
- have the right image for your company;
- not take sales away from your sales outlets, by giving away products they sell;
- not present storage or delivery problems;
- be within your budget;
- have that indefinable but very real spark of imagination and creativity that means outstanding customer appeal.

You feel like giving up the concept now? Don't. Explore the possibilities to the limit. Follow up thoughts that come to you, no matter how wild. Keep those parameters before you as guidelines for your thinking. In all probability, you'll get an idea that fits them beautifully—and if it's particularly strong on the last one, you're almost certainly on a winner.

Westpac recognise that they can make more of their service and offer their advice FREE.
Courtesy of Westpac Banking Corporation

The quest for knowledge

Here's another point to guide you. Perhaps the most popular premium of all is free information. This is why cookbooks, home medical tomes, handyman volumes and the like work so well in the premium role. According to pundits, this generation is almost totally concerned with the transfer of knowledge from one person to the next—so it stands to reason that free information can be a more powerful premium in more fields today than ever before.

This is especially true when you consider two other factors. First, we now have a wider range of information-dispensing media at our disposal, including such tools as diskettes, CD Roms, videos and seminars. Second, in tandem with our information-driven society, consumers tend to have narrower but deeper interests than they had even 20 years ago. They really want to know more about their special interest areas, not only from a knowledge point of view but to help them make wise purchasing decisions.

This is why more and more marketers are finding that premiums consisting of carefully targeted free advice can attract above average to very high response rates—and increase long-term product usage as a result.

Leave people time

Another vital aspect is one we looked at in Chapter 7. Leave people time

3M invite consumers to buy a library of tapes over time and build up a valuable FREE collection of best-selling books. *Courtesy of 3M Australia Pty Ltd*

to earn the premium. If you're asking for five proofs of purchase, don't end the promotion when most people would only have three. And if you're promoting the premium on-pack, set your closing date well after the last specially-printed pack should have cleared the shelves. If anyone slogs away to get the five (or whatever) proofs of purchase and sends them in, only to be told the offer closed last week, you'll have made an enemy for life. Don't risk it.

Budgeting

Now we come to the tightrope part of premium creation. If you're giving the item away, you don't want to spend the proverbial arm and leg on it. Yet if you don't spend enough, the item might well finish up shoddy and unappealing. So how much should you budget?

Surveys show that, on average, most marketers spend around 10% of the amount the customer has to pay to get the premium, multiplied by anticipated unit sales. In other words, if your product retails at $5 and you expect to sell 20 000 units through the premium promotion, your premium budget should be around $10 000. Our experience suggests that if you have a high-volume, high-turnover product, you can afford to put the premium budget up to 15% of your expected sales income. Anything over that should be treated with great caution. In fact, I'd go back to the drawing board at that point, and look for another premium idea.

'Slippage' may help

Back in our cashback discussion in Chapter 6, I referred to the 'slippage' factor. This, you'll remember, is the phenomenon where people buy extra product to get proofs of purchase, but either stop short of the necessary number or forget to send them in. So you get extra sales without paying anything for them. Happily, the phenomenon applies just as much to mail-in premiums as it does to cashbacks.

The chances are high that, because of 'slippage', your premium promotion will come in under budget. But let me repeat the warning I gave in Chapter 6. When you set your budget, don't take the 'slippage' factor into account. Sometimes, it just doesn't happen. Keep to the 10%–15% of projected sales level—and if 'slippage' does occur, treat it as a bonus.

The other way of increasing your profit from the promotion is to ask for more than the usual three to five proofs of purchase. Whether people will respond to this or not depends on the attractiveness of your premium and the speed of your product's purchase cycle. I have found, however, that people will wear a higher number of proofs of purchase if you throw in an additional lure, such as a sweepstake with an appealing prize. Such an addition makes your promotion a two-tiered one. Everybody who responds with the necessary proofs of purchase gets the premium—plus the chance to win something really attractive. Of course, the sweepstake prize has to be budgeted for, and weighed against the likely extra sales its presence will create.

Judging the response

Whichever way you go, there's no doubt that judging the likely response is one of the trickiest parts of your tightrope act. And here, I must admit, I can give you little generalised help for your specific situation. There are so many factors likely to influence the outcome. Your product's nature, category, price, reputation, normal turnover period and market position are just some of them. Others include the appeal of your premium, how much perceived value it adds to your product, the number of purchase proofs you're requiring, whether or not you're adding a sweepstake—the list goes on.

Ultimately, the ability to judge the likely response is a science—or perhaps an art form—in itself. This is why I would urge you to engage a good sales promotion agency to help with your free mail-in premium venture.

After the minefield

By this time, you may be feeling that a fairly daunting creative, mechanical, budgeting and response-judging minefield lies between you and your successful free mail-in premium. And in a sense, it does. Despite the obvious pitfalls, however, the crossing is well worthwhile. Many marketers have found that, to their very considerable profit.

1988 and all that

Among them was the 3M Company, in the eventful year of 1988. That was both an Olympic year and modern Australia's 200th birthday. So 3M offered its office equipment customers a unique premium—a set of four superbly designed coffee mugs, each carrying a large number '1', '9' or '8'. Put together in order on the shelf, the set spelt out '1988'.

This very imaginative premium brilliantly echoed other 3M advertising and promotional activities. It caught the mood of the times, and put the 3M name upfront in hundreds of offices and homes for years to come. Furthermore, it provided a strong spur to repeat sales. Because 3M customers were offered one mug free with every proof of purchase, they were powerfully motivated to collect all four. Somehow, mugs that said '1', '19' or '198' lacked the magic of a set that said '1988'.

Swimming in the waiting room

Another 3M division took advantage of the 1988 Olympics with a highly creative premium. Dentists who bought 3M dental products were offered magnificent, individually numbered prints of Olympic subjects—running, swimming and rowing.

Rather than have the artist sign these prints, 3M arranged for Australian Olympic athletes to sign them personally instead. Debbie Flintoff-King signed the last in the series just before she won gold for her country. This chance happening ensured the series' success.

All were ideal for hanging in the waiting room, where their contemporary appeal helped divert many a patient's mind from the ordeal ahead. Other dentists put them up in the surgery, or took them home for the lounge room. Wherever the signed prints were hung, they provided a lasting 3M presence in a subtle yet inescapable way.

Breaking new ground

Both the coffee mugs and the prints are excellent examples of premiums that broke new ground. They seized people's imaginations. They tied in extremely well with other Olympic promotional and advertising campaigns being run concurrently by 3M. They raised brand awareness among regular customers on a long-term basis. And they achieved a considerable increase in sales. You can't ask much more of a premium than that.

The Jampot Jamboree

In an entirely different market, the CSR 'Jampot Jamboree' helped turn the flagging sales of sugar around in the 1980s. The basic idea was that families were urged to make pots of jam for Boy Scout groups to sell as fundraisers. This, of course, involved buying sugar in considerably larger quantities than usual. In so doing, consumers were able to acquire a large number of proofs of purchase—which could then be exchanged for a very handsome, upmarket cookbook. In fact, if they persisted with the Jampot Jamboree, they could build up a whole library of excellent cookbooks.

All of this had a strong and natural link to the product. The cookbooks underlined the product's values, encouraged people to use more of it more often, and were extremely appropriate to the customers' needs, wants and lifestyles. In other words, they were absolutely ideal premiums. And they helped achieve a very substantial lift in sugar sales, at a time when the product was suffering from unwarranted (and later discredited) health scare claims.

You'll find more details about Jampot Jamboree and some related promotions in Chapter 15, which deals with cause-related marketing. The Jampot Jamboree certainly falls into that particular category. But first and foremost, the CSR sugar programme is an excellent example of an imaginative, creative—and highly successful—mail-in premium strategy aimed at stimulating purchase and product use.

Look for the home link

Some of the most successful premiums ever have been imaginative items that majored heavily on home-oriented pursuits like knitting, home safety and cooking. A particularly impressive example was a knitting book offered by Lever Bros for a mere two labels from Softly packs.

This wasn't just any old knitting book. From cover to cover, it was peppered with full-colour ideas from Jenny Kee, a top fashion designer known for her outrageous and brilliant use of colours. The promotion broke all response records. I wasn't surprised, because the premium was exceptionally well conceived, and had a perceived value well beyond that of two Softly labels.

If your product is used in the home, an imaginative home-linked premium could get equally spectacular results for you.

Give them a choice

One of the most effective ways to create a winning premium is to create several of them—and let your customers choose their own reward from a well-produced catalogue.

We did that very successfully for Apple Computers. In fact, we did it twice—for the corporate and educational markets. In both cases, we put the Apple logo on a whole range of appealing and appropriate items, and let the customers select the ones they wanted.

In the process, we learned two things.

The first—which I've also stressed elsewhere—is that you can't always assume that your market will go for a premium, just because you like it. Our Apple premiums were carefully chosen for their attractiveness through research. And we took bets in the office on which ones would prove the most popular.

We were almost always wrong.

Our second learning experience was that you shouldn't give your customers too wide a choice. If you do, you probably haven't done enough research into the kind of items they'd like. You run the risk of confusing them and making their selection too hard. And you can well create inventory problems for yourself or your client.

Keep the range down to a few thoroughly researched items and your multi-premium promotion should get excellent results.

The pack-linked premiums

Imagination is as vital to the creation of pack-linked premiums as it is to

Multiple purchase was the goal of this Black Douglas promotion. By packing an attractive glass into a Christmas gift box, Seagrams give consumers a strong reason to go on buying and collect a whole set at a time when spirit purchasing is at its highest.
Courtesy of Seagrams Australia Pty Ltd

their mail-in counterparts. Some would argue it is even more so—because the challenge of coming up with a memorable, useful, appealing, strongly branded premium that can be fitted on, near or in a pack is a formidable one indeed.

Budgeting is part of the challenge, because here there's no 'slippage' factor to act as a safety net for rubbery sales estimates. You can be sure of one thing with pack-linked premiums—you'll supply them with 100% of the sales you make. Furthermore, the free premium will often cost you more than a discount, and the expense and general hassle of attaching it to the pack may not be inconsiderable. Be sure to consider all these factors before you proceed.

On-packs that worked

Intimidating though the challenge may be, it is by no means unconquerable. Examples abound of on-pack premiums that combine creativity, practicality and strong branding support.

One of my favourites is Dettol's Home and Family Protection paperback book. Although fairly expensive (the free book is banded onto the 500ml Dettol pack), it expresses what the brand is all about in a way that is helpful and interesting to consumers. The information in the book also encourages increased use of the product in a variety of health care areas. And the book itself is a constant in-house reminder to buy

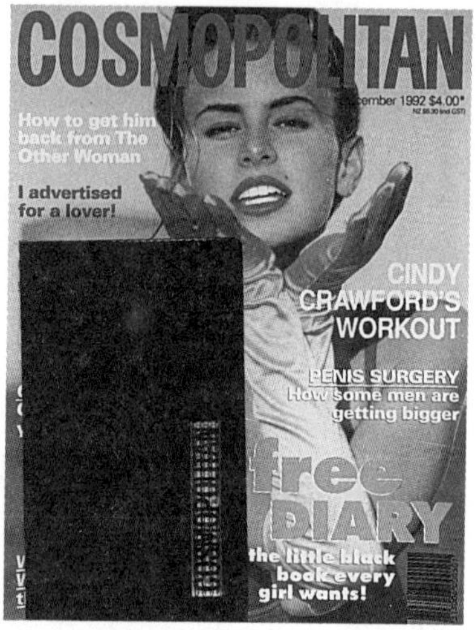

FREE on-pack premiums work best when they're appropriate to the wants of the target audience. They also promote trial as well as acting as a reward to buyers. They appeal to the target group, add immediate value to the purchase, create impact and interest and increase off-take instore. *Courtesy of ACP Publishing Pty Limited*

Dettol. This is a premium that really works in terms of reinforcing the brand's attributes. It's a brilliant way of achieving a short-term sales increase, heightened brand awareness and long-term sales too.

On-pack premiums are increasingly being used by publishers, who employ shrink-wrap technology to add value to their journals. Recent examples include a free Mozart CD fastened to *Classic Composer*, a free paint scraper on *Do it Yourself* and two free artists' paintbrushes attached to *Art & Artist*.

An obvious product link was achieved by Dulux Paints, when they attached a free paint scraper to each can. Nivea Sun Cream did it too, with their free beach towel offer. Almost certainly, there are plenty of potential premiums out there that will suit your product just as well. With a little thought and imagination, you'll unearth them.

Near-pack and with-pack purchase premium successes

A close sibling of the on-pack premium, the near-pack variety offers you much more flexibility in size and shape. Tactically, it can help you gain an extra display, additional stock weight and a short-term competitive advantage. It is often used today in conjunction with tailored in-store activity, and is managed by the sales force.

One of our successes in this area was a bright yellow, heavily branded PVC apron—a garish item that made a lot of sense when offered free with ICI Nilvern Wormer. Others I've admired for their obvious product links include:

- a free brush with shoe polish;
- a free garden rake with a lawn mower;

- a free tie—or even an extra pair of pants—with a suit;
- two pairs of spectacles for the price of one;
- a free bucket or paint tray with a can of paint;
- a free wallet, Parker Pen or calculator when you open a new bank account;
- free plant food with a plant;
- a free poster with a CD or cassette.

When the product arrived in the premium

3M Diskettes' file storage box was an excellent example of a really useful premium that tied-in strongly with the product. If you bought 10 3M diskettes, they came to you already packed in the box. And with them was another free extra—a pre-formatted diskette that not only offered additional value, but allowed the buyer to sample a new and normally more expensive product.

We put this promotion together for 3M at a time when the competition's research and development technology was lagging well behind. It helped 3M to establish a long-term sales lead.

Near-car premiums

Also in the near-pack category—well, sort of—was a series of premiums we offered in the UK to induce people to test-drive cars. If you test-drove a Toyota Camry, among these near-car premiums, for want of a better term, was an AA Book of the Road (with obvious motoring links). In Australia, we offered a Guinness Book of

Ford Dealers offer extra value by co-opting AEG, the top of the range tradesman's tool, to attract this specific target audience.
Courtesy of the Ford Motor Company

Ford dealers could have just cut the price—but by presenting the savings in a very imaginative way, they make the offer appear more attractive, valuable and exciting.
Courtesy of the Ford Motor Company

Records (because the car had a record number of standard features).

Another creative idea was given to anyone who test drove a Triumph TR7. It was an audio cassette by Noel Edmonds, a top DJ of the time and a well-known car enthusiast. On the cassette, Edmonds expounded the TR marque's history, and explained what the driver should look for in a test drive. With the cassette came a graphic booklet on this exciting sports car. Both were handed out free and without obligation to the prospect, immediately he or she agreed to the test drive.

Torches and first aid kits have been used, too, as test drive come-ons, because they can be very handy for most drivers. As well, we have used a number of leisure and sports items, even membership of sports clubs, as premiums with the actual purchase of the car.

Riding the sheep's back

Anxious to encourage embattled farmers to keep spending, Suzuki launched a novel form of discount on its four-wheel-drive utilities. It accepted wool as a trade-in. In advertisements in Victoria's farming newspapers, Suzuki Cars offered to accept any wool up to $2000 in value. This left farmers to come up with the balance in cash to take delivery of a new Suzuki Sierra utility.

It was not the first time Suzuki had tried these innovative tactics. Murray Wright, Suzuki's managing director, reported in the *Australian Financial Review* that Suzuki Cars had launched a similar campaign with considerable success during the beef crash in the 1980s.[1] It had then accepted steers in part-payment for vehicles.

The straight forward wool 'barter' offer would have appealed to those selling wool after the cut-off date for a government-sponsored scheme which topped up wool payments to the old floor. The timeliness of this deal reached the hearts and minds of a cash-strapped target audience. It cleverly helped clip the price of Suzuki's ideal farm vehicle in an appealing and imaginative way.

The magic word: FREE

Another borderline version of the near-pack premium is the product itself. Perhaps the most popular premium offer of all is simply your own product, *free*.

If you can think of a way to use your product or service to keep customers loyal or find new ones, run with it. You could cut your premium budget and save a lot of money, and you'll give your customers exactly what they want. These strategies are all based on the old Baker's dozen principle of 13 for the price of 12. They're appreciated, too. Over and over again, manufacturers have found that price discounts are what their loyal customers want most.

Ensure, however, that your offer lives up to its promotion. If you promise your customer a worthwhile tangible benefit, you really do have to deliver it. And remember that if you make too many free product offers for too long a time, your margins will start to suffer.

AT&T get prospects excited with their advertising which makes an offer of their own product; FREE calls for a month.
Courtesy of AT&T

Freebies galore

Keeping those two provisos in mind, it's interesting to look at the wealth of free product offers happening all around us. They're working for a very wide range of companies and industries—and they could well work for you.

Telecom and Optus offer free days of telephoning—up to two months of them if you stay loyal for at least two years. Mobile telephone retailers give away special upgrades in return for multiple purchases, or even a free telephone for your spouse or colleague.

Airlines offer free air miles. British Rail gave away a free ticket with each one purchased, which helped to introduce new travellers to the comforts of a modern high-speed rail service. Photocopying machine marketers offer free paper for a month or even a free rental period. Software manufacturers give free upgrades. Banks offer free financial advice as a door-opener to their financial services. And if you get two suits cleaned, your friendly dry cleaner will sometimes clean an extra pair of trousers for you, free.

A common ploy with hotels is to give away an extra night for every two you purchase. They're adept, too, at finding imaginative ways to use their leisure or dining facilities as free value add-ons. There's a valuable lesson here: a little creativity in its design can greatly increase your free offer's impact. In one growing trend, for instance, joint partners with affinity products are making offers neither could make alone, such as two weeks' car rental free (or at a nominal $1 more than the airfare) offered by an airline as part of a total travel package.

Another inventive variation is the offer of free credit rather than free product. CSR's PGH Pavers ran a 'Pave Now, Pay Later' promotion, with free credit over the period between delivery and payment. Many retail stores are offering up to nine months of free credit. Like free product offers, such strategies relax the financial burden on the consumer and make the buying decision easier.

McPizza premiums

Possibly the most common current example of free product premiums are those given away by fast food chains like McDonalds and Pizza Hut. Free french fries, free chicken nuggets, free Cokes, free gingerbread men with family-sized purchases are not only appealing to customers—they are almost certainly the cheapest items that the restaurants can give away.

However, McDonald's and Pizza Huts' premium programmes don't stop there. Both chains offer a huge and constantly changing array of items, all carefully researched to appeal to young children. The strategy is sound, because if you bring in the kids, you bring in the whole family. And every Junior Burger sold usually sells a Big Mac or Cheeseburger, fries, a cup of coffee, a Coke and maybe a couple of sundaes as well.

Many of the McDonald's and Pizza Hut items are self-liquidating premiums (see Chapter 9), usually created exclusively for the chain. They sell for a very small amount with virtually any purchase. Yet they're bought in such huge volumes that the selling price covers the whole cost of the promotion. The items range from licensed characters to dinosaurs to aliens to simple but ingenious toys. McDonald's often use their own Ronald McDonald and product-related characters in a host of creative ways—of which rubber bendy Ronalds and Big Mac 'transformers' are just two recent examples.

The lesson is that a mixture of different premiums, prizes and sweepstakes keeps the customers interested. A change of pace is almost a reward in itself. The kids can't wait to go back to see what new and exciting goodies will be on offer this time.

Adding appeal to point of sale

In some cases, near-pack premiums can be used to create a very attractive point of sale environment—one that not only looks appealing but cleverly underlines the product's image and attributes.

The classic example is Cinzano's outdoor parasol set. The tastefully branded umbrellas, chairs and table elegantly suggest the relaxed, refined lifestyle associated with leisurely martini drinking. The set is worth over $300, and is normally offered as a sweepstake prize rather than as a premium in the true sense of the word. However, the Cinzano people occasionally give one to store management in return for generous display space and a competitive selling price.

Display premiums

The logical next step from the Cinzano situation is to make the premium the whole basis of your in-store display. That means selecting it not only on the usual criteria, but on its display-creating abilities as well. Not an easy exercise—but one with great sales potential if you can do it.

Purists may object at this point, by saying that the items I'm now referring to are not really premiums, but more usually sweepstake prizes. They may well be right, but I'm unrepentant. While the items may be used as store customer sweepstake prizes, they're generally known as display premiums. That gets them a mention in this chapter as far as I'm concerned.

The Lux experience

Bob Bayley, a one-time colleague of mine in Britain, was a past master in their use. Typical of his creations was a Lux soap promotion we ran in the nation's top stores. This consisted of trendy Vogue baths piled high with Lux soap bars. The Vogue baths were sweepstake prizes with (you'll note) an obvious link to the product being promoted. The Vogue people benefited from the merchandising opportunity, while the piles of Lux soap bars in the baths disappeared like magic. By our estimates, they sold at least four times faster than they would have from a conventional display.

There's a not uncommon variation on this idea, in which a car or utility is brought into a store and stacked to capacity with bars of soap. The vehicle is supplied by a local car dealer, who gets considerable publicity throughout the promotion. A car or ute of the same model is the prize in a national sweepstake competition, in which people have to guess the capacity of the product stacked inside or on the tray. The entry forms are on leaflets at the point of sale or, better still, on the pack itself. Normally, the soap is sold at a discounted price, to cap off a well-rounded promotion for everyone concerned.

Nice one, baby

I've also seen baby product manufacturers use the same basic concept with great success. In those cases, they pile their products in and around naturally-linked display premiums like cots, playpens, prams and even paddling pools. Then the premium becomes a sweepstake for shoppers in that store at the end of the promotion. Meanwhile, it serves as an effective focus of interest in the store, and gains the baby products a lot more display space than they'd normally get.

Turning customers into safe breakers

One of the most successful display premium promotions I've ever run was for a Unilever household disinfectant. The product's claim was that it kept you safe from germs. So in a kind of enacted pun, we hired a flock of safes from Chubb, put them in stores, and piled the product around them. Then, for each purchase they made, shoppers were entitled to one spin of the safe's dial, to see if they could crack the simple combination and open the safe. If they could, the fortune inside was theirs.

The promotion captivated customers and the clients' sales staff alike. Many of the latter threw themselves into setting it up with such gusto that, in some stores, they buried the safes completely under product. In others, they piled so much stock around the safes that no-one could reach them. These hiccups were quickly sorted out—and then the queues of customers began.

For three weeks, we thought we were turning the nation's shoppers into safe breakers. Product sales doubled in comparison with the previous period. But as it turned out, the vast majority of our amateur safe breakers were unsuccessful. And I think we learned a lesson from that.

While the promotion worked brilliantly from the sales angle and created enormous excitement, I suspect it also created a lot of disappointment. The fact that so few of the customers actually won anything may well have soured many of them towards the brand in the long term. I now think you're much better off with a promotion that spreads the rewards widely or (in the case of premiums) gives them to everyone.

Castles of Coke

Yet another variant on the display premium theme is to use the product as the premium. Coke has done this very successfully on many occasions. They've used Coke cans and cartons to build huge in-store sculptures of everything from castles to cars, as a memorable and inescapable way of piling up stock in the store ready for a price-off sale. They've even built 'radio stations' of Coke cans, and had radio announcers present their shows from within these houses of cans in supermarkets and shopping malls. I applaud that. What better medium to highlight your product than the product itself—presented in such an extraordinary and dramatic form?

As we have seen, near-pack premiums and display premiums, their close relatives, come in every form from premium articles to sweepstake prizes to imaginative presentations of the product itself. But the aim is the same in every case—to give the product extra interest, impact and excitement. Few have done that more effectively than a Lever Bros promotion in the UK, way back in 1962.

A blooming success

This brilliantly creative venture remains one of the best known near-pack premium offers ever. It was an incredibly lifelike plastic daffodil, one of which could be taken free with every pack of Daz washing powder.

Massed in a dumpbin, the Daz daffodils made a giant splash of colour in the supermarket. Not only were they a powerful inducement to buy a pack of Daz—they kept people coming back for more, until a whole bunch of golden daffodils had been collected to the offer of 'Buy Daz, Pick a Daffodil Free!'. The benefits were in the immediacy of the rewards, the tangible evidence of the reward itself and the fact that *every* purchaser was equally rewarded. The fact that the items were colourful and unusual broke new ground with the consumer.

And what did people do with them? Most, I suppose, put them in vases. But not all. I well remember these yellow and green beauties poking their heads above the snow in the garden of my then girlfriend's mother. Mrs Antonio must have bought dozens of Daz packs to have obtained so many. Her family's clothes would have been the cleanest in the district!

Some years later, Lever Bros followed up this spectacularly successful promotion with a subsequent on-pack offer of free fresh-cut spring flowers from Interflora. The consumer had to send in proofs of purchase to obtain an Interflora voucher. This promotion would probably appeal more to today's environmentally conscious consumer—but I doubt it would have achieved anywhere near the success of Daz's dazzlingly imaginative venture of 1962.

In-pack premiums

Severely limited in terms of space, yet not without significant branding or usefulness possibilities, are premiums that go inside the pack.

The most regular users of in-pack premiums are breakfast cereal manufacturers. Their sets of cowboys, Indians, soldiers, animals and so on have kept the Hong Kong production lines humming for decades. Historically, the genre probably began with cigarette cards. Now collectors' items, these included beautifully produced flags of the world, test cricketers of the period, and even the Cunard fleet of ocean liners. Today, these nostalgic items have given way to rub off instant-win spot cards, or even things like holograms and lenticular pictures (pictures that change from different directions).

A good example of a creative in-pack premium is the free measuring spoon in a pack of flour. It's simple and inexpensive, yet it adds value to the product and gives the consumer a helpful product-use tool. Moreover, the spoon will be kept—and if well branded, it will serve as a constant reminder to buy the product again.

To me, the measuring spoon is a classic that establishes several criteria for judging in-pack premiums. It's easy and cheap to produce, fits comfortably in the pack and is relatively simple to handle at production stage. Above all, it's appropriate to the product and useful to the consumer. I realise that cowboys and Cunard liners have worked, even though they have nothing to do with breakfast cereals and cigarettes. But if it were my money, I'd put it on a useful, product-linked premium every time.

Reusable relevance

When it comes to relevance, however, probably no other premiums can match the reusable container. Design it attractively, and it will stay in the home for years—not only serving your customer in a highly practical way, but serving you as a constant reminder to buy. A reusable container adds value to your product and gives you a real difference at point of sale. Most importantly, experience shows that you can sell it and your product together at a premium price.

Flora Margarine produced a Tupperware reusable container in three colours, featuring a sunflower. Neatly named the Flora Storer, it contained 1kg of margarine and was sold with the line, 'After you've finished your Flora, look what you can store in your Flora Storer'. An accompanying leaflet then reeled off dozens of storage ideas. It was a well-planned and successful promotion.

Other memorable reusable containers come to mind. The Moccona coffee jar must be one of Australia's most popular storage containers. The CSR Sugar canister takes pride of place in many homes. Arnott's Biscuits and Cadbury's Chocolates are sold seasonally in beautiful tins and boxes. After the contents have been eaten, the containers become useful and attractive additions to the household. Many of the older ones are now sought-after collectors' items.

If your product can be packed in metal or glass, consider a reusable container promotion. You'll be hard-put to dream up another premium more relevant to your customers' needs.

Go fishing with a premium

The last of our premium categories is an entirely different one. Some will query whether the items concerned are really premiums at all. But I've included them here, because I believe they are.

Besides, I didn't know where else to put them.

They're generally known as trial premiums. People send them out on a fishing trip for prospects, before a sale has been made or even contemplated. They can take the form of personalised demonstration disks, solar calculators and other more or less hi-tech items. They're designed to stand out from the general run of brochures and letters, and are usually used in direct mail schemes to enhance response. In most cases, they are followed up by a phone call.

Currently, trial premiums are being used with good effect in the financial and insurance industries, to name two. I think their use will increase in the years to come.

Hi tech trial

A new concept called Uniloc™ is the trial premium of all trial premiums and it's turning the task of selling software on its head. This Australian invention, now owned by IBM, will be first used by WordPerfect to launch their software. The way it works is astonishing—you don't buy the programme until you've seen how it works.

When you've decided you want to become a user, you simply call a 1800 number and your credit card will be debited. You will then be issued with a unique number which will unlock the power of your programme and away you go! It's as easy that, and it's just the start of a revolution in selling software and information. We'll see a lot more of these 'Try and Buy' Uniloc™ trial premiums that convert to product, especially where electronic data interchange is concerned.

Why do some premiums fail?

Throughout this chapter, we've seen examples of highly successful premiums in many different categories. What I haven't mentioned are the premiums that fail. Let's face it—quite a few do. And the best way to ensure that yours won't is to think our way through a simple but vital question. Why do some premiums turn out to be flops?

It's not always an easy question to answer specifically. But through constant research of our own promotions and others, backed by regular information from around the world, we think we have some pointers towards an answer—at least in general terms.

Broadly speaking, it seems there are three basic reasons why a premium fails. One, people simply don't like it. Two, the premium's benefits and virtues have not been communicated clearly and compellingly to them. Or three, the effort required to get it outweighs its perceived value (see 'Toop's hoops', Chapter 3). Maybe too many proofs of purchase are required or some other barrier looms larger in the consumers' minds than the premium's appeal.

Be very careful, then, at those three points. Note every guideline I've suggested for premium selection. Make sure your publicity describes the item simply, clearly, honestly and attractively. And be certain you haven't made it too hard to get. Ask yourself—would I do all that to obtain it? If you wouldn't, probably few others will either.

The communication factor is particularly important when you don't have much space to announce the offer, as with on-pack premiums. In those cases, it's best to go for simple items of obvious quality and value—items that can easily be described in a few persuasive words. I've seen warehouses full of excellent premiums that simply weren't described properly or convincingly—or had too many hoops put between them and the customers. Get your premium right, describe it accurately and enticingly, and make it easy to get. Do all three—and yours shouldn't be a premium that fails.

Your premium checklist

Whether you go for free mail-in or pack-linked premiums, reusable containers or the trial variety, their likely success is governed by a number of points they all share. For the best chance of getting top results from your premium idea, run it past this checklist.

1. Are they practical in terms of sales tax, insurance, import restrictions, packing, storage and delivery?
2. Does their cost justify the likely return?
3. Would you like to receive them?
4. Are they useful to the recipients?
5. Are they innovative and original?
6. Will they seize your customers' imagination?
7. Are they appropriate and relevant to the recipients' lifestyle?
8. Would the recipients like to be seen using them?
9. Will recipients keep them for a long time?
10. Do they enable the recipients to 'spoil' themselves?
11. Do they convey the right image for your company?
12. Do they have a natural link with your product?
13. Do they offer you advertising extension possibilities?
14. Can they be linked with your current promotional activities?
15. Do they support your branding?
16. Will they be acceptable to your clients?
17. Can you afford them?

If your answer to question 17 is 'no', look for different premiums right away. But if it's 'yes'—and the answer to most of the others is too—press on. *Praemia*—booty and rewards—are within your grasp.

Notes

1. 'Suzuki discount scheme tracks wool for wheels', by Cathy Bolt, *Australian Financial Review*, 19 April 1991.

9

CHAPTER

Self-Liquidating Offers—Get Your Money Back

Self-liquidating offers or self-liquidating premiums sound rather like a suicidal version of Al Capone's capers on St Valentine's Day. But the name actually refers to a premium not unlike those we pondered in the last chapter. The big difference with self-liquidating premiums (or SLPs for short) is that you don't give them away. You charge just enough for them to recoup some or all of your costs.

Now that idea obviously has a lot going for it. Your premium budget is not locked into the normal 10%-of-product-sales limit, because your customers are sharing the cost. The key is to find unique items that are above-average value in the target audience's way of thinking. That means letting them spoil themselves with upmarket items like designer clothes, good cameras, or perhaps something highly desirable that's available only through the offer—all at irresistible bargain prices.

On the face of it, then, an SLP has to be the perfect promotion. It can be novel, attractive and memorable—yet cost you little or nothing at all. This is, however, the real world. And things in the real world are rarely as simple as that.

Trade coolness

The first SLP complication is the decidedly cool reception they tend to get from the retail trade. With some justification, the trade feels that SLPs cut across their sales of similar items elsewhere in the store. If, for example, you offer a full cutlery set at $10 with two proofs of purchase, the store won't sell many $120 cutlery sets while your promotion's on. And the extra sales they get from your product are unlikely to compensate them.

Hence the arctic reaction.

The non-self-liquidating SLP

The second complication is the relatively low consumer response to many SLP offers. Not infrequently, this can be down around 1% of on-pack promoted volume. The percentage can be even less depending on your communication medium. 'Take ones' or press, for instance, get results very different from those achieved by communication physically attached to the brand. Such depressing figures make it hard to achieve economies of scale in importing or manufacturing the premium. They also pose nightmares in premium quantity estimating and budgeting. Not to mention the embarrassment of having hordes of unsent-for SLPs lying around—plus the difficulty of explaining their presence to your management.

Few promotional tools, in short, have such fallout potential as the self-liquidating premium that doesn't self-liquidate.

The SLP secret: get it right!

All the above factors help to explain why SLPs have not been the most common promotional technique in Australia in the last decade or so. But enough of gloom and doom. An SLP can be a great way to increase sales, boost brand awareness, gain additional display space and build customer loyalty—if you get it right. Which, of course, is easy to say. But as scores of successful SLP promotions demonstrate so rewardingly, it really is achievable in practice. 'Getting it right' applies basically to two key areas—the SLP itself, and the price you offer it at.

Know your market

The first step towards selecting the right SLP is the same as for choosing the right sweepstakes prize (see Chapter 3). If you haven't already done so, get your researchers busy and find out as much as you can about your market. The more accurate your customer profile, the more chance you have of creating an item they'll really want to own. If it's something they can use, that's a good start. If it's made by a known and reputable manufacturer, so much the better. And if it has an element of novelty and imagination as well, you've probably hit on something your target market will find most attractive—especially if the price is most attractive too.

The price tightrope

It's in this second key area—the price you ask for your SLP—that you'll find yourself walking a tightrope. In my experience, SLPs are very price-sensitive. Much work is required to get it right when you set the price. You have to consider the total cost of obtaining the SLP, the number you believe you're likely to sell, and whether or not you want to cover 100% of your costs. You then have to juggle all that into the most attractive consumer price. Quite simply, the lower that is, the better—in proportion, of course, to the value of your SLP.

It's interesting to note from our observations that 38% of all SLPs currently have a consumer price tag between $5 and $9.99. Of the remainder, 20% are under $5, another 20% are $10–$19.99, and 22% are $20 and over. Occasionally, lower-priced SLPs are offered for something like $2 with no proof of purchase—or free with three proofs.

The big thing is not so much the actual dollars you charge. It's whether or not consumers will see your SLP as irresistible value. And if they do, you can look forward to sales well above the dismal 1% level we noted earlier.

Warming the trade response

Appealing to the consumer is one thing. As we've previously seen, however, most stores are pretty cool towards SLPs in general. Without their co-operation, you either have to promote your SLP solely through the media or forget the whole idea. So, how can you get the stores on side?

Quite easily, actually. Create an SLP that's unique to your brand and can't be obtained anywhere else. That way, the trade won't see it as a sales threat, and they'll treat it the same way they treat any other promotional idea.

Go for integration

If you're creating your own SLP—or for that matter, buying it off the shelf—there's another point to think of, too. It's the one I keep emphasising in every aspect of interactive marketing—complete integration of your total promotional effort.

In other words, choose an SLP that reinforces your brand image and values—one that's relevant to your product, useful to your customers and (if possible) echoes your above-the-line advertising theme. If you do that, your SLP promotion will not only bring you an immediate sales increase. It will help you build for the future.

Esso's immortal tiger

Among the most successful SLPs are those that do achieve this admittedly difficult goal of integration. Of these, the one that springs to mind most readily is an all-time classic. It became a sensational worldwide success as long ago as 1965. It emerged almost by accident out of a TV commercial. And probably no better example of a sales promotion device that brilliantly reinforced brand image and advertising theme has yet been devised.

I refer, of course, to Esso's immortal 'Put a Tiger in your Tank' campaign.

Esso had used the tiger in advertising on and off since it originated in Britain in 1953. Then, in 1964, came the American TV commercial that showed the tiger disappearing into a car's petrol tank. Only his tail was left visible. And surprisingly, it was not Esso or McCann-Erickson, their advertising agency, but an independent textile manufacturer who thought of the perfect SLP to support the commercial.

A tiger tail that attached to the petrol cap.

Esso agreed to the idea. The manufacturer produced a small batch for Esso service stations. They disappeared overnight. More were turned out. They sold equally quickly. Soon sub-contractors were hired to cope with what rapidly became an amazing and unprecedented demand.

Within five months, an incredible 3.5 million tiger tails had been sold. Many of these graced more than one car, as tiger tail thefts became an epidemic across the USA. In Britain, tiger tail shortages actually created a black market for the premium that saw prices rise from the normal one shilling per tail to five shillings. One Esso outlet in Guildford reordered his tails 15 times, while his Esso Extra sales rose by 15%.

Nor was tigermania confined to tails. Tiger colouring books, dolls, key rings, party glasses, polishing cloths, windscreen and bumper stickers, lapel badges, pencils, balloons and car mats all followed in quick succession. In the first five months, 2.5 million colouring books and 200 000 dolls were sold in America alone. Nearly 500 000 key rings were given away. What's more, every single item reinforced the advertising theme and brand image in the strongest possible way.

Almost 30 years later, few if any campaigns have matched the tiger for the sheer brilliance of its integration—and the overwhelming acceptance it received throughout the world.

Others that integrated

One that did come close is Marlboro. Their SLPs have reinforced brand values and extended their advertising with great success. The brand's macho outdoor image has been well underlined by leather jackets, hats, lighters and gloves, to name a few. If you could have bought all the SLPs at point of sale, you'd walk out of the store as the very personification of the Marlboro Man. All you'd lack would be a horse or now a 4WD. And a few rolling hills...

Another integrator was Pritikin bread, which offered the 'Pritikin Promise'—a book entitled *28 Days to a Longer, Healthier Life*. It was just $8.95, and was written by the famous doctor himself. That's another good example of an SLP that strongly underlines brand values—and does so in a very useful and positive way.

Penfolds Wine echo their expertise in wine by creating a unique premium offer that makes their advertising work harder. When promoted at the bottle shop check out, the offer of their authoritative book on wine gives Penfolds a point of purchase advantage and even more brand awareness.
Courtesy of The Penfolds Wine Group

Penfolds Wines have also gone the integrated book route with one of their SLPs. *The Rewards of Patience* sits on bottleshop counters and tells you all you need to know about wine for $9.99—plus your purchase of wine from Penfolds. This is a clever one, because the book not only creates display, but is in effect an advertising billboard for Penfolds at point of sale. In addition, it adds handsomely to brand values when promoted in the media. Like the Pritikin book, it delivers information the consumer wants.

Scotland the brave

Johnny Walker Red Label whisky is as Scottish as fields of heather. And the Johnny Walker people came up with a great SLP for it—a Johnny Walker jersey for little more than half the normal retail cost of such a sophisticated garment.

Note the number of coups they achieved. Because it was Scottish knitwear, the premium had a natural link to the Scotch whisky. It was extremely useful to its recipients. Its price made it a real bargain. And at no cost to Johnny Walker, it carried the brand name into the clubs and leisure areas of the nation. What's more, it made a perfect 'dealer loader'. Offered to bottle shop managers in exchange for a good off-shelf Johnny Walker display, it helped strengthen the brand's presence at point of sale.

You could almost hear the bagpipes playing 'Scotland the Brave'...

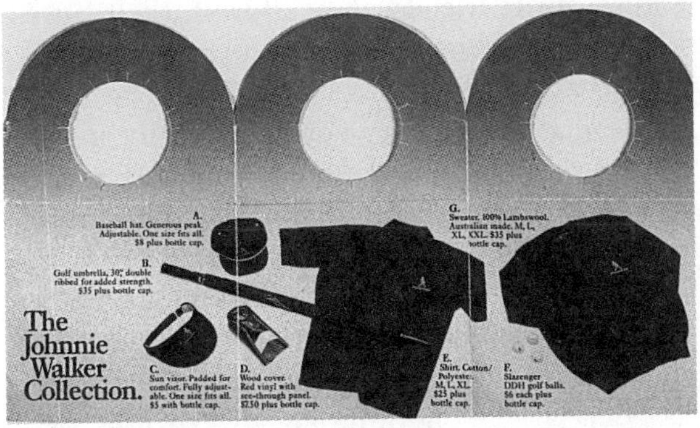

The Johnny Walker Collection is uniquely selected to appeal to and distinguish Red Label whisky drinkers.

These added–value, self–funding promotions are especially designed to reflect the brand's character. They can be shown physically at point of sale, where they increase on–shelf interest and impact. They can also be used as trade gifts to promote display. When worn by advocates of Johnny Walker, the red jerseys underpin brand preference and also act as a secondary advertising medium.
Courtesy of United Distillers (Aust) Pty Ltd

Beauty on the beach

While Scottish knitwear appeals to everyone, the Nivea range of skin care products is all about feminine beauty. The company reinforced its brand values with

Smarties' unique send–away, keep–sake offer especially created and personalised for a child. That's the kind of premium parents and grandparents are prepared to pay for, in addition to their purchase of Smarties multipacks.
Reproduced with the permission of Societe des Produits Nestlé SA, Vevey, Switzerland, the owners of the registered trade marks Smarties, Polo, Lifesavers and Nescafé

a very successful SLP—a beautiful Nivea beachbag in Nivea's corporate colours of blue and white. It was well promoted as an additional Nivea beauty aid for the beach. Like most good SLPs, it was excellent value, too—just $2 and two Nivea stickers.

SLPs in the confectionery area are not too common. But my agency achieved success for Rowntrees in the UK with a 'Me-book' SLP offered through multipacks of Smarties. This was one of those highly personalised books that makes the reader the hero. Through it, children could go on the 'Smarties Safari'—in a book that featured their own name, the names of their brothers or sisters and favourite friends, their address, their birthday and even the supermarket where the Smarties were purchased.

All this was theirs for less than the equivalent of A$12. The book, written by my friend and colleague Aubrey Watson, powerfully underlined brand values. It was in great demand from mums, dads and grandparents for their birthday and Christmas buying. Best of all, the promotion cost Rowntrees nothing, as all expenses were fully covered in the book's price. It allowed them the luxury of intensive consumer activity on the brand, to a target market they wouldn't normally reach (mums, dads and grandparents)—all without making a further dent in their promotional budget.

By buying Financial Times merchandise, readers associate themselves more closely with the world of finance.
Courtesy of The Financial Times

Old-world values

But one of my favourite SLPs was the one Sunlight Soap ran in their centenary year of 1985. All year long, the soap was packaged in a reusable centenary canister—a replica of the original 1885 tin. And for an extra $2.99, purchasers could obtain a unique set of 10 greeting cards featuring various Sunlight Soap advertisements and posters from the brand's early years. The whole venture brilliantly bolstered Sunlight's brand image of solid, long-established, old-world family values. Furthermore, it gained additional store display space, bigger stocking levels, wider distribution—and huge sales increases.

An entree to an image

An upmarket premium that carries the brand image to prospects and accurately reflects the target group's aspirations, has been cleverly used by Swiss watch group Tag Heuer.

A Tag Heuer watch is an expensive and exclusive personal possession. Its advertising is closely identified with sport. Tag Heuer attracts their audiences with an offer to would-be owners at an entree price very much less expensive than their premium-priced watches. They offer quality designer items such as sweat shirts and other sought-after sporting accessories at accessible prices, not at their normal wrist watch outlets but directly through the mail.

Their theme advertising is complemented with pop-up inserts in appropriate press. It offers these desirable items as a first step into Tag Heuer's exclusive imagery. The strategy introduces sporty prospects to the brand and puts them on track to the eventual purchase of a Tag Heuer sports watch. The promotion also allows existing Tag Heuer owners to enjoy another Tag Heuer branded product—not only a new addition to their Tag Heuer wardrobe but an endorsement of their original purchase.

This is a commendable and creative method of using the SLP technique.

The value path

Not all successful SLPs are completely relevant to the products. Some succeed on their sheer attractiveness and value, such as Benson & Hedges' wine vintages books and their even more famous *Restaurant Guide*. The wine book comes in deluxe English calico and soft cover editions for $21 and $7.50 respectively. The *Restaurant Guide* is available as a leather-bound volume for $22, or a gold soft cover book for $9.50. And all can be personalised to offer even more value to the consumer for just $2—a price that couldn't possibly be equalled under normal circumstances.

Retailers and SLPs

Also depending on value are the SLP promotions often run by stores (yes, the same stores that tend to be underwhelmed by manufacturers' SLP proposals). What they do is encourage repeat visits by offering such items as dinner sets and cutlery at almost unbelievably low prices, in return for so many proofs of purchase. Sometimes, the items are offered free if even more proofs of purchase are obtained.

Service stations are other retail outlets that frequently offer top-value SLPs—usually, with no proof of purchase needed. In recent years, these SLPs have included limited edition mug collections featuring football teams, American baseball teams' club caps, and character merchandise such as the Smurfs, available through BP service stations. All these items are not only exclusive to the stations offering them—they are sold at extremely low prices.

Perhaps today's biggest users of SLPs are another group of retail outlets—the fast food stores. They do very well with character merchandise and child-appeal items at prices that supermarkets and toy shops can't hope to match. Frequently, the items can't be obtained anywhere else—which adds the extra consumer appeal of exclusivity to their very low cost. As well, they are always available in sets, which encourages return visits.

The retail stores, service stations and fast food outlets all have an advantage over manufacturers when they push SLPs. They can—and do—display the actual merchandise, which obviously adds considerably to its selling appeal. Particularly when customers' children see their peers enjoying them.

If you're not a retailer ...

Unless you can talk your friendly store management into offering display space for your actual SLP—and I wish you luck—you basically have four ways of promoting it. On-pack. In a leaflet, which can be dispensed in-store. Media advertising. And various forms of point-of-sale display, usually involving the leaflet I just mentioned.

Or you can use a creative combination of all four.

One point to bear in mind is that, if you can't show people the SLP before they buy it, you're virtually in the position of a mail order vendor. The customer has only your word that the goods are as described. So you have to be prepared to make a full cash refund, if people demand it. That, of course, is just common sense anyway. You'd hardly risk losing a customer for the sake of a $10 refund.

The ageless SLP

Most SLPs are, for various reasons, fairly short-lived events. So let me end this chapter with an outline of my all-time SLP favourite. It was created in Britain in 1933. And at the time of writing, it was still going strong.

I refer to probably the most famous and certainly the longest-running SLP ever—the Robertson's Jams and Marmalade Golly Badges. You get these at very low prices with proofs of purchase. They're simple little enamel badges that feature an endearing character in an endless array of activities—playing cricket, riding a motor bike, skiing and hundreds of other things. They weren't new when I started collecting them avidly as a small boy. We swapped them endlessly at school. And when people build up a huge collection—as many have—they can sell them for surprisingly large amounts of money.

Robertson's Jams and Marmalade Badges have become part of Britain's culture. It's possible, I suppose, that yours may reach an equally exalted level. But I suspect you'll settle for an image boost—and increased sales.

At no cost to you.

Your SLP checklist

Basically, your SLP checklist is virtually the same as the premiums checklist in Chapter 8. I would add just these six extra questions:

1. Will your SLP be acceptable to the retail trade?
2. Is it made by a known and reputable manufacturer?
3. Can you offer it at a very attractive price?
4. If you have little media or on-pack space to promote your SLP, can the concept be mentally visualised easily by the target audience? If not, forget it.
5. If not directly relevant to your product, can it succeed on sheer attractiveness and value?
6. If people can't see it before they buy, are you willing and able to offer a full cash refund if they're not satisfied?

You can get away with a 'no' to question 2 (although a 'yes' is obviously better). But you do need 'yesses' to the rest, including most of those in the previous chapter's checklist. And if you get them, your SLP could well become what the concept, at first glance, promises to be.

An (almost) perfect promotion.

10

CHAPTER

Coupons, Cards and Clubs— Boomerangs in Repeat Sales

By and large, Australia is pretty well on par with the rest of the world in most areas of marketing. However, there are still one or two yawning gaps in our marketing armoury—and the whole area of couponing is one of them. Indeed, it seems that whenever couponing starts to emerge in Australia, someone hits it smartly on the head. Back in the 1970s, Green Stamps were gaining a real foothold. Their promise of free rewards just for shopping normally was attracting consumers. Their potential for building store traffic was being realised by retailers. Then in stepped Big Brother, with a ban on the whole industry.

The government's stated reason for intervening? Green Stamps were adding to the price of products, without contributing anything to the economy. Their real reason? Green Stamps were gaining popularity so rapidly that they threatened to become a secondary monetary system—

one beyond the ability of the government to control and manipulate. As governments don't like not being in control, Green Stamps had to go—and any excuse for their demise would do.

Enter Kerry Packer

The years rolled by. Then 1986 arrived—and with it, another attempt to introduce a large-scale couponing programme to Australia. It was well-thought-out and well presented. What's more, it was a personal initiative by a man who then as now stood astride Australian media like the legendary Colossus—Kerry Packer. Today, he is the richest man in Australia, and a man unused to losing. So, for Mr Packer, his *Smart Shopper Guide* was an unusual experience. Personally, I thought the concept was magic. The *Smart Shopper Guide* was to have been a full-colour booklet filled with price-off coupons on a vast range of merchandise, home-delivered across a wide socio-economic spectrum. It promised to stretch family budgets, make planning a shopping trip fun and establish cents-off couponing as a viable and valuable marketing tool in Australia.

The government had no worries about it at all. Everything seemed set for the arrival of a new marketing dimension—and another Packer triumph—until the retailers dropped the whole idea flat on its face.

Clearly, as the coupons had to be redeemed in the stores, it couldn't work without their co-operation. They simply weren't prepared to give it. They saw large-scale couponing—especially couponing originated by manufacturers—as a loss of control over their trade allowances and co-operative spending. They were worried about its effects on product mix, and the potential loss of their ability to control what the rest of us buy. They raised every legal, operational and cost barrier they could think of. Under their concentrated fire, the *Smart Shopper Guide* crashed in flames before it ever got off the ground.

Patting down the grave

Soon after, the Federal Government moved in swiftly to bury the smoking remnants and pat down the grave. It introduced legislation that makes coupons illegal if they involve a transaction between three parties.

Delivered through targeted door–to–door drops and direct mail, the 'Toys 'R' Us' catalogue offers product information and substantial savings to lure parents back into the store. *Courtesy of Toys 'R' Us USA Pty Ltd*

You don't have to be Einstein to see that three parties are indeed involved when a consumer cashes a manufacturer's coupon at a retailer. So, for the time being, manufacturers wanting to go the coupon route have to plot a somewhat circuitous course. They either have to handle the couponing directly with their customers, via direct marketing, or they have to arrange for retailers to issue the coupon on their behalf.

Both can be done. Coupon machines now available in the USA can print and issue a manufacturer's coupon in the store, for on-the-spot redemption. Because these coupons originate at the point of sale, they side-step the current Australian legal ban. Most stores in Australia would find them acceptable. The store would still be in control of the situation, and would enjoy increased store traffic.

However, the practice has yet to catch on here. From the manufacturer's point of view, it's still a lot messier than issuing your own coupons to your own customers for in-store redemption.

The dark before the dawn

Coupons, then, have an unhappy history in Australia. Yet despite the casualties and the obstacles, I can't help feeling that the current darkness obscuring them is the dark hour before the dawn—and that people involved in interactive marketing need to be aware of their very considerable potential. Why do I say this? For three reasons.

The first is the unarguable fact that couponing works. It's an easy and effective way to get people to switch brands and buy—which is why it's been a major sales promotion tool for decades in the USA and the UK. Second, targeted couponing door-to-door or personalised coupons in the mail are essential methods of building traffic to retailers. Third and perhaps most important, spectacular advances in barcoding, electronic 'smart' cards and database marketing have opened up huge new opportunities for coupon-led profits. And we need to look at those in a moment.

Meanwhile, a pause for a definition. What exactly do we mean by 'couponing'?

A technique for giving rewards

I like to define couponing as 'any technique that gives customers a reward for shopping in a particular store or retail outlet, on a continuing basis'. Clearly, that definition covers quite a bit of ground. It begins with the simplest and most traditional kind of coupon—the humble piece of paper that appears in an advertisement, a leaflet or the mail, offering you a discount on a specific product in a specific store. And it goes on to embrace the whole new area of database marketing in the retail environment—a multi-faceted development that opens up stunning new possibilities for retailers and manufacturers alike. The technology is now available to offer rewards to customers in a way that would have seemed positively Buck Rogerish just a few years ago.

Points for Purchase

Grace Bros, a major retailer, set the ball rolling in Australia with a simple scheme in 1991. Every time their account customers use their cards to buy anything in a Grace Bros store, they receive 'Points for Purchase'. The customers don't have to do anything apart from using their cards. There's nothing to fill in. Nothing to sign. Nothing to ask for. The points are credited to them automatically. Every so often, they get a

Grace Bros appeals to its customers through its retail outlets and catalogues. Customers can use the catalogue to order merchandise by phone or mail, or go into the store. They can pay in cash or by cheque, credit card or Grace Bros card, all of which makes purchasing easier. Shoppers who use their buyer card benefit from a points system that rewards their loyalty. At the end of the year, they get substantial savings in line with their levels of expenditure.
Courtesy of Myer Grace Bros Stores Limited

statement showing how their points are growing. Then, at the end of the year, they simply swap their points for whatever range of merchandise their loyalty to Grace Bros has earned.

With modern technology, such a programme is simplicity itself for the retailer to run. It could hardly be easier for the customer. And it gives the customer a powerful reason to shop at Grace Bros in preference to other stores, as often as possible. I believe Grace Bros are on a loyalty-building winner with this one.

Lavish rewards

My confidence in the soundness of Grace Bros' programme is all the stronger because of the success of similar store-based ventures in the USA.

The Nieman Marcus chain operates one that is notable for the scope and lavishness of its rewards. The customer earns one point for every dollar debited on his or her NM charge card. After 3000 points, they receive a special, personal InCircle card, a free newsletter, complimentary gift wrappings, magazine subscriptions and much more—even private nights when the stores are open only to InCircle cardholders.

Then, after 7500 points, the rewards really start to shine. At that point, they include things like crystal decanters and premier cookbooks. At 15 000 points, it's sterling silver, fine wines and free lunches. 30 000 points and above earn weekend holidays and the like. 45 000 points get you first-class airfare and accommodation breaks in a host of US cities. 75 000 points bring you a year's worth of invitations to glittering cultural, theatrical and sporting events. World travel options multiply from 125 000 to 250 000, with once-in-a-lifetime adventures going free for 500 000–1 000 000 points.

One *million* points? $1 million spent in one year in one retail chain? Apparently it happens. And perhaps this helps explain why.

Nieman Marcus is based in Dallas, Texas. I imagine JR would earn his 80-day Royal Viking Line world cruise in a matter of weeks...

The Frequent Shoppers' Advantage Club

Pitched at a much lower level—but with an interesting twist—is another US programme called the Frequent Shoppers' Advantage Club. Like the others, this club offers members purchase points on a wide range of products from more than 160 national brands. But the twist is that it's not confined to one particular chain. Club members receive a monthly statement of their total points earned to date and they can redeem them in a host of different stores. Within a year, they can easily build up enough points to earn a microwave oven or a colour TV. When you consider they're not spending a cent more than they would have anyway, the motivation to join the club is obviously very strong. The initial mailing in 1988 to 1 million selected households had a response target of 20%, or 200 000 members. This was 'far exceeded', according to Club executives. And it has continued to soar.

Such an operation would almost certainly be illegal in Australia under current legislation, because of its three-party nature. But it underlines the huge selling potential the technique offers. And it is definitely legal here when initiated by a retailer—or a retailer acting on behalf of a manufacturer or manufacturers. If you're in that category, I leave the thought with you.

Enter the 'smart' card

For all their promise, however, programmes like the Grace Bros Points for Purchase venture, Nieman Marcus InCircle and the Frequent Shoppers' Advantage Club are only scratching the surface of the new technology. The Grace Bros programme, for instance, still uses the same store card the customer has had for years. The next step—already in widespread use in the USA—involves not only a new card but a new type of card.

The so-called 'smart' card.

While this looks like any other store card at a glance, it's a quantum leap ahead. It includes a microchip that not only individually identifies the customer, but holds full details of the customer's purchase record to date for the year. So when the customer inserts the card into a reader at the checkout, several things happen.

First, the customer's name comes up on a screen, enabling the operator to say 'Good morning, Mrs Jones'—a personal touch appreciated by even the most blasé shopper. Second, the screen immediately shows the customer the number of purchase points he or she has earned to date. Third, when price-off promotions are happening, the discount on each item is automatically deducted from the price, there and then.

Instant gratification

So the smart card system means instant gratification and a high degree of personalisation for shoppers. It also keeps the lure of exciting prizes before them every time they shop. With various modifications, the system is now being used in a number of frequent shopper programmes in the USA and the UK—with results that can only be described as awesomely promising.

Points for petrol

One of these is run by Mobil outlets in Britain. They give their customers a magnetic striped card, which automatically registers the transaction every time the cardholder buys petrol and oil. When the points go onto the card, they're also redeemable automatically at a

With their paperless transactions, Mobil allows customers to accumulate points on a magnetic strip card. It's easy for customers to collect their rewards, as these points are redeemable at Argos, a well-known UK retail catalogue marketer.
Courtesy of Mobil UK

company called Argos, a catalogue operation with outlets all over the land. So if you're a cardholder and you want your rewards, it couldn't be easier. You just go into an Argos store and choose your merchandise. The points you use are deducted from your card. The merchandise is mailed to you within days. And you start piling up more points on your smart card the next time you stop for petrol. All over the UK, millions are now turning into Mobil stations. Exclusively.

Seeing is believing

An alternative to smart cards that contain a microchip is the optical memory card. This contains the kind of images used widely in the health industry to store pictures of medical conditions, from eyes to x-rays. These cards are the high capacity equivalent to floppy disks, but are much more durable, non-erasable and flexible. They are the top choice when data integrity, permanence and portability are important. Up to 4.1 megabytes of digital data may be recorded on a single card.

In France, a major initial LaserCard programme uses an optical memory card to record every item purchased by the cardholder during visits to a store. Bonus points, awards and discounts can be awarded to 'frequent shoppers' according to their exact shopping profiles. Issued annually, the cards record all purchases by barcoded UPC code, as well as date, store location and other pertinent data. Like cards with chips, they can be downloaded by erasing information until the 4.1 megabytes of information space is used up.

Building for the future

The really significant thing about all these programmes, however, is not just immediate sales or even an increase in customer loyalty. It's the customer database they enable the retailer to build—because there's no doubt whatsoever that direct marketing will be the dominant promotional activity for retailers and supermarkets within the next few years. The kind of databases the new technology makes possible can be personalised to an amazing degree. Individual shoppers' brand preferences, buying patterns, favourite shopping days and other indicators can all be recorded and instantly recalled. This is information that can be used to enhance the customer-to-store relationship and to deliver increased sales to the retailer.

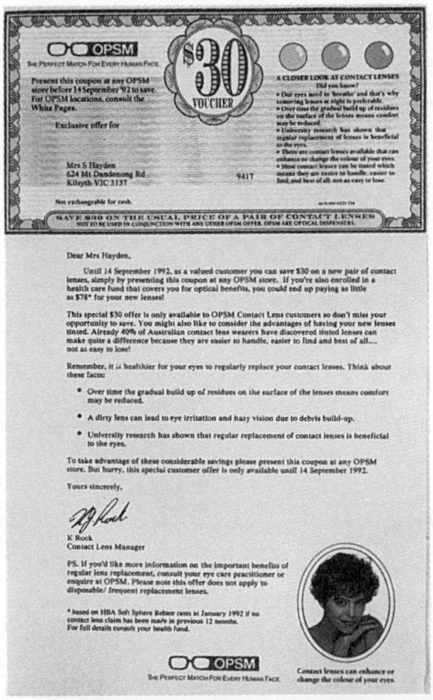
OPSM

THE PERFECT MATCH FOR EVERY HUMAN FACE

Present this coupon at any OPSM store before 14 September '92 to save. For OPSM locations, consult the White Pages.

Exclusive offer for

Mrs S Hayden
624 Mt Dandenong Rd
Kilsyth VIC 3137

$30 VOUCHER

9417

A CLOSER LOOK AT CONTACT LENSES

Did you know?

- Our eyes need to 'breathe' and that's why removing lenses at night is preferable.
- Over time the gradual build up of residues on the surface of the lenses means comfort may be reduced.
- University research has shown that regular replacement of lenses is beneficial to the eyes.
- There are contact lenses available that can enhance or change the colour of your eyes.
- Most contact lenses can be tinted which means they are easier to handle, easier to find, and best of all, not as easy to lose.

Not exchangeable for cash.

SAVE $30 ON THE USUAL PRICE OF A PAIR OF CONTACT LENSES

NOT TO BE USED IN CONJUNCTION WITH ANY OTHER OPSM OFFER. OPSM ARE OPTICAL DISPENSERS.

Dear Mrs Hayden,

Until 14 September 1992, as a valued customer you can save $30 on a new pair of contact lenses, simply by presenting this coupon at any OPSM store. If you're also enrolled in a health care fund that covers you for optical benefits, you could end up paying as little as $78* for your new lenses!

This special $30 offer is only available to OPSM Contact Lens customers so don't miss your opportunity to save. You might also like to consider the advantages of having your new lenses tinted. Already 40% of Australian contact lens wearers have discovered tinted lenses can make quite a difference because they are easier to handle, easier to find and best of all.... not as easy to lose!

Remember, it is healthier for your eyes to regularly replace your contact lenses. Think about these facts:

- Over time the gradual build up of residues on the surface of the lenses means comfort may be reduced.
- A dirty lens can lead to eye irritation and hazy vision due to debris build-up.
- University research has shown that regular replacement of contact lenses is beneficial to the eyes.

To take advantage of these considerable savings please present this coupon at any OPSM store. But hurry, this special customer offer is only available until 14 September 1992.

Yours sincerely,

K Rock
Contact Lens Manager

PS. If you'd like more information on the important benefits of regular lens replacement, consult your eye care practitioner or enquire at OPSM. Please note this offer does not apply to disposable/ frequent replacement lenses.

* based on HBA Soft Sphere Rebate rates at January 1992 if no contact lens claim has been made in previous 12 months. For full details consult your health fund.

OPSM

THE PERFECT MATCH FOR EVERY HUMAN FACE

Contact lenses can enhance or change the colour of your eyes.

The smart coupon

The direct marketing possibilities that result are mind-boggling in the extreme. Among them is a remarkable new development of the couponing technique itself. Just as there are smart cards, there

OPSM's personalised direct mail shot offered contact lens users savings at their usual store, and tracked their response.

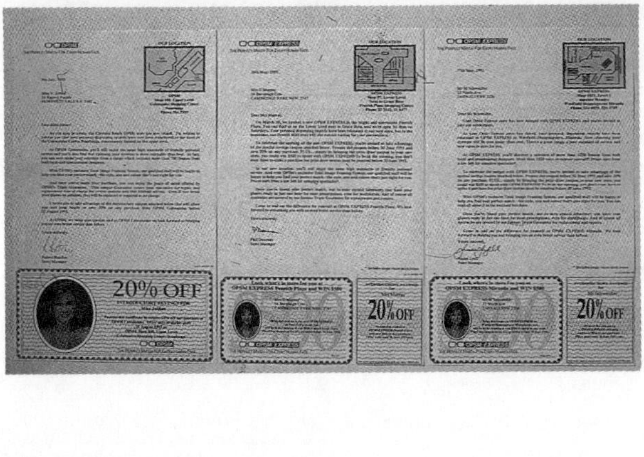

Direct mailed and personalised, these coupon offers point customers to new OPSM stores. Using unique numbers and bar coded devices, various coupon offers are tested and tracked with increasing cost–effectiveness, breaking them down by customers and individual shops.
Courtesy of OPSM Pty Ltd

are now smart coupons as well. This new generation of coupons looks at first glance much like those that have been printed in newspapers and leaflets for decades. But closer examination will reveal two significant additions: the recipient's name, and a barcode.

The first is drawn from the retailer's database. The second is born of very recent technology. Together, they create a totally individualised coupon, offering the recipient cents-off discounts on frequently-made purchases—with some others included to nudge his or her buying habits into wider areas.

Smart coupons might be mailed in batches of 50 or more at a time. Like the old kind of coupons, they're once-only cash substitutes that can be redeemed at the retailer or supermarket checkouts. But the personalising makes them much more effective, while the barcoding makes them much more controllable. They're the new era in couponing—and they're available for you to use now.

Revealing value

Coupons with a hidden value can have a huge and exciting appeal, as Toshiba found with a traffic-building promotion run by my friend Bob Bayley's Option One company in the UK.

The promotion was a multi-media campaign that included the coded coupon inserts in press, plus two TV commercials. As the first commercial explained, the inserts could be decoded by watching the second TV commercial at a particular time or by going into a Toshiba TV dealership to see it. The second commercial showed a red screen—and by holding their coupons against the screen, consumers could see the value of the prize they'd won.

It might have been $50 off a new Toshiba TV or an even more valuable prize. Either way, they then simply took the coupon into a Toshiba dealer to claim their price-off or the prize they'd won.

Part paying for education

Couponing or vouchers are used in other ways, too. Couponing has long been used by governments to facilitate the fair distribution of bread and milk in times of war, crisis and short supply. Tokens were often allocated according to the number of members in the household or for each child. Here's a little excerpt from the famous Aussie poem 'The Pub Without Beer', written after the battle of the Coral Sea and related by Dan Sheahan, which proves it.

> . . . some are sleeping their last
> in the land far from here
> And I feel alone in the pub
> without beer.
> They can hang to their coupons
> for sugar and tea
> And the shortage of sandshoes
> does not worry me.

The coupon concept was pushed heavily by Alan Toop with the British Government's then Education Minister, now Doctor Sir Rhodes Boyson, for use in education. The idea met with some success in the UK. I have seen recent press comments which suggest that coupons (or what they call vouchers) have curried favour here recently with the Liberals under John Hewson. The idea is to use your voucher to part-pay for your education, the voucher value being enough for the basic tuition. Put simply, if you want above-average schooling for your child, you can take your voucher and your child to a more expensive school, redeem the voucher and pay the balance in cash.

Safeway promote their double coupon deal creatively in the appropriate consumer press.
Courtesy of Safeway Supermarkets USA

Long live the dumb coupon

Of course, all the gee-whiz technology now available doesn't mean the end of what we might call the 'dumb' coupon, as the last example demonstrates. Indeed, most of the world's coupon promotions still depend on a little non-high-tech piece of paper that offers people a real and tangible reward. Or in some cases, two rewards.

The Vons supermarket chain on the USA's eastern seaboard has a policy of doubling the discount on all manufacturer-issued coupons. In other words, if you have a coupon with 30¢ off the price of a packet of washing powder, Vons will give you a 60¢ discount. They pass the first 30¢ back to the manufacturer, and absorb the second 30¢ themselves—because they have seen the value of attracting regular coupon-users to their stores. The policy has been so successful that Safeway, one of their major rivals, has been forced to adopt it too.

Helping a good cause

Another area where 'dumb' coupons are tremendously involved is cause-related marketing, which we'll look at in detail in Chapter 15.

If a cents-off coupon is redeemed by a certain date in that sort of promotion, the bearer not only gets the discount. The manufacturer donates a few cents to a particular charity as well. And those few cents, multiplied by millions of coupons, quickly add up to a very large sum of money indeed.

As we'll see in Chapter 15, some enormous promotions in the USA and Canada operate on this basis. Among them is the Variety Club of Canada's 'Cash for Kids' programme.

This massive undertaking is built around a huge schedule of full-page press advertisements. Each is crammed with price-off coupons from a wide range of packaged goods manufacturers. If redeemed by the due date, every coupon delivers a few cents to the Variety Club's efforts to help disadvantaged children. And, of course, it saves its bearer money—as well as boosting sales for its participating manufacturer and retail outlet. Once again, such an operation would probably be illegal in Australia, because it involves three parties. But it would be quite OK if initiated by a retailer, or if targeted directly to customers by a manufacturer. Delivered door to door, Civic Video's traffic-builder coupons have all the right ingredients—impact, value and a feeling of worth. Responders are tracked on Civic's database and receive further personalised and barcoded coupons.

Companies like Pizza Hut also create personalised and source-coded offers for their customers. Des-patched to homes and offices with pizza deliveries, they help create further sales, speed re-ordering and build loyalty.

So there's certainly still a profitable place for 'dumb' coupons. Especially if you use them with imagination, and keep a few basic principles in mind—most of which apply to smart and dumb coupons alike.

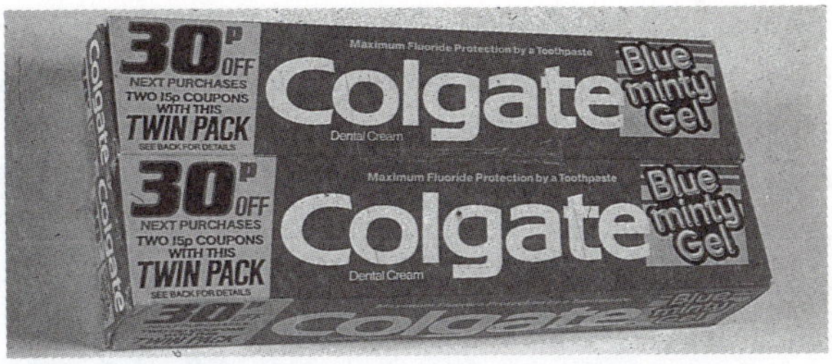

The brand manager's most popular method of couponing. Promoted on the pack, these money–off, next–purchase coupons add value to the initial purchase—but they can only be redeemed the next time the customer buys. That's impact with a twist—two promotional opportunities for the price of one.
Courtesy of Colgate–Palmolive Pty Ltd

Make it look valuable

If you're designing a coupon, make it look valuable in itself. Devices such as a scrolled border and a tasteful design with bank note overtones can help here. And don't try to be smart with the wording. Make the offer clear, simple and unmistakable. The more straightforward and immediate it is, the better.

How much off should you offer?

On grocery products, around 5%–15% of the purchase price seems to work best and be most productive. On large-ticket items, discounts of \$25–\$50 would be appropriate. The Sydney-based electrical retailer Bing Lee ran colour coupons for those amounts in newspapers in 1991, offering them as cash towards purchases of \$499-plus and \$999-plus respectively. But this is an area where experimentation is vital. Test a number of discounts, and see which one generates the most volume cost-effectively and profitably.

Four routes to the customer

Coupons, smart or dumb, can be personalised and barcoded with a unique number and mailed directly to customers via a database. While expensive, mailed coupons get higher redemption rates than those distributed by other means. In particular, US evidence shows they pull in about three times as many new product triers as those distri-buted in magazines.

Dumb coupons can also be distributed in newspaper and magazine advertisements or inserts. They can be attached to packs, in which case the offer applies normally to the next purchase of the product. This is the brand manager's favourite method, because the offer adds value to the promotional pack and helps create initial purchase. If the offer is pitched correctly, it will not only create the initial sale but also the next one, which in turn helps to establish habit and brand familiarity. Furthermore, the activity is directly measurable against pack units printed and distributed.

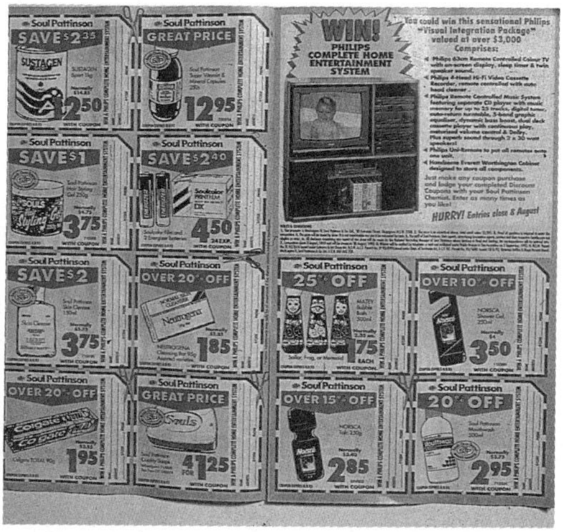

Through money–off coupons delivered door to door, Soul Pattinson create traffic and collect names for their database. They use these for their subsequent (and frequent) direct mail customer loyalty programmes.
Courtesy of Washington H Soul Pattinson & Company Limited

The misredemption problem

One of the big problems with couponing has always been misredemption, either through oversight or deliberate fraud. While database technology and barcoding reduce the risk, it's still very real and should constantly be considered. Bear in mind always that coupons are money.

With today's advanced copying machines, it's not hard for unscrupulous people simply to run as many copies of your coupons as they like. A good way to guard against this is to print your coupons in four colours. Then, trying to duplicate them is just too expensive to be profitable.

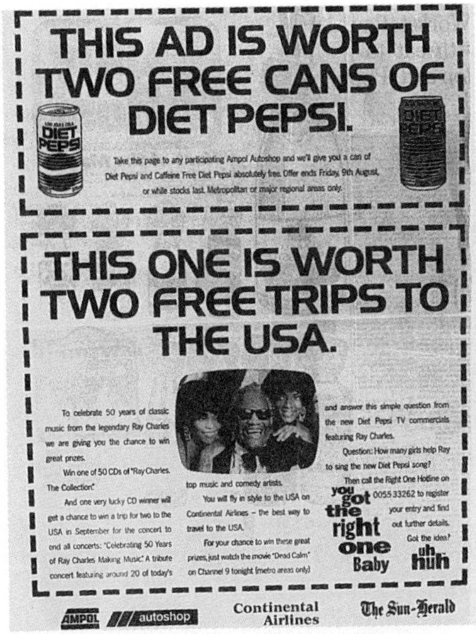

Featured in the press, this FREE trial couponing offer integrates with Pepsi's advertising. It encourages trialists to shop at Seven Eleven. The offer of a big trip to the USA to see a performance by Pepsi's advertising personality, Ray Charles completes the synergy and brand recognition.
Courtesy of Pepsi–Cola Bottlers Australia Pty Ltd

What coupons do best

Traditionally—and here the available evidence comes from experience with the dumb versions—coupons work best when they're used to give stagnating products a boost. They can reverse a slight sales decline, although not usually a long-established one. They can increase a declining market share, and kick-start a static product in a growing market. In short, the old-style money-off coupons have a pretty good track record in revitalising products that are performing below expectations. They have proved very effective, too, in leading people to try new products. They are, above all, dynamic in traffic building and encouraging customers to come into retail outlets.

Not a fan

Yet despite all this, I wasn't a fan of coupons just a few short years ago. I said so, too, in a few verbal battles in the advertising trade press. The problems of misredemption, delivery cost, wastage and so on seemed to me to outweigh the benefits.

My attitude, of course, had been shaped by my experience. When I was a brand manager with Unigate Foods in Britain, it was my job to find ways of increasing coupon redemption. Not only did money-off couponing on our brands take a big slug out of our budget, but everyone else was doing it. We had to get a good response to justify our investment, and stay ahead of the pack.

A time of testing

So we tried everything. We began by investigating the effect of varying the discount. We tested all money-off levels from a couple of pence right up to the product's full value, in cases where we had a significant product trial goal.

In all instances, the percentage redemption rate stayed stubbornly low. And the misredemption rate was quite high, especially as the discount grew. Eventually, the discount would reach the point where the coupon value exceeded the purchase price of the newspaper or magazine in which it appeared. At that stage, it became profitable for people to buy quantities of the publication and redeem stacks of coupons—illegally. They usually couldn't be stopped by the clearing house, over which we as manufacturers had no control either.

Adding a sweepstake

Realising there was no magic discount level, we tried other options. One was to insist that the proof of purchase was stuck to the coupon. This created problems with the trade. Another ploy was to add a prize draw component and offer people a big cash sweepstake incentive to redeem their coupons by a certain date. This was not only quite successful, but yielded us a fair crop of names and addresses. The trouble was, we didn't have the technology then to do much with them. It would be a different story today.

A convert to the cause

I finished my stint at Unigate Foods with a decidedly jaundiced attitude towards coupons, which I maintained for some years afterwards. But now, I must admit, I have become an enthusiastic convert to the cause. The advent of database marketing has, I believe, opened up vast new possibilities for couponing and its variants like smart cards and Points for Purchase programmes.

I am certain we will see coupons used in Australia more and more. They may be old dogs—but they have been taught some pretty stunning new electronic tricks.

Here's a coupons checklist, to help guide you:

1. Make coupons look like value for money.
2. State the coupon value clearly. Seriously consider actual money value rather than percentage off.
3. Make coupons as large as you can—the more they resemble paper money, the better.
4. Check with the media to ensure you have a solus position. Make sure, too, that other featured brand coupons on fast-moving consumer goods do not lift the total coupon value above the cost of the magazine or newspaper. Obviously, other coupons should not be placed back-to-back with yours.
5. Insist that direct-mailed coupons are properly and accurately personalised as well as barcoded for higher response, cost-effective collection and redemption, recording and tracking.
6. Show clearly the period for which the coupons are valid.
7. Ensure that a 'valid to' closing date is featured clearly.
8. Test media and offer values. Test and test again.

11

CHAPTER

Product Sampling—Trial-Gaining Offers

A picture, they say, is worth a thousand words. And even if that old cliche is put around by art directors, as claimed by copywriters (who naturally dispute it), it contains enough truth to ensure its survival. But if a picture does have that kind of impact, then putting the actual product in a consumer's hands must be worth a thousand of the best-lit, best-composed pictures ever taken.

That's why sampling is the most effective technique of all to obtain consumer trial and build a strong franchise quickly. At the same time, nothing beats it for generating positive response in the minds of the retailers. They regard strong initial purchases as the keynote of a successful new product. And once they think that way, you can confidently look forward to increased reorders and growing shelf space.

How can you best put your product into a customer's hands for this sales-inducing trial? There are a number of proven ways. The right one for you depends upon your product, your target market and your budget.

The door-to-door route

This is the most expensive sampling technique of all—but it's also the most effective way of getting your samples into the broadest possible cross-section of households. You can target an area with great accuracy, based on the demographics of your product.

Increasingly, a technique called cluster analysis and household definition is enabling you to reach your intended target grouping with ever-increasing efficiency. Using the mosaic classification systems (Marketfind and Streetfile are two such programmes, as are Apasco and MapInfo), you can determine where your market is most likely to live. And if you already have a powerful marketing tool at your disposal, in the form of a mailing list, credit card data or even warranty card data, you can match that information to give you a huge prospecting database.

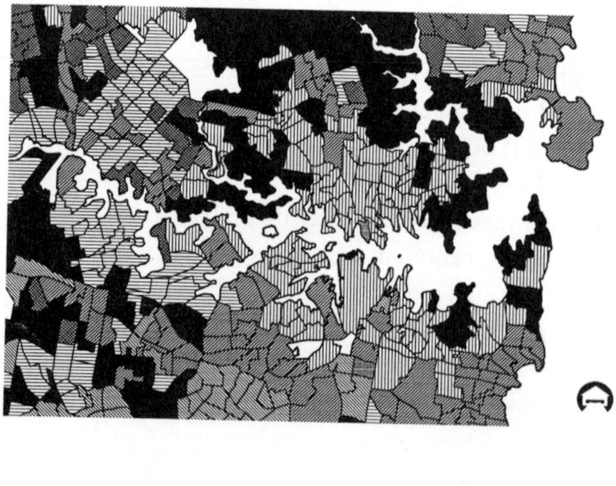

Now you can enrich your database with your customer's geo-demographic characteristics, as this representation of Sydney shows. Salmat's information covers more than 30 targeted dwelling and socio–demographic aspects.
Courtesy of The Salmat Group

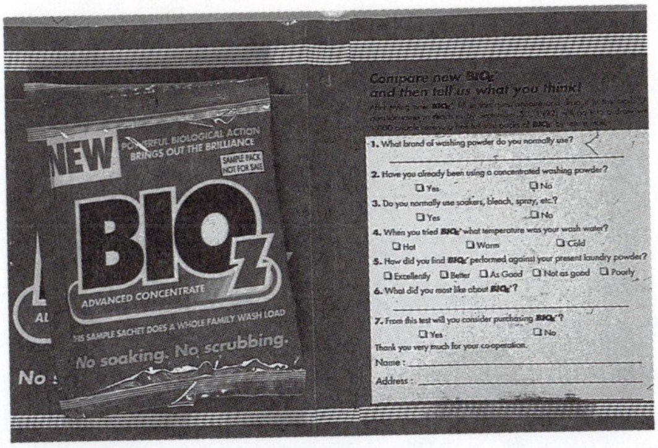

This targeted door-to-door launch, trial-sample promotion includes a sweepstake. The combination was designed to gain consumer trial and response through supermarkets and to build a database of trialists.
Courtesy of Belgiovane Atkinson Moses SSB and Kao (Australia) Marketing Pty Ltd

These geo-demographic systems classify people by where they live, down to Census Collector District (CCD) level. Each CCD (approximately 180 houses) comprises one of the 30 different lifestyle types, using information from the 1991 Australia National Census.

The system can pinpoint and target households very accurately. Then, by identifying neighbourhoods with a high proportion of your existing customers, you can pick out others with similar lifestyles or purchasing characteristics. There you can reach potential new customers via targeted door-to-door drops or database marketing methods. You can also add other data, including the White Pages, to give you a mailing list of prospects.

Just for you

Another new development now well under way in the USA will advance this process even further. Called 'Just for You', it's a household screening programme that identifies product users by direct mail. Additional data can be collected by questionnaires and phone surveys. This enables manufacturers to identify target prospects with great accuracy for sampling purposes.

Once your distribution area is selected, distribution crews take your samples right to the consumer's door. They either hang them on the door literally, or hand them directly to the consumer. The two techniques are known as 'ring and leave' and 'ring and hand in' respectively. Sounds good? It is—to the point where a much wider range of marketers is using it. Financial organisations, such as insurance and superannuation companies, are among the latest to go the door-to-door distribution route.

However, like most good things, it has its flaws. The main one you have to watch is your lack of control over the distribution company. Horror stories abound of finding piles of samples dumped in gutters or behind bushes by lazy or frustrated distribution personnel. This seems to be a particular risk when high-rise blocks are part of your chosen area.

Consequently, cross-checks of the distribution are essential. And it's an excellent idea to include your managing director's or marketing director's house on the route—and let the distribution company know.

Without telling them the addresses.

Rain, hail or shine

The door-to-door alternative to the distribution companies is the good old reliable postman. Many samples can be mailed in special mailers with detached labels. In this case, the postman puts the box and the label in the mailbox. Aim toothpaste, hair care sachets and soap are just some of the products that have arrived in mailboxes in this fashion. The postman can also deliver samples in a co-op mail piece. This works well if the sample's dimensions, weight and nature allow it to be mechanically inserted. Products as diverse as Band-Aids and dry salad dressing have been successfully sampled by this technique.

Once again, you can reach a broad cross-section of consumers through the mail—and at a lower cost than using the distribution companies. On the down side, the technique is limited to products that can survive a mail trip. It also usually needs a specially produced sample, and you have to allow for that when you cost the exercise.

What about long-term sales results? Little specific research information is available, but I've talked to a lot of experienced marketers who have carried out extensive in-mail sampling. They believe that around 70%–90% of samples received are tried—and that 20%–30% of triers actually go on to buy the sample product.

Thought-provoking results as these are, the results of research conducted by Dr Max Sutherland present a very different picture.

Closing the mailbox mind gap

When you pay for letterboxing a free sample or a brochure to a virtual 100% of households, you need to know how many of your target buyers in those households will receive it and whether it will register in their minds.

And among those who become aware of receiving it, you need to know how many will in fact try it—and then, how many will buy as a result.

Dr Max Sutherland, principal of Sutherland Smith Marketing & Research Consultants and a director of Marketmind Technologies in Australia, reported in *Ad News*, that research he has conducted suggests a fair amount of wastage.[1] But where does this occur? He demonstrates two examples.

Graph 1 shows that as a result of this mailbox drop, about 80% of the target buyers remained unaware that they had received a free sample of the brand. Only 17.5% became aware.

The net result was that 7.5% tried it; 2.5% bought the product as a result. Another 10% were aware of receiving the free sample brand, but did not try it.

Graph 1

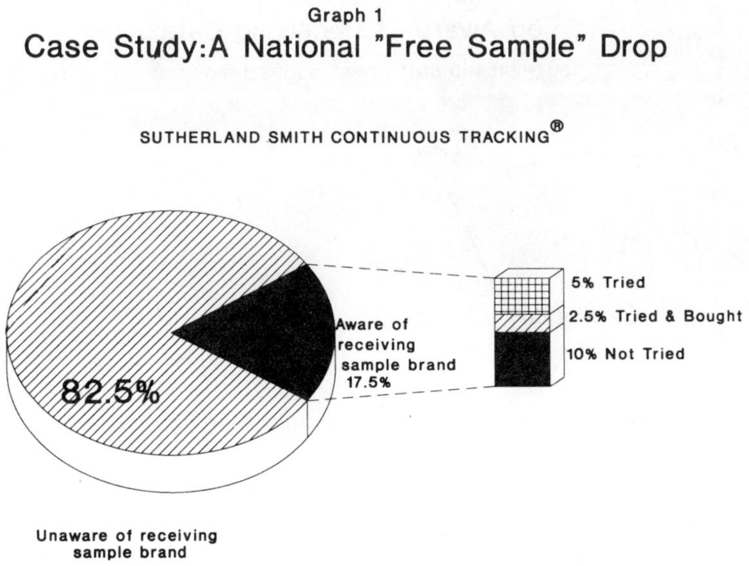

Courtesy © Sutherland Smith Continuous Tracking

This indicates that by far the biggest wastage is between the mailbox and the mind. More than three-quarters of the target buyers remained totally unaware of having received the free sample.

Dr Sutherland reports that this was not an isolated case.

Another example

Graph 2 shows another case—this time a 'saturation' drop of a catalogue.

In this case, the respondents were shown the actual colour catalogue and asked if they had received it in their mailbox in the last week or so—63% claimed they had not received it. Only 37% of households said they were aware of having received the catalogue.

Wastage reduces cost-effectiveness

Some wastage is in the delivery. But it is very difficult to know precisely

Graph 2

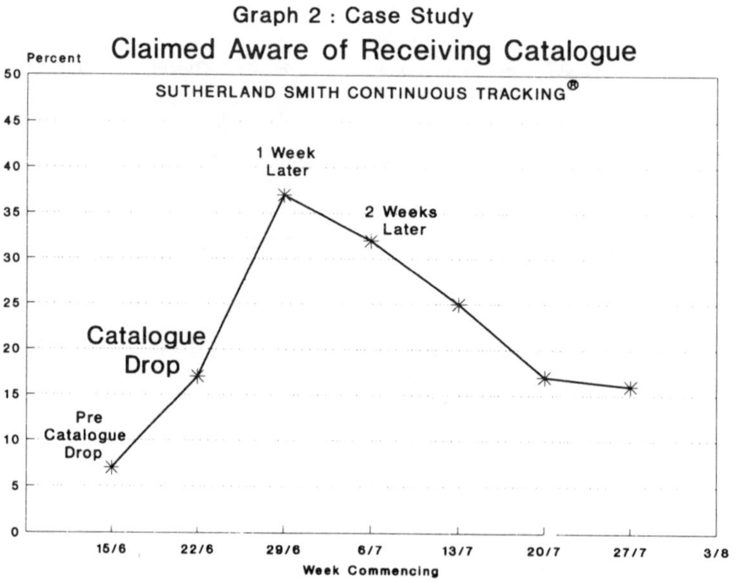

Courtesy © Sutherland Smith Continuous Tracking

what percentage never makes it into the mailbox. Salmat and Progress Press claim around 93% effective delivery.

Dr Sutherland concluded:

1. You need an independent auditing service to monitor mail drop delivery.
2. Door-to-door catalogues need more differentiation in executional style.
3. Marketers need to strive to own a style and to integrate their store with that style.
4. Consider TV and other media to generate interest and involvement and awareness of the drop.
5. As part of ongoing tracking, include measures of 'recall receiving' as well as 'looked through' and 'bought anything as a result'.
6. Learn from each change of execution style or product category inclusion as to what offer works and what doesn't.
7. Compare 'net awareness' results with other media rather than simply comparing cost per thousand 'delivered'.
8. The biggest gap is between the mailbox and the mind.
9. Continuous tracking can close the gap.

Where the customers are

The third sampling technique operates where your customers are—in the same retail store where later on, hopefully, they'll buy your product.

Clearly, the retail store is a great place in which to sample. Hordes of the people there are your customers, potentially at least. And if you can give them a favourable impression of your product in that buying environment, many will reach for it automatically when they see it there for real.

These points are fully understood by the Australian Dairy Corporation. As I write, the ADC is organising a $1 million in-store sampling campaign, jointly funded by manufacturers and the Corporation itself.

Retail stores and supermarkets lend themselves to a variety of sampling approaches. At least four are currently in widespread use, and there's another one emerging from the wings behind them. All are worth thinking about—especially if your product is any kind of food line.

Think small

The first approach is the traditional trial size at a special price. You make up a small pack of your product and sell it more cheaply per ounce or measure than the full-size retail pack. The store gets a 20%–25% mark-up, so they're happy to go along with you.

I remember one encounter I had with such an exercise—not professionally, but as a consumer. At the time, we owned a cat named Muffy. And Carnation Pet Foods launched a 12¢ trial sachet of Go Cat cat food. It was a splendid little affair, too. On one side, after it proclaimed 'Trial Offer', it told us to 'Give your cat the vote!'. Pondering the unlikeliness of this concept, we turned the sachet over. There on the back were three boxes, marked 'Wow! More! More!', 'Mmm' and 'Ho Hum'. Each represented a potential feline reaction to the Go Cat. When ticked and returned, they entitled us to receive 75¢, 40¢ and 20¢ respectively towards the purchase of future stocks.

Dutifully, we served Muffy the sachet, and waited for a reaction.

It started, frankly, as a 'Ho Hum'. But then she got the taste of it, and advanced swiftly to a very definite 'Wow! More! More!'. I can't remember if we sent away for our 75¢. Probably we didn't, in fact—experience shows that many if not most people don't bother responding to such offers. But we did go on to buy a lot of Carnation Go Cat dry cat food. With us as with so many others, brand loyalty was created by trial-size sampling.

Today, trial-size packs can be produced as perfect miniatures of the full-size version. Using technology under licence from Minipack Systems in the UK, Sydney-based company Sample Systems can produce pack miniatures in almost any shape and colour for liquids, powders and solids. Labels for both the body and cap are applied, and the pack is automatically sealed into a catchcard. It can then be bottle-collared to the pack or employed as a door-to-door letterbox sample.

Beverages and haircare industries use these little packs avidly—proving that miniature replicas can replicate sales on a scale out of all proportion to their size.

Think big

Also very viable is what you might call the 'big gift' approach—giving away a full-size retail pack either free or at a reduced price. The store receives a mark-up equal to or even better than normal.

Johnson & Johnson is one major marketer that uses the technique frequently. One year, they gave away no fewer than 4.8 million Stayfree Prima sanitary napkins in supermarkets and pharmacies throughout Australia. The long-term sales results more than justified this apparent profligacy. 'The only way we can convince the majority of women is to give them a sample,' said Clive Addison, J & J's Australian marketing manager at the time. 'Stayfree Prima lives or dies on the sampling programme.'[2]

If yours is a low-price, high-repeat-sale product with what you feel are demonstrable advantages, there could be a pointer here for you.

The demo route

For food products in particular, the most popular of all in-store sampling approaches is the demonstration. You hire someone to cook or otherwise prepare the product, and hand out samples—as near to your shelf display as possible.

If you're confident your product looks and tastes good, you can't go wrong with this approach. The Favourite Pillsbury Doughboy people have been using it for years to demonstrate their full product range. And now, thanks to the magic of the microwave, it's easier to do than ever.

Of course, the approach is not confined to food products. Cosmetics, perfumes, detergents, cloths—if you can show people why your product is better, the store is an ideal place in which to do so.

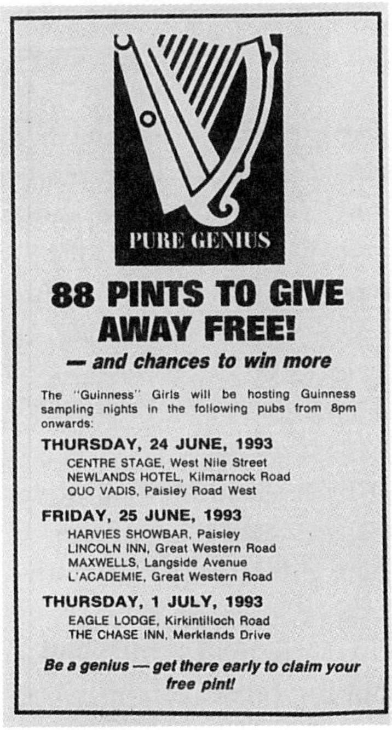

Creating a special sampling event helps Guinness to attract attention and boost pub–goers numbers, with the aim of changing these drinkers' buying habits.
Courtesy of Guinness Brewing Worldwide Ltd. The Guinness word, Harp device and 'Pure Genius' slogans are trade marks of Guinness

To gain trial, Ovaltine 'piggy backed' a drink sachet inside a Weetabix cereal carton. The link was logical—both products depend on milk for their consumption. The association with Royalty is a plus.
Courtesy of Weetabix Limited

The piggy-back approach

Another way to put your product in potential purchasers' hands is to piggy-back it with a related one on the store shelf.

A typical match of that kind saw a packet of Kellogg's® Rice Bubbles carry a free 60g sample of Pascall Sweets Marshmallows, plus recipes on using them both together. So the vast army of 'Snap, Crackle and Pop' fans received free marshmallows in the normal course of their buying activity—in a way that promised to widen the use of both products. That had to be a good deal for each manufacturer. And so, in practice, it turned out to be.

The piggy-back approach need not be confined to stores, either. Kleenex Tissues did well with a promotion that offered a free hayfever kit, including Oprex eye lotion, by mail.

The key to sampling in this way? Look for a host product with a natural link to yours—the kind of link that can, when skilfully exploited, increase the sales of both partners. The other manufacturer will quickly see the benefits and the stores will happily join in. Best of all, your product will reach thousands of potential new buyers in an intriguing, memorable and sales-provoking way.

Presence marketing

Our last in-store sampling route is a new one, first tried in Melbourne in March 1991. For want of a better title, we've called it 'presence marketing'—because you make your presence felt strongly and unmistakably.

The initial event saw the Good-O dog food people hold a full day of activities for dog owners and their pets in a shopping centre carpark. You could get your photo taken with your dog free of charge, have your face painted to look like your dog's, win prizes, collect free giveaways and so on. It was a lot of fun, and the manufacturers were happy with the result. I think it's an interesting concept, with a lot of potential for many product categories. You can certainly use it to concentrate promotional attention on specific geographical areas, and build consumer involvement.[3]

The technique is growing in popularity in the USA, where an organisation called Shopping Center Network sets up exhibits in major shopping malls around the country. They can use the events for sampling, product information distribution and coupon hand-outs. They have audiovisual facilities and trained personnel, and work with the shopping centre and the manufacturer to publicise the event.

More inventive

'Presence marketing' is a good example of the new thinking now going into the sampling medium. Some promising things are happening, as Anne Yeoman, general manager of the Sales Advantage, a Melbourne sales promotion house, observed in *B&T* magazine. 'Sampling is something manufacturers are using much more strategically, with most activity at point of sale,' she said. 'It is becoming much more inventive.'

To underline her comment, Yeoman gave the example of Sydney's 'Smart Store', the prototype supermarket of the future. She explained that a Smart Store demonstrator would actually show shoppers how to make an entire chicken meal, using perhaps eight products from the store. Many ways of cooking chicken and giving serving ideas would be included.

Woolworths has set up a separate division to handle sampling. National advertising manager Alan Holroyd told *B&T* that sampling was 'a growing area' of in-store marketing. Up to three demonstrations could now be run simultaneously in some of the larger stores.

'With demonstrations, basically everybody wins—the customer, the retailer and the manufacturer,' he said.[4]

Less reach, less cost

Like all other techniques, the various forms of in-store sampling have

A sample bag enclosing a FREE product which can be viewed through the bag is given away with any purchase from the Ambre Solaire instore display. The very clever idea not only draws attention to the display—it motivates the consumer to consider every Ambre Solaire item there, before choosing the most appropriate one to accompany the FREE gift. Brilliant!
Courtesy of ASDA Stores Ltd and Garnier Laboratories

their strengths and weaknesses. They don't reach nearly as many people as the door-to-door or mail avenues. But then again, they don't cost nearly as much. They offer tried and proven sales-building techniques for new products. They're particularly effective for foods of all kinds. And when people have to buy the samples, you get immediate consumer involvement in your brand.

On the other hand, in-store sampling is hard to police. The consumer may take your samples just for the low prices and never return. And if you go the trial-size route, you're up for the cost of the trial-size container.

Nothing's perfect in a world like this. The secret of success is to use the imperfect to best advantage. And with in-store sampling, many people have done precisely that.

Sampling or promotional offer

Link purchase has become an important feature for many supermarket chains. Some supermarkets promote the link via in-store coupons. Others simply promote the married products. The consumer benefit is worthwhile: when customers buy (say) three products, they get one *free* or at a big discount.

With more sophisticated retailers, the checkout system automatically deducts the benefit. Others rely on sighting the products, confirming the discount and deducting it from the bill at the checkout. Most promote the offer with specially-printed carry bags which carry the offer and are freely available on-shelf alongside the products on display. These carry bags identify the products and promote the link purchase offer to encourage trial purchase. The scheme also provides the supermarket chain with another way of saving the customer money.

The street-smart approach

If your product has wide general appeal, is small and compact and doesn't need to be cooked to be handed out, street corner sampling could be the approach for you. It's simplicity itself. Just hire people to stand near high-traffic areas such as bus stops and railway stations and hand out the product in all directions. This is a low-cost way to distribute vast numbers of samples in a short time. But, of course, it's non-selective in regard to demographics, and you're likely to get duplication if you do it more than once.

As I said, nothing's perfect …

Targeted sampling

In total contrast to the random hand-outs of street corner sampling is the highly planned, smart-bomb approach of targeted sampling. The technique is exactly what the name says. You identify a specific group of consumers—new mothers, university students, new home owners and so on —and deliver a sample pack to each person by hand or mail.

The pack contains a number of products of special relevance to people in those groups—or if not the actual product, details of a free or low-price offer. The Baby Bounty pack delivered to new mothers in hospital is perhaps the best-known example of the technique. There could hardly be a better psychological moment to hand a new mum your product—when she knows she'll need all the help and good advice she can get in the immediate future …

While many sampling techniques work best for new products, targeted sampling is an excellent way to introduce an established product to someone who's suddenly entered the market for the first time. It's reasonably economical, too, because the cost is shared by all the products in the pack.

Hills create awareness, enhance brand image and generate trial and leads for future direct marketing activity with TV advertising across the country. The 1 800 number allows immediate consumer interaction, stirred by a FREE trial offer. These premium products are sold only by veterinarians and specialty stores, whose traffic is enhanced by coupon offers contained in the trial pack.
Courtesy of Hills Pet Nutrition, Inc.

Media sampling

Another method of aiming targeted samples at your customers is to offer them through the media. Broadly, there are three ways of doing that.

The first is to put an advertisement in a newspaper or magazine, offering product samples from a group of manufacturers. The cost is shared by all the brands. The respondents normally have to send some money to cover postage and handling costs. The 'Value Pack' is an example of this approach. Promoted through full page colour advertisements, mainly in women's magazines, it invites readers to send in an order certificate. On this, they have to answer some questions from the advertisement. Or they may have to spend a little money to receive a sample pack of non-competitive products worth many times what they pay.

The second is via an offer-driven strategy using TV with an 1800 information and response number.

The third media sampling route goes beyond giving an offer of a product sample. It gives the product sample itself. Known as an FSI—'free sample insert'—or 'sample tipped on-page', this technique actually attaches a non-spillable or non-breakable product sample to a magazine cover or inside on a magazine page.

Hair shampoo is a favourite in women's magazines. Jif sponges also demonstrated how creative sampling and trial can be effected using this

Sony target potential customers for their new Sony mini disk by inserting the real product in the press most popular with their audience. After 'seeing and feeling', prospects are directed to stockists to experience the excellence in sound their new possession can deliver. To boost sales, Sony offer purchasers the chance to win one of 50 new mini Disk MD Walkmans.
Courtesy of Sony United Kingdom Limited

medium with a 'ticked in' sample of their product. Liptons Tea did it successfully with a tea sachet. Publishers stick in samples—free paperback book extracts '. . . the terrifying new thriller from the best-selling author'. Bound into magazines, they create awareness and familiarity. If compelling enough, they lead to another sale from the same newsagent.

There's another benefit. If the front cover features a well known personality—and the synergy is right between the personality and your product—your product can benefit from the exposure. Slazenger used this 'Covermount' strategy successfully with their new Slazenger golfball affixed to *Today's Golfer* which featured Jack Nicklaus, the world famous golfer and personality.

Offers like this one can be scheduled jointly by the advertiser and the publisher, in an effort to achieve product trial for the advertiser and additional impact and purchases for the publisher.

Hallmark's creativity in this kind of exercise is outstanding. They choose the right magazine to target their card-buying audience. And they make good use of the media itself. In true teaser fashion, the first page just reads, 'At Hallmark, we've always given free envelopes with our cards. Well, guess what . . .' When readers turn the page, the message continues, 'Now we're giving away free cards with our envelopes'.

The yellow envelope stands out strongly against the white magazine page. And under it is a humorous message for those luckless souls who

Trial sampling of a NEW golf ball attached to the front of *Today's Golfer* is directed straight at the right person—the golfer.
Courtesy of Today's Golfer

find the envelope has been removed by a previous reader or browser. They are told the full story of the promotion and how they can get onto the bandwagon.

On the back of the special envelope, Hallmark's 'big idea' gives an amusing set of instructions on how the reader can redeem a Shoebox greeting card of his or her choice. Also, of course, there are the vital database information-gathering questions: name, address, phone number, birth date, how many greeting cards purchased per year, where from, on what occasions? And a final check—did you lie about your age? Yes, no, I'll never tell!

This brilliant campaign achieves greatly increased awareness for Hallmark's Shoebox cards, builds their image and boosts store traffic. Even more importantly, it obtains much essential statistical information, to empower future offer-driven database marketing activities.

Sampling survey

Direct Marketing magazine reported that Pepsi-Cola received an overflowing response to a campaign that attempted to create a dialogue with consumers and convert Diet Coke drinkers.

After designating April 1992 as 'Uh-Huh Month', the company shipped 1 million consumers a case of Diet Pepsi. Pepsi targeted only those who had previously stated a preference for drinking Diet Coke. They gathered this information from a media challenge and responses to a survey on cola-drinking habits. Pepsi included a questionnaire in each case of Pepsi shipped. The survey asked the recipient's reaction to tasting Diet Pepsi and how they liked receiving samples at home. They were asked whether receipt of the sample would influence future cola-buying habits. Pepsi also wanted to know details about the whole household's cola-drinking patterns.

A free trial of Huggies with *Mother & Baby* magazine. Huggies target parents through a number of media, including specialist press. The parents could stay brand-loyal for up to 24 months or longer—a 'lifetime value' approaching $A1500. A second child doubles this value to Huggies. With amounts like these at stake, creating a relationship with these parents makes sense.
Courtesy of Kimberly-Clark Australia Pty Limited

Through this promotion, Pepsi amassed names and information about cola drinkers while it kept the lines of communication open and complemented its general advertising. Pepsi obviously sees the benefit of sending samples to highly-targeted prospects, because of the possibilities of a higher conversion rate among heavy drinkers of cola.

Less than perfect, but good

Media sampling allows you to target your prospects with a fair degree of accuracy. It also brings you a name and address for each sample you send out, so it helps you build a database.

On the other hand (yes, there are negatives here too), it operates slowly. It gets your samples into fewer hands than some of the other techniques. And if yours is an established product, you risk giving away samples to your present customers, which could be construed as a waste of money. The point, I suppose, is that the perfect sampling technique has not yet been invented. But meanwhile, there are some very good less-than-perfect ones to choose from.

And if you choose the right one for your product, the long-term sales rewards could be most significant indeed.

Your sampling checklist

Here's a checklist to guide you in your choice.

1. Is your product a new one with a wide general market and a substantial launch budget?

Consider door-to-door sampling through a reliable distribution company.

2. Is your product new and with wide appeal, but a less-than-substantial launch budget?

Consider mail sampling, if your product fits postal specifications. Or one of the in-store routes, if it doesn't.

3. Is your product new, a supermarket line, a repeat purchase item and being launched on a limited budget?

Consider one of the in-store sampling approaches.

4. Is it everything in (3) above, plus a food line?

Consider an in-store taste demonstration.

5. Can you see a natural link between your product and another popular household item?

Consider a piggy-back sampling approach.

6. Is your product small and easy to handle, with a wide general market and a limited sampling budget?

Consider street corner sampling.

7. Does your product have a sharply defined market whose members are identifiable and reachable?

Consider targeted sampling, either by direct distribution or through the media.

8. Do you want to track consumer responses or build a database for future relationship-building?

Consider a promotion which collects names, pertinent information, and also tracks response.

That, of course, is a fairly simplistic list. Many products will fit equally well into several of the suggested categories. However, it gives you an idea of the kind of issues to think about. Basically, the idea is to put your product into as many potential customers' hands as possible, in a way that maximises its sales appeal—and gets you the widest trial and penetration your budget can afford.

Notes

1. Dr Max Sutherland, 'Closing the Mailbox Mind Gap', *Ad News*, 14 February 1992, and 'Advertising and the Mind of the Consumer', by Max Sutherland, Allen & Unwin, 1993.
2. *B&T*, May 1992. 'Marketers Seek Trial', by Chris Pearson.
3. Dart Marketing Services, June 1993. '*Promotion Review*', by Matthew Jenkins.
4. *B&T*, July 1993. 'Everybody has their purchase price', by Sally Rawlings.

12
CHAPTER

Nine More Cost-Effective Ways to Higher Sales

As I planned this book, I discovered that all the basic sales promotion techniques I'm aware of either slotted neatly into a particular chapter, or formed the basis of one. That is, apart from the nine promotion mavericks we're about to consider. None of them seemed to fit logically under any of my headings, yet none had quite the detail needed to warrant a chapter of its own. So it seemed easiest to bracket the wayward nine into this one chapter.

While they're fairly diverse, they do have two points in common. They're all relatively inexpensive. And used properly and creatively, they all have very definite potential for boosting your sales.

1. Challenge promotions

In days of yore, knights confident of outperforming an opponent could challenge him to personal combat—usually, with a rich prize (or even a fair maiden) hanging on the outcome. Today, marketers confident of outperforming their rivals can do the same. And once again, a rich prize is

Toyota challenge consumers to get a better deal, with this targeted door–to–door offer. The creative treatment integrates with their massive media sponsorship of the Olympic Games, using an endorsement by favourite Aussie Olympic athlete, Robert De Castella.
Courtesy of Toyota Australia

at stake—the chance to win not only increased sales but the 'perceived value' battle as well.

The classic example is Pepsi and Coke. Fighting an uphill battle against Coke's much greater marketing expenditure, Pepsi made a landmark discovery. In blind product tests, a majority of people actually preferred Pepsi to Coke. So was born 'The Pepsi Challenge'. Pepsi set up sampling stalls in high-traffic areas like shopping malls and beaches in the summer. People were challenged to try the two drinks from unmarked containers and say which one they preferred. Here, too, the majority verdict went to Pepsi.

The results were, of course, widely publicised. Many of the tests were filmed and used as TV commercials. But Pepsi found they still had a problem. Experience showed that, even if people did prefer Pepsi in a blind product test, Coke's unmatched image and mystique often stopped the preference from turning into a sale. Despite that psychological barrier, however, 'The Pepsi Challenge' paid off well for Pepsi, on a comparatively modest outlay.

Challenge your consumer

Another way of using the challenge technique is to direct it not at your competitor but your consumer.

We did this very successfully for Cadbury's. 'Bet you a dollar you won't find a better chocolate bar' was our challenge to chocolate buyers. If they tried Cadbury's, but preferred another brand, they were invited to send in all the reasons why they liked the other one better. Cadbury's would then respond by sending them one dollar.

This sort of promotion is rather like the guarantee on a packet of soap flakes. Many people—including lots of brand switchers—buy the product to try it, but very few actually take you up on the challenge. So you pick up a swag of extra sales, at no cost to you beyond that of the promotion itself.

Comparing soups

We also used the challenge technique along slightly different lines for packet soups in the UK. The brand leader at the time by quite a margin was Swiss Knorr. We wanted to gain trial of a new product from our client, Maggi.

So we challenged the soup buyers of Britain to 'Compare your existing soup with a better one from Maggi *free*!' To do this, they had to send in the labels of their present soups, for which they would receive in return a pack or two of the new Maggi variety. The campaign was led by a sizeable media promotion, and drew a fairly large response. So we achieved three things. We sampled the new Maggi variety to a substantial cross-section of the market; we learned which brands and lines we were competing against; and we gained a useful database of trialists. That intelligence proved very useful in the future marketing of this particular Maggi line.

To promote interest and trial of their new product, Wall's Ice Cream demonstrate their confidence with a money-back guarantee offer in consumer press.
Courtesy of Wall's Ice Cream

Just pick up the phone

Both the Cadbury's and Maggi campaigns were extremely successful in their own way. Today, they could be made even more so—because now we have the technology to get responses not days later through the mail but instantly, through 1 800 or 0055 telephone numbers.

This technology, I predict, will mean a great increase in the use of the challenge technique by marketers wanting to mail samples of their products to consumers. Now they just have to tag their TV commercials with an easily remembered number instead of a more complicated mailing address. And because that makes it much easier for people to respond, marketers can expect a big rise in requests for samples. As a valuable bonus, this also means many more names for their databases.

2. Guarantees to sell

Since the beginning of the century, mass marketers and mail-order merchants alike have backed their products with a universally-recognised symbol of confidence.

The money-back guarantee.

Unilever and Proctor & Gamble have always been among the biggest users of the device, especially on their soap powders. Today, the guarantee has spread well beyond such traditional products, into such fields as cars and even fax machines.

A recent *Marketing Magazine* article by Michael Kiely pointed out that Xerox has a 'Customer Satisfaction Guarantee' that lasts for three years. It covers all Xerox products, from the smallest fax machine ($795) up to the largest laser printer (over $250 000). While not strictly a money-back guarantee, it offers to keep on replacing products until the customer is satisfied.[1]

Swapping cars

A similar plan is currently being offered in Australia by General Motors Holden. The newly-launched Holden Apollo (a re-badged version of the Toyota Camry) is backed by what the carmaker calls the 'Apollo Edge'. This is an upgraded customer satisfaction programme, part of which is a swap-if-you're-not-satisfied deal that breaks new ground in Australian automotive marketing.

The offer is open to buyers of the four- or six-cylinder Apollo versions (priced from $22 978 to $31 508). If they aren't happy with the car, they can bring it back within a fortnight or before they drive 500kms. They can then swap it for anything else in the Holden range, from a Barina to a Caprice. If they go up, they pay the difference. If they go down, they get a rebate. And they can keep on bringing cars back and swapping them as many times as they like.

Here again, buyers don't get their money back. But they are guaranteed ultimate satisfaction. Even if they have to go through the entire Holden range to get it.

A guarantee with a bite

Despite the growth of 'satisfaction' guarantees, there are still plenty of the full money-back type around. In the USA, Proctor & Gamble ran an unusual one for their Crest toothpaste brand. The promise was 'Better teeth protection or your money back'. A TV commercial invited viewers to phone in for a participation kit, which included an enrolment card. The consumer then went to the dentist for a rating on his or her dental condition, and agreed to use Crest toothpaste regularly for the next six months.

Five months later, P & G sent the consumer a dental check-up reminder. At the second visit, the dentist re-evaluated the guaranteed teeth, marked the check-up card accordingly, and returned it to P & G. If the consumer wasn't satisfied with the results, P & G refunded six month's worth of Crest, with proofs of purchase. A little complicated, but certainly a novel and imaginative use of the money-back guarantee.

Another Fortune 500 company on the guarantee trail is Kellogg®. In the UK, the cereal giant ran TV commercials offering viewers a money-back guarantee on new Golden Crisp cereal. The tag line summed it up by saying, 'An open box is an empty box, or your money back'. Also in the UK, Safeways is claiming to be the first retailer ever to offer a guarantee on the sweetness of melons.

The confused 20

In the previous section of this chapter, I touched on Pepsi's 'challenge' taste test clashes with Coke. Pepsi followed that up in the UK with a money-back guarantee to anyone who thought Pepsi wasn't the best tasting cola. Only 760 people asked for their money back. On an amusing note, 20 people thought it was a Coke promotion and demanded a refund because they thought Pepsi tasted better!

Powerful reasons to buy

Guarantees issue a challenge to consumers—a challenge to try your product, because you're extremely confident of your claims. At the same time, they make tangible the goodwill you feel towards your customers, and they're very reassuring to existing users. Those are powerful reasons to buy from you. If you really believe in your product, why not add to its sales appeal with a guarantee?

3. Insuring your promotion

If you don't want to take the risk, insurance is a way of protecting yourself financially against possible but statistically unlikely disasters. When this principle is applied to sales promotion, it becomes an extremely effective way to offer a prize considerably beyond your ability to pay.

The key to such schemes is to make them credible, believable—and fun. We've run several, including the Polo Mint Hole-in-One Challenge. This centred on golf, with the point of relevance being that Polo Mints, like Lifesavers, have a hole in the middle.

Trying for a hole in one

Entrants in this challenge had to decide where a golf ball hit by a particular competitor on a particular hole in a particular match would land. They indicated their decision by placing an 'X' on an entry form. The winners then had the thrill of watching a famous golfer trying to shoot a hole in one on their behalf.

If he'd succeeded, they would have shared in a prize pool of $1 million. As it happened, he didn't—but it wouldn't have worried Polo if he had, because they were insured against the possibility. If the hole in one had been achieved, the prize would have been paid by the insurance company, not by Polo.

Huge prize, low risk

By using insurance, our client was able to offer an unusual, exciting and very attractive promotion with a huge potential prize—without risking anything more than the cost of the promotional material and an insurance premium. The insurance company was happy to take the risk, because the golfer's chance of actually achieving the hole in one was obviously very small. And the contestants were happy, because they enjoyed the thrill of rubbing shoulders with a famous golfer and sharing the electric atmosphere of the hit-off.

Exactly the same idea was used successfully for Haig Whisky, who sponsored the Haig Golf Classic, and in New Zealand for Ford's One Million Dollar Drive. In Ford's case, people who took test drives were given the chance of having a hole in one hit on their behalf.

A free TV in four years

Toshiba had a creative—and apparently somewhat daring—use of insurance recently in the UK. They offered a guaranteed £400 cashback in four years time with every TV they sold. This was virtually saying—buy a Toshiba TV now, and four years down the line we'll give you a brand new one free. Or, if you prefer, bring in your set then and we'll give you back all the money you paid for it.

Now that's a formidable offer. It sounds like a very brave, if not foolhardy, move by Toshiba. But it was all covered by insurance—and the actuaries were quite sure that only a minority of consumers would actually get around to redeeming their guarantees after four years. They took several factors into account. People might still be happy with their TV when the four years were up. Or they might have bought another one in the meantime. Or inflation or new technology might have pushed the price of a new TV well over £400. Or they might simply have lost the letter of guarantee.

However, the offer was genuine. If purchasers took their TV, their proof of purchase and their letter of guarantee into a Toshiba dealer in four years time, their £400 would be cheerfully refunded. Courtesy of the insurance company. Here again, Toshiba found a way of getting money from nowhere.

Range Rover use the Limited Edition technique to focus increased attention on the product, and to underline its positioning as the top-of-the-range 4WD.
Courtesy of Range Rover and Weekes Morris Osborne/Masius Advertising.

Guaranteed sunshine

Insuring a promotion allows you to make the most remarkable claims. With my then colleague, Mike Lane, I ran a promotion in London for Nivea sunscreen products. We guaranteed consumers that, if they bought Nivea when they went on holidays in England or Scotland, they would enjoy days of sunshine rather than rain.

What we did, of course, was to take out insurance against above-average rainfall during various two-week periods throughout the summer. The promotion swiftly caught the imagination of British consumers. They bought Nivea in such quantities that the whole summer stock was sold out in a matter of weeks. The promotion achieved all its objectives. And as I recall, only two consumers claimed their payment for above-average rainfall! This was another case where a big offer could be made quite safely on a small budget, because it was covered by insurance.

4. The 'Limited Edition' technique

For higher ticket products, the popular 'Limited Edition' technique can be most effective. It's often used with cars, where a model with a personal link to a racing driver or other identity—or boasting above-average levels of extras—can be specially badged.

The JPS Black and Gold BMW, the Carla Zampatti Laser, the Limited Edition Range Rover and the Sportsgirl Barina are just a few examples.

Each one creates a promise beyond that of the standard vehicle. And the fact that there may be only 100 or even 50 of these special marques has tremendous appeal to people who want to feel different or distinguished.

Sometimes, the Limited Edition car technique is taken even further. Some sweepstake or chance-to-win promotions have offered the unique lure of one or two specially badged cars—the only examples of their kind in the world. Such initiatives can reap huge rewards, especially if the prize cars are customised to the market of the product running the sweepstake.

Toohey's, for instance, commissioned two Holden Camiras from GMH to mark their sponsorship of the Toohey's 1000 motor race. Cars were badged to reflect not only the race itself but Toohey's sponsorship of it. Offered in a sweepstake under a 'Win one for yourself and one for your mate' theme, they drew over 300 000 entries.

The Limited Edition idea added extra value and excitement to what would otherwise have been a fairly ordinary 'win a couple of cars' promotion.

5. Joint promotions

By 'joint promotions', I don't mean contra deals, where very attractive products such as holidays are obtained for use as prizes. Joint promotions are those in which different products with a common target audience and similar marketing objectives come together in one promotion. By doing so, they can usually share the costs, while their synergy can be used imaginatively to create extra opportunities for both brands.

The 'both' in that sentence is important. Successful joint promotions can never be a one-sided affair.

There's an ideal synergy between 'Wagon Wheels' and 'Hot Wheels', both in name and target audiences.
Courtesy of Westons Baked Foods. Hot Wheels copyright of Mattel

Apples and software

We ran a very successful joint promotion for Apple Computers and several software vendors. Entitled 'Apple Christmas Offers', it gave purchasers cashback vouchers worth up to $2000 on a Macintosh and $800 on an Apple Education Computer. The cashback savings could only be spent on nominated peripheral items, or on software from Microsoft, Lotus and Borland. And to make the deal even more attractive, the peripherals and software were available at up to 25% off normal prices.

'Apple Christmas Offers' gave purchasers an excellent opportunity to acquire a complete computer, peripherals and software package at considerable savings. It clearly benefited Apple, and it benefited the software people—even though they were selling against each other—because it reached Apple's extensive database. It gave the software companies a unique opportunity to sell directly to the core users of their product.

'Apples for the Students'

In 1992, Apple embarked on an even more ambitious joint promotion—this time with Coles Supermarkets. The promotion was imported from the USA through a local licensee. And it called for Coles to give Apple computer equipment worth over $8 million to schools across Australia. A total of 7800 schools—no fewer than 70% of all schools in the country—took part.

The idea was for schools to collect special yellow Coles checkout dockets. The dollar amounts on the dockets

Apple's joint promotion with Coles Supermarkets helped create high awareness and school sales for Apple. At the same time, the drive by concerned parents and friends to get computers for schools promoted loyalty to Coles Supermarkets.
Courtesy of Apple Computer Australia Pty Limited

became 'Registered Docket Values' (RDVs), the programme's basic currency. By collecting the dockets, the schools built up a 'credit account' in RDVs. They could then use these docket values to 'buy' Apple computer hardware and software.

A specially-produced 28-page catalogue of computer equipment available through the programme showed all prices in RDVs. It included just about every type of Apple hardware, printers, external disk drives and so on, plus over 1090 educational software packages. The 'prices' ranged from 5000 RDV for a basic software package to 345 000 RDV for a 2Mb computer with a 40Mb hard drive.

All the school had to do was collect the dockets and phone through with their RDVs an order for the equipment they could 'buy' from the catalogue with their RVDs. The equipment was then delivered. The school paid nothing in actual cash.

Estimates exceeded

Coles' original estimate was that 50% of Australian schools might take part. But with an offer as strong as this, I'm not surprised that the estimate was greatly exceeded. And because there was no upper limit on the number of computers they were prepared to give, the original equipment target of $8 million was swiftly surpassed. Two years into the programme, in fact, the hand-outs had hit $25 million—based on 3368 computers, 2143 printers and 15 000 pieces of software.

Pointing out that all this equipment went to schools that otherwise would not have had it, Coles spokesperson Sharyn O'Brien said, 'that makes us feel warm and fuzzy'.

Looked at in hindsight, the $8 million target was really very conservative. It would have been achieved if every child in 50% of Australian schools had collected $30 worth of dockets each week. As Coles' average docket figure across Australia is $96.68, and 70% of all schools joined in, it's not hard to see why the original target went through the ceiling.[2]

Brand manufacturers too

To give this already powerful programme even greater impact, Coles also invited 11 major brand manufacturers to share in it. Throughout the promotion's four-month period, Johnson & Johnson, Kleenex, Nestlé, Pal, Whiskas, Coca-Cola, Continental, Rexona, Colgate-Palmolive, Arnott's Biscuits and Smith's Crisps were all highlighted in-store with 'Bonus Buy' shelf talkers. When one of these products was bought, an asterisk appeared on the docket. The schools received an extra $1 credit for every asterisk.

With strong commitment from schools, pupils and families, extensive TV advertising, major brand support, Bonus Buy POS material and an Apple Computer in each of Coles' 372 supermarkets, 'Apples for the Students' had everything needed to be a winner. It involved a huge expenditure by Coles. But at the time of writing, it seemed this had paid off for them in terms of increased share of business—the real test of the promotion's success.

Keeping it in the family

Most joint promotions are far less ambitious than 'Apples for the Students'. Indeed, the most common format involves products within the same company. Typical was the one discussed in Chapter 3—the S. C. Johnson Spring Clean Sweepstakes, which embraced nine brands.

In the same way, many manufacturers link some or all of their brands into charity promotions and cause-related programmes (see Chapter 15). Such programmes make it easier to run a common promotion under one common theme.

The travel bug

My colleague, Derek Hughes of The Sales Machine, London, ran a successful joint promotion in the UK, with travel as the lure. The carrier was British Rail and the packaged goods manufacturer was Lever Bros. The purchase of selected Lever Bros products gave consumers the right to buy a British Rail ticket and get another one free.

The promotion was heavily supported with TV and press advertising. When it was over, British Rail had received five million ticket applications. They estimated that about 50% of these represented journeys that would otherwise not have been made. This meant huge additional

Persil Soap Powder promotes travel by British Rail and gains substantial ticket savings for their more regular consumers. The promotion ran again and again.
Courtesy of Unilever

revenue for them—and the sales results for Lever Bros were equally satisfactory. Not for nothing did one writer call this the 'grand-daddy of all joint promotions'.

Interestingly, of the six major promotions Lever Bros runs in the UK each year, almost all are joint ventures. British Rail has a history of success in them too, with different partners. Their first associate in a profitable travel promotion was not Lever Bros Persil soap brand, but Kellogg's® Corn Flakes.

6. Tailor-made promotions

This category is not about made-to-measure suits, but manufacturers' promotions created especially for one retail store or chain.

This trade marketing technique has been slow to catch on in Australia, for three main reasons. First, the trade puts pressure on manufacturers to discount prices, rather than find more imaginative ways of boosting sales. Second, money is then squeezed from sales force budgets to fund the discounts. And third, economies of scale can make it hard to justify the production of costly sales material for a comparative handful of stores.

Nevertheless, our clients have had real success with tailor-made promotions. The technique enhances negotiations with major buying groups. It can be an extra lever to gaining acceptance. And it can be a tactical trump when stocking or sales problems arise within a particular chain.

Normally, the tailor-made proposition is handled through the key accounts and national accounts salespeople, rather than the marketing department.

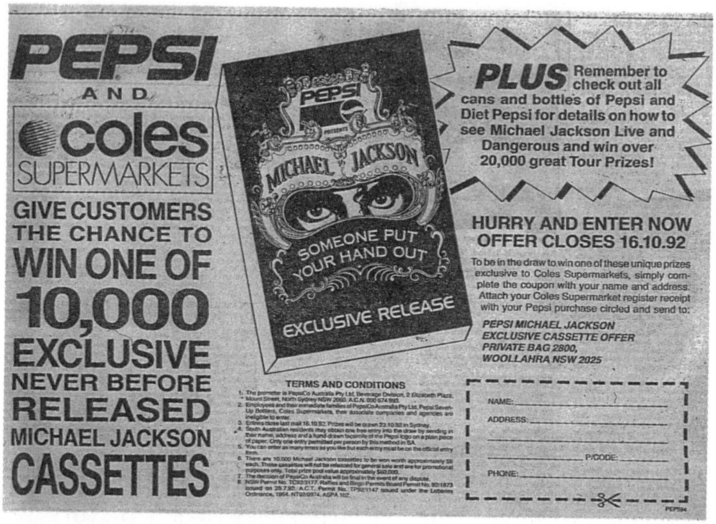

Endorsed by a block–buster personality, this Coles–only tailormade promotion enlivens the store's offer to New Pepsi buyers and attracts regular customers. *Courtesy of Pepsi–Cola Bottlers Australia Pty Ltd*

CSR's joint cake ingredients display incorporates Coles' own label flour. The inclusion of an own label product not only adds interest and surprise, but gains an extra commitment from the retailer. *Courtesy of CSR Refined Sugars*

The store as hero

Tailor-made promotions must look as though the store initiated them. They must endorse the retailer's selling themes and store proposition, if any. All POS display pieces must be in the store's livery and to their specifications. And if you can extend the promotion to help the sales of the retailer's 'own brand' products, so much the better.

Because of these factors, a tailor-made promotion is a good deal for the retailer. It adds extra interest, excitement and impact to the store's displays—at no extra cost, because the manufacturer produces all the

POS display material. At the same time, the approach can be very successful for you, if you're the manufacturer. It gains an unusual commitment from the store to your display, and normally gets you extra display space you wouldn't have otherwise. It reduces the pressure on you to discount your prices—yet, where price is the arbiter, increases the impact of your price promotion.

We created one of these programmes for Lipton's Tea and Woolworths. Called 'Win Wedgwood at Woolworths when you buy Lipton's Tea', the promotion underlined Woolworths' special commitment to Lipton's Tea buyers. It was negotiated to create above-average stocking and display for the brand, and communicated its features strongly throughout the promotional period.

The potential of tailor-made promotions becomes clear when you realise that, in Australia, 48% of all grocery turnover comes from just 650 retail outlets. It can make a lot of sense to focus your promotional efforts on one major chain. And because it shifts the emphasis away from discounting, it can be a lot more profitable too. As John David of David's Holdings was quoted in *Retail Grocer* as saying, 'Let's see more good old fashioned hard selling techniques, ideas, gimmicks, stunts and adventure that defuse the price emphasis . . .'[3]

7. Boost your response with the telephone

In Chapter 3, I discussed what we call 'Toop's hoops'—the number of steps a consumer has to go through to respond to an offer. The fewer the hoops, the better the response. And there's no better hoop-removers than 0055 or 1 800 telephone numbers. Picking up a telephone is much simpler than filling in a coupon, finding an envelope, addressing it, hunting for a stamp and going out to a post box. So these numbers virtually guarantee you an increased response—because they make action so much easier for your customers.

The 0055 numbers allow consumers to obtain information at their own expense. The 1 800 numbers allow them to reply to an offer at your expense. Some of our clients have used one or both numbers with excellent results. And those who employ the 0055 option also enjoy the money that is fed back into their budgets from the Telecom rebate.

The interactive telephone numbers allow you to add audio-

Kleenex tissues' highest usage is for colds. By positioning their tissues as a FREE help to hay–fever sufferers, the manufacturers empathetically extend usage to help an increasing number of sufferers in summer. Notice the clever use of the hayfever pollen-count hot-line to help sufferers prepare for the worst.
Courtesy of Kimberly–Clark UK

promotional and image-building dimensions to the response process. For instance, when callers phone in, you can play them a few seconds of your jingle or give them a very brief selling message before their call is actually answered. In fact, you can make a whole contest out of that aspect alone. We ran one where callers had to complete the words of a jingle we played them—or better yet, sing the rest of it! Then they had to provide proof of purchase, by quoting the brand, the barcode and use-by date on the wrappers. Only those who could do so were eligible to win the prizes.

Flexibility the keynote

The flexibility of 0055 numbers in particular gives you great scope for creativity. You can update the messages regularly—several times a day, if need be—just by making a phone call to the service's equipment. You can string different messages together in a predetermined order. And you can enable people phoning in to leave messages at the end of their calls—which allows them to enter contests and sweepstakes, place an order or make an enquiry.

There's no easier way to expand your database. But make sure the telephone response computer has a compatibility for disk data transfer to normal holding computers—or you'll have a major cost for manual transcribing from one system to the other.

Winning tickets to Wimbledon

Cafe Hag in the UK used the British equivalent of a 0055 number to give away 10 pairs of tickets to the 1990 Wimbledon Championships, plus two tickets to the Ladies' Final. The contest challenged respondents to 'play a game of tennis' with Wimbledon finalist Virginia Wade.

Her recorded voice served the respondent a series of simple questions on tennis. The sequence was organised so that progress was conveyed in the form of tennis scoring—'30-love to Miss Wade', and so on. The game went on until either the respondent or Miss Wade won. If the respondent emerged victorious, he or she went into the draw to win the tickets.

Sound effects throughout the game created a real sense of involvement. Miss Wade's voice added another intriguing element. One criticism was the game's length—at 25p per minute, it cost respondents over £2 to finish it.

Research potential

The 0055 telephone technique has interesting research potential, too. As I write this, Nestlé Australia is using it for Milky Bar chocolate to compare the promotional effectiveness of TV commercials and point-of-sale entry forms. Both media ask respondents to call a 0055-prefixed number—but it's a different number for each.

Which will get the greater response—TV or POS? Many of us await the results of the exercise with great interest.

Tomorrow's advances

In the near future, technological advances will enable the 'telephone computer' to become much more interactive. It will actually recognise minor tonal changes and so distinguish between key words. Voice response techniques are being used now in the UK, Australia and New Zealand, but these are really pioneering efforts. However, recent computer technology available on PCs can easily change typewritten copy into synthesised voice. This remarkable technology has only a little way to go before it will fully reap the technique's mind-boggling potential.

As my colleague and friend Peter Humphrey of Option One, London, puts it, 'The sophisticated usages will have to await the full availability of multi-frequency handsets and exchange facilities, with their ability for greater clarity (a bit like FM versus medium and long wave on a radio) that enables computers to recognise minor changes in the tone of voice and so to distinguish between key words.'[4]

At the moment, the best we can really do is to ask multiple-choice questions, or ask the caller to answer, say, four out of six questions correctly to win the prize. We can also give them the chance to gamble. They can go on and win a bigger prize by answering a harder question—but they lose their current prizes if they get it wrong. These techniques operate to 95%-plus efficiency, once the receiving computer has tuned into the respondent's accent and volume.

Make the most of today

Until the more advanced technology comes on line, there are still plenty of creative ways to use the technology we do have. Interactive telephone calls enhance your image and improve your response because they're easy for the consumer to use. They're immediate.

And they're about as one-to-one as you can get in present-day marketing.

8. Seasonality

In more product categories than is generally realised, seasonality is an important selling factor. The end of the tax year, for instance, finds some people with money and others without. The financial community can, and does, take full advantage of this phenomenon. It uses seasonal direct marketing and media advertising to offer investment opportunities on the one hand or loans on the other, depending on whether they're targeting group A or group B.

Clearly, the trick here is to identify each group of prospects correctly. Even the most dazzling investment opportunities will be regarded stonily by people who, at that time of the year, are battling to pay the day-to-day bills.

The most obvious example of seasonality in selling is, of course, the special promotions associated with Christmas, Easter, Mother's Day and Father's Day. Over 65% of retail sales in product groups like toys, perfume and chocolates are made at Christmas. Chocolate sales also boom at Easter, as do those in some less-evident categories. Hardware retailers, for instance, are now finding Easter a peak sales period. They're selling a lot of do-it-yourself items to people eager to work on their homes before winter arrives in full force.

Make the most of seasonality

With a touch of creativity, you can boost seasonal sales even further. Smarties proved this when they prepared special Christmas packs containing only red, green and white chocolates—the colours of Christmas. This was a clever ploy that made the most of a seasonal opportunity.

There are many such ways to capture additional sales at these times. Doubling your perfume counter space at Christmas, for example. Using post-Christmas sales to stock up with sales merchandise—items brought in especially to create bargains. Altering your product to give it a seasonal flavour. Creating products especially for seasonal selling periods, such as Easter eggs. And so on.

Of course, once you have a successful seasonal product, you may want to extend its sales beyond a three- or four-week period, once a year. And through the imaginative use of sales promotions, you can do just that.

Find the golden egg

Cadbury's did it brilliantly some years ago in England with their Creme Easter Eggs. They created 'The Chocolate Egg Mystery'—a two-tiered promotion that offered a chance to win one of 10 golden eggs hidden around well-known places in England, Scotland and Wales.

The clues to the golden eggs' whereabouts were contained in a beautifully illustrated book. This was sent to customers in return for several Cadbury's Creme Egg wrappers. It was worth considerably more than the required proofs of purchase, and the golden egg clues boosted its value even higher. However, it turned out to be somewhat unsound

Consumers collected proofs of purchase to get a FREE book—which gave the necessary clues to Win the Golden Eggs! This brilliant two-stage promotion gained initial trial, heavily promoted repeat purchase and maintained interest, suspense and intrigue.
Courtesy of Cadbury Ltd and The Marketing Triangle Ltd, © Nintendo Allied Filmmakers N.V.

environmentally. The number of golden egg seekers who rushed out to dig around places of historical interest threatened to damage many of them beyond repair. But the promotion did sell a lot of Cadbury's Creme Easter Eggs, well beyond the Easter period.

9. Put your customers to work

To run a promotion successfully, you usually need to put a lot of people to work. You can call on your staff, of course. And everyone at your agency, plus their suppliers. But occasionally, you need more hands still. When that happens, you might just be able to rope in a large group of people who'll not only work extremely hard for you.

They'll do so free, gratis and for nothing.

Who are these extraordinarily generous people? Believe it or not, they're your customers.

A labour of love

We've found that, when you run a cause-related marketing programme (see Chapter 15), your customers will willingly do the grass roots labour—if they see that, through their efforts, a cause dear to their hearts will prosper. And if that cause is their own children's well-being, their wholehearted involvement is even easier to obtain.

Money for jam

A typical example is the CSR 'Jampot Jamboree', which we met in Chapter 8, and will probe in some detail in Chapter 15.

Without pre-empting what you'll read there, the promotion was designed to sell more sugar. So we urged Scout groups to make and sell jars of jam. Naturally, they retained all the proceeds, and the groups that sold the most jars received reward badges as well as attractive prizes. And who put in the hundreds of hours of labour needed to prepare jars of jam by the thousands? Our customers, of course—the families of the Scouts. They not only bought the necessary sugar, but provided the vast amount of unpaid work required to make the promotion a huge success—both for the Scout groups and for CSR.

From jam to Apples

If you'll pardon a bad pun, the 'Jampot Jamboree' is money for jam. And the goal of another of our very successful essays in putting customers to work was money for Apples—Apple computers for schools.

Back in 1986, it was obvious that the Apple IIe computer was the best available for school use. But the big stumbling block to its widespread adoption was the obvious one. Money. Much as they wanted to instal Apple computers, software and peripherals, most schools and their associated Parents and Citizens' groups simply couldn't afford them. So we set out to help them raise the necessary cash.

We developed a package of enjoyable, creative and effective fundraising ideas that went well beyond cake stalls and the ubiquitous Aussie lamington drives. We mailed it to Parents & Citizens Association (P & C) groups and inserted it in P & C magazines. Within days, the vision had fired parents' imaginations. No fewer than 34% of all schools in Australia responded to the campaign.

The Apple Quiz Night

Probably the most ambitious of our ideas was the Apple Quiz Night. The concept here was for the P & C to hold a quiz night for parents, teachers

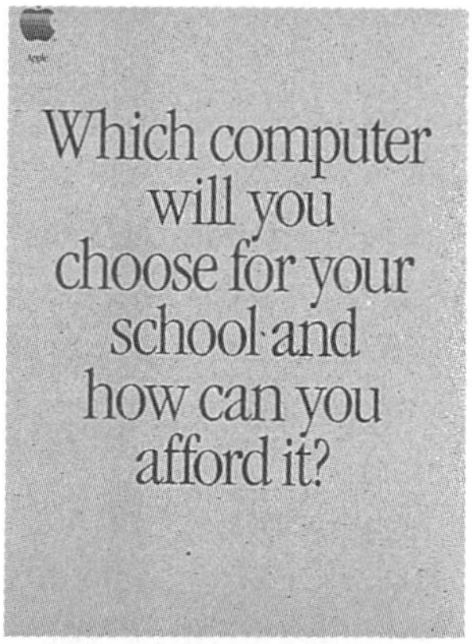

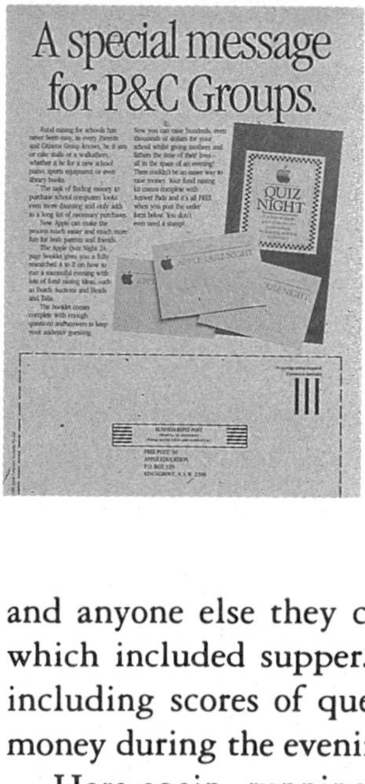

Apple Computer's corporate sell package was direct-marketed to school teachers. It included brochures and a video featuring testimonials from head teachers, educationalists, teachers and pupils who had used Apples successfully in class. The combination of endorsements proved a winner especially when linked with suggestions for raising precious funds to pay for Apple Computers.
Courtesy of Apple Computer Australia Pty Limited

and anyone else they could attract. There was a charge for admission, which included supper. The package provided everything they needed, including scores of questions and answers, plus other ideas for raising money during the evening (such as fines for smoking and drinking!).

Here again, running a quiz night and most of the other fundraising ideas demanded a great deal of time and effort from our customers—the P & C members and the schools who would ultimately buy the Apple computers. And they happily co-operated. Apple Quiz Nights provided evenings of fun all over the country. The other ideas were widely carried out. Apple resellers came to the party with very attractive deals on hardware, software and peripherals.

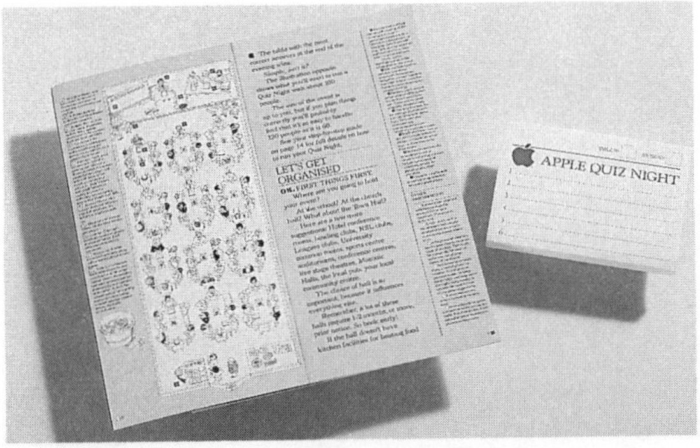

The Apple Quiz Night was an alternative to traditional walkathons and lamington drives. It provided an easy–to–understand, convivial, user–friendly method of raising money for computers.
Courtesy of Apple Computer Australia Pty Limited

The results were overwhelming. Apple went into 'back orders' for the next 18 months, and IBM was forced to withdraw its competing school computer from the market—even though it was $300 cheaper than its Apple rival.

So there's the principle. Run a promotion that will benefit the customers' children or a cause they hold dear, and a large, highly motivated workforce can be at your disposal.

Free.

Employees give up their time

Under some circumstances—and with sufficient motivation—you can even get your employees to work for nothing. We managed that when the 3M Company became a major sponsor of the 1988 Australian Olympic Team. With 3M's American background, there was great PR value for the company in being seen to raise substantial sums of money for Australia's athletes.

A 3M fundraising kit. Using these, 3M strengthened its Olympic involvement throughout the company by raising $135 000 for Australia's cause through their employees' efforts. The top staff fundraising team won a trip for all members to Seoul.
Courtesy of 3M Australia Pty Ltd

So 3M employees were asked to go out and fundraise, largely in their own time. But there was a very attractive carrot. The seven who raised the most were given trips for two to Seoul to see the Games, while the runners-up received overseas holidays to other exotic destinations.

With that motivation added to subtle but definite management pressures, the employees went into action. They organised cricket matches, theatre parties and a host of other after-hours activities. Within weeks, they had raised a very creditable $125 000. The programme's aim of strengthening 3M's image as a concerned Australian company was achieved—and the labour and goodwill had all been provided free. The only cost was some overseas trips and a few tickets to the Games.

So, if your promotional idea needs many hands to make it work, don't overlook the possibility of getting them for nothing—or next to nothing. Offer the right psychological or tangible carrot, and a free labour force could be yours.

Imagine the budgeting pressures that would remove . . .

Notes

1. 'Satisfaction Guaranteed', by Michael Kiely, *Marketing Magazine*, August 1993.
2. *The Sun-Herald*, 9 August 1993.
3. John David, *Retail Grocer*, 1984.
4. Peter Humphrey, Option One, in a letter to Martin Williams.

13
CHAPTER

The Arts and Sport in Selling

What do you have in common with medieval Popes, 16th century English dukes and the de Medici family of 15th century Florence? Precious little, you may say. But as a practitioner of modern marketing methods, you might be nearer to them than you realise. You may even be following in their footsteps.

These people and others like them had one thing in common. They all practised patronage. Because of their financial support, penniless geniuses were able to create some of the world's greatest artistic and musical masterpieces. True, many of them enjoyed lording it over their protégés—which is why 'patronising' is now such a negative word. But they didn't always have it their own way. The spectacle of Rex Harrison's Pope Julius II bellowing at Charlton Heston's Michelangelo to hurry up with the Sistine Chapel ceiling—and getting an equally spirited reply—has become a cinema classic.

Patronage, then, was the vital spark that lit much of old Europe's creativity. And in today's hard-nosed business world, the practice goes on—only today, we call it sponsorship.

Why did our medieval forebears pour their money into other people's endeavours? Sometimes, for genuinely altruistic reasons. Sometimes, because of personal admiration for the composer or artist concerned. And quite often, to boost their own images in the eyes of the populace at large. They wanted, in short, to be seen as 'good blokes'—perhaps for their egos' sake, or to soften community perceptions of them before they imposed new taxes!

Measuring the returns

Today, companies go into sponsorship ventures from an equally wide spread of motives. They may genuinely want to give something back to the community, or they may have been dragged into it by a good cause's tenacious fundraiser. But if the venture is to have real sales promotion value for the sponsor, it needs to be looked at carefully. In cold financial terms, what sort of a return can you expect from it?

That may seem a reasonable question—but it's actually the hottest potato in contemporary sponsorship practice. Measuring the returns from sponsorship has always tended to be a too-hard basket item. Even when large sums of money are involved, sponsorships have too often been handed out on nothing stronger than the managing director's whim. In such cases, virtually no thought is given to their likely benefit to the company, or even how such a benefit could be measured.

Over the years, in short, sponsorship has been the stronghold of ad hocery. And that attitude remains widespread. As recently as the late 1980s, the Hill & Knowlton sports marketing division conducted a survey of Western Australian companies involved in sponsorship. Many were giving more than $100 000 a year. Yet a staggering 68% of them had no procedures in place to check the value of their sponsorships. How many of those companies would spend $100 000 on advertising without monitoring every stage of the campaign? How many would pay an executive $100 000 a year without demanding accountability for performance?

Sales the key to measurement

I believe firmly that, wherever possible, *sponsorship today should be made as accountable as any other part of the marketing mix.* I say 'wherever possible' because, as we'll see in this chapter, some forms of sponsorship have long-term networking goals that don't lend themselves to immediate measurement. But if sponsorship is linked directly to a product, measurement should be possible through the only criteria that ultimately matter. Sales.

Don't equate TV and press coverage of the event with success—even if your logo appears often and prominently. Instead, take a close look at your sales results and see if they go up during the sponsorship period.

Pepsi sails to sales

A classic example of measurability was Diet Pepsi's sub-sponsorship of the ANZ 12 Metre Challenge sailing event on Sydney Harbour in 1990. The Diet Pepsi logo was featured on the boats' jibs, in the media centre and on the support boats. Diet Pepsi also backed its sponsorship with a promotional campaign. The result? A 40% increase in Diet Pepsi sales while the races were on, and immediately afterwards.

Not all sponsorships, I emphasise again, are as readily measurable as that. Indeed, there are many, especially in the non-sporting field, where it's almost impossible to establish a direct cause-and-effect relationship between sponsorship and sales. But don't let your flint-hearted accountant rule them out on that score. Whether they're directly measurable or not, carefully-planned sponsorships are well worth looking into. They can be a cost-efficient way to enhance your corporate profile. They can link your company and brand with your customers' lifestyles and aspirations. They can create a difference for your product, boost the effectiveness of your total promotional programme, and put you in touch with people who can do a great deal for your business.

Basically, sponsorships can do all this for you in two vital areas.

The 'good bloke' motive

The first area is one that hasn't changed since the Middle Ages. But interestingly enough, recent psychological studies show that the desire to be seen as a 'good bloke' is very rational from a commercial viewpoint—for quite irrational reasons.

Let's say the local shopping centre has two butchers, with meat of equal quality. Butcher A's meat is cheaper, but he's a real grouch. Butcher B, on the other hand, is a very pleasant person. Don't we tend to buy from butcher B—even though it costs a little more? On the face of it, that's an irrational—or emotional—buying decision. We're there to buy meat, not to enjoy the butcher's company. But after two years of study by Harvard University researchers, we can at least understand why we act the way we do.

The studies showed that, even in corporate buying situations, 80% of the buying decision is governed by the right-hand side of the brain. The brain's left side hardly gets a look in. It influences only 20% of the buying decision.[1]

Emotions rule

Now that's very interesting, because the right-hand side of the brain is the seat of our emotional actions and attitudes. Its left-hand partner looks after the rational, logical and analytical part of our nature. You'd think our buying decisions would originate there—but as we have seen, 80% of the decision is made on the other side.

The emotional—or irrational—one.

In other words, the emotional aspects of a buying decision are four times as important as the rational factors. It's easy, then, to see why a favourable perception of a company can have a very favourable impact on the sales of its product. It's all to do with right-brain dominance. So now we know why, in business and commerce, it pays to be seen as a 'good bloke'—and sponsoring a popular community happening is an effective way to get yourself seen in that light.

The 'rubbing shoulders' syndrome

Another reason for going the sponsorship route is what I call the 'rubbing shoulders' syndrome.

Sponsoring a sporting event or cultural activity gives you the chance to 'rub shoulders' with people who can benefit you in business. It may happen in a box at the cricket, at a surf club annual meeting or at the

Sponsorship of the USA Tennis Open is handled in a way that maximises the investment for many sponsors.

opening night of the ballet. But wherever it is, you find yourself mixing with people in a non-business atmosphere of excitement and enthusiasm. It's the perfect setting for networking—rather like joining a select club, where you mingle with people in just the right environment for building relationships and creating business opportunities.

Having a sponsor's box at the cricket is an excellent example. It lets you give your clients and suppliers a pleasant day or night at a glamorous event. The ground is electric with emotion and enthusiasm. It's an experience everyone shares and remembers. And not only can you 'rub shoulders' creatively for hours—your guests can do the same with people who can benefit their businesses as well. Few events could be better calculated to polish up your 'good bloke' image. So if you want to benefit from right-brain dominance and the 'rubbing shoulders' syndrome, sponsorship is a good way to go.

The first decision

But before you sign on someone's dotted line, you have to make a basic decision. Do you want to major on 'rubbing shoulders' with a fairly small group, like the surf club committee or opera goers? Or do you want to be seen as a 'good bloke'—a good corporate citizen—by most of the community?

If the latter, be prepared to spend money. Sponsorship can never be your major communications thrust. It is always and only a complement to it. For every $100 000 you spend on sponsorship, I believe you need to spend at least another $100 000 on more conventional promotional activities. And your sponsorship venture mustn't happen in isolation from them. It must be an integral part of your total promotional programme. It must tie in closely in theme and message with everything else you're doing.

Only then, in my view, will you get real benefit from your sponsorship dollars.

The exception

However, as with most rules, there's an exception. If you're a small business with a local clientele, sponsorship could be a creative way to spend a large slice of your promotional budget.

Imagine you're an electrical retailer in a suburban shopping mall. Sponsoring the local football team might well do more for you than little advertisements in the local papers or leaflets in letterboxes. It would certainly help you to be seen as a 'good bloke'—which, as we've noted, can activate right-brain dominance in your customers and sway their buying choice. Provided, of course, that your demeanour in the shop matches the 'good bloke' image you're spending money to create!

Four avenues to follow

Now let's assume you're somewhat larger than the electrical retailer. You're keen to try the sponsorship route. You want both the 'good bloke' and 'rubbing shoulders' benefits. In other words, you want wider exposure to your target audience, and you want to meet the right people. Like most of us would be, you're inclined to support an event or cause that appeals to you personally. Yet because you're running a business, you don't want right-brain emotions to win the day entirely over left-brain pragmatism. Where do you put your money?

Basically, there are four avenues you can follow—sport, the arts, science, and good causes. And the more you spend on sponsorship, the more discerning you should be in choosing between them.

Match the event to your market

The key to success is actually pretty obvious. You choose the kind of event that appeals to your target market, suits your product's image and fits your marketing objectives.

In sponsorship, alcohol is NOT small beer. Marketers have to be as alert and vigorous as the athletes to capture viewers in the fiercely competitive field of sports sponsorship.
Courtesy of Carlton & United Breweries, Tooheys Ltd and Lion Nathan Breweries

If, for example, you're looking for reach and you're selling a low cost product with wide general appeal, sports sponsorship may be the avenue for you. If your product is an upmarket one, artistic events could suit you better. If you have a technical product, science-type sponsorships would be possibilities. And if your main aim is to be seen as a good corporate citizen, put your sponsorship money into good causes. There are plenty of those around—the Children's Hospital, the Red Cross or the environment, to name three. AIDS research is another one—but to date, most sponsors of AIDS research have preferred to remain invisible.

Put in more than money

Once you've surveyed the field, you'll almost certainly find a promising candidate for your sponsorship money. And that's the time to stop and consider a vital point. To get positive results from your sponsorship, you must be prepared to put a lot more than money into it. You must be prepared to commit large amounts of time and marketing expertise to it as well.

That means treating it as seriously and professionally as you treat all your other promotional activities. It means monitoring it constantly, to ensure that your name, logo, product and so on are being featured exactly as agreed. It means developing reliable ways of measuring its results, if that's possible. It means thinking about extensions—spin-off consumer and trade promotions, staff motivation programmes, hospitality functions and so on.

It also means being willing to keep it going for several years at least. The longer you stay with your sponsorship, the better the results you can expect—and the better, incidentally, for the event too. If its name chops and changes from one year to the next, its image will become confused and tarnished. Then its value as a sponsorship property will drop.

Are you prepared for a beyond-money commitment like that? If not, I'd frankly advise you to give sponsorships a miss. And if you are, there's still one more question to ask. Will your key staff be as enthusiastic about your sponsorship proposal as you are? Without their wholehearted support, you have a problem. They're the ones who have to attend your sponsored events—almost always in their own time—and rub shoulders with your clients and other VIPs. If your people are lukewarm about the event, their lack of enthusiasm will almost certainly communicate itself. So be sure to take your top people's nature and interests into account when you choose your sponsorship.

If they're bronzed outdoor types, they may be fish out of water at the ballet. Or, of course, they may be right at home there. The point is—be sure your key people are comfortable with whatever it is you're planning to sponsor. You need their dedication to the project as well as your own.

Sports: where the big dollars go

In Europe and the USA, according to a *B&T* magazine estimate, around 10% of all marketing budgets are channelled into sports sponsorships. In Australia, by contrast, the figure is about 5%. So while we have a long way to go to catch the northern hemisphere in this regard, the money spent here on sports sponsorships is still quite substantial. Here and abroad, in fact, sports are where the big sponsorship dollars go. The success stories show how well the approach can work—when all the essential factors we looked at a moment ago are in place.

Ford courts its customers

Back in 1985, Ford Australia became exclusive sponsor of the Australian Open tennis tournament. It was an ideal choice. The wide appeal of tennis matched the wide appeal of the Ford product range. The sponsorship offered maximum exposure of the Ford name at the event, and on national and worldwide TV. It opened up 'rubbing shoulders' opportunities in courtside boxes. It was tightly integrated with Ford's total promotional programme.

And it worked so well that Ford recently renewed the sponsorship through to the end of 1995—in a deal estimated by B&T magazine to be worth some $10 million.[2]

The sponsorship goes well beyond the Australian Open, too. It also provides funds for the satellite tournament circuit for younger players—a canny move that not only encourages the up and comers, but keeps the Ford name well and truly before them as they near car-buying age.

Local football too

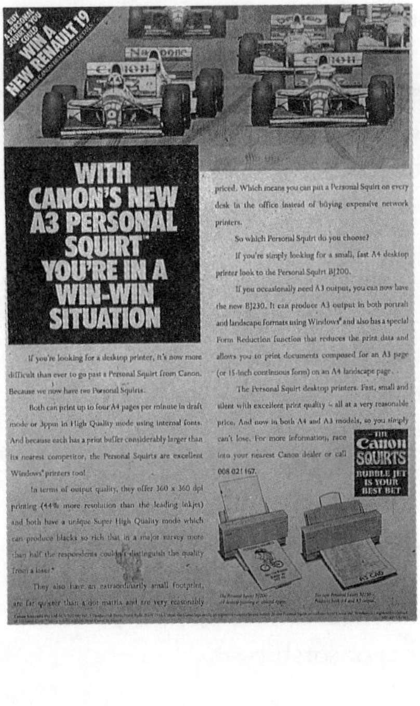

Interestingly, Ford sponsors another sport besides major tennis. In a scenario reminiscent of our mythical suburban electrical retailer, the automotive giant also supports its local Geelong Football Club—and has done so for nearly 30 years. It's a logical association, according to a senior Ford executive. The company is Geelong's largest employer. The sponsorship strengthens its links with the local community, and it ensures that the company is seen as a 'good bloke' on its local turf.

Success in technology sells. Canon capitalise on their prowess on the race track to promote sales in the office.
Courtesy of Canon Australia Pty Ltd

CUB: international and local

Like Ford, Carlton & United Breweries sponsors not only major national sporting events—the Melbourne Cup, the Adelaide Grand Prix and the Australian Football League—but supports local community sports as well.

The sponsorships, however, are not thrown around willy-nilly. Each has a carefully researched purpose, and targets an audience compatible with CUB products. The Melbourne Cup, for instance, screens in 35 countries, while the Adelaide Grand Prix has a worldwide TV audience of 600–650 million people. The company believes that sponsoring both events has played an important part in making Foster's an international drink.

Checking results through research

Nevertheless, CUB is not prepared to maintain sponsorships without making every effort to check their effectiveness. It is currently conducting extensive market research aimed at establishing which parts of the programme are working and which ones aren't. Those in the first category will be maintained and strengthened. Those in the second will be relinquished. In my view, that is the professional and responsible way to conduct a sponsorship programme. Like any other promotional activity, sponsorships that don't provide a return waste your money. It's as simple as that.

Targeting women

One way to get good results from sponsorships is to target your audience accurately. Johnson & Johnson have done that very cleverly for their range of sanitary protection products. They sponsor the annual netball World Series and a school netball education programme. The players are aged 12 to 35—the exact target market for the products. So the sponsorship keeps the product well and truly before the primary users—and does so from an early age, with the possibility of creating lifelong brand loyalty.

In the USA, Tide detergent targeted its female audience in a particularly imaginative way—through a racing car sponsorship.

On the face of it, that seems a strange decision. Motor racing is a very masculine type of activity. All the other car racing sponsors were male-oriented products like beer, motor oil and men's clothes. And surveys showed that 59% of the TV viewing audience were men. To Tide's sponsorship planners, however, that meant that 41% of the audience were women—and no-one else was speaking to them at all. So Tide filled the gap, with a product sponsorship that millions of women saw and identified with throughout the car racing season.

Two-level sponsorships

Here in Australia, Mitsubishi Motors has added an interesting twist to sports sponsorship. The car giant is putting around $3 million a year into sponsoring not just a sport but the telecasts of major sporting events. Its traditional sponsorship dollars go to the National Basketball League. And they're substantial enough to give Mitsubishi naming rights to this core dimension of a fast-growing sport.

In addition, however, Mitsubishi sponsors telecasts of AFL (Australian Rules) and Rugby League matches in all mainland capital cities. On those occasions, while its name doesn't appear on players' clothes or signs around the ground, it does come up regularly in the commercial breaks. It also features in a sponsorship acknowledgment at either end of the telecast. So for TV viewers at least, the link between Mitsubishi and the sporting event is still strong.

Does this two-level approach give Mitsubishi the best of both worlds—the 'good bloke' image of helping basketball to grow and develop, plus the harder-sell thrust of associating their advertising with key sporting events? Perhaps, if the car maker's sales results are any guide. For the first four months of 1993, they soared 19.2% above those achieved in the same period in 1992.

Louis Vuitton goes to the races

In the late 1980s, luxury luggage manufacturer Louis Vuitton entered the Australian market as a virtual unknown. Four years later, it was a household name among its affluent customers. And the company attributes its massive gains in awareness to sponsorship.

Its first step was to put its money on the horses—not, I hasten to add, through the TAB or the bookies, but as sponsors of one of the biggest events in Australia's racing calendar. The $301 000 Louis Vuitton Mackinnon Stakes is run at Melbourne's Flemington Racecourse on Victoria Derby Day, during Melbourne Cup week in November.

'This sponsorship is a major activity in our marketing programme,' says Louis Vuitton's Australian chief executive, Julia King. 'It continues the company's tradition of support for cultural events, including sporting events such as the Grand Prix de Paris, and the arts worldwide.'[3]

As well as horse racing in Melbourne and Brisbane, Louis Vuitton Australia has sponsored several art exhibitions in the eastern states. More on those later in this chapter.

Small can be beautiful

So far, our sports sponsorship examples have involved giant multinational companies. Are there success stories involving the little people—our electrical retailer and others not much larger?

There are.

The hero of one such story was a little US popcorn manufacturer called Smartfoods, Inc. The company had virtually no money for advertising. So in a move that added new meaning to its name, the company used what money it had to sponsor local ski, windsurfing and bike teams. Each of these teams dressed in Smartfoods clothing and gave away some 6000 samples at their various events.

In just five years, Smartfoods sales leapt from $35 000 to $20 million. That, I think, is a classic example of what well-thought-out, well-targeted sports sponsorships can do.

Sponsorships plus

Another way of getting top results from your sponsorships is to combine them with something else.

Shell did that in Australia in 1992. As a sponsor of the Australian Olympic Team, they invited customers to buy a $2 sticker at any Shell station. The money went to the Olympic Team, and the buyer's name went into a sweepstake draw. The prize? A trip for two to the Games in Barcelona. This device focused consumer attention on the sponsorship, enhanced Shell's 'good blokes' image—and gave the consumer a chance to win an extremely attractive prize. It made the most of the sponsorship in a simple yet highly creative way.

In upstate New York, Kodak used the 'sponsorship plus' technique to turn what looked like a pretty mundane sponsorship into a winner. The film giant had agreed to sponsor the Rochester Pro Bowling event—but the Kodak people knew they wouldn't get vastly increased sales from a little Kodak mention in event advertising and signs at the alley. So they added two other elements to the promotion. Calling the whole thing 'Pin Money from Kodak', they offered every purchaser of two rolls of film a $2 rebate and two free games of bowling. That gave both the event and Kodak a giant boost in exposure. It also gave the customers two very definite benefits. The result: while the sponsorship and the promotion were on, Kodak's regional film sales exceeded the average for the period by a remarkable 267 000 rolls.

That's an example of building on a sponsorship to create an even more effective promotion. And it well illustrates a point made by leading sports sponsorship marketer Bob Pritchard.

Success through sponsorship doesn't just happen. You have to make the sponsorship work for you.[4]

A widening scene

Kodak's support of the bowling tournament illustrates another trend in sports sponsorships. The sponsorship dollars have traditionally gone to major sports like football, tennis, cricket, golf and car racing, because of their widespread appeal and huge media coverage. But today the scene is becoming much more diverse. What used to be thought of as minor sports are actively seeking sponsors through specialist sports marketing agencies. They know they need the money and the commitment of powerful backers to grow and develop. In the process, some are growing rapidly in prominence and popular appeal.

Basketball is Australia's most spectacular recent example. Now widely featured on television, it is catching the imagination of a rapidly growing public, both male and female—a point not lost on Mitsubishi Motors, who as we saw earlier are now sponsoring it. In the summer, the unlikely sport of beach volleyball is now snapping at basketball's heels, thanks to sponsorship from Diet Pepsi and Nescafé. Other sports like baseball, table tennis and squash are still in the hoping stage. And I think there are real sponsorship opportunities in some of these so-called 'minor' or new sports.

By getting in with one on the ground floor, you could well grow with it—and benefit in an economical way from its increasing popularity.

Sports sponsorship works best when your product has an obvious link with the game being played. Examples come readily to mind: tennis shoes for tennis tournaments, The NSW State Lotteries Soccer Pools' sponsorship of soccer on SBS-TV, Suntan lotion for surf carnivals. And lots more.

But what if your product has no obvious sporting links? The answer may lie in research that strives to match target markets with the followers of a range of sports.

Pioneered in Australia, the research is designed to help companies identify the sports that appeal to their particular customers. It also seeks to find out just how the fans of a certain sport enjoy it—whether they play it, read about it, watch it on TV, go to the ground or whatever. The results can be very helpful indeed.

For example, one early research project by AGB Research revealed that beer drinkers in Australia tend to follow cricket, tennis, rugby league, Australian rules, fishing and golf. What's more, 70% of them stay home to watch rugby league on TV—but 66% go to the ground to watch cricket. The implications: beer manufacturers should sponsor the sports listed rather than others. And posters and promotions at the ground could work better for them at cricket matches than at league games.

The ultimate sports sponsorship

The ultimate in sophisticated sports sponsorship is, of course, the Olympic Games. They're watched and read about by hundreds of millions, all over the world. And today, with staging costs soaring into the billions, sponsorship is vital if the Games are to be held at all. The International Olympic Federation is well aware of that fact, and it acts accordingly.

Years before each Games, it begins to promote the sponsorship opportunities heavily around the world. Using beautifully produced brochures and sophisticated marketing techniques, it outlines the array of benefits sponsors will receive. And they really are quite impressive.

First, there's permission to use the world-famous Olympic five-rings symbol in your advertising, with all its associations of integrity and achievement. Then there's the right to call yourself an 'Official Sponsor' of the Olympics. There are also several significant marketing opportunities, such as advertising space in official IOC publications. The chance to be featured in IOC TV and film productions. Access to exclusive official merchandise and premiums for use in your own promotions.

Plus, of course, complete product exclusivity.

See the conquering hero . . .

Above all, the Olympics can put your product name on worldwide TV, where it's seen by millions and basks in the reflected glory of the Olympic athletes. Think about that, and you can understand why a certain Australian Prime Minister loved to be seen with sporting stars—the winners, anyway—in their moments of triumph.

If nothing else, he understood the value of being seen as a 'good bloke'. And if you became an Olympic sponsor at Atlanta or in the big build-up to the Sydney 2000 Olympics, millions of people would see you—or your company—in the same way.

A morale booster

Sponsoring an event like the Olympics can also bring you big dividends in the employee relations field. The 3M Company, a worldwide Olympic sponsor in 1988 and 1992, encourages its staff to take part in Games fundraising, to help Australia's athletes in their final training. This acts as a morale booster, by linking 3M's far-flung staff in a common purpose. The energy and enthusiasm it unleashes and the teamwork it promotes spill over into the employees' everyday work. And their feelings toward the company are warmed. The benefits to 3M are many and obvious.

Over its long association with The Games, 3M's Olympic sponsorship has been directed at key business decision makers. For the Seoul Olympics, 3M offered dealers and distributors the benefits of stocking 3M brand advertised products which carried the endorsement of the Olympic symbol—plus a chance to go to the Games, if they reached volume targets.
Courtesy of 3M Australia Pty Ltd

David Wylie, director of 3M's Olympic sponsorship programme, commented, '3M and the Olympic movement are a natural alliance. Both are global in their scope. Both strive for competitive excellence. That synergy was the key to our successful worldwide sponsorship in 1988 and 1992, which helped to build our company by increasing the awareness and favourable response to 3M brands and products, our people and our services.

'The Olympic commitment to competitive excellence—to go faster, stronger and higher—is a philosophy we share at 3M. Using our corporate positioning of "In-novation working for you", a comprehensive advertising campaign, harmonised with public relations, sale promotion and other marketing activities, crossed every 3M division.

The result was a campaign that united our employees, business partners, customers and end users as part of the "Winning Combination".'

Shoulder-rubbing par excellence

One of the best perks of Olympic sponsorship is priority access to first grade tickets and accommodation. That certainly opens up some of the most prestigious 'rubbing shoulders' opportunities in the world. If you can't rub shoulders creatively at the Olympics, you can't rub them anywhere.

There's another 'good bloke' benefit of sponsoring an event like the Olympics, too. You can share the warm inner glow with your customers. Telling them that a percentage of their purchase money helps the national Olympic team can make them feel part of the event. The 3M Company goes even further and invites its best customers, worldwide, to be its guests at the Games. However you do it, involving your customers in Olympic fever can be a powerful marketing ploy. It not only makes your customers feel good—it tends to associate you, in their eyes, with the pinnacle of endeavour and achievement.

Which is a pretty good image to have.

From de Castella to Domingo

But perhaps your product appeals to a public more at home in the concert hall than the sports stadium. If so, a wide range of artistic sponsorship opportunities is open to you—and many astute Australian companies are already taking advantage of them. Some, in fact, have found artistic sponsorships the ideal answer to their marketing problems.

Epson Computers and Printers are one. When Epson was new in Australia, it had to convince the PC market that it was here to stay. It also had to establish a high profile to help it break into the corporate PC market and establish solid credentials there.

Sponsoring the Sydney Symphony Orchestra turned out to be an excellent way to achieve all those aims. The venture has been so successful for Epson that the company is now the orchestra's major sponsor. As such, it enjoys many benefits. Chief among these are naming rights (the

Epson Master and the Epson Mozart Master Series are examples). The Epson name also appears on SSO programmes and brochures, and in every advertisement, article and media review. The company's banners hang in the foyers on concert nights. And the company gets complimentary tickets—which it uses to the full on 'rubbing shoulders' occasions.

A creative match

Another Sydney Symphony Orchestra sponsor, the State Bank, has creatively matched its sponsorship to its marketing goals. It sponsors the SSO's regional touring programme. This ties in perfectly with the State Bank's far-flung branch network. And it puts local branch managers into the 'rubbing shoulders' business, because they get special entertainment privileges when the orchestra is in town.

Sydney? Not us

In Melbourne, a law firm sponsored the Melbourne Symphony Orchestra to help overcome a crippling handicap—the perception that it was basically a Sydney firm. Its sponsorship package included the opportunity to entertain clients at a special evening's performance. The orchestra turned on complimentary drinks at interval, a superb supper and the chance to meet and mingle with the artists. This proved to be a memorable night indeed. Besides the sheer enjoyment of it, much productive rubbing of shoulders took place among company personnel and guests alike.

Racing into the arts

We noted previously that Louis Vuitton, the prestige luggage manufacturer, has put its sponsorship money on horse racing in a big way. But in a move that reflects the quality and appeal of its products, the company has also sponsored several important art exhibitions. These include the 'Suleyman the Magnificent' exhibition in NSW and Victoria, the 'Magic of the Paris Opera—Three Hundred Years of French Style' at the Art Gallery of NSW, and the 'Toulouse Lautrec' exhibition at the Queensland Art Gallery and the National Gallery of Victoria.

'Although Australia may be in the throes of recession,' chief executive Julia King commented, 'business has rarely been brighter as consumers with cash embraced known brand names and the solid values of quality.'[5]

Louis Vuitton has achieved remarkable gains in awareness through sponsorships. And these have been matched by something even more important—consistent sales increases. When that happens, you know the sponsorships have been extremely worthwhile.

A family affair

Mitsubishi Motors is another company whose sponsorships extend from sport to the arts. We looked earlier at its involvement with basketball and sports telecasts. Over in Adelaide, the motoring giant is also a major sponsor of the Adelaide Symphony Orchestra's family concerts. Its aim is to link the 'quality' of the orchestra with its cars. And it specifically targeted the family concerts for a match-the-market reason—its cars are largely designed for the family market.

These sponsorships didn't just fall into the Symphony Orchestras' laps. They marketed themselves vigorously and well to potential sponsors. Sydney's handsome brochure promised each sponsor 'an individually designed and serviced package of benefits tailored to match its particular Corporate and Marketing objectives . . . There are many varied sponsorship opportunities. One of them will suit your business.'

This commercial awareness is in marked contrast to some areas of the artistic world, where the benefits of sponsorship have yet to be appreciated. A glaring example in my experience was that of a stage director who refused to have a potential sponsor's pack on a table during a key scene—even though the sponsor's money could well have determined whether the production proceeded or not.

Move over, Mr Royce . . .

Sometimes, artistic sponsorships enable a company to be a 'good bloke' to its customers in a very practical way—by offering them a rare and sought-after benefit. In one recent Sydney case, the benefit was not only rare. It couldn't be obtained otherwise for love or money.

For many years, as regular patrons knew to their cost, you just couldn't park at Sydney's world-famous Opera House. Incredibly, although the place was (and is) an internationally publicised symbol of Australia, patrons had to jostle for parking in crowded city streets, compete for spaces in small nearby parking stations—or park in a larger one some kilometres away, and ride to the Opera House by bus. Even today, it's a good 10 minutes walk from the new Opera House car park to the entertainment halls.

The only parking within the Opera House itself is for senior management, some performers and a handful of mega-VIPs. Members of the general public have no chance whatsoever of parking in the hallowed grounds.

Unless they happen to drive a Toyota Lexus.

Part of Toyota's sponsorship deal with the Opera House is that people who own their top-of-the-range vehicle can indeed park there. And not only that—they are shown to undercover parking places right opposite the main stairs. An Opera House representative then greets them, and escorts them all the way to their seats—while drivers of lesser breeds like Rolls-Royces, BMWs, Mercedes and Porsches are searching for places in parking stations, and preparing themselves for a brisk walk.

Giving your customers such VIP status is what I call a stylish benefit. And Toyota can offer it only because of their sponsorship.

Opportunities in science

It's a far cry from Domingo treading the Opera House boards to white-coated boffins pottering around in scientific laboratories. Yet the field of science provides smart companies with many good product-linked sponsorship opportunities.

Pharmaceutical giant Burroughs Wellcome, for instance, sponsored the first Chair of Pharmacology in Australia at the University of Western Australia. They also give a wide range of research grants to Australian medical establishments, for such tasks as antibodies research and the study of how toxic substances damage cells.

Such activities, when discreetly publicised, help to present the company as one deeply involved in medical research. And that image certainly can't hurt the sales of its pharmaceutical products.

Sydney's Powerhouse Museum lies on the border between science and entertainment. So it's not surprising that its sponsors come from both the technical and general product areas. Here, aeronautical giants such as Boeing, Northrop, McDonnell Douglas and Rockwell International mingle as co-sponsors with Coca-Cola, Coles Myer, Greater Union and other general consumer-oriented marketers. It's all part of the complex marketing process that makes us feel at ease with airlines operating Boeing 747s and McDonnell Douglas DC10s. And leads us to order a Coke when we're settled on board.

Last but not least

Last but by no means least of the categories is that of the good cause. And here, image-boosting sponsorship opportunities abound. Among them is the chance for local companies, large and small, to show a commitment to the local community. Nor do they need an obvious product link to do so. For example, the restoration of the Sir Joseph Banks Pleasure Gardens brought large sponsorship dollars from local giants ICI and Kellogg®, plus lesser amounts from small local businesses.

On Sydney's northern beaches, Apple Computers sponsored a local surf lifesaving club. There was no obvious link between the two, apart from the geographical one. The same be-seen-locally-as-a-good-bloke principle leads Ford to sponsor its local Geelong Football Club, as we saw earlier. And a development of the principle has seen the appearance of planter boxes and other beautification items, each bearing the name of the local sponsor, on Sydney railway stations.

Good causes are also plentiful beyond the local level. McDonald's sponsor parents' accommodation at the Children's Hospital—not only a 'good bloke' activity but a natural link, because children make up the bulk of McDonald's customers.

Back to the wild

As conservation issues move further into the spotlight, they are bringing more and more corporate sponsors with them. And both the companies and Australia's endangered wild creatures are feeling the benefits.

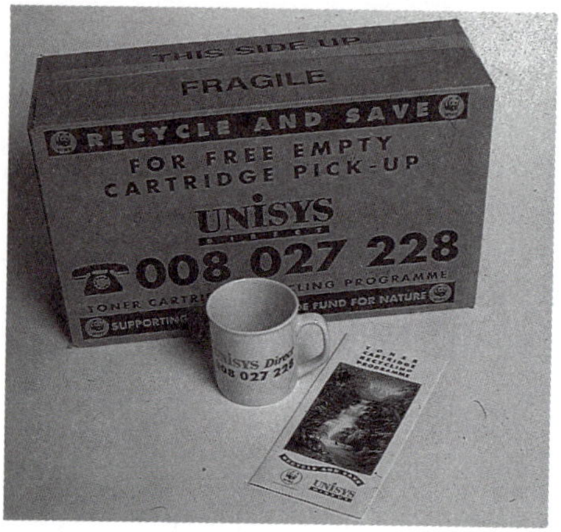

Unisys wished to promote recycling of their laser printer cartridges. No better endorsement than the World Wide Fund for Nature. The bonus for office users—a FREE World Wildlife Unisys Direct coffee beaker for each laser printer cartridge recycled.
Courtesy of Unisys Australia Limited

The orange-bellied parrot, for instance, lives more comfortably in Tasmania, Victoria and South Australia because ICI Australia is helping the World Wide Fund for Nature to implement a conservation plan for it. Westpac is sponsoring research into the ranges and status of Australia's rarest birds. And in the outback, the bilby and the numbat have a better chance of survival—now that New World Properties Pty Ltd are helping the World Wide Fund for Nature to set up control areas where the animals can repopulate.

The World Wide Fund for Nature, Australia, incidentally, is another of the groups actively seeking to woo corporate sponsors. In a well-produced promotional brochure, it points out that sponsorship of conservation activities can bring a host of benefits to the sponsor. Among these, it lists increased corporate awareness, strengthened brand loyalty, improved community relations and added credibility for new product launches.

A vital proviso

In all sponsorship activities, it is important to protect the integrity of the activity being supported. If it is cheapened or its identity threatened, the sponsorship could rebound on the sponsor's head.

The Melbourne Cup has been a cherished Australian institution for decades. Many people feel that calling it the Foster's Melbourne Cup undermines its traditional identity. Will Foster's arouse resentment in some parts of the community through its sponsorship? The jury is still out on that one.

Medieval trend-setters

Probably, neither Pope Julius II nor Lorenzo de Medici realised they were setting a trend when they sponsored Michelangelo's Sistine Chapel ceiling and Botticelli's Birth of Venus respectively. Your sponsorship may or may not help to create an enduring masterpiece.

But it can certainly help to beautify your bottom line.

Your sponsorship checklist

You may, for reasons of personal interest, be very keen to sponsor a certain activity or event. Or you may be under pressure to do so from a persuasive promoter. In either case, consult this checklist before you act.

1. Are you clear on your sponsorship objectives?
2. Does the activity or event have a link with your product?
3. Is the public perception of it a positive one?
4. Is it watched, attended, shared in or enjoyed by your target market?
5. Will your sponsorship raise your image in their eyes?
6. Is the activity or event free of close identification with a previous sponsor?
7. Will it create good 'rubbing shoulders' opportunities for you?
8. Can you measure its results?
9. Will it give you tangible benefits, such as naming rights, programme advertising, on-site displays or merchandise?
10. Will it have PR possibilities that reach beyond the immediate audience into your target market?
11. Will it be a natural extension to your main advertising and promotional activities?
12. Are you prepared to commit yourself to it for a considerable period of time?
13. Are you prepared to put a great deal of effort as well as money into it?
14. Will your key personnel commit themselves to it enthusiastically?
15. If you're not sole or main sponsor, can you get your money's worth from your participation?

16. Is its cost within your budget?

If the answers are positive, the project is worth serious consideration. Work out a way to measure its results if you can—but even if you can't, they could be quite considerable in the long term.

Notes

1. Allen Konopachi, Harvard University, 'Are You Selling in the Right Hemisphere?', *Industrial Marketing*, 1982, pp. 38–39.
2. 'Sports Sponsorship', feature, 'Sponsors Seek Top Performers' by Chris Pearson, *B&T*, 9 August 1991.
3. Julia King, quoted in article by Michael Lynch, 'Louis Vuitton to back the Horses', Marketing Section, *Financial Review*, November 1992.
4. 'Gambling on Sports Sponsorship', by Bob Pritchard, *Marketing Magazine*, August 1991.
5. AGB Australian Research, quoted in article by Chris Pearson, 'Sponsors Seek Top Performers', *B&T*, 9 August, 1991.
6. Julia King, op. cit.

14 CHAPTER

Interactive Media, Offer-Driven Advertising and PR

One very effective way to boost sales and build brand identity is to give your promotion a media dimension—and to strive for total integration of your message across all the media you use.

The first step to success in that process, of course, is to choose the right media for your product and purpose. Doing that to good effect calls for a sound understanding of the capabilities of each medium, and how they can best be integrated for maximum impact.

You may well have an excellent idea of today's media options and how they work. But most of us aren't yet as familiar with the new electronic media that are about to join them.

These new developments will revolutionise our industry. Some, indeed, will revolutionise society at large. Their impact will be enormous—at least as great as the introduction of television. What's more, they're not decades away. Most are just around the corner. And if we don't start understanding them quickly, we'll soon be one with the dodo whose sad fate we contemplated in an earlier chapter.

So before we look at some very imaginative uses of today's media, let's take an overview of those waiting in the wings—or in some cases, available right now if we recognise their potenial.

First among the latter is the fax machine—the 'how-did-we-ever-do-without-it?' bundle of ingenuity that now sits in all our company offices.

Faxes: high response, high impact

Today, the fax is becoming an increasingly attractive business-to-business direct response medium. We first used it to receive responses from direct mail promotions. We sent out in-bound Fast Action Fax Response forms in mailing packs for our information technology clients. We were fascinated to see that over 60% of our responses came through the fax, rather than the telephone or the mail.

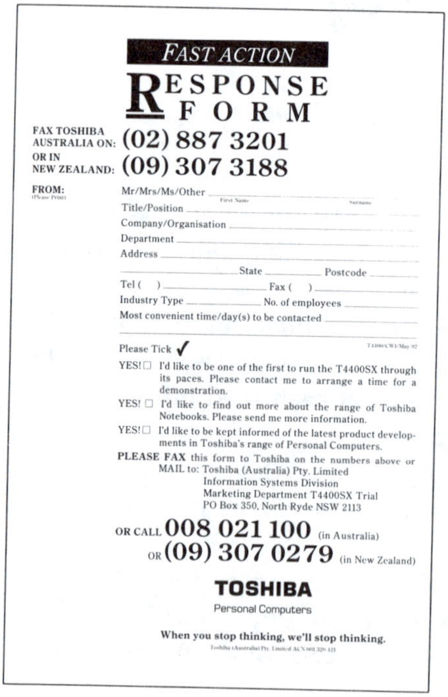

React first via fax or phone for a 'test drive' of the new T4400SX.
Courtesy Toshiba Information Systems

As an outbound direct response medium, the fax can sometimes make even more impact than a direct mail shot. Our client Unisys Direct has used outbound faxes with great success. The secret, we've learned, is to have a clear offer that delivers a recognisable benefit on a well-known product—or at least on one featured in their catalogues. Unisys also programme their faxes to go out at night, when lower rates make the medium even more cost effective.

A friend of mine has discovered another example of the fax's communication powers. He uses it to chase payment on his overdue invoices. He writes 'strictly confidential' boldly and prominently on his faxed appeals for payment. This, he says, ensures they will be read by the widest possible audience. He tells me the response to his debt collection activities has improved dramatically!

The interactive revolution

Even more revolutionary in their potential than faxes are the various rapidly-approaching forms of interactive television. These, of course, will not just be another media option. They will radically alter the relationships between consumers, the media and the advertiser. In fact, as I observed earlier, they could well change all our lives to quite a mind-blowing degree.

In the USA, EON's TV Answer came on line in 1993. This technique leads the trend towards automated ordering systems with automatic data-capture capabilities. TV Answer provides users with a black box, programmed with their demographics and financial information. They can use it to order a product they see advertised on TV, without even involving their credit cards. Their response is automatically recorded, processed and billed directly to them. Millions of transactions per hour can happen without clogging the telephone lines.

Interactive game, set and match

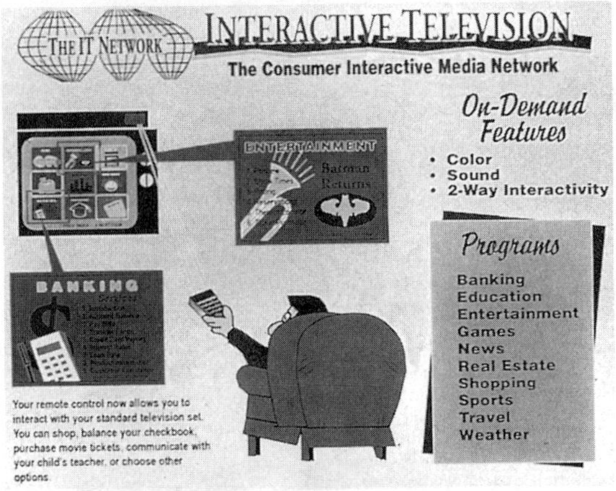

Now you're in control of what you want to watch, when you want to watch it.
Courtesy of The IT Network

Gene Bylinsky in *Fortune* magazine reported that Interactive Network Inc., a public company in Mountain View, California, has a system in use today. He reported that the company has deliberately chosen games and sports as a wedge into the much larger business of information delivery.[1] Those committed to the medium are heavyweights—the original investors include GE's NBC, United Artists and A. C. Neilsen.

The technology relies heavily on digital data processing. In a control room, specialists called 'data jockeys' analyse live and prerecorded TV shows. The trick to making the process interactive is to supply information—the choices for a basketball star's next move, for example—to subscribers at just the right moment, precisely synchronised with the events on the TV screen.

The data jockeys transmit the data to nearby FM radio stations, which relay the signal to subscribers over an unused segment of the FM bandwidth. At the rate of 9600 bits per second, the data pours into a portable $199 control unit that looks much like a laptop computer. During a telecast of, say, a basketball game, the data jockeys supply play calls. The viewer makes his or her choice on the control unit and can't change his or her mind after that. If the viewer picks the right play, he or she is rewarded with an instant message on the unit's screen.

At the end of the show, the viewer plugs his telephone jack into the control unit, where the results have been stored. The unit automatically transmits the data to the central computer. A few minutes later, a return

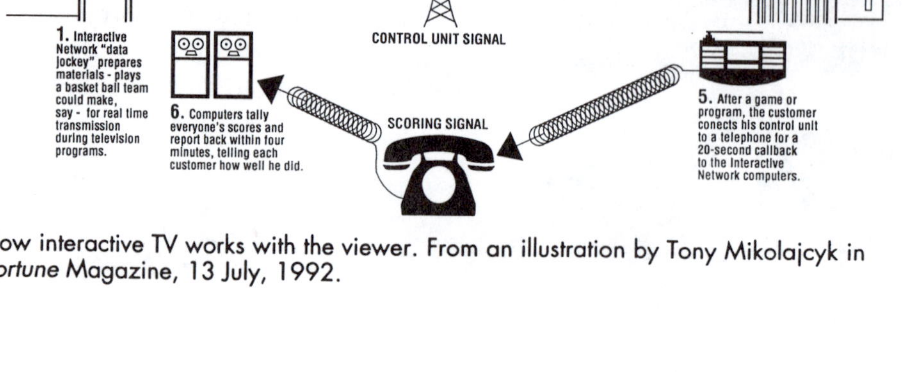

How interactive TV works with the viewer. From an illustration by Tony Mikolajcyk in *Fortune* Magazine, 13 July, 1992.

signal displayed on the unit's screen tells the viewer how he or she ranked against other subscribers watching that game—and if he or she has won, say, a trip to the basketball semi-finals Final Four or a Hawaiian vacation. Cost: $15 a month, plus a few dollars extra to compete against other viewers for prizes.

Worldwide programming

Other techniques related to EON's TV Answer and Interactive Network Inc. are also emerging. One of these is Direct Broadcast Satellite technology (DBS), which is currently undergoing development and testing. US advertising agency Backer Spielvogel Bates Inc., in their BSB Projections 2001 study, said, 'Current advancements in DBS systems have already produced some dramatic results. The most notable feature is in the area of spatial broadcasting.'[2]

In other words, DBS will permit global programming. Integrated with digital compression, it will give the viewer an absolutely overwhelming range of entertainment choices—possibly hundreds of thousands of them by next century. It's the most astounding example yet of the rapidly increasing proliferation and fragmentation of the media. (DBS can cover approximately 15.2% of the world using a single transporter.)

One consequence, of course, will be a viewership split into far more subcategories and subcultures than ever before. This will demand vastly greater creative versatility from advertisers and agencies. Messages will be targeted to individuals, based on their lifestyles and demographics—much as is happening now with direct mail shots built on databases. This will make advertising much more target specific. Advertising waste will be minimised or possibly even eliminated.

The system's interactive capabilities will be as advanced as its programming range. Programmers and broadcasters may even be able to poll subscribers individually on their viewing preferences—and allow viewers to select their entertainment in advance on a daily, monthly or yearly basis. The interactive device may well be a combination of TV, personal computer, phone and fax, miniaturised to the size of a modern TV set.

TV Answer beams its message to cell sites. From there the message is distributed locally to each user by fibre optic telephone line/cable.
Courtesy of EON/TV Answer

Just around the corner

Those interactive capabilities, however, don't have to wait for DBS. They can also be brought into the home by a technology that's literally just around the corner.

Fibre optics.

This system can receive messages via the telephone cable, store them until they've been viewed on a PC/TV or even print them out. Its abilities will make it another valuable medium for a wide range of offer-driven sales promotion activities. For example, the consumer will be able to respond to a TV commercial, and have a barcoded coupon printed immediately on the fax component of the interactive device. The coupon will then be redeemable at retail outlets. From now on, obviously, offer-driven consumer promotions and high-tech are inextricably bound together—a process that will become faster and easier still when ordering by phone gives way, as it will in the near future, to ordering by a PC linked to the TV.

Interactive Television Australia already has this technology available. It plans to install interactive TV fibre optic systems in 250 000 Australian homes by 1995. This will enable those households not only to buy advertised goods directly, but to enter competitions and take part in game shows, all without leaving their couches.

The technology has significant financial implications for the television networks. According to the *Australian Financial Review*, Interactive Television Australia believes it can take over a $400 million slice of current direct-response advertising—the kind that now requires people to clip out coupons or use the phone.[3] Personally, I think that is a little optimistic for a new technology that still has to work out how to keep current home telephone lines open during game shows. But it does underline what is certainly an unstoppable trend to easier offer-driven communications and shopping at home.

Optus Communications has also declared its interest in the shop-at-home-by-TV field. Optus has announced that it has established a joint venture with Media Management Holdings to launch a free-to-air home shopping channel. The channel will operate via satellite, with distribution by cable through Optus Networks Pty Ltd. Optus plans to develop the service across Australia and the Asia Pacific region. It recently absorbed Demtel, Australia's largest telephone/TV direct marketing business, and will use Demtel's experience in its expansion phase.

If Optus enters the fray, can Telecom be far behind? The answer is no. Telecom has signed with News Limited and with the Seven and Ten television networks to roll out cable TV and other broad band domestic services.

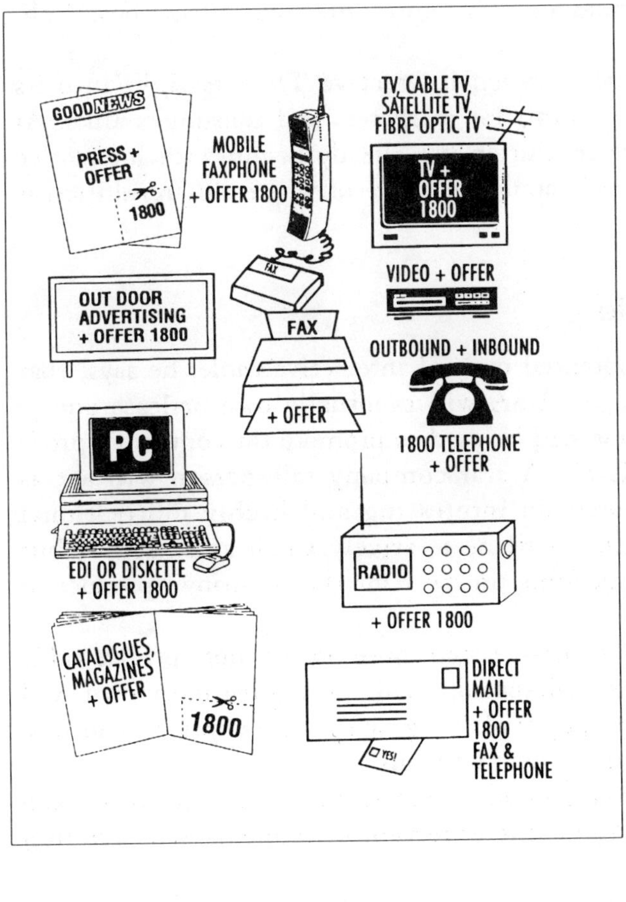

Interactive media hardware, mobile fax phones, mobile computers and electronic data interchange suggests mobility will be the key to the success of the information 'super highway'. Marketers will have to work hard to capture customers with offers enticing them to use their media.

The sky's the limit

Those who enter the interactive field,

whether by cable or fibre optics broadcasting, can look forward to rich pickings. This is confidently pre-dicted by Al Eicoff, chairman of Chicago-based A. Eicoff and Company, now an Ogilvy and Mather subsidiary.

The Eicoff Company specialises in using broadcast media for immediate, measurable results. In his profound book, *Eicoff on Broadcast Direct Marketing*, Eicoff emphasises the remarkable success already being achieved by the infant interactive media. In particular, he says, it can sell much more expensive items than normal direct response TV. Experienced direct marketers limit their direct response TV offers to products with a top price of $39.95. On interactive cable, products priced at over $500 have been sold successfully. The conversion rate from some cable enquiries has been five and six times more profitable than those from normal TV channels.

This again suggests that, when interactive TV gets right into its stride, the sky will be the limit for marketers and consumers alike. Al Eicoff adds, 'This selling revolution has already begun with interactive cable, and direct marketers should be aware of where this revolution is heading.'[4]

Companies on cable

So huge is the selling potential even of interactive cable, he says, that every major company in the USA will eventually own or lease one or more cable channels. These will be used to promote the company's products in depth and in detail. A star company salesperson will act as presenter and offer viewers an interesting and highly motivational presentation. The audience will be relatively small and narrow, but everyone in it will be a genuine prospect for the company's product or service.

A car manufacturer, for instance, will have one or more private cable channels featuring its best salesperson. This persuasive individual will motivate the viewers to buy, by explaining each model's options, features, benefits, prices and advantages over its rivals.

But how will the viewers know where to tune? In a quantum leap away from present practices, the entertainment media will act in a support role to the interactive channels. Viewers will no longer see 15- and 30-second commercials filled with morphing cars, marching bands and dancing girls. Instead, the commercial in entertainment programmes will set forth the basic offer and add, 'For more information, turn to Channel 26'.

When viewers in the market for new cars turn to that channel, they will receive a complete, interesting, informative presentation of product features and benefits—and be able to send for detailed literature just by pressing a button.

Which, of course, will give the car company the viewer's name and address for targeted follow-up. You can see how the whole process will integrate to form an enormously powerful selling tool.

Predictions come true

Al Eicoff made some predictions back in 1988. They sounded like science fiction then—but many are starting to come true. A selection of news items in the Australian advertising trade press on just one day—8 October 1993—echoes several of the predictions made five years earlier:

- Bell Atlantic and other US phone companies will now build advanced fibre optic networks, after the US Federal Court lifted a ban on phone companies owning TV companies. AT&T will sell and carry interactive programming in tests with cable giants Viacom and Time Warner. Bell Atlantic will deliver 384 TV channels into homes within 12 months.
- The Interactive Network in the USA will bring 20 hours of entertainment a day to Chicago from November 1993, and to other major cities by March 1994. Subscribers will have the choice of 100-plus channels. All televised Chicago sporting events will be fully interactive. The cost: $US299 for six months, plus $US15 a month for complete programming. The service will be launched by a 30-minute 'infomercial'.
- Here in Australia, Qantas plans to introduce interactive TV to its first and business class sections. Passengers will be able to respond to duty-free shopping offers with their credit cards, and have the goods delivered to them when they leave the aircraft. They will

also be able to play video games, and perhaps games of chance. Nissan Australia has already signed to become the first major advertiser to take advantage of this new way to reach a wealthy market.

- In London, Rupert Murdoch's Sky Channel has spent £2.5 million to launch its new subscription-based multi-programme package. It has also introduced 24-hour TV shopping on the network. In a hard-sell approach, a presenter offers items at a big discount—which is only available before an on-screen clock ticks its way to zero.

The shopping channel is being provided by Barry Diller's QVC company—Quality, Value and Convenience. QVC is now turning over billions in the USA, and has moved successfully into Mexico and Latin America.

'Information Super Highways'

It's snippets like these, I think, that show just how quickly the interactive revolution is spreading. And for the next few years anyway, fibre optics will spearhead its impact on our lives. While not having DBS's potential for introducing hundreds of thousands of entertainment choices, fibre optics will certainly give us 300 or more TV channels, thanks to a technology called digital compression.

Those channels, moreover, will do far more than multiply viewers' options. They will be 'Information Super Highways', said Rupert Murdoch, chairman and chief executive of News Corporation, in his address to the world in September 1993.

'Choice is only one of the characteristics of the new communications era,' he went on. 'The others are equally extraordinary, converging and interacting. Five of the world's biggest industries—computing, communications, consumer electronics, publishing and entertainment—are converging into one dynamic whole.'

Combining satellite technology with telephone networks, digital 'Information Super Highways' will give consumers fast, simple access to communications, TV shows, movies, sporting events and information services, on an interactive basis. What Mr Murdoch didn't say was how advertisers would be able to use these dynamic new services. Consumers will certainly have to pay for them, as advertisers will be less able to reach such fragmented audiences cost-effectively.

As with DBS, advertising in these personalised media will be fragmented, as we have seen, but extremely targeted and very worthwhile for the niche marketer. But how will marketers who target mass audiences get a look-in? Eventually, they will have to learn how to break their markets into groups and sub-groups. In the short term, however, one option for them may be to help subsidise the service to the consumer, or to sponsor (to the advantage of the customer, not the brand or service) certain programmes or even the leisure activities the 'Information Super Highways' will open up.

Planet-wide forums

These leisure activities may prove to be one of the new technology's most influential contributions to the world. Among them will be planet-wide computer networks of enthusiasts who will come together electronically in 'forums' to discuss their special interests—news, aviation, music, science, social issues, computers themselves and hundreds of others.

Some of these networks already exist in embryonic form. What's more, they're growing rapidly. *Time* magazine estimates that 12 million people in the USA and 20 million worldwide now go home and plug into a home PC system, instead of watching TV.[5] CompuServe Pacific offers subscribers 400 on-line forums and 47 services to help them learn how to use the network—all for an introductory price, including software, of $A5. Internet, the largest US system, is used by 5 million people in 50 countries—and it has begun to accept advertising.

But if these networks are growing rapidly now, they'll really take off when the 'Information Super Highways' come on line. The new technology will add TV and vision components to the present computer bases, and give them a 'virtual reality' dimension that vast numbers of people will find irresistible. I confidently predict that retailers like McDonald's will lead the way in enabling customers to talk to their fellow McDonald's buddies across Australia and around the world.

Clearly, the existence of such sharply defined and rapidly growing special-interest groups creates another opportunity for advertisers and their agencies. But the opportunity won't be maximised by rushing in and blasting away with slick 30-second commercials. The advertising will have to be handled in a style that makes it more inviting, more watchable and more relevant to the group's specialised area of interest.

Enter the 'infomercial'

One way of doing that is already making an appearance in the USA and elsewhere. This is the 'infomercial'—a programme-length TV or radio commercial lasting anything up to 30 minutes or even longer. Great creative skills are obviously needed to fascinate viewers for that long, and give them all kinds of chances to respond through constantly repeated phone numbers and other devices. Equally obviously, skills of a like order are required to handle the ordering, back-up and fulfilment parts of the process.

The content of infomercials made to date has usually come from a brand property, looked at from an oblique direction. Volvo, for instance, ran a successful one on safety, linking a wide coverage of motoring safety aspects with their existing safety positioning offers. Other marketers have taken the stars of once-popular soapies, and created specials where the product is given an equal star billing.

Infomercials aren't for everyone yet, but there's no doubt they'll be used more and more—and not only in the new interactive media.

Back to the present

The potential of interactive TV, fibre optics, shopping-at-home, planet-wide computer networks and all their gee-whiz compatriots is exciting, mind-boggling—and perhaps a little scary. But for the moment, we have to use the media options we have at hand—and, of course, we'll continue to use them long after the newcomers are in full cry.

So now it's back to the present, and on with the job.

Time and again in this book, I've urged you to build promotional offers of any kind around brand values and identity. I know it's not easy. I

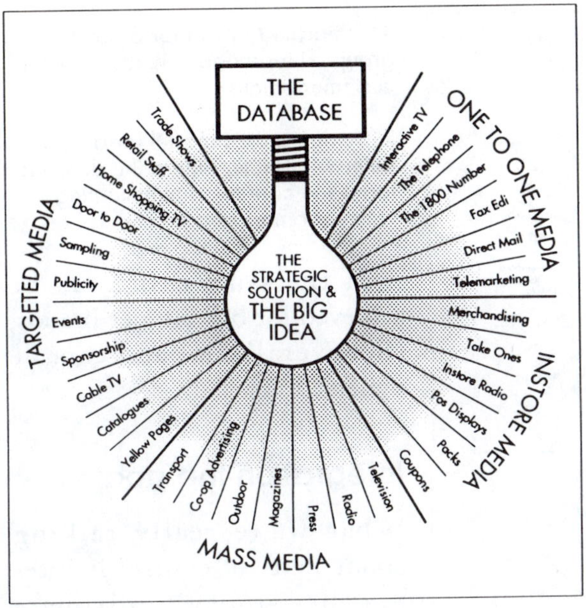

The database is central to knowing the customer as an individual and integrating all your communications across each of your marketing channels.

know it's the ideal rather than the norm. But it can be done. And when it is, you're very likely not only to achieve the immediate sales boost you're seeking, but to strengthen your brand identity for the future.

The simplest and most effective way to build a promotion on brand values is to link it strongly with the brand's media advertising. That sounds easy when you say it quickly. There are, however, two practical difficulties.

First, to break through today's clamour and clutter, an offer-driven sales promotion venture almost inevitably has to go beyond the brand's image. Second, most advertising media propositions are somewhat intangible. It can be very hard indeed to translate them into powerful offer-driven advertising and PR strategies.

Using a well-known presenter or a favourite cartoon character can make it much easier. It becomes easier still if you do what I firmly believe should always be done—deliberately create a mainstream advertising approach that will readily and effectively adapt to below-the-line promotions. Many brands and services don't have the budget for lengthy media campaigns. Their money is maximised if their brand proposition can be compellingly echoed in promotions, competitions and sweepstakes.

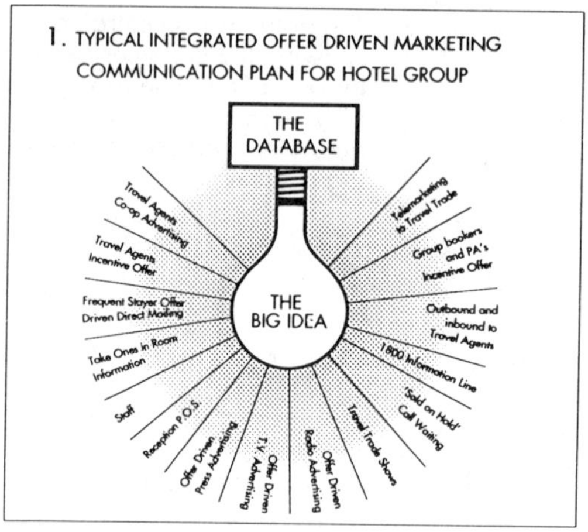

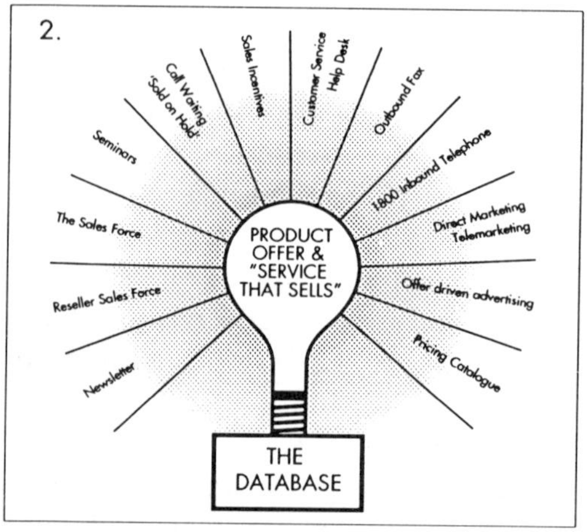

1. Integrated model for a hotel group. The database holds the vital customer details.

2. An integrated model for a computer wholesaler where the database forms the core to communicating with customers and prospects.

If the same thing can be achieved for big budget brands, the overall impact can be massive indeed.

Integration the goal

What we're really talking about here, of course, is integration—today's ultimate marketing goal. Integration means that everything you do, from major TV campaigns to the smallest on-pack promotion, says the same thing in the same way. It builds a consistent brand image and identity, no matter how diverse your actual advertising and promotional activities. Everything fits together, everything is planned and everything builds on and reinforces everything else. No matter where your message appears or the immediate response it seeks, it strengthens and confirms your existing image in your market's mind—because they know at a glance it's from you.

Take the symbol of the light bulb (Figure 1) as a model. From the information contained in the database comes the strategic solution—the 'big idea' that makes a powerful offer based not only on the target market's known wants and preferences, but on the brand proposition and image too. Then the 'big idea' is expressed through every facet of the campaign—obviously, in a form appropriate to each medium but conveying the same offer, the same mood, the same message and, where possible, the same graphics every time.

Few if any campaigns, of course, would have all the components of that ideal model. Figure 2 shows a typical offer-driven integrated marketing plan for a hotel group. Figure 3 shows the same for a computer wholesaler. Basically, it's the same picture—the 'big idea' coming out of the database information, and flowing through into every campaign segment.

Its consistency reinforces the message to trade and consumers alike, no matter which parts of the campaign they see.

Jerry Reitman, vice-president of Leo Burnett, brought integrated direct marketing into that agency in the USA. In an article in *Ad News*, K & D Bond's chairman Ian Kennedy quoted Jerry as saying, 'integrated advertising is a commitment to a common voice. Doing this requires a team that understands the brand, its distinct targets, and the multitude of tools available to reach those targets. And most importantly, they must know how to combine these in ways which are profitable for the client and consistent with the essence of the brand.'[6]

'Tremendous recall'

When you do achieve graphic and verbal integration across a range of media, the net result is 'high impact and tremendous recall of both the ads and the mailings'. So says Ernan Roman, author of *Integrated Direct Marketing.* And he has firm ideas as to how integrated advertising, mailings and telemarketing should be scheduled in a campaign.

'Through testing,' he says, 'we've learned that the mail should hit one week after the ad, that telemarketing should begin within 72 hours of the mailing, that follow-up mailings to a positive respondent should go out within 24 hours, and that a telemarketing call should follow up the second mailing within three days. This scheduling retains awareness and interest. Longer gaps in time erode the possibility for a sale.

'Adjusted for the medium, all the messages speak with one voice. Thus the benefits of the offer are reiterated again and again, whether via print, mail or phone.'[7]

On this sort of schedule, according to Roman, double-digit response in a compressed time frame is achievable—if the integration is strong enough. And as anyone with any experience of direct marketing knows, double-digit responses are extremely high. The chance of achieving them is a powerful motivation indeed for going the integrated way.

Who does the integrating?

However, at this point in time, you'll rarely get a wholehearted commitment to integrated marketing from advertising agencies. Their whole thinking is just too strongly focused on media. Rather, an integrated marketing orientation will come from clients themselves and from the new kind of agencies whose skills are in database manipulation and interactive offer-driven strategic marketing.

MLC enhance their competitive fixed interest offer with a $20 000 bonus offer to investors. The campaign theme is integrated into press advertising and direct mail to prospect investors and investment advisors.
Courtesy of MLC Life

The debate over who should control integrated marketing—the agency or the marketer—surfaced at a recent conference in Chicago. Both parties agreed on the wisdom of the integrated approach, but they stood on opposite sides when discussing who should do the integrating. According to *Ad Age*, Gary Moss, Campbell Soup Company's vice-president of advertising, told the conference, 'I don't believe any advertising agency has the expertise to see the role integrated marketing needs to take'.[8]

Unhappily, I think he's right—at the moment, anyway. Hopefully, some of the brighter

Clever use of a special radio broadcast around selected poster sites extols the virtues of the Forbidden Planet musical. Drivers who pass the site and switch to 9.99 FM hear a sample of the show's lively music—plus the box office 1 800 number they can call to book their seats. Inserts in targeted media offer test drives and other inducements to help lift sales of Toyota's new vehicle. Toyota is the show's major sponsor.
Courtesy of Kevin Jacobsen Productions

people in traditional advertising agencies will soon start thinking outside the square. When they do, they'll realise that media advertising is now just a part of a much greater communication whole—in which integration can create a dynamism and effectiveness beyond the sum of its parts. And at its core you'll find a relational database driving the entire communications package.

It follows that the more dimensions you give your advertising and promotional activities, the greater degree of integration you can achieve. And in my experience, adding a media dimension to a sales promotion or direct marketing event is one of the most effective ways of doing so. It increases not only integration but awareness, interest, response and—most importantly—sales.

Match media to your needs

The exact degree to which that happens, however, depends very much on the kind of media dimension you add. A PR event, for instance, can give you greatly increased product recognition, but rarely an immediate sales surge. Of course, that might not matter. Your most urgent need might not be quick sales as such, but heightened brand awareness—or altered brand perception among your target audience. In those cases, engineering a PR event could be a good way to go.

The kind of event I'm thinking of here is not a sales promotional offer in the strict sense of the word. It doesn't ask you to buy the product or take part in some kind of contest or happening. Rather, it puts the product before you in an excellent and enviable light. It seeks to increase your awareness of it and enhance its image in your mind. But by its very nature, it doesn't urge you to turn your newly-created awareness into buying action.

Giveaways as PR

The most common of these PR events are the ones where a product or service is offered as a free giveaway or as a contest prize. It might be through a nationwide TV game show, a local radio station, a women's magazine or a newspaper. Whatever the medium, the product or service gets considerable exposure and has its selling points well and truly extolled.

CSR create events in shopping malls with the help of The Variety Club and its wonderful stars. *Courtesy of CSR Refined Sugars*

The media themselves often initiate such promotional offers and sell the concept to marketers. A variation of the basic idea involves a contest, in which viewers, listeners or readers are invited to buy the product or service. If they do, they have a chance to win a prize—often one as attractive as a holiday, or even a car. The prize element is normally supplied by another part-sponsor of the promotion, who in turn gets valuable PR for the holiday, product, car or whatever the prize might be.

This variation can increase sales for you, because contestants have to buy your product or service to have a chance to win. In general, however, such PR promotions tend not to generate an immediate sales boost. They happen too far away from the point of purchase and rarely offer the consumer a compelling reason to go and buy the product now. Unlike promotions that take place on or around the pack, they miss the vital motivating 'bridge' between customer and product. But then again, they're very good for raising awareness. So if a media representative suggests one to you, be sure you understand what they can and can't do, and relate that to your immediate needs. Otherwise, you could finish up with a promotional event that does a lot for the radio station or newspaper that initiated it, but very little for you.

Create your own PR event

Of course, you can always look to add a PR dimension to a directly sales-oriented promotional event. We did it with our Variety Club 'Bake a Cake for Variety' promotion for CSR. Eric Laakso, CSR's marketing manager for refined sugar, co-opted Nissan—who as joint sponsors were responsible for assisting with funding the Variety Club's Sunshine Coaches from money raised through the promotion.

Eric convinced them of the benefit of driving a Variety Club bus from Perth to Brisbane, towing a two-metre high birthday cake. Its route included the largest shopping malls in Adelaide, Melbourne and Sydney, and the major country towns in between. The bus was driven by a number of

A new approach for Nescafé, the '$20 000 for a good ideas' promotion encourages talent among young people, to attract sales and acceptability from this difficult–to–target group.
Reproduced with the permission of Societe des Produits Nestlé SA, Vevey, Switzerland, the owners of the registered trade marks Smarties, Polo, Lifesavers and Nescafé

Variety Club stars and personalities, including Tony Hasham, Stuart Wagstaff, Brian Henderson and Jeannie Little. The stars drummed up huge media coverage on regional radio and TV and in local press, as well as their personal appearances in shopping centres across Australia. Meanwhile, country and suburban newspapers were eagerly recording the 'Bake a Cake for Variety' fundraising efforts of their local groups and ladies' auxiliaries.

We estimated that the total PR coverage was worth over $200 000—probably as much as the total budget of the whole promotion.

A giant yawn

Such large-scale media coverage of a promotion, I must emphasise, is not easy to achieve. Your event must be unusual and newsworthy before the media will cover it. You'll normally need some kind of human interest dimension that sets it far apart from the general run of sales promotions. Otherwise, fascinating as the promotion may be to you, it will be a giant yawn to editors everywhere. However, if you do manage to come up with a breakthrough idea, you can look forward to extensive media coverage and a very significant boost in awareness—which, if you handle it correctly, can be obtained from part or all of your target audience, as you choose.

Nescafé: a younger image

A classic example of such a promotion is the Nescafé 'Big Break' Awards, conceived by the company of my ex-partner, Leo Schofield. It has been created to strengthen the perception of Nescafé among younger people, where the brand is relatively weaker. So its aim is to build brand loyalty for the long haul, rather than to achieve quick short-term sales.

The 'Big Break' promotion offers just that—the 'big break' of their lives—to talented young people aged 16–21. When they enter, they describe their dreams of achievement in their particular fields—which might be business, fashion design, music, the theatre, software development, environmental research or just about anything else. The entrants have to convince a panel of expert judges that their idea, project or talent could succeed with some cash support.

The judging panels select what they believe are the eight most promising ventures. Each of the young people concerned is then awarded $20 000 by Nescafé, to help turn the dream into reality.

Nationwide coverage

The promotion is currently an annual event. It is heavily publicised in media advertising, on pack, at point of sale and through PR. But the real pay-off comes when a Commonwealth Government minister announces the winners. Nationwide media coverage follows, propelling the Nescafé brand to centre stage in TV, radio, press and magazines. In particular, it gains huge awareness among younger people—where it is becoming seen as a caring brand that takes a real and practical interest in Australia's youth.

And where it is quietly but surely developing a market that could stay with it for decades.

Spectacular though it is, the 'Big Break' sort of promotion is not for everyone. Its purpose, let me repeat, is not to gain immediate sales but to create warm perceptions of the brand among young people. However, it is possible to come up with a promotional idea as brilliantly original and newsworthy as the 'Big Break'—and link it directly to product sales. Union Carbide demonstrated that back in 1982, with the 'Glad Bag Fashion Awards'.

High-fashion garbage

Now Glad Bags, as you probably know, are plastic garbage bags—one of the lowest-interest product categories imaginable. And at the time, they were being soundly thrashed at the checkout by lower-priced generics. Union Carbide stepped up TV advertising for Glad Bags, with no measurable results. So Rod Larkin, then of Union Carbide, and Roger Maynard's agency went for a really left-field promotional idea—a fashion awards event for 'clothing' made from Glad Bags.

A coup was achieved when they gained the support of the 'Mike Walsh Show', then Australia's top daytime TV programme. Gripped by the sheer originality of the idea, the 'Mike Walsh Show' agreed to promote it heavily. They contributed two weeks of 'teaser' spots, a

20-minute launch segment, daily segments for five weeks totalling 140 minutes, and special coverage in their Melbourne Cup and Miss Australia features. This meant that the 'Glad Bag Fashion Awards' story reached five million people a week through 140 stations for five weeks. In 1982 dollars, that was worth $350 000–$400 000. And the promotion's total budget? Just $22 000.

A staggering 10 000 people sent in entries. Each one used many Glad Bags. Thousands used complete Glad Bag bulk packs. Comedienne Jeannie Little acted as Glad's presenter, giving the promotion another dimension of fun. Fashion parades were held all over Australia. Extensive media coverage was obtained in trade and consumer press. Jeannie was widely interviewed on top radio stations. She even assisted at some sales presentations to major accounts. Imagine the surprised look on the Coles buyer's face when Jeannie turned up with the local 'Glad' state manager for a sales call.

The winning fashions were modelled on the 'Mike Walsh Show' by the reigning Miss Australia and the seven Miss Australia finalists. The prizes of a Ford Meteor car and seven Kriesler colour TV sets were supplied by their manufacturers. The promotion won the Best Low Cost Promotional Award in the 1983 ASPA Awards.

The purpose of the whole promotion was to fight the generics by stressing the quality, value for money and versatility of the extensive Glad Bag range—and it worked. Glad Bag sales showed a dramatic growth at a time when the brand was given no other promotional support of any kind. Significantly increased promotional space was obtained as well.

Advertising: the media dimension you control

When your product needs a prompt and sizeable sales boost, you may come up with something as daringly novel as the 'Glad Bag Fashion Awards'. Then again, you may not. But that's not the end of the world. You

Among the vital ingredients for Family Recipe cakes is an egg. The media chosen to promote the idea of making the cakes was an obvious one, the egg carton. Eggs' high in–home penetration ensured awareness and increased the impact of press advertising and point of sale.
Courtesy of The Uncle Tobys Company Limited

can readily meet your goals with a high-impact promotion that gives people an immediate reason to buy—a price-off, cash-back, sweepstakes or similar venture with strong on-pack, POS or in-store promotion. If you budget to add media support as well, you can look forward to even better results.

But remember this. Unless your promotion is devastatingly original, just sending out press releases about it is most unlikely to get you any column centimetres or air media time. The only way you can guarantee media coverage is to use the media dimension you can control—advertising.

Your advertising might run in press, magazines, radio or TV, depending on your budget and the style and duration of your promotion. But there's no doubt that, if you have everything right at the distribution, stocking and POS levels, media advertising support will increase your promotion's effectiveness. I've often seen sales targets set higher in expectation of a boost from a promotion—and then, handsomely exceeded even further because of advertising. Conversely, I've frequently seen them fall below expectations, when advertising support was weak or non-existent. But, of course, advertising is not of itself a magic path to success. There's no point in pouring money into media unless your POS promotion, stock levels and distribution are all working for you. I'm always surprised at how many otherwise intelligent marketers fall into that trap.

Don't let yourself be among them.

When media is a must

You can get away—mostly—without media support in FMCG (fast-moving consumer goods) promotions. Strong on-pack with POS messages are usually enough to get a satisfactory result. But as with any rule, there are exceptions. If you don't use your pack, you have to use media to get your offer across. Great successes have also been achieved by promotions that use advertising to target children—who then put pressure on mum to go out and buy. This technique has proved particularly effective in promotions for impulse lines.

But if advertising can be an optional extra in on-pack FMCG promotions, it never is in promotions involving services or high ticket items. In those situations, it's a must. Service products in particular have no packs to carry sales messages. Nor do they enjoy the promotional possibilities of a supermarket environment. If you're designing a promotion for a service product, strong media support is the only way you'll get an outstanding response.

That was true even for the 'World's Biggest Offer', as British Airways called their mindboggling post-Gulf War promotion. This huge worldwide venture offered no fewer than 50 000 free trips to London. These could be taken from virtually every country on the British Airways network. Despite the attractiveness of the offer, however, the whole vast promotion would never have succeeded without massive TV and press advertising that pointed consumers to a phone number or a sweepstakes address.

If the 'World's Biggest Offer' needed advertising support to succeed, how much more does yours?

Riding the media wave

Another approach that can be very creative is what I call 'riding the media wave'. It involves taking a current media event and building a promotion around it. A highly successful 1983 promotion by the then NSW Permanent Building Society remains typical of the technique.

The primary aim of this promotion was to obtain 15 000 new children's accounts, with an average of $20 in each. The secondary aim was to encourage the children to develop a savings pattern—so that the total deposits in their accounts would grow to $600 000, or $40 per account, after six months.

'Star Wars' wins a sales victory

To achieve this, the Building Society's agency, then run by my ex-colleague David Sherbon, developed a promotion with a Star Wars theme. As *Return of the Jedi*, the third movie in the Star Wars trilogy, was about to be released at the time, the theme was extremely topical. And it had great appeal to the target audience—children from four to 14.

A 30-second TV commercial featuring Star Wars characters launched the campaign. It was backed by screen advertising in theatres where *Return of the Jedi* was showing. When children opened an account with $20 or more, they received a special Star Wars passbook, a classroom pack of Star Wars items—a pencil sharpener, rubber, ruler, badge and sticker—and a large Star Wars poster for their wall. Then, whenever they made further deposits of $2 or more, they received a sticker of a Star Wars character to go on their poster. In this way, they were encouraged to keep on saving. All Star Wars account holders could also win prizes in special sweepstakes, including movie passes to *Return of the Jedi*. And a highlight was the personal visit to many Building Society branches of Darth Vader himself, armed not with a light sabre but a pen to sign autographs.

The results were nearly as spectacular as the Star Wars movies themselves. Over 20 000 accounts were opened (33.3% above target), with total deposits of $2.3 million (an incredible 283% above target) and an average balance of $70 (75% above target). Riding the media wave paid off handsomely for the NSW Permanent Building Society, on quite a minimal promotional budget.

A media smorgasbord

TV and local press advertising, plus letterbox drops around the branches Darth Vader was visiting, made up the media dimension in that promotion. But, of course, there's a whole smorgasbord of other media you can use too. Press, magazines, radio, direct mail and PR are the main ones. Inbound and outbound telephones and faxes are growing in popularity and as we have seen, the coming interactive media will open up many exciting new possibilities.

Capitalising on this smorgasbord demands the fullest possible exercise of our creative powers. Very often, in fact, offer-driven advertisements, brochures and air media commercials can give you even more scope for creativity than straight product spots. We saw an example back in Chapter 10—the Toshiba multi-media promotion in the UK, undoubtedly one of the most imaginative to appear in recent years.

I think its sheer brilliance earns it another mention here.

The campaign story was that Toshiba TVs are best because they have better 'Thingamybobs' inside. Special 'Thingamybob' cards offering prizes ranging from £20 000 cash to Toshiba TVs to £20 cashbacks were distributed through Toshiba outlets and selected press inserts. The card also gave the appearance times of a Toshiba TV commercial. To find out whether their card was a winner, contestants had to place it against the TV screen while the Toshiba commercial was running. Part of the commercial was a red background. When the card was held against that, the prize details on it could be read. You then knew right away whether you were an instant winner. In a brilliantly original fashion, this promotion achieved enormous synergy between itself and the TV campaign. Deservedly, in my view, it was a huge success.

Continental Cup–a–Soup combines worthwhile prizes and interaction with Sale of the Century, Australia's top rating game show, with entry via Woman's Day, Australia's No 1 women's magazine. *Courtesy of Unilever Australia*

Whistle and you'll get an encore!

Also highly creative, in my modest view, was a radio promotion we did for Encore, a then-new liquor brand. The task was to get awareness and display for Encore in bottle shops. Our solution was a 45-second radio commercial built around Humphrey Bogart's famous last words, 'Just put your lips together and whistle'. The commercial invited customers to go into their bottle shop, and whistle as loudly as they could. Each Encore display had a whistle-sensitive battery-operated sonic key finder attached to its header card. When people whistled, it beeped back—leading customers to the point of sale display and the Encore stand. And if the customer was an inveterate key loser, he or she could get a key finder free by sending in two bottle tops.

Our promotion won the ASPA Gold Award for that year's most creative use of radio.

Continental winter warmer

An outstanding example of Unilever's efforts to boost instant soup sales to take advantage of winter usage was Continental Cup-a-Soup's 'Sale of the Century Game Bonanza'. This broke new ground by being the first commercial sales promotion to appear in conjunction with Sale of the Century.

The popularity of Australia's No. 1 rating game show was teamed with the circulation of Australia's No. 1 weekly women's publication, Woman's Day. Together, they provided maximum reach and frequency to the offer's target audience. The media mix also provided excitement and a Big Idea.

A double-page centre spread was run in Woman's Day for three consecutive weeks. This contained a game card and explained how to play the Continental Cup-a-Soup Sale of the Century Game Bonanza.

Complementing the magazine advertisements was a special television campaign. Using 15 second spots, it urged viewers to watch Sale of the Century, buy the product and play the game.

The prize pool was designed to be appealing and relevant across the brand's target audience of teens through to adults. As well as a seductive $85 000 prize pool, the promotion also contained a second hook mechanic—an attractive $5 000 cash jackpot for consumers who played for five nights running.

To play, entrants had to watch Sale of the Century. When the Continental Cup-a-Soup and Sale of the Century flash appeared on screen, they had to write on their game cards what the three contestants' scores were at that point. To help them, the scores were freeze-framed for 10 seconds.

The prize pool included:

- a family holiday to Disneyland;
- a $5 000 shopping spree;
- the opportunity to "live as a millionaire" for a week;
- a family holiday to Kakadu National Park.

Created by Ogilvy & Mather, the promotion drew 89 000 entries, all of which involved a purchase. The promotion achieved a redemption rate 110% above the average.

An essential element in the campaign's success was close co-operation between The Grundy Organisation, producers of Sale of the Century, and Channel 9. The advertising was placed to coincide with the show. This achieved maximum integration of instore activity, magazine advertising, the TV campaign and publicity—a major factor in reaching the brand's awareness and sales objectives.

I think the Continental Cup-a-Soup campaign had many interesting features. Among them were:

- a strong link with Sale of the Century, Australia's No. 1 game show;
- a strong link with Women's Day, the No. 1 women's publication;
- innovative entry methods via the magazine advertising;
- maximum TV viewer interaction;
- an excellent range of prizes;
- a structure that meant entrants had to purchase the product to participate;
- a "second hook" of a $5 000 cash jackpot;
- powerful reasons for the trade and salesforce to boost stocks and displays;
- a framework that minimised the price factor, to Continental Cup-a-Soup's advantage

Tieing in with the soapies

Recently, another creative new way of using the media for promotions has emerged. Press advertisements or TV commercials invite viewers of popular soapies to watch out for a particular product in the show—and to phone a 0055 (user pays) number when it appears to enter the draw.

Raguletto pasta sauce went this route on Channel 9's 'All Together Now'. When viewers saw a character in the show making a pasta dish, using Raguletto sauce, they had to phone the 0055 number and name the dish. This happened for two weeks in a row. The Raguletto brand was not mentioned in the script at any stage, and the offer was not advertised in either of the two episodes in which the pasta was used. However, a commercial did appear at other times. It featured a character from the show, who explained how the offer worked.

Telecom had a similar promotion in 'E Street' on Channel 10. Viewers had to ring the 0055 (user pays) number when they saw a Phonecard being used. The product was not highlighted in any way, beyond its obvious usefulness in the scene's context. The promotion was held in NSW only, and viewers in other states would not have noticed anything special about the scene. In this case, promotional commercials appeared during the show. One was aired immediately after the scene in which the phonecard was used. But neither the Raguletto nor the Telecom promotion was supported in-store in any way.

Channel 7's 'Home and Away' was used by Arnott's Snack Foods in a slightly more complicated manner. The product packs contained cards with one of 70 entertainment trivia questions. A character from the show casually gave the answer to one question each night. If you had a card with that question on it, you then phoned the 0055 number to enter the draw. This offer was highlighted in 'Home and Away' promotional spots and had its own segment in a commercial break near the end of each night's show.

These three promotions were certainly creative. But is there a downside to this kind of venture? To what extent will viewers see such tie-ins as crass commercial gimmicks that destroy a show's integrity? Time, I imagine, will tell us that.

By promoting mateship and in–pub camaraderie, Tooheys underpin their 'Having A Tooheys Or Two' advertising campaign and sponsorship of the 'Tooheys 1000' popular car endurance race, with a big offer: Win one for yourself and one for your best mate. *Courtesy of Tooheys Limited*

Sponsorship and the media

Few promotional events lend themselves more readily to a media dimension than large-scale short-term sponsorships. Our client, ITT Sheraton Pacific Hotels and Resorts, for example, ran an excellent promotion to get maximum benefit from its sponsorship of the 1992 Australian Olympic team. Its intriguing theme was 'Sleep at a Sheraton, and Wake Up in Barcelona'. The mechanics were simple. Everyone who spent a night at a Sheraton hotel went into a draw to win one of three trips to the Barcelona Olympics, plus 15 five-star Sheraton holidays. Sheraton holidays could also be won by the travel agents who took the bookings and the secretary or assistant who made them.

This integrated promotion was heavily advertised on TV and in leading business magazines. A large part of the budget was devoted to direct mail, including solid targeting of Ansett Golden Wing members. As well, the offer was featured in every Sheraton hotel. Few business travellers in Australia would have escaped the 'good blokes' message of Sheraton Pacific Hotels' Olympic sponsorship—and the chance it offered them of winning very attractive prizes. And as we saw in the last chapter, being seen as a 'good bloke' triggers a warm reaction in the right-hand, or emotional, side of consumers' brains—where 80% of buying decisions are made.

Some other Olympic sponsors followed a similar route. The 3M Company was one, although their 'Win a Trip to the Olympics' promotional effort was directed at the trade through trade media, rather than to the general public. But the intention was the same—to capitalise on their huge top sponsor Olympic involvement through 3M's extensive outdoor and trade communications, with all its potential for enhancing

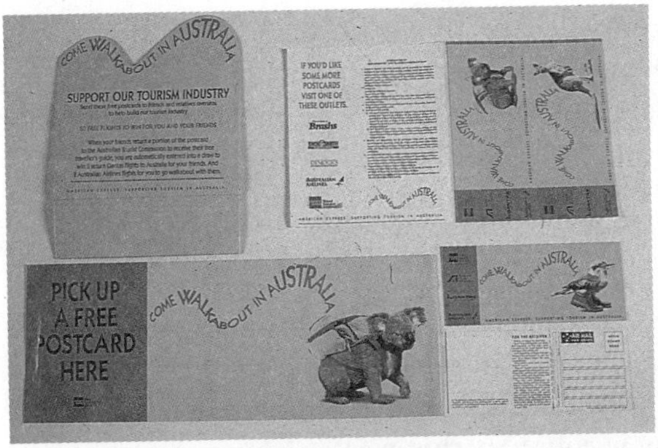

American Express and The Australian Tourist Commission bring tourists to Australia by using TV, press, point-of-sale and free postcards to send to friends overseas. The benefit to the postcard recipients: a chance to win a trip downunder FREE.
Courtesy of Australian Tourist Commission

their image and building future sales. And the media dimension was essential to achieving their goal.

The same principle underlies Toohey's sponsorship of the Toohey's 1000 motor race in Bathurst. The accompanying promotion goes beyond on-pack displays in bottle shops to include outdoor posters, radio and TV. It offers not one but two sports cars—'Win one for yourself and one for your mate'. The media plays a key part in drawing a response to the promotion. Again, the aim is to underpin the advertising theme and to project Toohey's as 'good blokes' whose interests parallel those of the target market.

A boost for Australia

I could go on with examples of promotions strengthened and boosted by a media dimension. But let's just look at one of the biggest held in Australia to date—an immense effort to boost the Australian tourist industry, involving the Australian Tourist Commission, American Express, Qantas and Network 10.

Between them, they have produced five million postcards that highlight the charms of Australia as a tourist destination. The idea is that Australians send the cards to friends and relatives overseas. Then, if the friend or relative returns a cut-off coupon from the card to the Australian Tourist Commission in Sydney, the sender is entered into a prize draw. Moreover, the friend or relative has a chance to win two of 20 Qantas tickets to Australia, plus two tickets to any Qantas domestic destination once they've arrived.

One million postcards were mailed to all American Express members in Australia. A further three million were inserted in newspapers. TV commercials pushed the remainder, while special promotional material on Australia went to 12 million Amex cardholders in the USA, the UK, Germany, Japan, Singapore, Hong Kong, Italy, Taiwan, Malaysia and Canada.

If the campaign boosted tourist figures by just 2%, estimated Tony Thirlwell, then of the Australian Tourist Commission and now of the New South Wales Tourist Authority, an extra 48 000 tourists would come to Australia each year. They would inject $90 million into the community and create 1800 new jobs. So this was an enormous venture indeed, with great potential for Australia. And it was made possible only by its very large media dimension. More and more in modern sales promotion, an old cliche is gaining new validity.

It pays to advertise.

Notes

1. 'Technology to Watch', by Gene Bylinksy, *Fortune* magazine, 13 July 1992.
2. Backer, Spielvogel and Bates, Inc., *Projections 2001*. BSB Inc., 1993.
3. News item, *Australian Financial Review*, 14 September 1993.
4. Al Eicoff, *Eicoff on Broadcast Direct Marketing*, P13, NTC Business Books, Lincolnwood, Chicago, 1988.
5. News item, *Australian Financial Review*, 3 September 1993.
6. Jerry Reitman, quoted by Ian Kennedy in 'Direct Marketers Diary', *Ad News*, 28 January 1993.
7. Ernan Roman, *Integrated Direct Marketing*, McGraw Hill, New York, 1988.
8. Gary Moss, vice president advertising, Campbell Soup Company, quoted in *Advertising Age*, September 1993.

15
CHAPTER

Cause-Related Marketing—A Good Cause Can Help

One of our most basic human drives is the need to feel good about ourselves. So if a sales promotion technique could do that for us, it would obviously be a pretty potent selling tool.

Just such a technique does in fact exist. It's called cause-related marketing. And it takes us further down a previously travelled road—because it's at least a first cousin, if not a full-blown sibling, to the sponsorship technique we probed in Chapter 13. Sponsorship, you will remember, enables a marketer to be seen as a 'good bloke'. And as 80% of a buying decision originates in the emotional, or right-hand, side of our brains, that perception is very often enough on its own to clinch a sale.

Cause-related marketing advances the process by another vital step. It not only garlands a marketer with 'good bloke' laurels. It enables customers to see themselves in the same light—because it allows them to regard themselves, quite legitimately, as significant donors to a worthwhile activity.

Even though they don't have to contribute a single cent towards it.

How buyers become donors

The concept behind cause-related marketing is simple. When people buy the product, the manufacturer donates a small percentage of the purchase price to a particular cause—community, charitable or environmental. It might only be a few cents at a time, but it quickly adds up to a substantial amount of money.

I'm sure you can see why people respond to an idea like that. Most of us would love to give more to deserving causes. Usually, though, in the real world of bills, mortgages and price rises, it just can't be done. Then all of a sudden, along comes a kind, understanding company that makes it possible. Without requiring us to spend an extra cent, they give us the warm inner glow that comes from genuinely helping someone—just by making purchases we would probably have to make anyway. We're strongly impelled to repeat buying, because the more we do so, the better we feel. And as we buy, we build an image of a warm, caring, socially involved company—which, of course, gives us all kinds of right-brain support for our new purchasing patterns.

Psychologically, in short, cause-related marketing has a lot going for it. You could confidently expect it to create brand switching, increased sales and a concerned corporate identity on the one hand, and raise real money for good causes on the other. And as I've found through more than 20 such ventures, it can indeed do all those things—as long as a few pertinent points are borne in mind.

Before considering those, however, let's look at some real-life examples.

A miracle for children—and the manufacturer

Children in distress tug at everyone's hearts. Since 1985, Johnson & Johnson in the USA has used this unarguable fact to raise hundreds of millions of dollars for children's charities—and to increase its own sales very substantially in the process. It does so through an extremely large promotion called the Children's Miracle Network. This massive venture begins each year with a day-long live telethon from Disneyland. Featuring the USA's top stars, the telethon reaches a quite staggering estimated total of 68 million families. And it's followed up with magazine advertising, elaborate in-store product displays and, increasingly, free premiums. These all highlight the campaign's second major thrust—the offer of millions of price-off coupons that not only give worthwhile discounts to buyers, but direct more money to children's charities every time one is redeemed.

Naturally, ongoing publicity focuses on the growing sums of money reaching and benefiting children in need. Johnson & Johnson's customers feel good to know they're helping in such a tangible way. They appreciate the opportunity to enjoy the warm inner glow. And Johnson & Johnson's image as a company that really cares for children grows every year.

Sad relevance

The Children's Miracle Network isn't Johnson & Johnson's only annual cause-related programme. The company runs a number, one of which is called 'Shelter Aid'. It's sadly relevant to one of the more disturbing developments in American society—the need for more and more women to seek shelter for themselves and their children, to escape domestic violence.

Through the same combination of promotion, redeemable price-off coupons and strong POS product displays, Johnson & Johnson is meeting an increasingly significant portion of that need. So the company is performing a very worthwhile community service—as well as achieving a sizeable sales boost.

Jerry the giant

For all its vastness and huge outlay from Johnson & Johnson, the Children's Miracle Network is actually eclipsed in size and cost by Jerry Lewis' giant 'Easter Seals' telethon. Sponsored by Nestlé and Nescafé, this is the largest telethon of them all. Many other manufacturers take part besides the major sponsor, and a wide range of deserving causes is supported.

The Easter Seals telethon is also followed up by massive press advertising that spreads no fewer than 150 million price-off coupons across the USA. Here again, buyers save money with these, and their favourite charities benefit when the coupons are redeemed. But unlike the exclusively Johnson & Johnson Children's Miracle Network, these coupons cover products of all kinds from dozens of different manufacturers. They can be redeemed in a host of retail outlets, to support many different charitable activities. Probably no other cause-related marketing venture in the world spreads the benefits to as many customers, companies and causes as the Easter Seals programme.

The wave of the future

Certainly, there'll always be warm support for programmes that help children in need, support medical research, give shelter to homeless families and so on. But in the future, I believe environmental issues will increasingly become linked with cause-related marketing. Issues such as saving the rain forests, protecting marine mammals and cleaning the atmosphere will be seen as increasingly urgent. Indeed, one environmentally-oriented cause-related programme has already become something of a classic in Australia.

American Express and the koalas

It would be hard to imagine two more contrasting images than the fast-moving, sophisticated, global American Express company and a koala sleepily munching in a gum tree. Yet a few years ago, they came together very successfully—because each had problems the other could do something about, through cause-related marketing.

American Express' problems included a proliferation of competitors, fluctuating foreign exchange rates that discouraged international travel, and the perceived 'foreignness' that goes with its name. The koala's problem was a more basic one. Survival.

The way ahead for both parties proved to be a cause-related marketing programme that raised $200 000 for koala research in just three months. American Express committed themselves to donations to the

American Express enables people to support Australian causes without spending an extra cent. The plight of our Koalas and concern for their well-being gives the brand a sympathetic reason to gain support from outlets that take the card, outlets that might take it, and from their members too. All can contribute to the cause simply by using their Amex Card, no excuses! American Express also add a $50 000 sweepstakes American Express Travellers Cheque offer, as a further encouragement to use the card on every occasion.
© 1993 American Express International Inc. All rights reserved. Reprinted with permission

project for every single use of an Amex card, for each $100 of Amex traveller's cheques purchased, for each new cardholder and for each travel purchase made at an American Express office. And they offered their members more than a warm, fuzzy, koala-shaped inner glow.

Substantial prizes

Every time a cardholder did something to generate a donation, he or she was entered in a sweepstake. The prizes were substantial, too—from $50 000 in American Express travellers' cheques and Qantas flights anywhere in the world to Apple computers and *The Complete Book of Australian Mammals*.

An intensive mailing launched the campaign to all members. It included items such as an endorsement letter from the Minister for the Environment, a brochure on the koala's plight and a koala merchandise sales catalogue. This was backed by a seven-week press advertising campaign, community service announcements on television, extensive point- of-sale material and billing inserts. It was quite a programme, but it paid off. Average card member spending increased. New card sales went up significantly over the budget. Traveller's cheques sales soared almost 30% above previous levels. Service establishment signages exceeded budget by 15%. Extensive press coverage reflected the goodwill the promotion gained for American Express.

And many of Australia's battling koala colonies were given new hope for the future.

Tangible results

Now both from the koala and American Express viewpoints, those are very tangible results. And to me, they effectively squelch one common objection to cause-related marketing—namely, that it achieves little but image enhancement. Some, however, will be unconvinced. Surely, they will say, the American Express campaign succeeded only because of a large and intensive promotional budget, plus the opportunity to mail directly to a known target audience. What about branded products without a database market? Can you link them with a cause in such a way that both cause and product benefit?

Yes, you can—as long as you're prepared to invest money in the programme and stay with it for the long haul. If you are, my experience suggests you should never underestimate the kind of results you can get. Take, for example, the classic case of Ronald McDonald House.

That venture started out as a cause-related promotional element of McDonald's marketing mix. A few cents from every burger went to set up houses where parents could stay while their desperately sick children were in hospital. Little or no promotion took place outside McDonald's own tray mats—yet over the years, the programme has been enormously successful. Ronald McDonald Houses now abound in cities around the world. They have contributed hugely to McDonald's sales and family-oriented image. They have grown beyond being a promotional element to become part of the total McDonald's product. And they have unquestionably done immense good in thousands of very difficult family situations. What was needed to get those results? A clear corporate commitment to investing the necessary money—plus a determination to hang on for the long term.

CSR's long-running cause–related strategy reversed a slump in sugar sales. It convinced many that making cakes, desserts and jams (high usage areas for sugar) was indeed 'a natural part of life'.
Courtesy of CSR Refined Sugars

Let them eat cake

We took the same approach when **CSR Sugar** faced a significant sales decline. The problem was that housewives, the younger ones especially, just weren't making cakes, desserts and jams like their mothers did. Many lifestyle factors lay behind that decline, including a big increase in the number of women in the workforce, an abundance of convenience foods and more eating out. The health suspicions that touched upon sugar at the time didn't help, either. But whatever the cause, the result was the same—a sugar sales slump that had to be reversed, on a fairly minimal budget.

We felt it could be done, through a long-term cause-related marketing programme. Eric Laakso, our client contact at the time, and I devised one that ran for many years, in a number of distinct segments.

The first of these was called, 'Bake a Cake for Charity'. Sugar purchasers were invited to return a 50¢ symbol from the pack. In return, CSR then donated 50¢ to a charity nominated by the purchaser. They also sent the purchasers a free copy of the *Bake a Cake for Charity Cookbook,* consisting of donated recipes notable for their appetite appeal.

Next came 'Add a Little Variety'. This time, the emphasis was on puddings and desserts, and the money went to the Variety Club—an organisation composed of Australian and overseas showbusiness personalities who raise money to supply Sunshine Coaches and other equipment to help disabled children. Moreover, the personalities donated their favourite recipes to CSR. So after purchasers had returned six symbols, they received a bonus—a very desirable *Entertainers' Cookbook*, absolutely free.

Further variety still was added in Australia's Bicentennial Year, when buyers were urged to bake plenty of birthday cakes for big occasions. They were also invited to send $2 themselves to the Variety Club for its work. A unique reward was offered—a personally-signed birthday card from Paul Hogan, Cliff Richard or some other helpful star, mailed directly to whoever the donor nominated.

Money for jam

Following these, the campaign moved into its longest-lasting phase. Our big idea, CSR's 'Jampot Jamboree', invited Australia's 140 000 Scouts and Cubs to make and sell jam to raise money for their groups. To launch this new development, we contacted every Scout and Cub group in Australia by direct mail. CSR gave cash prizes, plus gold, silver and bronze woven award badges, to the groups that collected and sold the most pots of jam. And, of course, the groups themselves retained all proceeds from their sales.

The same basic cause-related promotional principles applied to this aspect of the campaign. The purchaser again returned on-pack symbols, to obtain a free jam-making cookbook. And the lure of helping a good cause was not only still there, but was greatly strengthened by the unique appeal of Scout and Cub groups.

Above-average sales for the product quickly resulted and were maintained. 'Jampot Jamboree' was soon joined by its Girl Guide counterpart, 'Candy Capers'. Together, they remained part of the Australian Scouts' and Guides' calendar for many years.

This fundraising kit was sent directly to all Scout groups to encourage them to make pots of jam!
Courtesy of CSR Sugar Ltd

The proof of the pudding

Why did both become such firm fixtures? For one simple reason. They worked—both for CSR and the Scouts and Guides. For the latter, they became indispensable fundraisers for literally hundreds of groups. And for CSR, they and the earlier schemes not only halted the sales decline. They lifted sales by up to 6.7% in every period during which they operated, and greatly enhanced trade relationships as well. In other words, both the causes and the manufacturer genuinely benefited.

I believe that's what good cause-related marketing is all about.

Choose your cause with care

So, how do you go about creating an effective cause-related marketing programme that's right for you? There are three vital aspects you have to get right: the cause, the contribution level, and the premium you offer as a repeat purchase mechanism. Of these, the cause itself is probably the most critical. Choose it with great care—and make sure it meets these eight essential criteria:

1. *The cause should be well-known*, especially to your target market, and totally reputable.
2. *Its work should appeal to your target market*. It should be the kind of worthwhile activity they would want to support.

3. *It should operate nationally*, to allow you to run the promotion in all states, and to avoid complications in distributing the funds.
4. *It should be a newsworthy cause*. This will give you extra PR opportunities in TV, radio, newspapers and women's magazines.
5. *It must enable you to tell the customer exactly what his or her money will do*. Express the goal as a clear mental picture—a Sunshine Coach for disabled children, a humidicrib for the Children's Hospital, a research project to help koalas, or whatever it might be.
6. *The cause must obviously be a very worthwhile one, yet be mentally digestible too*. However desirable it might be, one that is too poignant can be a complete turn-off in this kind of promotional activity.
7. *It must be acceptable to the trade*. And if it is, this is a powerful extra plus. Often you'll find key trade figures are personally involved in it. Our experience is that cause-related marketing can enhance the trade's attitude to your company at every level from management to shop floor.
8. *The cause should, if possible, be complementary or relevant to your product*. An ideal example is dog food and Guide Dogs. On the other hand, cream buns and Freedom from Hunger would obviously be mismatched. Use your common sense here.

An excellent recent example of matching cause to product is the smash hit musical *Miss Saigon*. Cameron MacIntosh, its producer, distributed part of the proceeds, plus theatre-goers' donations, to Vietnamese refugee relief programmes through his MacIntosh Foundation. This very strong link added an extra dimension to patrons' perception of the show—and helped them express the remorse that so many in America now feel towards the Vietnam war.

Keep contributions realistic

From the cause itself to your contribution. And here there's just one point to watch. Keep your contributions realistic. If they're too high, people will suspect the product's price has been inflated. If they're too low, you will appear miserly. Either way, participation will not be maximised. Go for a contribution of around 1% of your purchase price, and you'll be pretty right.

What's in it for me?

Lastly, there's the question of a premium. And this is a vital one. It's true that cause-related marketing gives purchasers a warm inner glow that no other promotional technique can deliver. Yet in my experience, the addition of a premium to encourage repeat purchases—often over a range of products—is the key to real sales success in this kind of exercise. Several examples spring to mind:

- A free sticker with one proof of purchase for Dettol, in their bid to raise $25 000 for the Red Cross.
- Free badges with three proofs of purchase for Kimberly-Clark, who gave donations to a wildlife project.
- A free Matchbox model Variety Club bus with three proofs of purchase of Kellogg's® Variety® cereal, which gave substantial amounts to Variety to help needy children.
- A free Grant Kenny training book for three proofs of purchase of Kellogg's® Nutri-Grain®, when purchasers helped our Olympic team training.

And so on. If you add tangible personal gain to the warm inner glow, people respond—often, at quite spectacular levels.

It's interesting, as we saw earlier, that cause-related promotions in the USA tend to offer a price-off coupon in place of a premium. The Johnson & Johnson and Easter Seal extravaganzas do, and they're the biggest in the business. Coupon redemption across a wide variety of products and services is basic to Variety Club fundraising efforts for disadvantaged children in Canada, too. The coupons are offered in press advertisements and must be redeemed by a certain date to deliver the benefit.

But for the reasons we noted in Chapter 10, coupon-related techniques are all but impossible to use in Australia. I can't help feeling that the premium is a better idea anyway. Everybody looks at a proposition and says, 'What's in it for me?' The premium tells them—and powerfully reinforces the psychological appeal of a cause-related programme.

What's in it for you?

Naturally, being human, you'll probably look at your proposed cause-related promotion and ask the same question—'What's in it for us?' Well, after 20-odd very successful programmes and about $6 million raised for great causes, all I can say is cause-related marketing can offer you substantial image enhancement, strengthened trade relationships and lasting sales increases—plus a real opportunity to do some good in this world.

That combination of factors, I believe, makes it well worth considering. I think you'll find the warm inner glow just as enjoyable as your customers will.

Your cause-related marketing checklist

To gauge the likely success of your cause-related marketing programme, test your planning against this checklist:

1. Can you select a cause that is complementary or relevant to your product?
2. Is the cause well and favourably known in the community, and completely reputable?
3. Will its work appeal to your target market?
4. Does it operate nationally?
5. Is it newsworthy?
6. Are its goals clear and easy to communicate to your target market?
7. Are they acceptable in a promotional environment?
8. Will they appeal to the trade?
9. Can you set your contributions at 1% of product purchase price?
10. Can you allocate an adequate budget and time frame to the promotion?
11. Can you offer a premium to generate repeat sales?

A 100% 'yes' score is not only a clear go-ahead but a pretty certain indication of substantial benefits to come for you.

And for a good cause too.

® Registered Trademark Kellogg (Aust) Pty Ltd, Authorised User

16

CHAPTER

The Sales Force—Make An Offer They Can't Refuse

Picture this cartoon that appeared some years ago in a business magazine. Two downhearted sales management types are standing in an office. Gloomily, they contemplate a plunging sales chart and a map with pins showing where the sales representatives are. 'Maybe we'd do better,' says one, 'if we took the pins out of the map and stuck them in the salesmen.'

What he was advocating was, in fact, a sales force incentive programme—even if in a somewhat crude form. And today, the need he saw to spur the sales force on to greater efforts has become a multi-million dollar activity in its own right—one that every producer of goods and services needs to consider very carefully.

Quickly measurable

Sales force incentive programmes are probably the most rewarding sales promotion techniques of all. They offer huge and exciting opportunities for creativity. Their effects are usually immediate and often far-reaching. What's more, they're quickly measurable. You very soon know whether you've caught the imagination of your sales force and the trade—and if so, whether that feat is being translated into increased sales.

The fascinating thing about sales incentive programmes to me is that they deal with people and what makes them perform. For some people, the best motivation is peer group recognition. For others, it's travel or special items they normally wouldn't buy for themselves. For others again, it's straight monetary gain. Selecting the right spur for a particular group is an absorbing exercise.

The grass is greener . . .

A properly planned sales incentive programme will significantly lift the performance of most sales forces. With some, however, there's a deep-seated morale problem that needs to be overcome in other ways. By that, I don't just mean the envy of the opposition that seems to be almost a sales force norm. Talk to most sales personnel, and they'll tell you that their rivals have better cars, better mobile phones, better merchandisers, better training, better working conditions and better commission structures.

In reality, most such comments are little more than a litany based on hearsay. But every now and again, they contain a germ of truth. In those cases, better on-the-job training, better equipment, better sales aids and better merchandising techniques could do more to boost morale, performance and job satisfaction than any sales incentive programme. Indeed, the Carlson Marketing Group, the world's biggest merchandise motivation company, believes motivation awards and training are part of the same process—one aimed at showing people how to unearth and use their skills to achieve the best possible results.

There's certainly something in that. But in my experience, a good sales incentive programme can further boost the effectiveness of even the best-trained, most contented sales force. And the reason, I believe, is hinted at in a quote by famed sociologist, William James. 'Most people,' he observed, 'exert only 15% of their combined education, know-how, skills and aptitudes in their work.'

Your staff—working at 15% capacity

I'm sure Mr James wasn't thinking of sales incentive programmes, but his remark certainly underlines their potential. In other words, no matter how good any of us is, we can always work harder and perform better. The potential exists, in theory anyway, to lift our game by a mindboggling six times. The point is recognised by General Foods in Australia and many US companies, which put management through self-development courses to help them tap their unused skills and aptitudes. Greater motivation—the kind supplied by sales incentive programmes—can have the same effect. So how would your bottom line look if each of your salespeople became up to six times more effective?

Think about that for a moment, and your next question will follow almost automatically. How quickly can I get my incentive programme started? The answer is, not too quickly—at least, not until you've thought it through thoroughly. Based it on some well-proven principles. And given your sales promotion agency a comprehensively detailed brief.

The three-tiered sales force

A good way to start your thinking is to recognise that your sales force, if it's like most, is a three-tiered affair. It's made up of three different groups of people. Group one is your top 10% of sales stars—outstanding performers who pursue excellence every day, and catch it more often than not. Group three is the bottom 10%—the plodders who are unlikely to improve, and who really should be doing something else. Group two is the other 80%—the average performers. They're out there slogging away, never setting the world on fire but never failing disastrously, always turning in figures that are—well, just average.

And they're the most important group of all.

Why? Because it's with them that your real potential for improvement lies. The top 10% are stretched to the limit now. You won't get much more from the bottom 10%. But almost all the middle 80% are capable of a big lift in performance. Quite a few, in fact, could easily push their way into the top 10%—if they were given the right motivation to do so.

The importance of the middle 80% is underlined time and again in our research. This is why they're always the primary focus of our sales incentive programmes. Recent work by Geoff Minter of Minter Research on our Toshiba programme confirmed the predominance there of medium achievers—and the huge sales increase that could and should follow, when they're properly motivated.

But how can you inspire your middle 80% to lift their game?

More harm than good

Not by sitting them down in a sales meeting to watch a high-flyer get the 'salesman of the year' award. True, such a first-past-the-post sales contest might be great for your top performers. And true, it's comparatively cheap and easy to organise. But from a long-term viewpoint, it actually does more harm than good.

To start with, those top performers would have given it all they had anyway. So your investment in the contest will bring you few, if any, extra returns. Second—and even more seriously—it totally ignores the vital 80% who represent your main improvement potential. They know they don't have a hope in a first-past-the-post race, so there's absolutely no reason for them to try harder. Furthermore, if any contest progress report reaches them, it will only be figures that confirm their also-ran status. More probably, they'll hear nothing at all until the contest is history—and they're sitting at the sales conference watching the all-too-predictable result. And yawning. . .

In short, then, the traditional sales contest approach has several crippling flaws. It motivates only your top few stars, who probably don't need much extra motivation. It offers no carrot whatsoever to most of your sales force. Any progressive scores along the way only demoralise them further. And finally, when everyone does hear the full story, it's all about past events—when what should be happening is a firm focusing of their attention on the future.

Divisions and jealousies

Equally seriously, the traditional sales contest divides the sales force. It arouses jealousies and cuts across involvement and commitment. It does this because it pits people in the same company against each other, instead of uniting them in the common cause of building company sales—a goal in which each one's self-interest becomes very much a secondary aim.

Powerful objections can also be made to 'chance-to-win' sweepstake schemes. These, we have found, are the least popular—indeed, the most widely despised—of all sales force incentive programmes. Our research shows conclusively that offering a seductive prize when the chance to win it is obviously remote is a major demotivator, rather than the opposite. Admittedly, the technique can work up to a point if it overlays lesser guaranteed-to-win gifts and prizes. Nevertheless, our general rule is to avoid games of chance as sales motivators at all costs.

The vital clues

It's important to understand the weaknesses of these kinds of sales contests. Once we do, we have the clues we need to design a really effective sales force incentive programme—or for that matter, a programme to motivate your dealers, distributors or retailers, because the same principles apply.

Get your goals right

The very first thing is to decide exactly what you want the programme to achieve, in terms of units sold, share of mind gained, income, turnover or profit. Only by setting measurable goals can you tell, at the end of the day, whether the venture has been successful and cost-effective.

So make your goals clear, precise and realistic. Don't aim vaguely for 'increased sales'—set exact target figures of items to be sold or extra dollars earned. But at the same time, avoid fantasy. Don't, for instance, go for sales increases that simply can't be achieved. When goals are too high, you get the unhappy situation where six months of hard slog may indeed boost sales over last year, perhaps even against market trends—

yet profit projections aren't met, because sales still don't reach the artificially-inflated target. It's far better to set your sights at more modest levels and get a pleasant surprise at the end. So go for goals that will, with above-average effort, give you a realistic, worthwhile and measurable return, over and above the programme's cost.

Spread the rewards around

Now let's start looking at it from the participants' viewpoint. The first thing they'll probably ask is: what's in it for me?

As we've just seen, programmes that reward only the known top-notchers motivate no-one. So a successful programme must offer every participant an equal chance to win some very attractive awards. Above all, it must gain the enthusiastic involvement of all those in the average 80%. They're the group where major improvements are possible. Just a

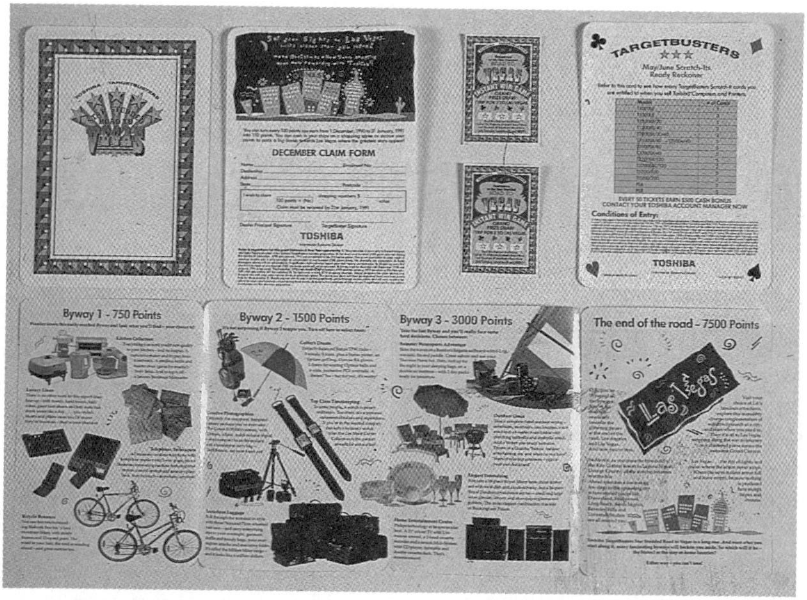

Viva Las Vegas—a great destination to aim for, with merchandise rewards for those who fall short of going the whole distance, and 'booster' sprint promotions along the way.
Courtesy of Toshiba/Australia Pty Limited

small performance lift from each of them will boost your overall figures most significantly. That's true no matter who the participants are, because the 'average 80%' rule applies as much to dealers, distributors and retailers as it does to your own sales force.

However, even when a programme seems on paper to offer everyone an equal chance, it's wise to check the results in practice. The most democratically-designed programmes can, on occasions, finish up rewarding just the top-liners.

That happened to us with the 'Toshiba Targetbusters' dealer incentive programme. We had run it for three years, and achieved considerable success in sales terms. But then we noticed that, out of 700 resellers, it was largely the same 100–120 dealer principals and their spouses who were taking off for wonderful places every year. David Henderson, Toshiba's general manager, and Lesley MacLennan, Toshiba's marketing and communications manager, decided to survey their reseller network and sales force, to determine attitudes towards the programme.

Not surprisingly, they found that both groups wanted the results threshold lowered to enable more people to share in the prizes. The research also showed that animosities had developed because of the programme, which was in real danger of becoming a demotivator.

At the same time, a few calculations revealed that, while the regular 100–120 prize winners contributed a notable percentage of Toshiba sales, an even larger volume was coming from those outside the winners' circle. So the appropriate changes were made to the programme format. Today, David Henderson and the Toshiba

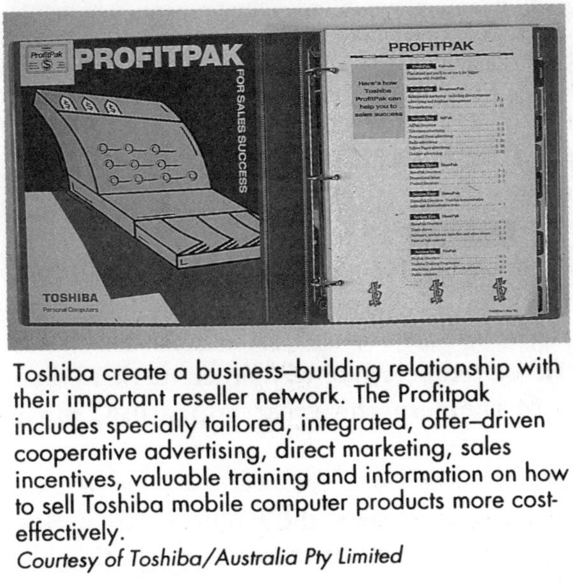

Toshiba create a business–building relationship with their important reseller network. The Profitpak includes specially tailored, integrated, offer–driven cooperative advertising, direct marketing, sales incentives, valuable training and information on how to sell Toshiba mobile computer products more cost-effectively.
Courtesy of Toshiba/Australia Pty Limited

management team have an even higher participation level in the Targetbusters programme, and happier salespeople at company and reseller levels.

We'll look at Targetbusters a little more closely later in the chapter.

How to get them involved

There are six essential steps to gaining the enthusiastic involvement of all potential participants:

1. *Offer the right awards.* We'll deal with that in detail shortly.
2. *Make the sales targets realistic and achievable for everyone.* Award points for individual improvement, and design a handicap system to iron out differences between territories and situations.
3. *Keep the programme simple and understandable.* We make it easy for participants to handle administrative chores like recording their sales figures. We also ensure that the prize details—what is awarded for each achievement level—are clear and obvious. The KISS principle (keep it simple, stupid) is very important in sales incentive programmes. If the whole thing sounds too complex, many potential participants will simply give it a miss.
4. *Make the programme the right length.* That, basically, is however long it takes to give the participants time to achieve your sales goals. Within that parameter, keep it as short as possible—maybe around three months, and certainly no more than six months. Beyond that, participants' enthusiasm will flag. They need to see some tempting carrots not too far down the road.
5. *Bear in mind that your incentive programme is first and foremost a marketing tool.* Just like any other marketing programme, it needs a solid selling effort behind it. So don't simply announce an incentive programme, give the details and leave it at that. Treat your sales force, dealers or retailers like any other market—and sell the programme to them in the most appealing, most compelling way you can.
6. *Provide your resellers with the same marketing tools you'd use in their situation.* Your resellers often don't have the resources to employ marketing staff like you can. Give them the tools to do the job. Peter Drucker said, 'Marketing is simply a method of reducing

sales costs'. Pass on your knowledge to help their productivity and keep them selling profitably on your behalf. If you pass on your knowledge it will be appreciated.

An exciting launch

A good way to start selling your incentive programme is to launch it with style and flair at a sales, dealer or retailer conference. Make it an exciting event right from the start. Decorate the venue with travel posters, if travel is one of your awards. Have attractive, imaginative leaflets on hand with programme and award details. Show the awards in full living colour. Many companies produce videos or stage glamorous floor shows, to give the launch an extra dimension of movement, excitement and memorability.

And when the launch is over, your selling of the programme isn't. Remember, you're not rewarding people for the past, as in a sales contest. You're motivating them to work harder now and in the future.

Consequently, do everything you can to keep the enthusiasm bubbling. One method is write regularly and personally to all participants, using the magic of modern database techniques to detail their current achievements against their targets. That's a good way to encourage them, if they're doing well—or to urge them to lengthen their stride, if they're behind. Assure the stragglers that they have a chance to be winners, right to the very end.

Sales people need to be stimulated with their performance versus target on a regular 'drive cycle' basis. A simple computer programme charts their progress towards their ultimate goal, refreshes their interest and informs them of their next task.
Courtesy of JCT Australia Pty Ltd and Brother Industries

Keep dangling the carrots

Use these mailings, too, to keep the carrots dangling before them. Paint tempting verbal pictures of the awards just around the corner. And for extra impact, include teaser items as further reminders of the joys to be won. Such items can be purely fun—such as a message in a bottle, plastic blow-up palm trees, cocktail straws or mock boarding passes, if your award is a trip to Hawaii—or more practical items, such as sunglasses or coffee mugs. Usually, the more imaginative and creative they are, the greater their impact. But whatever form they take, their task is the same—to focus attention on the awards, and to keep the programme's momentum charging ahead.

With our Japan Airlines travel incentive programme for Brother Club typewriter and sewing machine dealers, we mailed participants monthly with the latest figures on their individual performances. We included items themed to their award destination (Hawaii) to maintain the excitement among them and their spouses. We also sent similar letters to dealer principals, to keep them up to date on how their employees were doing. This was very relevant information for them, because their own chances of winning a trip depended heavily on their salespeople's performances!

We created even more interest by giving the letters an unusual twist. We not only gave the salespeople their performance data to date, but we charted each person's progress towards Hawaii on a map. Our clever computer programme allowed us to plot their progress from start to destination according to their sales successes. An aeroplane crossing the Pacific showed how comparatively close (or far away) they were from their destination.

Through this database promotion, many more dealerships reached their target than in previous years. Over 30% more had sales people who qualified for the trip. Our letters were a very simple way of gaining extra attention for the programme. They showed that Brother Club headquarters were treating each salesperson as an individual, by sending him or her a personal letter from the sales manager—even though more than 700 people were involved.

Break into a sprint

Another proven pot-boiling technique is to offer incentives along the way. You can do this by holding 'sprints', or mini sales incentive programmes, within the main one. Keep them short and sharp—a maximum of two months. Offer attractive awards to the winners. And make the additional results count towards the main awards at the end of the whole programme.

If those main awards are extremely enticing, we've found they help to maintain momentum by themselves. We also get good results by including a lower level of prizes that participants can obtain at any stage of the programme. All they have to do is cash in sales points they've earned up to that time. They can cash in their entire total for an item they really want—or hold enough points back to keep themselves in the hunt for the major prizes. We've found that the best incentive programmes of all are those where goals can be achieved more easily and the rewards come fast and often. The ideal formula seems to be sprints overlaid on a longer programme.

Choose your awards with care

Now comes the really crucial question. What should you offer as awards? What kind of carrots will best motivate your sales staff, dealers, distributors or retailers?

Don't always throw money

Interestingly enough, experience suggests that money is not always the best incentive. True, people usually say that money is what they want most. True, it's a powerful motivator for the kind of personalities that become high-flyers. But from the incentive aspect, it has one big drawback—there's nothing really special about it. Money, after all, is what people are paid all the time. And it slips through the fingers so easily. Any extra earned in an incentive programme tends to disappear quickly on mundane household bills. Then it's soon forgotten.

Big sales signal bigger rewards. When Toshiba sales people sell a million dollars worth, they can select from premium quality gifts.
Courtesy of Tosiba/Australia Pty Limited

So within days or weeks, people have nothing left to show for their special efforts. What's more, when they receive additional money, they quickly come to expect it as a regular right—and can cause problems if they don't continue to get it. Yet there'll always be a place for money in incentive programmes, especially if you can find imaginative ways of handing it out.

Let them spoil themselves

Generally speaking, the secret of giving effective incentives is to let people spoil themselves. That means offering them something they would really love to have but would not normally buy, for one of three reasons. They can't afford it. Or if they can, they won't buy it because it would seem like an extravagance. Or it might even be something that money can't buy. So if you offer it to people for nothing but extra effort, they'll go flat out to make it theirs.

And that's what motivation is all about.

The four basic incentives

What are the alluring 'somethings' that people will gladly go the extra mile to get? Basically, they fall into four categories. Money. Travel.

Merchandise. And recognition. Each one has its own particular strengths. Sometimes, you can build a very effective incentive programme on just one of them. More often, your programme will include two or even three. How, when and why do you use each? To start answering that, let's look at all four categories in more detail.

Money: the high-flyers' carrot

Cash is obviously the easiest prize to offer. It frees you entirely from hassles like contra deals, prize selections and award brochures. Sometimes, when speed is essential, its immediate availability makes it the only choice. And because high-flyers' personality types tend to include a component of risk-taking and lack of conservatism, money can be an extremely attractive carrot for them. People like that generally have high aspirations—and extra money will help them achieve the lifestyle they're seeking. You won't motivate them with a prize below their aspiration level.

That said, however, cash as a general motivator suffers from the limitations we noted a moment ago. There's nothing different or memorable about it. It quickly goes on everyday expenses. It doesn't maintain motivation over a long period. And in the amounts that high-flyers expect, its value is drastically eroded by tax.

But as I said, sometimes you're stuck with money, if you haven't time to organise anything else. In those cases, you can overcome some of cash's failings by presenting it in an interesting way.

We had a Toshiba promotion that was designed to run out a product line coming to the end of its life cycle. The idea was to motivate reseller representatives with an extra bonus for each machine they sold. So we dressed up the promotion with scratch cards. The resellers received five of these every time they sold a machine. If they collected 20 cards, they received a further bonus, over and above their scratch cards' total cash value. This Australian campaign outsold all other Toshiba subsidiaries throughout the world.

Travel: the award everyone wants

There's no doubt that, of all four categories, travel is the one that motivates more people more of the time. Just about everyone likes to travel, and the chance of doing so free certainly drives most sales staff, dealers and retailers to lift their game.

There are, however, several points to watch.

The first is cost. Travel is the most expensive of incentive awards. It takes huge slices out of a budget. Realistically, will the programme generate enough extra income to justify your outlay? On anything but high-ticket items, you have to sell a lot of product to cover the expense. And you can't string out the programme over a long period to do so, because you'll find it impossible to maintain the momentum. But you're confident the outlay can be covered? Then remember point two. Everyone in your incentive group must have a genuinely equal chance to gain the points necessary to win the trip or trips. Otherwise, as we saw earlier, the programme will actually be a disincentive to most.

Point three is obvious but sometimes overlooked. Be sure to include spouses or partners in the trip, because this adds to its motivational impact in two ways. It makes it a more attractive proposition for the participant—and it turns the spouse or partner into your ally. Obviously, a holiday-hungry spouse or partner will put more pressure on the participant to perform than you ever could.

Make sure the spouse knows

For years, we used sales meetings as the occasions for telling salespeople about the trips they could win. And for years, we found that spouses or partners were very surprised when they discovered they were off on a holiday to a glamorous destination. The salespeople just weren't telling them about the programme, in case they didn't win. So we were losing all the motivation pressure a spouse or partner can bring to bear.

The solution? We started to mail the programme information directly to the salespeoples' homes. The results were spectacular. And as a bonus, we bypassed not only the office system but any management people unhappy about outsiders motivating their sales personnel. Today, it would be very unusual for us to send letters anywhere else but to the salesperson's home. Our messages are designed and addressed to include a spouse or partner as well as the salesperson, as both will share the award. And two heads are always better than one, especially when they're working together.

Bondi or Bermuda?

Basic to the whole concept of a travel award is choosing the destination. It's a choice worth agonising over, because it plays a big part in determining your programme's effectiveness.

The first deciding factor, of course, is your budget. It may or may not run to faraway places like Tahiti, Hawaii, Disneyland or Las Vegas. The overseas destinations are very motivating, but they're also quite expensive. Local destinations cost less, and—provided they're exotic enough—can also be highly tempting. They have other advantages, too. Because they're cheaper, you can have more winners, which means a wider spread of motivation. And because they're closer, you can make the trips shorter—which not only saves additional money, but is less disruptive to work.

This last point is important. As early as the late 1970s, our research showed that incentive trips longer than a week or 10 days—and sometimes even less—created problems. Sales managers didn't want their staff away from work longer than that. The salespeople themselves didn't want their territories covered by other, perhaps less able, stand-ins.

As well, the potential trippers had usually made their own holiday plans for other times—and the grandparents didn't want a further lengthy period of looking after children or pets. In other words, longer sales incentive trips were just too hard. Their negatives soured something that was supposed to be exhilarating, enjoyable and rewarding. For that reason, most travel incentive specialists now advise that the winners should be sent as far as the budget allows, in the shortest possible time frame.

The best of both

Of course, if you can afford it, you can have the best of both travel worlds—an overseas jaunt for the ultimate winner, with local hops for the runners-up or as 'sprint' prizes along the way. Or you can hold a special two- or three-day conference at an exotic local location for, say, the top 50% of your performers under your handicap system. Spouses and partners are also invited, and the winners of the major travel awards are announced during the function.

The 'horizons' principle

A helpful aid for destination selection is what one writer calls the 'horizons' principle. This means you should always choose a destination beyond the participant's 'horizon of expectation'—yet within his or her 'horizon of comprehension'.

Don't, in other words, pick a destination where the participant and his or her family would normally go for their holidays—somewhere nearby and fairly cheap. That's within their 'horizon of expectation'. Instead, select one beyond that horizon—a place where the participant would love to go but normally wouldn't, for reasons of cost or perceived extravagance. It's the same principle we saw earlier of allowing participants to spoil themselves.

On the other hand, don't put the destination beyond the participant's 'horizon of comprehension'. Don't choose a destination so exotic that the participant would never have dreamed of going there, wouldn't know what to expect or do, and would be quite uncertain of whether he or she would enjoy it anyway. Between the two horizons lies plenty of scope for creative choice—which should be exercised in the company of a travel agent skilled in the planning of incentive travel.

Behold, the taxman cometh

One thing to remember with travel—and indeed, with all incentive awards—is that they may be taxable in the recipients' hands. Missing that point would, of course, totally destroy the whole point of having them. No-one would thank you for a trip to Disneyland if they were hit with a $5000 tax bill on their return. So you have to pay any tax that the rewards attract, and you need to build a tax contingency into your budget. Consequently, your tax advisers should be involved in the early stages of planning your incentive programme.

One way to reduce—and perhaps even eliminate—the tax problem is to build a business component into your travel award. You might have the winners visit overseas parent or branch offices for familiarisation. Or they could perhaps attend a major international sales conference or annual general meeting. If you do this, be sure to include plenty of free time at the destination—and to arrange some enticing stopovers before and after the business component.

Make it memorable . . .

Whatever form the trip finally takes, it has to be a brilliant package. Travel, hotels, transfers, optional tours—all must be first rate, because what you are actually awarding is a memorable experience. The travel winners have to come home thoroughly satisfied with their trip—even if it was part educational—and eager to go all out to win the next one. If they come home unhappy with anything, some of that unhappiness will be directed at you. This is another reason to plan the whole venture through a travel company with a proven track record in the incentive travel field.

. . . or forget planning altogether

The other way of planning the package is to take precisely the opposite direction—and not plan it at all.

Instead, you could make the awards travel vouchers, good for any destination, tour package or cruise the winner chooses. This is not only much easier for you. It can actually add to your programme's impact, because travel vouchers allow participants to work towards their own travel dreams—and increase their motivation to be a winner. They also involve the participant's spouse or partner—and sometimes the whole family—in planning the desired trip. That, as we observed earlier, creates a pressure to perform that you can never hope to equal. What's more, travel vouchers make excellent 'sprint' and along-the-way awards. Give them out in denominations of, say, $250. People can accumulate them and aim for a big holiday, or settle for an earlier, smaller trip.

Keeping the world's hottest secret

Another way to add impact to travel incentives is to give them an extra dimension that can't be experienced otherwise. We did this most successfully back in 1979 for Maxwell House Coffee. Entitled 'Dateline Dallas', the incentive was a trip to Las Vegas, Hollywood, Disneyland and Los Angeles. There was nothing unusual in that. But the programme contained a very imaginative and totally unique extra.

At the time, 'Dallas' was the flavour of the moment on TV in Australia and across the world. And we all knew that JR (played by Larry Hagman) was about to get shot. So our special incentive was to challenge the salespeople to discover the answer to one of the world's most burning questions—'who shot JR?'.

Of the 400 salespeople eligible (with their spouses) to win the trip, the top-scorer and spouse had the chance to have dinner with Larry Hagman and discuss JR's impending demise. This highly topical programme meant huge recognition for the winner, a uniquely entertaining evening they could talk about for years—and the answer to the world's best-kept secret. The whole incentive programme was exciting and easy to theme. And it held every participant's interest right to the very end.

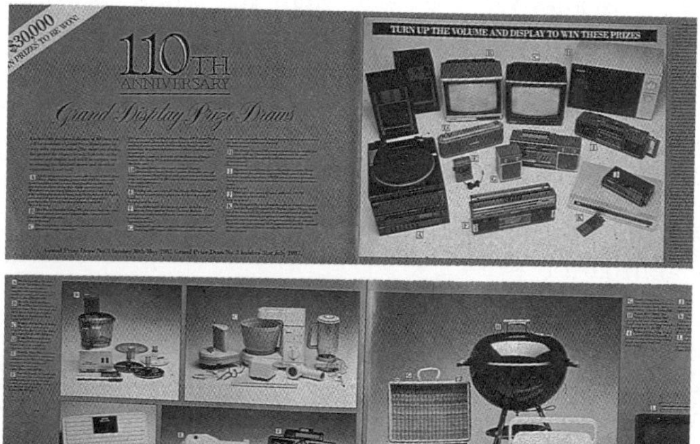

This bottle shop trade promotion was designed to increase McWilliam's stock levels across their product range. The more McWilliam's product retailers took, the better the gifts they could choose. If they also created a McWilliam's display, they gained entry into an attractive prize draw. So the promotion had two aims: 'get into the store, get out on the floor'.
With permission of McWilliam's Wines Pty Ltd

After all, who could resist the chance to be the person who had to keep a provocative secret from the whole world?

Travel, then, is the big motivator. But it's certainly not the only one. Merchandise items can give you a very effective—and much more economical—programme on their own. Or you can blend them with travel awards to create a well-rounded programme with something for everyone.

Merchandise: more than just economy

In recent years, spiralling travel costs have moved merchandise closer to the centre of the incentive stage. Quite obviously, you can buy a lot of fountain pens, bone china sets and windcheaters for the price of a ticket to Fiji.

Let alone Disneyland.

Merchandise also eliminates the additional costs travel incentives can impose on the winners. Almost always, they have to spend money on things like new clothes, new luggage and other items essential for their trip that the prize doesn't cover. Those extras can sometimes take a little of the gloss off their success. Merchandise incentives do away with that problem altogether.

However, the rise of merchandise has not been for economic reasons alone. The evidence is growing that merchandise items, creatively chosen and presented, can be powerful inducements in their own right. Indeed, many experts claim that, even if travel is the big prize in your incentive programme, you should spend 75% of your budget on merchandise items for along-the-way awards. If the items are exciting and obviously good value, some people will actually choose them over the travel prize itself—not just for their intrinsic worth but for the ongoing evidence of success that they provide.

Back to basics

What kind of merchandise, then, will motivate people in this potent way? To answer that, begin with the basic principle we laid down earlier: the strongest incentives are those that allow people to spoil themselves. Add another of our basic principles—that motivation is increased when spouses or partners or families would like the items too—and the list starts to write itself. Camera equipment. Video camcorders. Bicycles. Cordless telephones. Car phones. Bone china sets. Crystalware. Outdoor furniture. Sporting equipment. Kitchen appliances. Luxury linen. Compact discs. Designer clothes and accessories. Video machines. And so on, to the limits of your imagination.

Don't, however, offer too many options. We have found that the less choice we give people, the more successful the promotion. When there are too many things to choose from, the programme can be a disaster. It seems that when the choice is too hard, people find it easier to do nothing!

Apart from electrical goods—which are often the most desirable—you may be able to save up to 20% when you buy prestige merchandise from a supplier. This money can be fed back into the budget to reduce the programme's cost or to provide even more generous prizes.

Five points to check

The actual merchandise, of course, needs to be very well chosen from the long list of possibilities. What might appeal to you might not—in fact, probably won't—appeal to your sales force. So test. Ask your salespeople what they'd like. Or approach someone who knows them well. But don't just settle for asking your sales director—or his or her spouse!

Some experts suggest a five-point check list, to help you judge the suitability of incentive merchandise. Four of the points are from the participants' viewpoints, and the fifth is from yours.

1. Is the merchandise memorable, rather than mundane and commonplace?
2. Is it shareable, in the sense of appealing to others in the family?
3. Is it personal?
4. Is it useful?
5. And from your viewpoint—is it reasonably priced?

If you get a 'yes' to all five questions, you're on a winner. You're pretty safe with four or even three 'yesses'. But if you get five 'nos', then you'd better think again.

Speak to an expert

One thing to watch with merchandise is the ordering, storage and delivery problems it can create. It's vital to have supplies always on hand, so that the prize or gift can be sent immediately when a participant redeems it. This seemingly simple task calls for a level of planning, experience and specific expertise not usually found in client companies. Consequently, it makes sense to speak to an expert—by consulting a sales promotion company that knows how to determine such a programme's objectives, organise trouble-free delivery of the goods and analyse the final results.

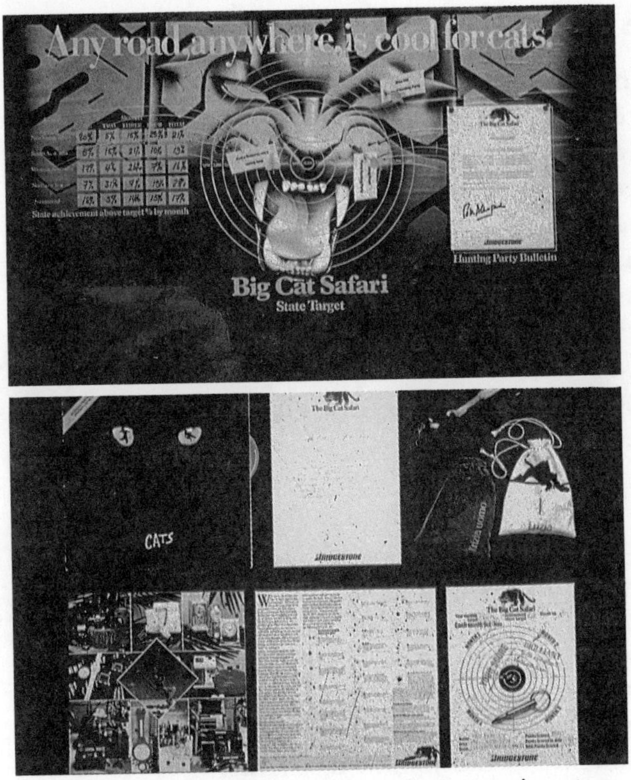

Bridgestone's 'Big Cats' advertising theme translates into a 'Big Cat Safari' of big prizes and holidays to motivate Bridgestone dealer sales people and their spouses.
Courtesy of Bridgestone Australia Limited

The Big Cat Safari

One way to add potency to your merchandise incentive programme is to theme it. When it ties-in directly with your current advertising theme, the programme is unmistakably linked to your brand or service—and it can put extra mileage into your advertising budget as well.

This is exactly what we achieved for Bridgestone Tyres. The Bridgestone consumer advertising at the time claimed that Bridgestone's Big Cat

Tyres gripped the road 'like cats'. So our sales incentive programme became the 'Bridgestone Big Cat Safari'. Dealer salespeople and their spouses received a Big Cat catalogue, showing the attractive merchandise and Big Cat Safari Travel holiday prizes the promotion offered.

Along the way, they also received regular teaser interest-boosters like porcelain cats, Big Cat cologne—and items such as a bullet and a target with a bullet hole in it, to symbolise their ability (or lack of it) to hit the target. On an extremely low budget, the six-month incentive programme increased the sales of Australian-produced Bridgestone Tyres by over $1.2 million—a rise of around 120%.

Motivation at arm's length

Many incentive programmes like the Big Cat Safari focus on the sales force not of the client company itself but of its dealers or resellers. In such cases, the client has no direct control over the salespeople being motivated. Close co-operation with the dealer principal is essential to get maximum action from an arm's length sales force. And one of the best ways we've found to ensure pull-through in such situations is to motivate the reseller's customers.

The key to that is getting hold of the reseller's database and using it creatively. As database techniques become ever more sophisticated, we can communicate by mail and phone not only with the reseller's sales force but with their customers as well.

The power of 3

A good example is the 3M 'Power of 3' programme. We run this through participating 3M master distributors who have their databases in trust with us. We contact their customers directly four times a year with a range of consumer incentives. We also offer incentives to the distributor's sales force, and further motivate the distributor principal with performance-over-target incentives and volume discounts.

So in this case, distributor principal, sales force and customers all receive incentives to stock, sell and buy 3M products rather than other brands or generics. The programme has helped 3M magnetic media products to increase their market share significantly in just three years. It has justified a switch of funds to relationship-building.

Less tangible merchandise

Also in the merchandise category are less tangible, but no less valuable, financial products. Insurance bonds, for instance, have been used very successfully as motivators. So have traveller's cheques, which overcome the drawbacks of offering money by giving it a glamorous, jet-set image. And among the most attractive incentives are cash vouchers of various denominations. Like travel vouchers, these can be accumulated towards one large purchase, or exchanged for smaller items as quickly as they are won.

The magic of vouchers is that they look like money, and so seem to have an intrinsic value of their own. But they can't be spent on boring, quickly-forgotten items like the gas bill. They can only be exchanged, in participating stores, for a wide range of memorable, spoil-yourself-style goods or services. Their flexibility means that few, if any, other incentive devices so readily invite family participation in deciding how they will be spent. And from your point of view, they save you all the problems of storage and distribution.

Divide the spoils

Vouchers are also divisible. When more than one person is responsible for a sale, vouchers can be used to reward them all—in a way that a stubbornly indivisible item like a mantle clock can't. But in selling a voucher incentive programme, we've found we have to stress the desirability of the items the vouchers can obtain. For all their resemblance to money, vouchers are really only pieces of paper. Their motivating power is most effectively kindled when you stress the rich rewards their possession can bring.

You can create your own vouchers, and integrate them closely with your corporate or brand image. Or you can simply select from a wide range of off-the-shelf gift vouchers that can be exchanged for anything from alcohol to hardware.

One such voucher is the Australian Bond—not to be confused with the now-defunct Aussie Bonds that used to be a government-run savings plan. Australian Bonds can be used for any incentive programme, large or small. They can be expended immediately or saved and accumulated for a more expensive reward. And from an incentive point of view, they have the advantage that they can't be exchanged for everyday items like food and liquor. They can only be exchanged for the kind of goods that remind winners—and their friends and family—of the outstanding effort that was made to obtain them.

Extending the budget

A very creative use of vouchers was achieved some years ago by the Benson & Hedges Company. For a long time, they had incentivised their van salespeople with merchandise gifts linked to sport, household items and electrical goods. Then the increasing price of such merchandise started to make the whole idea unprofitable. But the company didn't want to drop its incentives. What could they do?

My friend and ex-colleague Aubrey Watson came up with a highly ingenious way of making the budget go much further. His solution cut the promotion's costs by 25%—yet increased sales over the previous period by 22%. To my knowledge, this was probably the first true database-controlled promotion.

Saving stamps

When the salespeople earned points for sales, they received a coloured postage-sized stamp. This matched a small section of one of six Benson & Hedges poster advertisements displayed in the promotion's 'Win Gold' brochure. So as the salespeople collected more and more stamps, they could complete the advertisement like a jigsaw puzzle.

Each advertisement was given a cash value. And when the salespeople had a completed one, they could claim whatever it was worth. They would then receive a voucher for that amount, redeemable at the department store of their choice.

The stamps were given out apparently at random, which meant that a certain amount of luck was involved. However, the despatch was controlled in reality by a computer program held on what was then a very large mainframe. Consequently, the sales manager could influence the scheme to benefit particularly hard-working representatives.

Merchandise replaces advertisements

Research after the promotion underlined its success, and showed it had been interesting and fun for the salespeople. However, it also showed that the representatives would be even more motivated by pictures of desirable merchandise rather than Benson & Hedges advertisements. So the second time around, we called it 'Picture your Prize'. Instead of the advertisements, the salespeople had to complete pictures of tempting items—which they could then obtain at wholesale prices.

Shares in a 'company'

Another imaginative idea we ran in the UK was one for an insurance company. While this didn't use vouchers as such, it did use their first cousin—elaborately-produced 'shares' in a fictitious company created especially for the promotion.

At the start of the program, each insurance salesperson 'bought' shares in this 'company' according to his or her success against target sales. The shares exchanged throughout the scheme were always sold to the salesperson at par value, but their value increased in line with the 'company's' value—which went up steadily as the representatives' combined sales consistently exceeded their targets.

The end result: the salespeople not only received the face value of their shares, but almost 2.5 times that amount when the 'company' was 'sold' back to the insurance company. What's more, they also received a bonus, according to how long they had held the shares—which were then swapped for their value in the company stock at par. This was an unusual incentive campaign that really caught the imagination of the salespeople concerned.

Make it look good

When you've selected your merchandise or vouchers, remember the importance of selling the whole programme to the participants. Among other things, that means producing an attractive merchandise catalogue, which has two main jobs. It must show each item at its most tempting. And it must clearly explain the awards that are available at each level of sales points. Having such a production before them—and receiving constant reminders and progress reports—will help maintain participants' enthusiasm throughout the programme.

If you go the voucher route, you can still produce a prestigious catalogue. In fact, you have to—because as I've already stressed, vouchers are only pieces of paper. Your catalogue must illustrate and describe things the vouchers will obtain, and include a list of stores that accept them. The actual vouchers need to be well packaged and presented, so that they make a visually appealing award in themselves.

The final point about merchandise is a vital one. Make sure the items are delivered to winners swiftly and in perfect condition—or the disappointment you'll generate will cut across the effectiveness of all your future programmes.

Here again, to get anywhere close to running a flawless merchandise-based incentive programme that achieves all your goals, you need professional help. Within your own organisation, you're most unlikely to find either the range of specialist skills or the time required to make it happen.

Recognition: the psychological carrot

The third incentive award category is recognition—and while it may seem initially to lack the motivating power of travel or merchandise, it certainly should not be discarded lightly. Just look at the eagerness with which actors pursue Academy Awards. The opportunity to gain real recognition in your peer group's eyes can be a very motivating one indeed.

But to be successful, recognition awards have to be done extremely well. They have to be (or appear to be) a personal initiative by the company's most influential person—probably the chairman or managing director. They need to be publicised throughout the organisation via meetings, bulletins, memos and prestige brochures. And they must involve some kind of tangible token that tells the world about the winner's achievement. This could be a superbly designed certificate, plaque, trophy or lapel pin—something that can be displayed in the office or the home, or (in the pin's case) worn. Devices such as letters of appreciation from the chairman are very gratifying for the recipient, but they need to be backed by a lasting and visible proclamation of the feat.

Lend Lease, a client of ours, does this very well. Their Chairman's Awards are attractively mounted, and each state winner receives a handsome trophy with their name engraved on it. The winners are further rewarded by receiving a special prize, usually a grant to further their education or involvement in some worthwhile activity. They're also introduced to the whole Lend Lease organisation, through a Pacific-wide satellite link beamed to every country where the company has an office.

McRecognition

McDonald's, the purveyors of immensely popular burgers, also know how to motivate staff through recognition. Go into any of their restaurants, and you'll see the salespeople of the week, month and year displayed in photos on the wall. You'll also see them going about their tasks like all the other staff—but as they do so, their names and pictures are up there for everyone to see and applaud. And rightly so. They'll have worked hard to get their awards.

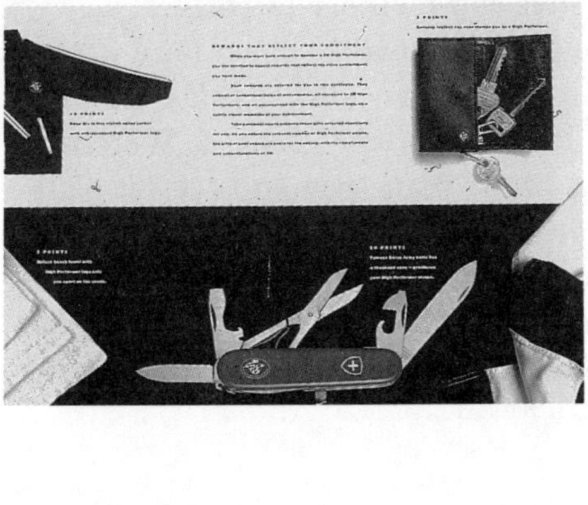

3M Automotive trade incentives were closely geared to recipients' known preferences.
Tasteful 'High Flyer' personalisation added a powerful recognition factor to merchandise that rewarded the sales forces of 3M and their resellers for outstanding sales achievement.
Courtesy of 3M Australia Pty Ltd

See the conquering hero . . .

As the whole aim of recognition awards is to make the recipient a hero or heroine, everyone in his or her working world needs to hear about the winner. House journals, newsletters, company bulletins and the trade press should all be used to spread the story far and wide.

Sometimes, it's possible to include a recognition factor in merchandise awards. Recently, for 3M Australia, we added a small, tasteful '3M High Performer' logo to sports jackets, sports watches, business shirts, business organisers, Akubra hats, sports bags and other merchandise awards. This personalised the merchandise in a unique way, and made a strong but subtle visual statement of the owner's status.

To personalise merchandise in this way costs almost nothing—yet it can pay you dividends in recognition-driven motivation for years. Other popular items for this purpose include plaques, trophies, silver ashtrays and beer mugs, all of which can easily be engraved with the reason they're being awarded, and the date. Be careful, though, that the awards aren't ostentatious. A cheap and vulgar item, we've found, is distinctly unmotivating. The article has to be something the winner can display with pride to colleagues, friends and family.

'Personal Best'—personalised

One of the most successful recognition schemes we have run was a 3M Company plan called 'Personal Best'. We selected a short list of merchandise items that were above average in desirability and perceived value. These were to serve as performance awards for 3M salespeople and the 3M dealer sales force, for selling diskettes and memory cartridges.

All the salespeople were invited to put their names down for a particular item—something they'd be proud to own and display in their homes for years. They could choose from a carriage clock, a Waterford crystal decanter, silver coaster/slides, a Mont Blanc pen and crystal glasses. These were all positioned at various points levels, representing different sales targets. When a salesperson's individual sales target was achieved, he or she received the previously-chosen award—which was heavily personalised with his or name or initials and the date of the presentation.

Recognition awards can be the most economical of all. But used in the right situations—which professional assistance can help you identify—they can give you a quite extraordinary return for a comparatively modest outlay.

Target: Vegas!

Earlier in this chapter, I mentioned our 'Toshiba Targetbusters' incentive programme. Because it has a lot of points worth noting, I'd like to cover it now in a little more detail.

The 1990 edition was called 'Toshiba Targetbusters—the Star-Studded Road to Vegas'. The participants were the sales personnel of Toshiba's distributors, Australia-wide. And the programme was an excellent example of much we have covered—a blend of travel and merchandise awards, with 'sprints' thrown in. A system of 'sales points' was devised to give all participants an equal chance, no matter where they lived and worked. A total of 7500 points earned the major award—a trip for two to Los Angeles and Las Vegas.

A tantalising choice

Throughout the programme, participants faced a tantalising choice. They could accumulate their points and try for the 7500 level. Or they could use them along the way for smaller travel and merchandise awards, all of which were described and illustrated in colourful catalogues.

At the 750-point level, participants could swap their points for a five-star country weekend for two, an outing for two to a top-rating show with limousine travel and supper afterwards, or a superb dinner for four. Alternatively, they could choose from a collection of kitchen appliances, a luxury linen pack, a cordless telephone or his 'n' hers mountain bicycles. At 1500 points, they could opt for one of three weekend interstate packages, or a set of golf clubs and accessories, an up-market camera package, prestige watches or a luggage collection.

When they reached 3000 points, their choices widened. Participants could take a five-day holiday for two in one of six destinations—Micronesia, Sabah and Sarawak, Vanuatu, New Zealand, Alice Springs and Ayers Rock, or Kakadu National Park. If they preferred merchandise, they could select a sailboard with many accessories, an outdoor furniture setting, bone china and crystalware sets or a home entertainment centre.

Or, of course, they could choose to retain their points, and keep on striving for 7500. Naturally, once they took any award at any level, their points went back to zero and they started again.

The Camel sprint

A sales 'sprint' within the programme added extra excitement. The sprint offered the uniquely Australian award of a weekend in Alice Springs, attending the famous 'Camel Cup' race meetings. The chance of seeing the dauntless dromedaries lumbering around the track—not to mention the attendant pleasures of a weekend in Australia's Red Heart, such as climbing Ayers Rock, visiting the Olgas and staying in the swish Sheraton Hotel—proved very effective as an additional motivator.

The Targetbusters programme was warmly received by its participants. And as I mentioned earlier, it's now being extended to give even more dealers and resellers a chance to visit lavish destinations and share in great entertainment. But this first Targetbusters venture outperformed all others we had run up to that time. It showed that prizes carefully selected for their outstanding quality and value will always be winners. And most importantly, it more than met Toshiba's targets for it. With the right professional assistance, your sales incentive programme can do the same.

Your incentive programme checklist

Keep the following questions in mind when you sit down to plan your incentive programme. And if your agency does it for you, use the questions to evaluate their proposal.

1. Have you set clear, precise, measurable goals for your programme?
2. Does it give every participant an equal chance to win awards?

3. In particular, will it appeal to the 'average 80%' of your targeted participants?
4. Are the sales targets realistic and achievable by everyone who applies themselves?
5. Is the programme simple and understandable in format?
6. Does it keep participants' paperwork to a minimum?
7. In duration, is it long enough to achieve your targets—yet short enough to maintain the participants' enthusiasm?
8. Will you sell it strongly to all potential participants?
9. Are you planning to keep all participants informed of their progress throughout?
10. Will you do so in a way that encourages front-runners and stragglers alike?
11. Are you planning 'sprints' within the main programme?
12. If you're selecting travel awards, are they beyond the participants' 'horizon of expectation'—yet within their 'horizon of comprehension'?
13. Are you including spouses/partners in the trip?
14. If you're having merchandise awards, will they allow people to 'spoil' themselves?
15. If there's a recognition dimension, will the winners receive permanent visible mementos of their achievement?
16. Will they be presented as heroes or heroines to everyone in their working world?

If you get a 'yes' to all or most of these questions, you can confidently expect outstanding results from your programme—and a sales, distributors, dealer or retailer network eagerly awaiting the next one.

17

CHAPTER

Business Gifts and Offers that Get Action

The premium offers we looked at in Chapters 8 and 9 have a first cousin—one so closely related in form and function that the distinction between them sometimes blurs. This lookalike relative is known as a customer incentive or business gift, depending on the exact task it performs. If it's something the customer earns for ongoing loyalty, it's a customer incentive. And if you give it away to create a warm inner glow, with no sales strings attached, it's a business gift.

Mind the minefield

Either way, this multi-talented item has another point in common with sales force incentives. It shouldn't be rushed into without careful planning. Selecting customer incentives and business gifts can, in fact, be a positive minefield for the inexperienced. Sales tax, insurance to cover storage and non-arrival, import restrictions, packing and storage considerations, ease of delivery, order and reorder lead times, prices in relation to quality—boring as they may sound, these are some of the key factors to be borne in mind. And as we'll see, they're just the beginning.

3M carefully select their business gifts to maximise exposure for the 3M brand
Courtesy of 3M Australia Pty Ltd

Rewards for loyalty

The first of our two categories—customer incentive offers—is the art of rewarding your customers for staying loyal. It gives them a positive reason to go on buying from you—because as they do so, they build up customer points which can be swapped for tempting gifts.

Avis Rent-a-Car, for instance, ran a customer incentive programme where carefully selected gifts became more and more attractive as the rental periods lengthened. This was really a programme within a programme. It was designed to be exclusive to members of Ansett Airlines' Golden Wing Club. They enjoyed the lowest Avis rates to start with. But if they rented for at least 15 days in a 12-month period, the extra rewards began. Clocks, cameras, portable radios, a bubble gum dispenser or books on wine and cooking for 15 days rental. A tennis racquet, carrybags and further choices for 25 days. An expanding range of goodies, including a barbecue, outdoor furniture and an exercise bike, for 35 days. And fine wine, an espresso coffee machine, a superb leather bag and other enticing options for 50 days.

Repeat sales earned

Entitled the 'Regular Renters Bonus' programme, the promotion was very successful. And deservedly so. This was a situation where repeat sales were the goal. And the programme earned them—by giving people powerful reasons to bypass the other car hire desks and head for Avis. Not just once, but every time they landed.

The lesson, then, is clear. If your business runs on repeat sales—if you have a service or product people have to buy regularly but could buy elsewhere—a customer incentive plan could work brilliantly for you. Put yourself in your customers' position. You find you can get some sought-after rewards without spending an extra cent—just by always buying the same brand, or constantly patronising the same outlet. Wouldn't you do so?

A customer incentive add-on

In Australia in 1987, the 3M Company demonstrated the truth of two sales promotion axioms: a customer incentive plan can often be the ideal add-on to a sales incentive programme. And very successful promotions can be created around current events.

At the time, Olympic fever was building up throughout the country. The 3M Company was a major sponsor of Australia's Olympic team. Every 3M product sold helped to get the Australian team to the Games in Seoul. Consequently and logically, the 3M Automotive Trades Division ran a sales incentive programme for its distributors, based on 3M's Olympic involvement. Like all good incentive programmes, it was simple. Distributors aimed to reach their 3M sales target each quarter. If they did, each sales team received 100 3M Olympic Points—which team members could then exchange for a range of merchandise from a catalogue.

Selling efforts reinforced

That provided considerable motivation for the teams. And in the race to reach their targets, their selling efforts were reinforced by a customer incentive plan. This also took advantage of growing interest in the Olympics—and an important psychological principle. Probably, we've all imagined ourselves breasting the tape or splashing to victory before a cheering Olympic crowd. And if we can't do that, we want others to do it on our behalf.

So the plan enabled customers to fulfil their wishes. For six months, all cartons of 3M Automotive Trades and Marine products contained special Olympic Games gift tokens. These reminded customers that their purchases were helping the Australian Olympic team. But as well, customers could collect the tokens and exchange them for gifts from a customer gift catalogue, supplied to them by their distributor.

A double-ended freight train

For the 3M Occupational Health and Safety Division, repeat sales were the name of the game. So the situation was made to order for a customer incentive plan. The whole promotion was like a freight train climbing a mountain, with engines at each end. The distributor incentive programme pulled the sales from in front. The customer incentive plan pushed them from behind—while a good dose of patriotism and topicality added power to both. Not surprisingly, the promotion achieved excellent results.

What would you like?

What kind of gift would make me loyal to one brand or outlet? That's the question to ask yourself when you plan one of the crucial parts of your customer incentive programme—choosing the gift.

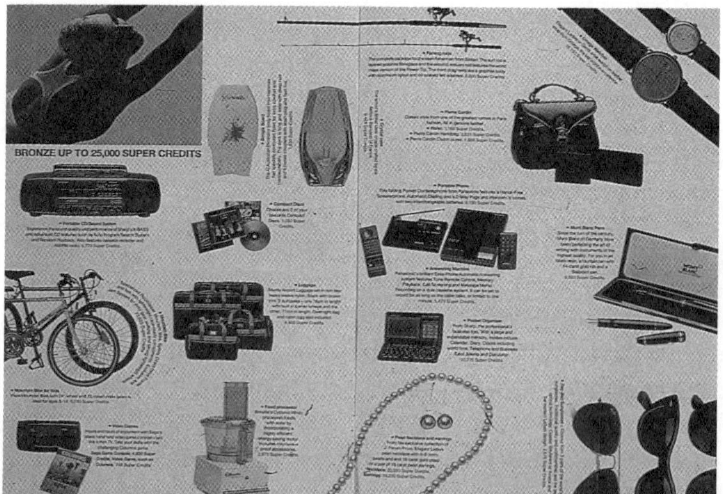

Appropriate 'Gold', 'Silver' and 'Bronze' gifts encourage business customers to continue buying from 3M, because they're given a choice—a wider range of gifts, or fewer, more valuable ones.
Courtesy of 3M Australia Pty Ltd

If the item you have in mind would appeal strongly to you, that's a point in its favour. But as your tastes may not be shared by the whole population, run these by-now-familiar questions past it too. Is it useful to the recipients? Is it appropriate and relevant to their lifestyles? Will they like to be seen using, wearing or drinking it? Does it enable them to 'spoil' themselves?

Then, from your point of view, consider these questions—many of which we've also met before. Is the item's image right for your company? Does it have a natural link with your product? Does it offer you advertising extension possibilities? Will it avoid conflict with your clients? (Offering free T-shirts, for example, may not be wise if your clients are clothing stores.) Is it practical to buy, store and deliver? And perhaps most basic of all—can you afford it?

Once again, get an overwhelming majority of 'yesses'—with no 'no's' on the obviously vital questions, like the last one—and you can look forward to a highly profitable promotion.

Christmas morning revisited

Remember the thrill of waking up on Christmas morning and seeing

Special merchandise items carefully chosen for Apple buyers allow them to demonstrate their special affinity with the brand.
Courtesy of Apple Computer Australia Pty Limited

the bulging pillowcase at the foot of your bed? Or your feelings of anticipation as the family handed you your birthday presents? The point is, we all love getting gifts. And the pleasure doesn't diminish as we grow older.

This is why business gifts, carefully chosen and well presented, can do so much to create goodwill and build customer loyalty. At the same time, they can be subtle yet powerful promotional pieces for you. If they're the kind of items people use regularly, they not only keep your name before your clients, but link it with the pleasant experience of receiving a gift. Consequently, business gifts have traditionally included items like key rings, paper knives, pens and rulers. While predictable and pretty unexciting (would you fall on your knees in gratitude to someone who gave you a paper knife?), such items still have their place. They definitely get 'yes' answers to the first and last of our check questions—they're useful to the recipients and they're almost certainly within your budget.

The Coca-Cola people have had worldwide success with business gifts that are not only useful but a lot more imaginative than most of the above list. Indeed, many of their hand-outs have become cult items among Coke vendors. They include bar mirrors, Coca-Cola clocks, bar mats, straw dispensers that sit on milk bar counters (right where the buying decision is made) and even refrigerators. These items are given away free to Coke outlets when their sales reach a certain figure. They're welcomed by the Coke sellers, who regard them not only as useful sales builders but as evidence of achievement.

Coca-Cola seek maximum exposure in milk bars and wherever the brand is sold via signage and special business gifts like refrigerators and straw dispensers. They encourage consumers to carry their name too, by giving away Coke-branded clothing and accessories. Coca–Cola design special premiums to give their brand name the greatest possible exposure.
Reproduced with the permission of The Coca–Cola Company, owner of the registrered trademarks 'Coca–Cola' and 'Coke'. Courtesy Bladon Australia Pty Ltd

The walking billboard

Traditionally popular as business gifts, too, are T-shirts, caps and other wearable items that display your logo or brief selling message in a tasteful form. Here again, Coca-Cola is well to the fore. There's a Coke company in Hong Kong that does nothing but churn out Coke-linked clothing items for global use. Coke has even expanded into the designer clothes area, to ensure that appropriate clothing can be worn wherever their brand is sold.

Of course, you don't need to go as far as designer clothes to create an effective gift. Simple clothing items will score fairly well on the 'yes' scale, not only from the recipient's angle but from yours. They certainly have good advertising extension possibilities—the prospect of squads of walking billboards spreading your message at no extra cost is not unattractive. Such items are easy to obtain, store and despatch. And very probably, you can well afford them.

The oddball ideas

Occasionally, because of the nature of your product, it's extraordinarily difficult to link a gift idea with it. What, for instance, links naturally with a toilet cleaner? That's what I had to ask myself when we launched one—a toilet cleaner that rejoiced in the name of Swish.

Like Toilet Duck, its main competitor, Swish had a curved spout for cleaning under the toilet rim and it cleaned the whole bowl effectively. In other words, it was just as good a product. But Toilet Duck was well established. Swish was the newcomer. I felt an effective gift could help give it the unique identity it needed. But what could that gift be?

Well, the principle is this. If you can't link your gift idea directly with your product, look beyond the pale. Go for the left-field idea—the useful but oddball item that will give you an attention-grabbing talking point. In Swish's case, it proved to be the Swish Loo pencil holder.

The sheer unexpectedness of creating a desktop pencil holder in the shape of a toilet worked. It was aimed at the trade, who received it well. They talked about it and put it on their desks. It helped us to get excellent distribution, superb on-shelf siting for the brand—and lots of sales.

So if you really can't link a gift with your product, don't despair. Go for the wild idea. It's not easy. But if you get it right, it can work brilliantly.

The upmarket alternative

The other way many companies go is upmarket. Prestige pens, clocks, watches, sports bags, golf umbrellas—all of which can carry your name or logo elegantly—are widely used as gifts for preferred customers. They can be expensive, admittedly. But over the years, they've proved their worth as goodwill builders and cementers of relationships.

Divisible gifts

Sometimes, the decision to buy your product can be made by more than one person. In the professional videotape market, for instance, the chief engineer, director, producer and purchasing officer can all have a hand in it. How do you distribute business gifts in that situation?

Quite simply. You go for the divisible gift—a device we employed to very good effect in a promotion we ran for 3M professional videotapes. Called 'Keep Mumm with 3M', it was designed to boost tape sales among production houses. We offered a crate of Mumm Champagne with the 3M tapes, to help the studios celebrate a successful production. We also added award-winning wines for those who bought above-average stocks of the 3M product. Staggering sales quickly demonstrated the soundness of the strategy.

Subsequent research showed that the booty was indeed divided up among the relevant recipients. In some cases, it was used to swell stocks at the office Christmas party. Since then, 3M has very sensibly ruled out alcohol as a business gift—but we've yet to find a substitute as popular or as effective with this particular market!

Wanted: originality

Increasingly, the trend today is to more imaginative and original gift ideas. Around the world, enterprising sales promotion companies are putting in the extra effort needed to come up with truly individual premiums. Their goal is to create one-off gifts that reflect a company's image, product and message far more strongly than standard items can—while still retaining the basic essentials of usefulness, relevance, affordability and so on.

It's not hard to see why. If someone gives you a birthday present that's not only useful but is just right for you—something unusual and unexpected they've obviously taken a lot of trouble to find—don't you appreciate it more than socks or stockings?

The right medicine

Typical of the new wave in gifts was a memo roll that Evans Medical, a British pharmaceutical company, distributed to chemists. Evans had been advertising in the pharmacy journals, with the message, 'For high quality drugs at low prices, pick up the phone and call your wholesaler.' Their sales promotion agency came up with an ingenious gift—a memo roll shaped like a security medicine container. It carried Evans' advertising message, and dispensed paper that featured the advertising's visual device of a phone-shaped pill bottle. Every time pharmacy staff pulled out a sheet of paper, Evans' advertising campaign was strongly reinforced.

The basic idea, then, is to put your promotional message on a piece of office equipment—which is not only useful but unique, distinctive and memorable.

Avoiding the throwaway risk

VNU Business Publications in England did just that when they acquired *Accountancy Age* magazine. They wanted to convince advertising agency media buyers of the magazine's potential. The traditional route would have been to produce a brochure. But however glossy and appealing such a brochure was, it risked being glanced at and thrown away—or at best, filed, reported *Promotions and Incentives* magazine.[1]

Wanting to avoid that risk, the company's sales promotion agency devised an imaginative gift and delivered it personally to 250 media buyers. It was a very modern, stylish telephone address box—the kind of item anyone would happily keep on their desk. And it incorporated all the magazine's essential data in pithy, read-at-a-glance form. So instead of progressing swiftly from hand to wastepaper basket or filing cabinet, the *Accountancy Age* facts and figures sat semi-permanently on the desk, and steadily wormed their way into the media buyer's consciousness. That's probably the next best thing to whispering them into the buyer's ears every night as he or she sleeps—and rather easier to arrange.

Blurring the lines

Earlier, we observed that the line between gifts and incentive items frequently blurs. Such a blur certainly surrounded another imaginative item created by VNU's agency. Was it a business gift, an advertising device or an incentive tool? You be the judge.

The occasion was a trade exhibition. The task was to persuade visitors to call at VNU's stand and absorb details of the company's information technology publications. And VNU lured them in with a brilliant ploy—an invitation to play 'VNU Challenge'. This was an absorbing cube game, not unlike the Rubik's Cube that fascinated and frustrated millions a few years ago. However, the VNU cube cleverly promoted the magazines' names and selling points to players as they manipulated it. And to take the impact well beyond the exhibition, sets were given away to selected visitors to intrigue them further in their offices or homes.

Results beyond goodwill

Business gift-giving, in short, can involve a lot more creativity than simply opening a catalogue and plonking a finger on a likely item. But whether you follow the custom-made or the off-the-shelf path, your give-away can get results that go well beyond generating goodwill. It can do a solid selling job for you as well.

Case study: the BA mug

A British Airways gift distributed by BA's sales force worldwide reinforces its 'feeling good' TV campaign—the one in which people from all continents come together to form a smiling face. The gift is a heat-reactive Magic Mug in five colours, supplied by Imbrex/Prince William Pottery. A smiling globe appears on it, as it does in BA's commercial, when the mug is filled with a hot drink.

One of a catalogue of items, this is the most heavily requested of all BA's offerings, which also include T-shirts, block pads and paperclip holders.

So choose an item that people will want to keep. Make sure the message echoes what your current advertising is saying. And what you spend on gifts will add to the effectiveness of your advertising dollars.

Replacing the product

In some cases, the ability of a customer incentive or business gift to extend product awareness can be taken to the ultimate. It can reach the point where the incentive or gift actually replaces the product.

The classic example is Dunhill. As a cigarette company, the brand spent a fortune to establish itself as the most prestigious on the market. In the process, it also established itself as a bespoke gentleman's outfitter and accessories store, offering superb clothing and merchandise items to customers via its prestigious London store.

Then the world changed. Cigarette smoking started to become socially unacceptable. As the process accelerated, Dunhill began to switch its advertising emphasis from its cigarettes to its upmarket clothing and accessories stores—which it opened in the most prestigious addresses capital-by-capital. Today, for many people, the brand is just as well known for very elegant clothing and merchandise, with never a cigarette in sight or mind. That has to be one of modern marketing history's most sophisticated examples of the tail wagging the dog.

Red nose, red face

As we have seen, relevant creativity is one of the rules for outstanding incentive or gift success. But there's one thing we all know about rules. They were made to be broken.

One of today's best-known incentives is immensely creative. Its effectiveness has been quite extraordinary. Yet its relevance to its product—or its purchaser's needs and lifestyle—is, frankly, non-existent. This is the famous 'Red Nose'—the very visible symbol that has made the annual appeal of the Cot Death Association such a huge success.

Cot Death, or Sudden Infant Death Syndrome, is an awesomely tragic subject. Most of us would rather push it right out of our minds. So the Red Nose was developed to lighten it—and to break down our mental barriers to the charity's appeal.

The incentive comes in three forms. There's the Red Nose itself, the 'Too Chicken to Wear a Red Nose' badge and the much less embarrassing Red Nose for the car. As well, considerably larger Red Noses appear on houses, buses, ferries, trucks and other unexpected places. The results: tremendously increased awareness—and millions more dollars—for the Cot Death Association's work. So sometimes being a little silly can help a lot!

Innovation the key

The Red Nose might lack obvious relevance to its product, but it certainly has everything else. Its sheer innovation has seized the whole community's imagination. It doesn't just identify with its product's promotion—it *is* the promotion. Almost everybody identifies it immediately with its product. And its costs are absurdly low for the results it gets.

So here's another case where daring originality has paid off handsomely. But in charity work and every other product category, the search goes on for ever more innovative incentives. If you can create one that seizes your customers' imagination, integrates strongly with your current promotion and supports your branding, the search will be well worthwhile. In your case, it will end very profitably indeed.

Check the checklist in Chapter 8

Not only are customer incentives and business gifts the first cousins of sales incentives—they're related on the other side of the family to premiums as well. That fact becomes clear when you check the checklist in Chapter 8. Every question there relates with equal force to customer incentives and business gifts. Go through them carefully—and evaluate your incentive/gift idea in light of the answers you get.

Notes

1. 'The China Syndrome', by Robin Cobb, in Market Survey, *Promotions and Incentives* magazine, February 1993.

18

CHAPTER

Your Database—The Way To Relationship Marketing

It's long been said that the secret of getting on in life is not what you know, but who you know. Never has that been truer than in present-day marketing. Do you know who your customers are? By name? Their marital status? Number of children? Personal likes and dislikes? The kinds of selling offers they'll respond to? The types of gifts and recognition items and services they'll appreciate most?

No?

Then you'd better start learning. Because if you don't, it won't be long before your competitors do. But don't let that learning challenge daunt you. The truly startling thing is that, with modern computer techniques, all those points mentioned above and many more can readily be gathered onto your customer database. The information can be obtained through direct marketing techniques, outside rented lists, telemarketing, coupon response from advertising and sales promotion, and other avenues such as your sales force.

Start with basic customer information as shown in the example below:

Title *(Mr, Mrs, Ms, Dr, Rev)* **First Name & Initials**
Last Name **Suffix** *(BA, LLB, FAMI, etc.)*
Address

City **State**
Postcode
(Street numbers and post codes can reveal a lot about the type of housing and socio-demographic group)
Telephone
Postal/PO Box address

Sex
(Many names and titles such as Professor and Doctor disguise the person's sex)
Age/Birth date
Company name
Company address
Fax number
Mobile phone
Work phone
Pager number
Email coding **Source Code**

Obtaining all that is very much an ideal. However, get as much of the above as you can. Then leave space for many different fields on your relational database . These could include demographics, seasonal factors, household income, family size, ages and sex of children, car make, spouse's role and so on. You'll also want information like the results of the last contact or mailing, the customer's reaction to offers, his or her previous sales patterns, transactional patterns and any other data relevant to your situation.

The kind of things the local grocer used to keep in his head.

Gradually, your list will become segmented. A startlingly detailed profile of your personal market-place will begin to emerge. And as new technologies like interactive and two-way TV come into daily use, the process will not only become easier but increasingly relevant.

A word of caution. Never collect information that cannot be used to help your marketing effort. Information goes out of date quickly and is expensive to enter. Assess what you need carefully, before you touch a key.

Let your customers drive you

The implications of this customer-centred approach are immense. Even today, most marketing people are product-driven. Ask them how many units they produce and sell, and they'll have the answers at their fingertips. But ask them who their customers are, and you're apt to get a blank stare, a shuffling of feet. And silence.

Which leaves a huge question unanswered. How can you give your customers exactly what they want, if you don't know their personal tastes, preferences and priorities? It's a bit like your circle of friends. Probably you're all roughly in the same socio-economic group. But you're all individuals, with very distinctive characteristics, likes and dislikes. So up to a point, you modify your behaviour, tone of voice, gestures and so on, depending on which friend you're with. To get maximum satisfaction from your relationships, you speak to and treat each of your friends in subtly different ways.

Today, you can do exactly the same with your market. You can tailor-make your sales pitches and marketing efforts for different segments of

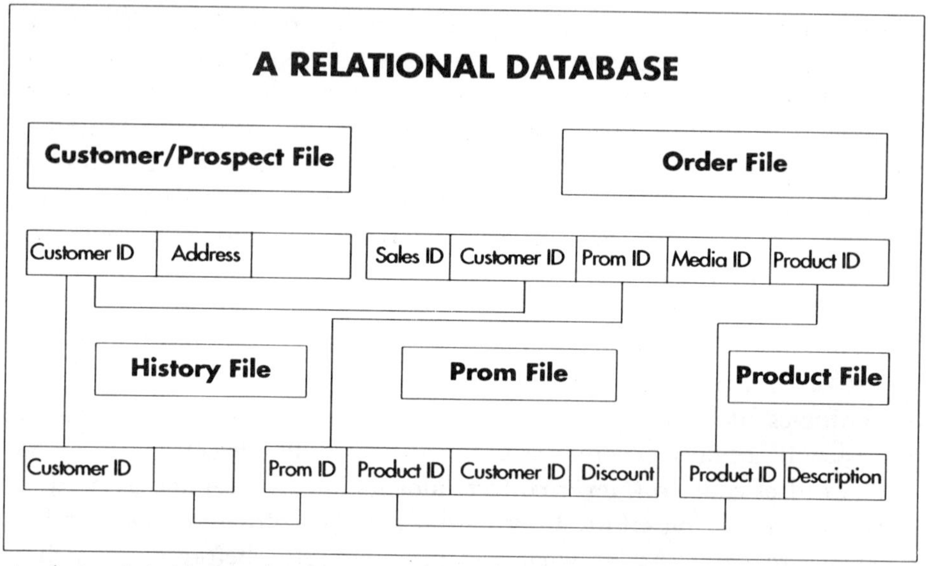

A relational database means that several files can be linked. An example of the kind of structure you could develop is shown above. You can see that the customer or prospect file can be linked to the sales history file, the promotion file, the order file and the product file. This allows you to cross-reference client information, and gives you unimpeded access to it.

your database at different times. While that certainly helps you to make immediate sales, it also does something far more significant still. It enables you to build mutually fulfilling long-term—even lifetime—relationships with your customers, just as your consideration of their individuality does with your friends.

This is the quantum leap forward that modern databases have opened up to us. The marketing potential of personalised long-term or lifetime relationships with customers is mindboggling for three main reasons—all of which must be fully grasped, if you don't want to wither and die on the marketing vine.

Customers are easier to keep than get

The first reason is that it takes five times the energy and budget to get a new customer as it does to keep an existing one. So anything that binds existing customers to you makes a valuable contribution to your bottom line.

But there's much more to it than that. A disproportionately small number of your customers generates a very large proportion of your income. The old 80/20 rule—that 80% of your business comes from 20% of your customers—is a remarkably accurate generalisation. Sometimes, your prime spenders are an even smaller proportion of the whole. Here's what strikes me as a really mindblowing statistic: current research suggests that just 12 000 people make 70% of all business flights flown within Australia.

I also heard recently of a cat food company in Belgium whose database disclosed that 16% of its purchasers provided 65% of the brand's sales. Clearly, if even a small proportion defected, a large part of the company's business would disappear. The cat food company needs to keep a very close relationship with their top 16%, and develop strategies that maintain and increase this key group's loyalty. And now, they can—just as you can in your situation. For the first time, you can now positively identify your top spenders. You can pinpoint your best customers—and because you can also discover and record what makes them tick, you can move to keep them yours, far more effectively than ever before.

Consider their 'lifetime value'

The third reason why building long-term customer relationships is so crucial hinges on the real value of your best customers. What is their true worth to you? $5.85 for a packet of washing powder? 85¢ for a can of dog food? $2 for a private bus fare? $30 000 for a new car? That's the old pre-relationship way of judging a customer's value—and it grossly underestimates the true figure.

If you can keep the washing powder customer's loyalty for 10 years, he or she is worth more than $5000 to you. The dog food buyer is worth at least $4000 over the same period—or a staggering $8000, if he or she is from one of Australia's many two-dog families. The private bus passenger, travelling both ways each day, has a 10-year value of $9600. And the car buyer? With a new car every three years, plus servicing, plus at least one second car at some stage, $135 000 over 10 years would be a conservative estimate.

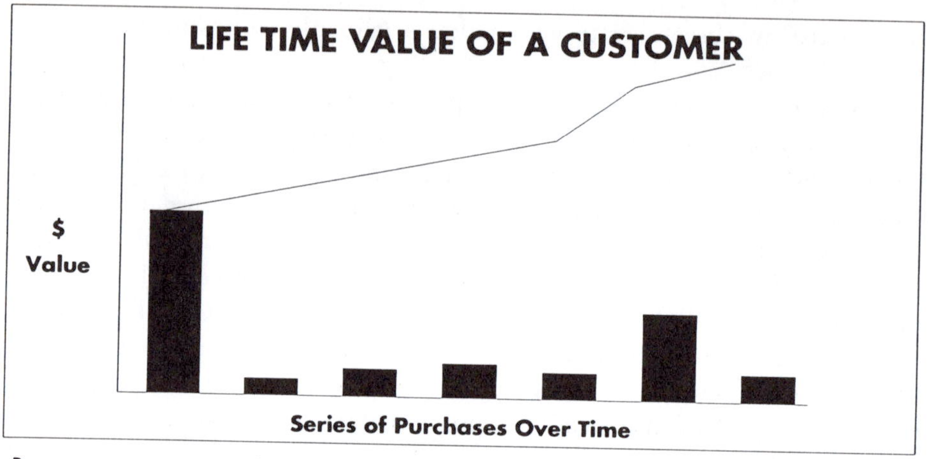

Because a customer makes a series of transactions and not a single purchase, he or she has a surprisingly high Life Time Value.

Once you start valuing your customers along those lines, the worth of each one hits you as never before. And building a lasting relationship with them—your best customers especially—becomes the obvious way to a prosperous and profitable future.

Don't follow the dodo

This is why, to today's shrewdest marketers who understand the full implications of the microchip revolution, the old idea of 'transactional'

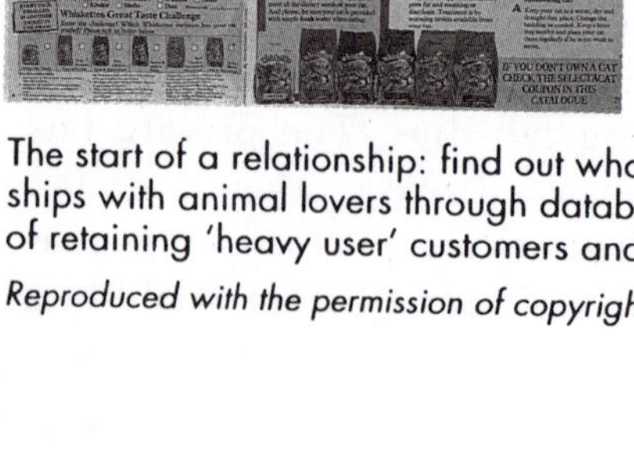

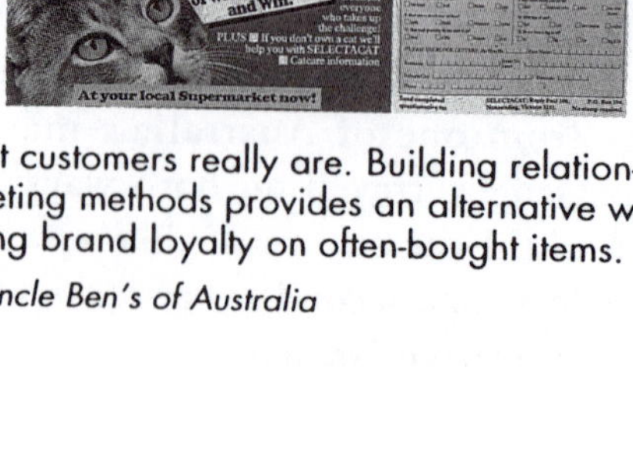

The start of a relationship: find out who your best customers really are. Building relationships with animal lovers through database marketing methods provides an alternative way of retaining 'heavy user' customers and enhancing brand loyalty on often-bought items.

Reproduced with the permission of copyright owner, Uncle Ben's of Australia marketing—making a sale and moving on—is as dead as the proverbial dodo. Now all their thinking centres on 'relationship' marketing—the customer-driven, database-empowered approach that regards every good customer as a crucial business asset, and seeks to win his or her commitment to a mutually beneficial, ongoing relationship. Indeed, one marketing authority insists that, without such a carefully cultivated personal relationship, the customer loyalty everyone pursues so avidly simply cannot be maintained in today's environment.

Are you following the way of the dodo? Or are you looking at your customers with long-term eyes? Are you investing money in the media, in-store, in packaging, direct mail and the telephone, to turn your customers into friends?

Your future, in large measure, depends on the answer.

Retention the priority

This new understanding forces a re-think of one hallowed marketing emphasis. Chasing new customers used to be the top priority for most businesses. Now the priority has changed to relationship-building with the top 20% of your customers, and working on the next 25% to upgrade them. A smaller effort should go into the following 25%, while the final 30% are probably not worth bothering about. Chasing new customers has dropped even lower down the list.

Yet there's an irony here. Once you're doing extremely well with customer retention, you'll tend to do better with acquisition too. You'll have learned so much about the likes and dislikes of your target audience that you'll automatically have a deeper understanding of what new prospects want—and be able to attract them more effectively, even though it's no longer your top priority.

Cultivating the relationship

The 'why' of relationship marketing becomes obvious after a few minutes' thought. Then it's time to turn to the harder part—the 'how'.

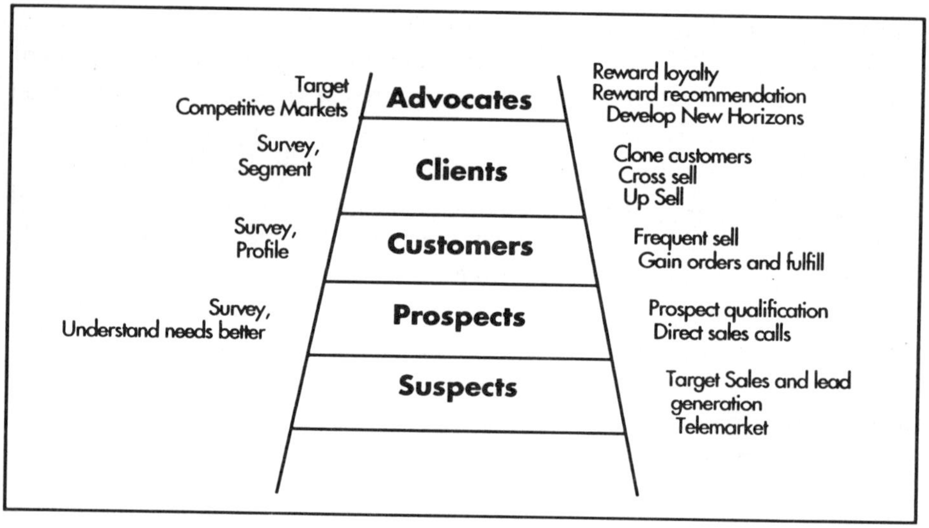

Murray Raphel's Relationship Ladder: climb it and turn prospects into customers, customers into clients and clients into advocates of your business. The 'Relationship Ladder' is the basis for a new book by Murray Raphel called *Up the Loyalty Ladder* (William Morrow Publishers, New York).

Actually, it's not all that hard once you consider what relationship marketing really is. It's simply going beyond regarding your customers as a huge faceless mass and getting to know them as people.

Getting to know their tastes, predilections, priorities, motivational triggers, wants, needs and hopes, on an increasingly individual basis. And then moving to meet those requirements—not only with your product, but with caring, customer-driven support services too.

That's relationship marketing: and to date, no-one's come up with a better way of doing it than through some form of a frequent buyers' club—a structure that gives a customer a feeling of belonging, provides tangible rewards for loyalty and (if I could add a dimension that many clubs still lack) offers opportunities for personal recognition too.

Flying high

Perhaps the best-known examples of such clubs are the 'Frequent Flyer' ones—the airline versions that offer passengers points for so many miles flown. As the points pile up, they can be redeemed for further flights,

British Airways reflect their advertising theme and sell the benefits of their exclusive executive service in an effort to look after their best customers. It's important for them to keep the custom of regular business travellers, who account for a high % of turnover and profitability.
Courtesy of British Airways

holidays, or attractive merchandise. As well, the clubs seek to pamper members with extra services. Typically, these include their own departure lounge with business and refreshment facilities, faster boarding procedures, priority baggage collection and special club magazines.

Widely used in the USA, Europe and Australia, Frequent Flyer Clubs have proved very successful. They have certainly justified the faith placed in them by the airlines, who stuck to them even when so-called marketing gurus were pooh-poohing the concept in international magazines.

Relationships—or rewards?

More recently, however, other marketing identities have put up a more thoughtful critique of the clubs, in light of relationship marketing principles. Do the clubs really build relationships, they ask, or do they simply offer customer incentives? Would the customer's loyalty to the airline continue if the club stopped—or would he or she just seek the same benefits elsewhere?

A very good question. And one, I believe, that can be answered positively if the club delivers the extra dimension I mentioned above—by going beyond rewards to personal recognition. Some airlines have already woken up to this. They have developed ways of making club members feel loved, such as automatic upgrades to higher classes whenever seats are available. Thoughtful touches like those, in my view, are what make the difference between incentives and relationship-building—because they say 'you're important, you really matter to us' far more eloquently than gifts alone.

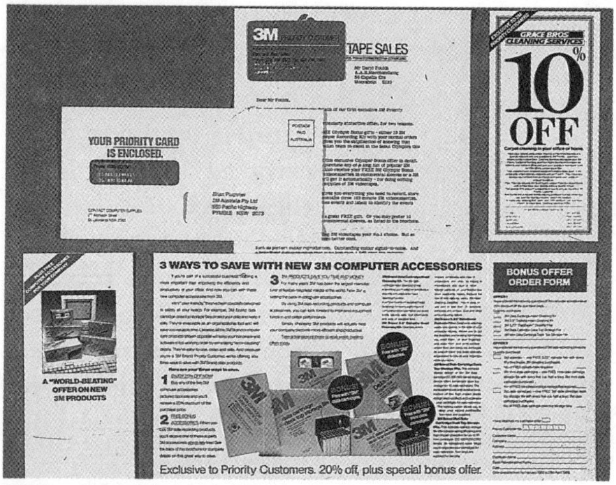

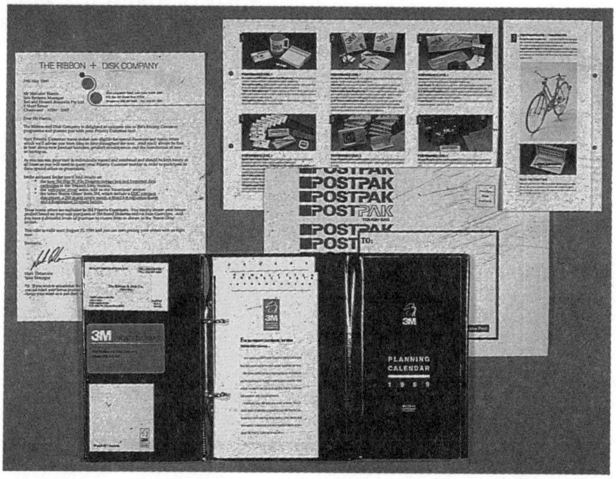

3M employ their 'resellers' databases to reach the end users of their products individually and proactively with regular offers, through their Priority Customer relationship marketing programme.
Courtesy of 3M Australia Pty Ltd

Priority customers

It's possible, we've found, to communicate the same sense of recognition to people through devices like plastic cards. Our 3M 'Priority Customer' programme (see also Chapter 20) has worked on that basis now for several years. We simply send known business purchasers of 3M disks, diskettes and data cartridges a plastic '3M Priority Customer' card, bearing their name, company and an identification number. When ordering 3M supplies, they only have to phone and quote their name and number to receive priority service. As well, they get appealing gifts for purchase points earned, plus special price-off deals, regular newsletters and advance information on new 3M products.

The programme has boosted 3M Office Supplies' market share very significantly. It would probably have worked pretty well if we'd called it the '3M Keyboard Kapers Klub' and just offered the gifts, deals and information. But what makes it magic, I am certain, is personalisation and the title—plus the individually named and numbered plastic card that confirms the recognition the title implies.

Go for recognition

So that's one point I'd emphasise about running frequent buyer clubs of any kind. If you possibly can, include some factor that doesn't just reward people but recognises them as someone special. It could be the club name or a plastic card. Or it could be a simple act that adds to their comfort, convenience or sense of importance.

American Express achieved something of a coup in that area a few years ago in America. For some time, the American Express people have been well aware of the importance of relationship building. They stratify their customers through green, gold, 'Optima' and corporate cards, and offer appropriate relationship-building incentives to each group. These include low-price insurance, a wine club and special rewards for introducing a friend.

But as well, American Express has two actual frequent buyers' clubs. Through the first, called 'Buyer's Advantage', members receive exclusive extended warranties on electrical appliances and other household goods, when they buy them on their cards. The second club, appropriately named 'Applause', allows members to obtain the best seats in the house at the most popular musicals and stage shows. And it was through Applause that American Express gave its members recognition in a big way.

Realising that the hit musical *Miss Saigon* would be booked out for months after it opened, the American Express team moved in early and bought huge blocks of tickets. They offered these at normal prices to club members—and so enabled them to jump the queues and see a sold-out show at very short notice, while their friends waited for months. It was a brilliant move that made club members feel important, privileged and appreciated. I'm certain American Express strengthened many key relationships through that one act of recognition.

Personal experience

Go for recognition, then, wherever you can. I believe it's enormously

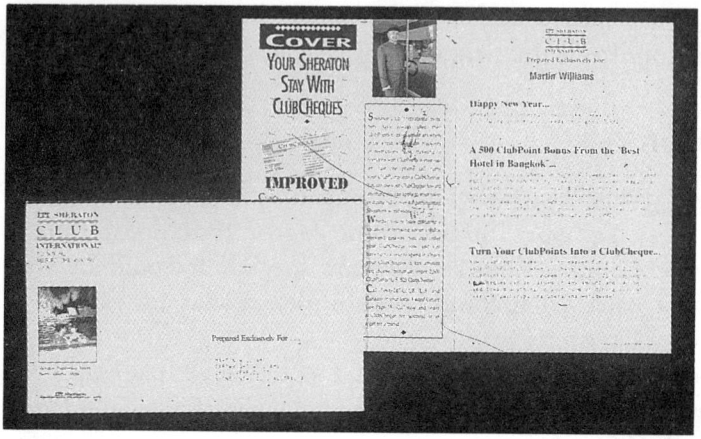

Sheraton, directed from Boston USA, mail their database worldwide from Holland. Each customer is updated regularly with pertinent offers and Frequent Stayer points exchangeable for stays and upgrades as well as merchandise. Points are awarded on staying or spending time at a Sheraton. This relationship scheme is credited with being the best of its type anywhere. *Courtesy ITT Sheraton Pacific Hotels and Resorts*

strategic. And my reasons for saying that are not just the detached observations of the professional who's involved in clients' projects and has read the research. I can say it from personal experience—because I know how good it feels to belong to a club that goes out of its way to make me feel appreciated.

This club is conducted by our client ITT Sheraton Pacific Hotels and Resorts. Built on a sophisticated database programme, the Sheraton Club International is run from Boston, USA. It communicates with me and its other members through mailings despatched worldwide from Holland.

When I open my distinctive Sheraton envelope, I find a personalised A5-sized catalogue containing a message directed very relevantly and individually to me. The catalogue is full of useful offers from all over the world, many of which appeal to my particular interests. There's also a record of the points and bonus points I have received, as well as deductions for any I might have used in upgrades, special holidays or even Grace Bros department store vouchers.

I welcome these mailings, and feel part of the club they represent.

Once a year, the club mails me my Gold Card. When I book into a Sheraton hotel, the card is run through a machine. The hotel retains the receipt, which records my presence. The information is processed and sent to Boston, and the details will show up in a subsequent mailing I receive.

My membership is paid by annual fee. Alternatively, the fee can be swapped for points accumulated throughout the year. Each hotel in the group contributes towards the points system. This means that the scheme always has money to still pay out, even when people cash in their points over a relatively short period.

Taking recognition further

The very personalised nature of the Sheraton Club International's mailing pack gives me the individual recognition I appreciate. But, of course, recognition can be taken much further than personalised elements in a mailing. In some special circumstances, it can even be the whole basis of the club.

The Bank of Boston, for instance, offered their wealthiest customers membership in a luxury service club that gave them priority entrée to the region's most notable events. Superbly produced direct mail pieces invited them to the best seats at prestigious concerts and polo matches, and to privileged browsing at exclusive art auctions. From this recognition, relationships have developed—relationships that have come to be worth millions to the Bank over long periods of time.

The Bank of Boston Club approach takes personal recognition to the ultimate degree. But however you make your best customers feel appreciated, do so by showing them the same kind of consideration you show to special friends—because that's what you want those customers to become.

Give up the guesswork

Let me emphasise a second key to frequent buyer clubs' success. Don't just guess at what your members would like by way of recognition, rewards or new products. Find out for sure. How? By asking them. You are now entering into a relationship with them. And two-way communication is basic to any relationship worth the name.

So make full use of the information-gathering sources I outlined at the start of the chapter, plus your database's recording power. You'll soon have a pretty clear picture of what motivates and gratifies the various segments of your market. Then all you have to do is give it to them.

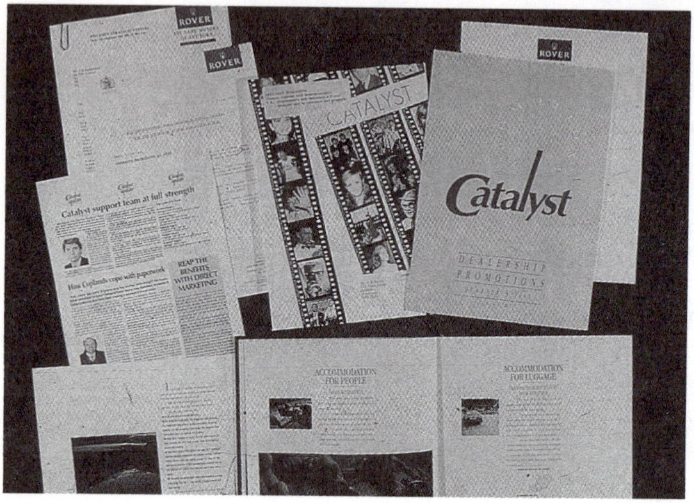

A totally personalised communication medium, Rover's uniquely configured Catalyst magazine appeals individually to each customer's interests. It comes from the dealer quarterly to help build the relationship for future purchases and service business, throughout the vehicle's life. The magazine gives unique insights into new advancements in technology and features, keeping customers abreast of these. Rover also makes pertinent offers designed to warm customers for their next purchase. These offers and communications intensify 30 to 36 months from the initial sale, just when a new purchase can be expected.
Courtesy of Rover UK

Introducing the Catalyst

This approach has led to the creation of a breakthrough relationship marketing programme in Britain. Back in 1980, Austin Rover began a database marketing venture, aimed at the buyers of its cars. It mailed them a welcome letter and a warranty at the time of purchase, and followed up with service reminders, accessory discounts and various offers throughout the car's life. Then, when the average time for buying a new car approached, the mailings became sales messages. And they plugged the virtues of whichever car the Austin Rover people thought was the most likely replacement choice for the customer concerned.

The whole programme worked fairly well, but it had three weak points. It drew very little information from the customers. It simply guessed at the time when they were likely to buy a new car. And it guessed at what model that car might be. Eventually, Austin Rover's agency decided that, with modern computer resources, guesswork wasn't good enough. They needed to base the programme on accurate information. Further, they wanted to know more about the customers, so they could make the programme's offers and rewards as appealing as possible. The best way to get all that data, they decided, was to ask the customers themselves.

The personalised magazine

They hit on an ingenious way of doing so. They created a handsome lifestyle magazine called Catalyst. To receive their free copies, customers complete a simple questionnaire that covers their present car, why they bought it, when they're likely to replace it, and what model they're thinking of next.

As well, they're asked to indicate their special lifestyle interest from four categories—home and garden, food and drink, sport or travel. Catalyst has an in-depth section on each of these, but only the one chosen by the customer is included in his or her copy of the magazine. So the publication is totally personalised to the customer's lifestyle. The company knows the kind of offers each customer will appreciate most. And it has solid information on which to base its next sales approach.

Enter the VIP

That approach begins with telemarketing from the dealer, when the customer's nominated replacement time draws near. If the response is positive, he or she is sent a VIP (Vehicle Information Portfolio) on the indicated replacement model. This fully personalised pack contains an invitation for a test drive, plus purchase incentives aimed at the customer's established lifestyle preferences. And, of course, once the purchase has been made, the whole process starts all over again.

Dramatic success

Catalyst has been dramatically successful since it began. The first issue drew a response rate of nearly 40% of all names in the database. The key to its success is its quality. The editor is Michael Parkinson, all articles are written by top journalists and experts on various subjects, and the acceptance of prestige advertising provides a substantial production budget. The products and services it offers, known as the 'Catalyst Collection', are not only targeted at the reader's known interests, but are innovative and imaginative too (would you like a session in a DC10 flight simulator?). It's no wonder many more marketers and agencies in Britain are considering how to adapt the Catalyst concept for their own use. It's yet another indication that the more you can learn about your customers, the better the relationships you can build.

And the better your relationships, the better your long-term sales.

The concept spreads

Actually, using personalised editions of magazines to build relationships is not all that new. *Farm Journal* in the USA has employed the technique since 1982. Now, however, the idea is spreading. In 1992, *Newsweek* became the first major consumer magazine to adopt it.

Ian Kennedy, one of Australia's best-known direct marketers and chairman and founder of K&D Bond Direct, reported on the trend in *Ad News*. He wrote:

> 'In the USA in the magazine subscription business, progress has been made by *Farm Journal* which, since 1982, has been targeting different regions and different types of farming with a mix of editorial and advertising material. *Farm Journal*, with a circulation of 800 000 subscribers per month, still goes out in 9000 different versions, with selectively bound advertisements and editorials. *Newsweek* last year was the first major consumer magazine to offer customised editions and for $5 a year readers can choose from four feature sections. *American Baby* has used selective binding since 1986 to better target advertising. Commencing with the issue this month, *Child Magazine* in the US offers a customised editorial section called 'Your Child Now'. There are 16 different sections, each based on the birth date of the child, which the magazine has on its database. Selective binding together with ink-jet imaging, provides a unique way to foster relationships through personalisation. It may provide a way for you too.'[1]

Mass market relationships

Well, you say, now we're getting down to the nitty gritty. Relationships can certainly be built with the comparatively small number of frequent flyers, millionaire bank customers or Austin Rover owners. But those magazines Mr Kennedy mentions are dealing with mass markets—where most of us have to operate every day. Can relationships really be built with the millions who buy high-turnover, low-cost grocery products every day from supermarkets?

They can, and they are—as L&K:Rexona Pty Ltd are currently demonstrating in Australia, through the 'Omomatic Club'.

Well-thought-out and attractively packaged, the Omomatic Club is rapidly bringing thousands of householders onto a relationship database. It's attracting them through heavy on-pack promotion, plus direct mail to buyers of related products like front-loader washing machines. Once recruited, the members are retained by regular benefits such as cash-backs, movie tickets, prizes and sweepstakes. They receive a newsletter packed with practical washing and fabric care hints. And if they need advice on specific problems such as stains, they can call a free club 1 800 Helpline and speak directly to laundry experts.

The Omomatic family

Those are just the kind of benefits needed to make members feel part of the family. They give them a good reason to stay with one product in a

Unilever market directly to niche 'front loader' washing machine consumers via a special Omo Club. Regular benefits, tips and information are direct-mailed to high users as a cost–effective alternative to mass marketing methods. *Permission of Unilever*

me-too market. But here's the real point from the manufacturer's angle. Every time members send in on-pack Privilege Vouchers to claim a cash-back or prize, they're asked in the gentlest way for information too. Where do they buy Omomatic? Do they use a fabric softener—and if so, which brand? How many times a week do they wash? What brand of washing machine do they have? How many children under 15 live at home?

And so on. Seemingly unrelated questions that, over a period of time, will build into a remarkably complete picture of each of thousands of Omomatic users. That picture will enable L&K:Rexona to target their customers ever more closely with product improvements, offers and prizes—and keep them in the family for decades to come.

Know why you want the names

At this point, let us digress for a word of warning. The Omomatic Club is succeeding because L&K:Rexona know exactly what to do with all those names. Too often, however, marketers gather names onto databases without a clear idea of why they want them. This can be costly and unproductive. Unless you can add factors like past buying performance, competition entry history and so on—data that defines the customer's relationship to your product—a list of bare names won't be much help in building long-term loyalty and sales. Names are valuable only if you know how to use them to make money from continuous sales to satisfied customers. That's what loyalty building and relationship marketing are all about.

You also need to be a tad wary when you collect heaps of names from a competition. It's not uncommon to get 300 000 or more names from a single promotion. And if it costs 35¢ to enter each one, you're up for a staggering $105 000 just to get them into your database. That could use up half your next promotion's budget on its own—not to mention the extra cost of eliminating duplications and unclear names. Then, you're facing around $90 000 for postage, even at discount rates, to communicate with people about whom you know nothing—apart from their names and the fact they entered your competition. I'm not saying you shouldn't do it. But when you have a stack of names and hardly any data on them, you do need to weigh the costs very carefully against the likely benefits.

Coke and the kids

Returning from our digression, it's obvious from the Omomatic Club that market size, purchase price and product turnover are no barriers to the creation of a relationship marketing club. Coca-Cola is also busily proving that, with the launch in Australia of 'Club Coca-Cola'.

An extensive national mailing introduced the club to the company's target market of 12–18-year-olds. For an annual fee of $20, they were offered a 'welcome pack' containing an identity card, baseball cap, back-pack, skysurfer poster and the first issue of a quarterly club magazine, *The Watch*. The magazine deals with music, fashion, films and the environment. It also contains promotional offers, discounts and editorial contributions all designed to build two-way relationships and strengthen Coke's bond with its core market. Its one weakness might be that, unlike the USA and Europe, Australia doesn't have coupons to keep the boomerang effect going and customers coming back. However, keep an eye on Club Coca-Cola. It might be the start of a new wave in the cola wars.

Pepsi plays a new card

Speaking of cola wars, an imaginative new shot was fired recently in the American theatre of operations by Pepsi. And the interesting thing was that, while this very large campaign was certainly relationship marketing, there was no club structure as such involved—just a plastic card, intriguingly called a 'Gotta Have It' card.

The venture began with double-page direct response advertisements in top national magazines, backed by TV commercials. Readers were invited to send for their Pepsi 'Gotta Have It' cards, in return for a proof of purchase. The cards, it was explained, would entitle them not only to cut-price Pepsi, but to healthy discounts on the products and services of nine major companies. These included Reebok, Avis, Eddie Bauer (clothing), MCI, Norwegian Cruise Lines, Blockbuster Video and Kentucky Fried Chicken. Discounts were also available on amusement parks, long-distance phone calls, catalogue merchandise and more.

The response was incredible. Over 20 million people returned coupons, asking for their cards. Millions more obtained them through Pepsi packs. *Direct Marketing* magazine (USA) reported that, in the summer of 1992, 40 million Americans flashed their 'Gotta Have It' cards at participating establishments all over the country.[2] And, of course, regular in-store promotions, newspaper inserts and direct mail followed up the cardholders, offering them special inducements not only to keep on using their card—but to keep on buying Pepsi.

A brilliant idea, and one with years of relationship-building potential in it.

More non-club relationships

The 'Gotta Have It' card shows you can build effective database relationships with customers even if you don't have an actual club structure. Others have proved that, too. Here in Australia, the retail stores are doing it more effectively all the time.

Grace Bros, Myer and David Jones, for example, keep in regular touch with customers through their databases. In particular, they target customers whose patronage seems to be flagging. These defaulters are plied with tempting offers designed to bring them back into the stores more often. But the regular customers aren't overlooked—a constant flow of attractive catalogue items seeks to sustain their regularity, if not increase it. Here again, the offers are matched as closely as possible to the occasional and regular customers' known buying preferences.

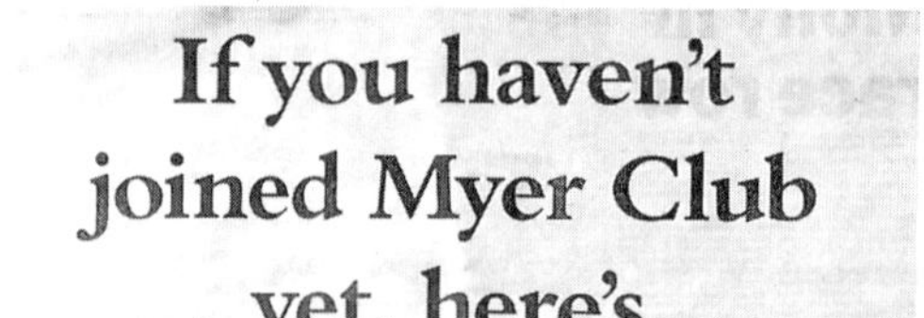

Pay $30 and join the Myer Club—then reap the benefits of buying up bigger and staying loyal.
Courtesy of Myer Stores Ltd

In the entirely different field of optometry, our client OPSM are improving their data capture processes, to help them build productive customer relationships based on individual personal data. BBC Hardware, another client of ours, have also grasped the concept of building customer loyalty through relationships. BBC operate a programme that successfully pinpoints their best customers. This will allow them to make relevant offers to different customer segments, according to those customers' previous purchasing histories. Offer-driven communications like these are highly effective in retaining a solid core of regular customers—in an effort to keep them away from Mitre 10, K-Mart and Woolworths.

A destination, not just a store

Ikea is another retailer that fully understands the importance of relationship-building. Tom Peters' book *Liberation Management* explains how Ikea has raised the service concept to an art form, capturing customers for whom a trip to the store is part entertainment, part value hunting.[3]

A model for 1990s marketing, Ikea knows they have to offer a destination rather than just a store. Most of their outlets are remote from shopping malls or even out of town. A visit often means almost a day's outing for the family. On the average, customers spend three hours at Ikea, instead of the one they usually spend at the competition. To add to their shopping experience, Ikea have a huge concentration on baby welfare, from food to changing rooms to strollers for hire. For toddlers, they also provide the 'ballroom' thrill of plunging into a pit filled with soft plastic balls—something few kids can resist.

The customers' tool kit

Once the children are settled, customers can pick up their special Ikea action kit—catalogue, tape measure, notepad and pencil. They have to assemble the furniture, a feature that saves them heaps of money. The kit adds to the DIY mood, and helps the customers feel that their contribution is valuable. The catalogue's distribution is targeted more and more carefully. It is designed to create the excitement of great rooms filled with furniture at unbelievable prices.

Rent a Christmas tree

Ikea abounds with other traffic-building, relationship-creating schemes. One of the cleverest is a 'Green Christmas'—Ikea's Christmas Tree rental. For as little as $20, customers can 'rent' a 5–7 ft Douglas Fir. Astoundingly, they can return it to Ikea after Christmas and get a $10 refund. In addition, they can have the tree ground up for garden mulch. Some Ikea stores even offer 'bounce back' coupons, good for a free seedling later in the year. So up to three customer visits can be generated by this one promotion. At three hours per average visit, it obviously opens up significant extra sales and profit opportunities.

The PR value is huge, too. The $10 refund offer is a big talking point at Christmas. And the promotion certainly solves a problem most of us face—what to do with a used Christmas tree.

The Ikea family

Ikea also run a frequent buyers' club—a very successful one called the Ikea Family. Membership is open to anyone who pays a $15 annual fee, or makes a one-time purchase during the year of at least $150. The privileges of membership include special discounts on merchandise and meals at Ikea cafés, plus a newsletter and travel packages. Ikea Family members can also earn the right to trade homes worldwide for use on overseas holidays.

Ikea is a current retail marketing success story. With such an emphasis on relationship-building, it's not hard to see why.

Wooing vets and pets

Yet another of our clients—Ciba Animal Health—is establishing the value of relationship marketing in a different kind of context again. The company's products are mainly specialist drugs used by veterinarians in routine clinical procedures. The drugs are sold only in veterinary clinics. The two key markets are the veterinary surgeons themselves and pet owners.

'We are increasingly moving to relationship marketing for both audiences,' says Ciba's Jeremy Cocks. 'This is a logical move because there are fewer than 2000 veterinary clinics in Australia. Our communication to them aims to provide information and to support the activities of our sales force.

'Our relational database gives us the constant flow of up-to-date information we need to sell our product benefits to vets and pet owners alike. It also allows us to target the pet owners with offers designed to increase customer traffic through vet clinics. Our strategy is based on getting to know our pet owning target audience, and to build relationships over a wider group of veterinarians.

'Mass marketing cannot deliver this to us cost-effectively, nor with the accountability we require in the 1990s.'[4]

Broadening the picture

Cross-selling is another effective non-club way of using databases, as marketers like Procter & Gamble, Coca-Cola, Nestlé, Nabisco, Kraft and General Foods have demonstrated in the USA and Europe. These giants are spending millions on developing databases of householders who have the potential to buy across their full range of products.

This Ciba–Geigy direct mailing includes an envelope and a personalised mail pack. The mailing is personalised to the pet, the customer and the veterinarian, which in turn creates greater involvement and interaction. It builds customer relationships through veterinarians and their database of pet owners. More pets being kept comfortable and healthy, long–term, means more on–going sales and profits. *Courtesy of Ciba–Geigy Australia Limited*

Through such databases, they can not only work to create loyalty to their key products. They can cross-sell, break existing purchase patterns on competitors' brands, trial new products and conduct research—all within what is virtually their own 'private' market-place. If you have multiple brands and a good database, you can do the same.

The Air Miles phenomenon

While all these non-club examples of relational database marketing are well worth studying, I still think the club approach is the one that maximises a database's potential. But what if you don't have the resources to launch and run a club? In that case, you might have to rely on someone else to do the job for you.

In Britain at least, even that facility is now in full swing.

Known as the 'Air Miles' programme, it's a frequent buyer club like all those we've considered—with one very significant difference. It's not run by a company to boost its own sales. It's run by an independent operator as a service to any company, large or small, that wants to offer its customers a frequent buyer club.

So far, more than 130 UK companies have taken up the opportunity. They include oil companies, retailers, food stores, restaurants, financial institutions and service companies of all kinds. So when consumers become Air Miles members, they immediately start earning points for purchases almost every day of their lives. Only they don't earn points. They earn what the club name implies—air miles. Every time they buy a participating product or service, they earn so many miles of air travel, mainly on British Airways and two other smaller airlines. In a matter of weeks, just by making everyday purchases, they can run up enough miles for round trips to places like Paris or Brussels. It's a tremendous consumer lure, and one that is paying off very handsomely indeed for the companies involved.

Two-way promotion

Air Miles runs its own TV, print and direct-mail promotion for the service. And the sponsors promote it among their customers as well. This two-way promotion has sent consumer awareness of Air Miles soaring from zero to 80% in just over three years—a remarkable performance that underlines the vast potential of such a third-party frequent buyer club.

Round about now, however, I wouldn't be surprised to hear you interjecting. Surely, you say, all this is straight consumer incentives. How does it build customer relationships—especially when the contact between manufacturer and customer goes through a third party?

That's an excellent point. And the Air Miles people have come up with an excellent solution.

Targeting known buyers

Every two months, they send the members a statement. This shows them all their club-linked purchases for the period and the air miles they currently hold. As well, these mailings can include special promotions from sponsoring companies. The sponsors can't obtain Air Miles members' names for their own mailings—but they can reach them very selectively indeed through the Air Miles packages.

Recently, for instance, Austin Rover used the service to mail a test drive offer to known Shell petrol buyers—and only to known Shell petrol buyers. So as well as building customer loyalty and offering major sales boosts, Air Miles is helping its sponsors with the customer relationship-building process too.

Walking taller and taller

Stan Rapp, chairman of Rapp and Collins, reported in *B&T* on a new relationship marketing programme by a niche athletic shoe marketer that looks like a real winner. It's called the Saucony Walking Club. And in Stan's view, it is a serious effort by Saucony to provide what a member needs to achieve his or her health and fitness goals.[5]

People join by buying a pair of Saucony walking shoes at an authorised Saucony Walking Club retailer. There they complete a 12-question enrolment form. Valuable customer profiling information then goes into Saucony's growing customer database.

Members receive a kit which includes the 40-page *Saucony Walking Handbook*, a customised walking workout guide, a progress log and other goodies. An innovative feature is the 'Milestone Awards Programme'. Whether the goal is to lose 20 pounds or walk a mile in less than 15 minutes, Saucony offers awards and recognition at each individual milestone reached.

According to Stan, this is one of the most comprehensive, customer-focused relationship marketing programmes he has seen anywhere—certain to win loyalty and enhance Saucony's brand image in the walking shoe segment.

To sell running shoes, Saucony has a different approach. Runners go through shoes fast. In less than two years, Saucony has enrolled 70 000 men and women in a frequency marketing programme called the 'Extra Miles Club'. With the purchase of four pairs of shoes, for example, members get a free jacket. The more shoes you buy, the bigger the reward you get.

Saucony uses different subsets of direct marketing to address the individual needs of different market segments. They provide both an excellent product and a caring relationship after the sale. This commitment to relationship marketing is just one of the many marketing initiatives which led to a 50% jump in Saucony's sales in 1992 and a further 50% gain in the first quarter of 1993.

Wayne Elley of Elley Brian Edwards in Melbourne, a database marketing consultant, underpins such strategies as this:

> 'We are seeing a shift from the product emphasis to a service emphasis for all types of organisations. Marketing communications are serving to progressively educate the prospect or customer, to create a lead and to develop loyalty. This type of marketing is designed to establish relationships and communicate in a way that is more targeted, personalised, informative, interactive, timely and long term.'[6]

Get started now!

As we've seen, there are many ways that customer relationships can be cultivated. But however you're going to do it, the vital thing is to start now. Every day you delay, customers could drift away—with potentially catastrophic results. As Warren McFarlan of Harvard University said recently, 'In five years there will be two types of company—those who use a computer as a marketing tool and those who face bankruptcy.'[7]

Your first step is to identify the data you'll seek to obtain on each customer. Collect only the information you need to know—information that will help you understand your customers better, and provide the basis for a growing relationship with them. And be clear in your mind what you're going to do with it!

One final word. The database is not an end in itself. To make it work in relationship-building, there has to be a company-wide commitment to the programme. Your relationship-building plans have to be a priority for your whole organisation. Getting that process to work takes quite a bit of time and effort. Which is another reason for starting now.

If you don't get to know your customers soon, they soon won't want to know you.

Relationship-building data

Below you'll find listed some information vital to building a relationship. Build this information over time, and only collect the information that you know you can use to better direct your marketing efforts.

- purchase history (RFM) recency of purchase (R) (date of last purchase)
- frequency of purchase (F) (how often has the customer purchased)
- monetary value of purchase (M) (the weighting of importance you apply to each of the R, F and M variables will vary from organisation to organisation, whether a business or a consumer entity and even between products)
- purchasing ability, past records, non-payment
- family make-up, education
- age, sex, professional status
- occupation of family members, ethnic make-up
- leisure interests, travel, property, sports, what car they drive
- responsiveness to direct mail, to telemarketing, to existing product offers

- media interest, magazines read, TV, radio, newspapers
- special reports, compliments, or complaints

One last word—never forget your source code. This is often the most important method of finding out what marketing action and offer-driven activity is working most cost-effectively for you. It will also show you how to personalise your subsequent communications appropriately.

Relationship marketing checklist

1. Can your customers' lifetime value measurement produce enough incremental margin to create sufficient profits to sustain a relationship marketing programme?
2. Are you prepared to get into it, keep it going and sustain communications?
3. Will your customers perceive value over and above competitive offerings?
4. Is senior management committed to database principles and keeping existing customers loyal through direct marketing, telesales, customer service and the sales force (retail staff)?
5. Can you profit from spending energy and resources in marketing to niche segments?
6. With some products and especially services, it's easy to find ways to give a dollar reward. How easy is it for you?
7. How prevalent are relationship-building techniques in your industry? Assess what your competitors need to do to take away your customers. Now go and stop them doing so!
8. If marketing is becoming more and more directly aligned with computers and communication—is it not sensible to embrace technology now rather than later?
9. Are you in a strong enough position to take the bad results with the good and withstand criticism in the often slow build-up to profitability and success?

Notes

1. 'Direct Marketers' Diary' by Ian Kennedy, *Ad News*, 26 March 1993.
2. 'Direct Intelligence' feature, *Direct Marketing* magazine, Hoke Communications, July 1992.
3. Tom Peters, *Liberation Management*, Macmillan, London, 1992.
4. Jeremy Cocks, letter to Martin Williams.
5. 'Defining the Marketing Boundaries', by Stan Rapp, *B&T*, 2 July 1993.
6. Wayne Elley, at Database Conference, September 1993.
7. International Market Report by Peter Peskett, *Direct Marketing International,* June 1993.

19
CHAPTER

Questing for Customers, Lead Generation and Direct Marketing

Getting the right people to the right place at the right time in the right mood to buy is a problem that preoccupies most retailers. It is likewise a problem for the marketers who rely on retailers to distribute and sell their product or service. Both groups know they need to attract people with money to spend, rather than browsers or 'tyre kickers'.

In the 1980s, retailers tried everything from mass advertising campaigns to rub-off spot games with top dollar prizes to free continuity premiums for coming in and buying in-store. They promoted deep price cuts by word of mouth and in catalogues inserted in newspapers or delivered door-to-door. Only a few achieved success. Most were not successful in maintaining the impetus. Traffic after a time simply dropped off. To compete and to provide what the customer wanted, the retailer had to purchase smart and in extremely large quantities (as well as maintaining a relatively low overhead). This mass marketing approach has led to very similar price points and an overkill of 'on sale' items the whole country over.

The end of the mass market

Now the mass market has gone. The day of mass media exercises designed to attract a larger homogenous customer group is over. Timothy J. Keane of Retail Target Marketing Systems in Waukesa, Wisconsin, wrote to me and made the point most persuasively. His comments present his company's thoughts on the current retail scene. They were also picked up in *Direct Marketing* magazine in its July 1991 issue. I believe they merit close consideration.

> 'Homogeneity in consumer goods marketing is now a thing of the past. The market is fragmenting into smaller niche groupings. With less money around the pressure is on to find customers and to attract them and increase their loyalty, as well as enlarge the basket size of those customers with whom retailers already have a relationship. The pressure is on to use information-based target marketing.
>
> 'Just to underline this, Faith Popcorn's 1992 report states:
>
> > "The key to making the 90s work for you, will depend on how quickly you learn the new ways of this decade. Perfect packaging, beautiful product shots, cleverness, style over substance, or hype, just won't work anymore. The key to your customer will depend on how much extra you can actually deliver. Product plus, plus, plus. Your consumer databank will become your most vital resource. Companies will set up new departments devoted to finding ways of opening dialogues with consumers and keeping them going. Even the vague term 'customers' will be obsolete. You'll call them by name."
>
> 'So, you see, successful retailers must now look at the consumer in a new way—as small groups of individuals with their own separate needs and wants. And they must employ means which individualise their approaches towards their customers.

'In this environment, the retailer needs to differentiate himself with other than just merchandise selection in order to survive. Because, if merchandise is similar, and price is similar, what's left is differentiated customer service.

'To quote an Ernst & Young retail newsletter:

"The high quality customer service is at the heart of the retail business."'

To prosper today, serve the customer better

'Today's consumer expects outstanding service and will bring increased loyalty to retailers that provide it. The store that can provide all the elements of good service—high touch, personalised selling, wide selections of sizes and styles of products; attentive follow-up and so forth—will keep the loyalty of customers for as long as they can maintain their differentiated service standard.

'What does this have to do with information-based target marketing?

'One definition of customer service is providing the right product, at the right price and right time, with the right delivery, through the right medium, and with the right creative message.

'That is also the definition of relationship marketing.'[1]

Timothy is right, of course. The world over, the only way retailers can now differentiate themselves is through customer service. Information-based relationship marketing has a great contribution to make to that process. It provides the tracking information necessary, in human terms, to communicate with customers in high touch, personalised ways.

Mine gold from existing customers

For all retailers—banks, food stores, supermarket groups, financial institutions, hardware retailers and so on—the marketing tools are now available to mine gold from existing customers. In the 1990s, retailers must use these tools to target their customers and prospects very accurately. Today's highly competitive retail market environment demands that management uses detailed customer-based information for decision-making. Coupled with an 'aisle walking shop floor management style', this will help them understand not only their customers but the staff customers have to deal with—a very important point if the relationships being built are to be mutually rewarding and lasting.

Buyers with more to spend

Marketers too can now track their customers in new and innovative ways, to enhance a wide range of marketing programmes.

Our client, Thomson World Trade Exhibitions, for example, holds Expos twice a year in Melbourne, Sydney and Brisbane for retail buyers. The events happen in spring and autumn to cater for Christmas and winter buying respectively. And Thomson WTE have found a new way to target and attract their market.

In the past, they advertised the events. Then they saw the possibility of individualising their approach, once they had captured their previous customers on a mailing list. At that stage, we turned their mailing list into a relational database capable of holding enough relevant information on their customers. This has not only cut the cost of their marketing effort, but has made it considerably more effective. The big advantage is that they can now target their best customers precisely. These people are owners of

World Trade Exhibitions target retailers to buy from their trade exhibitors with a customer membership card. This allows ease of entry to their exhibitions and tracks attendees for future segmentation and specific offer-driven direct marketing action.
Courtesy of Thompson World Trade Exhibitions

retail stores of all sizes in the gift, toy and jewellery fields, plus a special group of departmental store buyers. As a result, we have increased the quality of buyer traffic, the exhibitors have enhanced their sales, and more space is being taken at Thomson WTE's Expos.

What's more, Thomson WTE can now track their visitors from Expo to Expo. They can tell how often they've been and to which trade they belong. They can pinpoint their strengths, weaknesses, wants and needs. Very importantly, they can attract tradespeople by obtaining lists of their relevant target groups and mailing them individually with special offers. This has proved extremely effective in building awareness, boosting the Expos' image and increasing existing and new visitor traffic.

Leveraging the customer database

John Goodman, writing in *Direct Marketing* magazine, bears much of this thinking out. He said:

> 'Customer-driven marketing information is a key corporate resource! Customer information gathered from previous purchases or enquiries enables a business to mould their marketing strategies around what the customer is currently telling them they want most from their business. As many will agree, a key ingredient of successful retail marketing today is to stay flexible and be able to adapt or change your business to meet the current needs of your customers. Those who understand the needs of their customers best, will be capable of catering to them best.
>
> 'The vehicle to "listen" to your customers and create a dialogue with them is the customer database. Those businesses which are able to reshape and redefine their marketing direction based on information derived from their customer database will hold a distinct competitive advantage over those who have either waited too long to build their database or those who have not been able to integrate this information into their entire marketing mix.
>
> 'In short, today's customer is a moving target, and the customer database allows you to reach this target. The marketing database is a key corporate asset and every customer-driven business needs to leverage this resource.'[3]

Strength, security and performance

MLC/Lend Lease are another major group who improve their service by tracking their customers. For the last four years, we have collaborated on their 'Investor Updates'. These are presentations that allow customers to hear of the performance of assets and investments, and gain reassurance of the strength and security of the company acting on their behalf.

The Investor Update is managed by a group of people under Lend Lease's Project Control Group system. These leaders direct each Update's proceedings under the guidance of our client Lend Lease Corporate Projects.

The Update lets investors hear the top people in the company, from the Managing Director to the heads of each investment group – in other words, the people actually running the business. Investors can question the presenters directly in open forum in Sydney, Melbourne, Adelaide, Brisbane and Perth. They like this open style of management, for which Lend Lease is well known.

The information collected from surveying the database gives the knowledge to select the investors who would be most interested in attending. It has also contributed to the information provided in the Update sessions themselves. As well, it has helped to match the sessions and support material to the actual needs and wants of the MLC/Lend Lease investors.

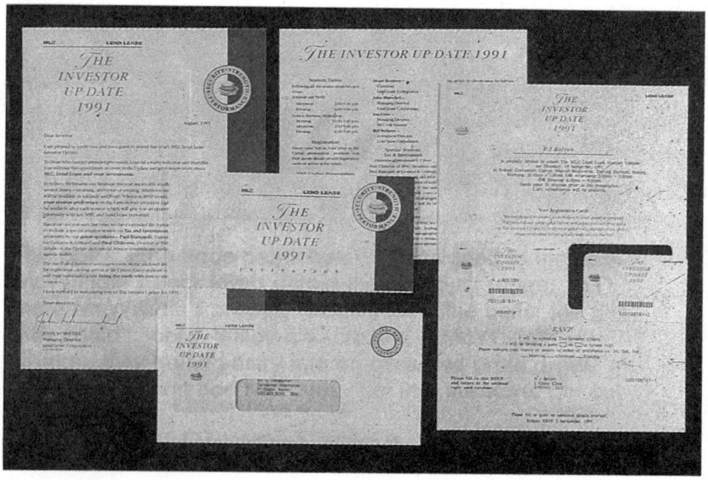

Personalised bar coded entrée cards trigger a higher response to Lend Lease's FREE investors' seminars. The personalised entry cards also allow for tracking of responses and follow up. *Courtesy of Lend Lease Corporation*

The combination of targeted database marketing and our relationship marketing tactics has steadily increased response and customer traffic year after year. MLC/Lend Lease also know the value of consistency. They have embarked on a strategy they are reluctant to change. Their investors like the format. They appreciate the informality and the quality of information they get. The result has been increased investment and progressively enhanced confidence in Lend Lease and its management.

Building a customer database

Recently, the Datascope system, pioneered by Hans Aigner of Applications Software Company Inc. in Washington DC, has been very successful in helping serious niche marketing organisations to build their customer base and create unique relationship marketing models. Widely used by retailers and financial institutions in the UK and USA, Datascope allows us to analyse a customer database using proprietary software and advanced modelling and scoring techniques. This analysis pinpoints the segments where promotional effort is most likely to be productive. By evaluating customer purchasing trends department-by-department, we can predict future buying patterns store-by-store, and adjust the merchandise mix accordingly.

Proven performance

The Datascope database system also allows retailers to leverage their information and select the most promising of a wide range of market profiles, based on demographics, lifestyles, shopping histories, annual expenditure and store allegiance. This ensures highly targeted and responsive customer marketing campaigns in every store. Retailers can track their marketing efforts more easily than ever before, and individualise their approach to customers and prospects. In addition, they can measure the success of each marketing activity. The effectiveness of catalogues, targeted door-to-door offers, couponing, advertising specials, sales and deep price-cutting activity can now be judged very accurately from one customer to the next.

Our retail and finance clients regard these tools as essential in planning their longer-term marketing and merchandising policies. And they're right to do so. Anyone who wants to remain competitive in the 1990s needs to be aware of the sophisticated business analysis resources available to them today. There's no point in going to prospects who aren't in a position to buy, or don't have the money.

Tomorrow's marketer

My friend David Simmons of Intermark Marketing Services in the UK has become adept at using Datascope database methods to gain profitable extra sales and significant productivity increases, particularly in the insurance industry.

David combines his special skills in insurance, direct marketing and computing to develop offer-driven direct marketing programmes. He has introduced direct marketing to many of the country's largest insurance companies. To me, David typifies tomorrow's marketer—a multi-talented person with skills in computing, direct marketing and offer-driven marketing, plus in-depth knowledge of the product, the customers, how they respond and what makes them respond.

Increasing loyalty through lifestyle

For retailers, one of the most interesting results Datascope can achieve is reactivating dormant customers and returning them to profitable purchase levels. The programme can also be used to target cash shoppers and others who don't use the store credit card—until now the primary source of customer information.

Its most important role, however, is to secure the long-term loyalty of existing customers. Right behind that comes the targeting of high potential prospects, based on the similarity of their profile to that of the retailer's best customer. By analysing the store's catchment area and using geodemographic overlays, we can select the housing type and socio-economic grouping most likely to harbour these hot prospects (see Chapter 11).

As well, the Datascope information can target a retailer's best prospects as a way of gaining market share more cost-effectively. In such cases, we overlay external information on existing data, to help identify these promising non-customers and target them for fruitful acquisition.

With Datascope and systems like it, retailers and marketers in general now have a method of assessing the effectiveness of current marketing efforts, of predicting the success of future ventures—and of avoiding people who are less likely to buy.

Lead generation

Questing for customers is not, of course, an activity restricted to retailers. It's a must for most product manufacturers and service suppliers too. While it's true that an existing customer is always the best prospect for a future sale, it's also true that a steady flow of leads is needed if a business is to grow.

Like anything worth doing, a lead generation campaign has to be done well. The consequences of a badly handled campaign can be profound—much worse, in fact, than if you'd done nothing at all. This is especially true when it's very successful and generates more leads than you can handle.

All the prospects you fail to service properly in that situation will almost certainly be lost to you, sometimes forever. But if each and every one is followed up promptly and efficiently, you'll convert a high percentage into clients who could stay with you for years. You'll enhance not only your sales but your reputation.

The first aim, then, is to create a lead generation campaign that matches the capacity and capabilities of your follow-up procedures. In my experience, it's better to obtain a lower number of leads with a higher-than-average conversion per lead to sales. The way to success is to 'profile' each lead accurately—that is, to gauge its potential for short- and long-term sales—and to co-ordinate the efforts of your telemarketers and sales force. Great sensitivity and understanding are also needed in allocating leads to sales people. Who gets the best leads? Who gets the less promising ones? How do you avoid favouritism?

Speed the secret

Before that sales management decision, however, comes your immediate response to the coupons and phone calls your campaign generates. And here, speed is the key. Customers—new customers especially—expect a fast turnaround to fulfil their expectations. If they're interested in your product or service, they'll be searching the media and finger-walking through the *Yellow Pages* to see what your competitors have to offer, too.

To get their business, you have to be one jump ahead all the time.

One hand on the phone

Rather than send in a coupon, more and more consumers today will call your 13 or 1 800 number or even your fax machine. And if they're responding to a radio or TV commercial, most will phone within seconds of the commercial's airing. Our experience suggests you can expect quite a few calls. If you experience an overload, they will have to be qualified later (but not too much later) by telemarketing.

To start with, however, someone in your office or telemarketing bureau will have to be poised, as it were, with one hand on the phone—ready to give the full product story immediately in response to calls. That story, moreover, will need to be a lot more extensive than the content of a TV or radio commercial. In terms of volume, it will be more like a letter or a long-copy press advertisement. But the 1 800 answerer will need to have it at his or her fingertips.

The Automobile Association aim at the lucrative over 50 years market and are prepared to pay to get them with desirable and worthwhile offers to turn prospects into customers.
Courtesy of AA UK Limited

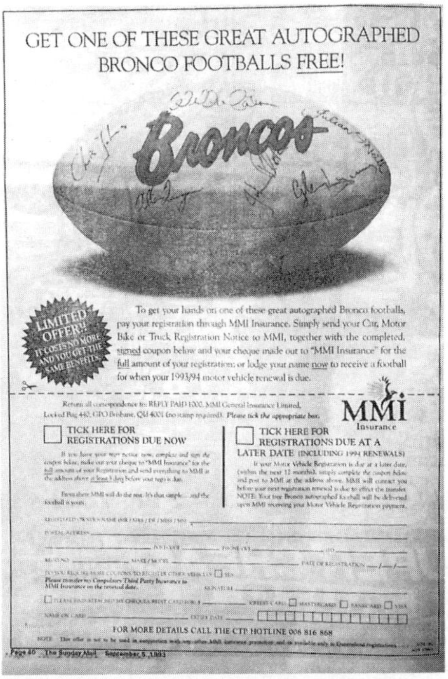

MMI offer first-comers a chance to enhance their insurance purchase with a FREE football specially autographed by the local team.
Courtesy of MMI Insurance Group

The NRMA generate interest and emergency calls for every need not just motoring breakdowns. Your call for help, could lead to a lifelong association with the NRMA.
Courtesy of NRMA

If he or she has to go away, get it all together and call the prospect back, you'll lose many potential customers.

Leading callers to buy

One company that's handling telephone enquiries extremely well is Cellarmasters, Australia's largest wine distributor. It's using sophisticated screen and software techniques to provide full information without delay, and to lead callers through the order and selection processes.

Cellarmasters is also using an interesting technique called predictive dialling. The computer decides when to phone prospects, because it knows from previous order and reorder patterns when they're most likely to be at home or in the office. The machine does the dialling. When the phone is answered, the customer's name and phone number appear on the screen. The telemarketer then takes over to establish the formalities, re-introductions and needs.

Predictive dialling, Cellarmasters has established, can be more cost-effective than mailing catalogues and following-up. A properly-run telephone fulfilment service can increase your profits even though seller and customer may never meet each other. I know of two people at Oracle in North Sydney who sell merchandise worth over $3 million a year on the phone, and never see the colour of their customers' eyes!

The pages of profit

A moment ago, I mentioned the *Yellow Pages*. They deserve more than a casual mention. Are you in them with a permanent listing and a high-impact advertisement? No? Then you should be. Just as your lead generation efforts can drive prospects into the *Yellow Pages* to check out your competitors, the reverse is true. Someone else's lead generation campaign can also drive prospects into the *Yellow Pages*—where your insertions should be waiting to snare and divert their attention to you.

If you're a medium to large business, the *Yellow Pages* are a vital part of your lead generation efforts. If you're a small business, they're absolutely indispensable.

It's interesting to note that Telecom's *White* and *Yellow Pages* are now available in CD–ROM. Telecom Business Finder version 5 is available on diskette. And it's incredibly proficient in data storage—so you can access vastly more information easily and quickly. You can even download the information after a selection and name count, print labels and dial telephone numbers directly from the disk. Other systems available in Australia include Disk 4, OZ on Disk and Desktop Marketing.

Lifting lead quality

Lead generation strategy was discussed in depth at the Pan Pacific Marketing Symposium in June 1992. In the experience of most delegates, a blend of advertising, direct mail and telemarketing generates more high-quality leads, loyalty, retention and revenue than any one technique on its own.

Typically, it was agreed, a good lead generation campaign begins with advertising—both general and direct response. The aim here is primarily to create awareness, credibility and leads, with some degree of revenue as a secondary (but still important) goal. The direct response advertising component must obviously include couponing, an 1 800 phone number or both.

No more than one week after the first advertising appears, the initial direct mail piece must reach the prospect. It has four basic objectives—to build on the advertising's impact, heighten product awareness, generate qualified leads or sales via a response device (a business reply card (BRC) or 1 800 number), and pre-condition the prospect for a follow-up call.

Then, within 24 to 48 hours after the mail drop, outbound telemarketing commences. Apart from its obvious role in strengthening the overall campaign, its objectives are incremental leads and sales, generating qualitative data (including the reason for 'no interest' answers) and reinforcing replies by mail or 1 800 responses. A good call creates a 'halo' effect that can often motivate later action by people 'not interested' at the time of the call.

Personalisation begins

Even in the initial communication stages, enough prospect information can be gathered to personalise the ongoing communication process. Areas of interest or needs, for instance, may have been identified, buying triggers clarified and the buying time cycle established. If so, the prospect's interest can be aroused with individually targeted information. Follow-up action can then be planned for the time when it's most likely to lead to a sale.

This kind of process is now taking place at AT&T with very encouraging results, said Ernan Roman, leader of the 1992 Symposium, in *Marketing Magazine*.[4]

> We're trying to manage all of our prospects—even the non-responders—and move them from cold to warm to hot,' explained AT&T's Jon Weise. 'We're focused on improving the

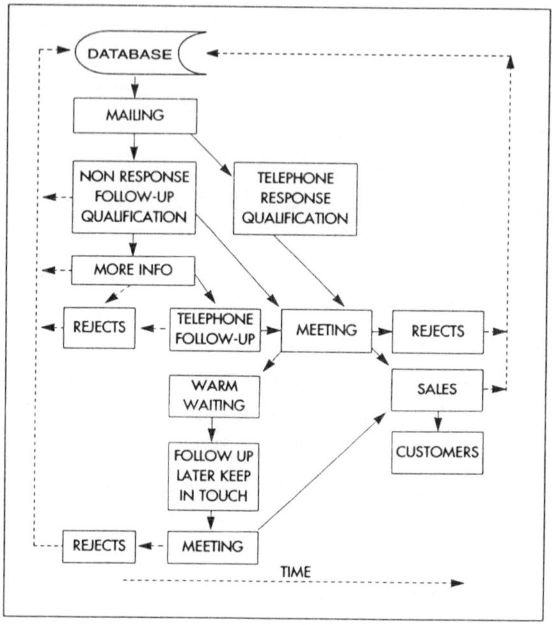

A typical lead generation pipeline used by financial and high-tech marketing organisations. It demonstrates the processes involved in leading customers closer to a face-to-face meeting.

quality of our prospect information so we can increase our close rate. It's a process that occurs over time and ultimately improves our relationships both with prospects and our own customers.'

The lead generation pipeline

A similar procedure is shown in the following figure. This is the 'lead generation pipeline' similar to that used by our information technology and financial clients, to guide them from prospecting to sales.

Note how the pattern echoes those we've already discussed. The initial approach to the prospect is made by an offer-driven advertisement (or an offer-driven direct mail pack or air media commercial) containing a response coupon and/or a 1 800 phone number. The prospect responds by phoning or returning the coupon. The manufacturer replies with direct marketing and telemarketing, which open the way for a face-to-face sales call, a demonstration and, if all goes well, a sale. Those who don't respond are followed up on a carefully-planned schedule using a combination of telephone and mail.

But as in all well-run campaigns that have enjoyed sales success, the process doesn't stop there. Next comes a survey, by phone or mail, to find out if the customer is really satisfied. If the answer is no, swift

Targetted via rented lists as well as AV Jennings' own database, this lead generation mailpack attracts prospects to FREE information seminars and offers a discount to encourage the process. *Courtesy AV Jennings*

remedial action is initiated. If the answer is yes, the company may see the possibility of further sales—and proceeds to enter everything they've learned into their marketing database.

Information input

At every stage in such a process, vital information about the lead's potential can be gleaned. The right questions will tell you how far off the likely sale is, the total expected revenue, the payment method, other brands being assessed by the prospect, and so on. It's essential, of course, that the information-gathering procedure be carefully monitored, to ensure that neither salesperson nor prospect come under any hardship or pressure.

Complications creep in where leads are created by the marketer, but have to be followed up by a wholesale sales force. In those cases, a thorough yet easy-to-follow report form has to be devised. In fact, I'd go further and say that developing such a strategy is well worthwhile in every situation. It makes the telemarketer's job easier, gives the sales force confidence and simplifies the task of transferring information into the database.

Try it—you'll find it helps to keep the whole process on track, throughout the often quite long gestation period before a lead becomes a money-spending client.

The aim of these procedures is to reduce the cost of prospecting and selling. The use of prospecting lists obtained through interactive offer-driven media or by rent builds the database of suspects and 'cold' prospects. Then comes the mailing and subsequent response. Non-responses are followed up with telemarketing and the results returned to the database. Positive and interested 'warm' prospects go on to a face-to-face meeting, in an effort to turn them into paying customers.

Pre-sale rewards

Another way to keep the process moving is to offer your sales force rewards at various stages before the sale itself. With some of our information technology clients in particular, we have created incentive schemes that reward sales personnel for achieving a demonstration and subsequent follow-up. These usually take the form of sales points that can be exchanged for merchandise or cash.

Obviously, an even bigger reward awaits those who clinch the sale itself. But we have found that rewarding sales people progressively—especially those regarded as playing a back-up role—can lead to above-average success.

In recent years, we have amassed evidence of the effectiveness and cost-efficiency of direct marketing lead generation programmes, based on qualified mailing lists, in the information technology industry. And when they involve resellers as well as marketers, sales forces and telesales staff, their impact is maximised.

We have also demonstrated the power of targeted advertising as the prime lead-generation medium in the insurance and various business-to-business markets. And both in direct marketing and advertising-based programmes, measuring results along the way has helped us redefine and shape the whole lead generation process much more cost-efficiently.

Multiplying your best customers

If your current client list is on a database (and if it isn't, it should be), you have a good profile of your best customers. That gives you a great start in hunting for more just like them. You can target your potential markets very precisely, and go after the prospects who offer you above-average profit potential.

What's more, the modern media explosion gives you more ways to reach them than ever before.

Business-to-business communication now includes mail, phone, fax, computers, electronic mail, electronic data interchange, mobile fax-phones and pen pads, as well as traditional advertising media.

Consumers can be reached in their homes by almost all the above media, plus interactive TV, normal TV, radio, press, magazines, letterbox drops and door-to-door. You can reach them in stores via POS, in-store radio and video, brochures, leaflets, trolley posters and demonstrations. Radio, poster, outdoor, mobile phone and transit advertisements can speak to them while they're travelling by car and public transport. And there are many other often overlooked opportunities—events, trade shows, sporting activities, user groups, seminars, social gatherings and affinity groups, to name a few.

An offer they can't refuse

So where do you start? Despite the proliferation of new media opportunities in the above list, I think it's best to start with the more traditional ones—press, TV, radio and direct mail. But wherever you start, your lead generation advertising will be greatly strengthened if you make your prospects an offer they can't refuse. Give your offer good image associations, of course—but a purely 'image' campaign will rarely match the results of an offer-driven approach that promises tangible benefits as well as information, if people respond right away.

That response, needless to say, should be sought via a 1 800 number, a mail-in coupon or fax number, to make it easy for prospects to take advantage of your offer—and have their names added to your list of leads.

Incidentally, I can't understand why every company that woos customers doesn't have a 1 800 number today as part of its communication mix. It makes it so simple for customers and prospects to contact you. In fact, the only reason for not having one would be that you're not geared to handle the calls—in which case, you could, and should, employ a bureau to field calls and process requests on your behalf.

Direct marketing the Easifax way

Moving on to the newer media, here's one that enables you to send a direct response message to a list of up to 20 000 customers in a matter of minutes.

It's called Telecom Easifax. You just give Telecom a database of your customers' fax numbers and other details. In fact, you can give them up to 900 separate lists, based on your target subsets.

The scanned image of your message is sent with optimum speed and quality. It is retained in the Telecom computer until despatched to the last name on your list. If Easifax can't get through to a number, it will keep on trying. Eventually, if the number proves resolutely impenetrable, Easifax will generate a non-delivery report. You don't pay for unsuccessful attempts.

A few tips. If you send your message overnight, you can cut your costs by up to 30%. Don't use too many black areas in your design—they slow the process down and increase the expense. And always include an attractive offer in your message. Not only will it boost the response—it will deflate the annoyance some people feel when you use their machine and paper for unsolicited advertising.

Easifax is an Australian success story. Now sold overseas as one of the world's smartest fax systems, it is becoming an essential tool for cost-effective, highly targeted direct marketing. Others, however, such as Singapore's SingCom, are not far behind.

Word of mouth

Probably the most effective way of obtaining new customers is the oldest one of all—one that was widely employed not just in medieval times but in ancient Rome and Greece.

Word of mouth.

Modern research confirms the strength of this age-old ploy. Mintel asked 7000 people in several European countries what was the biggest factor in influencing them to try a new brand, according to an article by Michael Kiely in *Marketing Magazine*. Personal endorsement and recommendation by family and friends was a runaway winner, specified by 60% of respondents. Next came discounts and coupons at 44%, sampling and free trial at 37% and advertising at 36%.

In short, word of mouth emerged as the most powerful form of promotion, with offer-driven marketing coming second. The success of direct selling organisations like Amway, Nutri-Metics and Rawleighs (see Chapter 1) would seem to bear this out. Satisfied customers like to tell others about their good fortune. It helps to validate their original decisions, and demonstrates the astuteness of their choice to their friends.

But how can you persuade your customers to sing your praises to others? As Shakespeare put it—aye, there's the rub. I think the clue is in the adjective 'satisfied'. Add a sufficiently attractive offer to a quality product, exceed your customers' expectations, and you should make them happy enough to spread the word. True, there's no way of knowing who they'll tell. So you can't gather those potential customers onto a database. Or not immediately, anyway.

You may have to wait until they buy your product—and hopefully, become word of mouth promoters themselves.

Direct mail lists

There's no better direct mail list than your own list. But clearly, if you're questing for new leads, your list needs to be refreshed and expanded. This means going to a reputable list broker and renting or buying one.

Such lists can be segmented very precisely in the UK, Europe and USA. As yet, however, few consumer lists in Australia are well segmented, either by area or individual households—although our business-to-business lists tend to be much better.

The main things to look for in a list are an affinity with your product or service and a similarity to your present customers. Make sure the broker has removed people who don't want to receive list mailings. You should also try to determine the list's current deliverability—that is, the number of people who are still likely to be at the addresses shown for them. A figure of 95% in this regard is normally regarded as acceptable.

In addition, ask for an indication of how well this list responds to mailings. Talking to a previous user could help you here. It's important, too, to check the list against yours, to eliminate any prospects you may already have. This avoids embarrasment and crass wastage.

A good independent list broker will assist you in developing your strategy. The broker will also point you to lists with telephone numbers for follow-up, and help you avoid the traps so many have fallen into before you.

Lists beat creative . . .

If asked whether the list or the creative is more important in direct marketing, most people would probably go for the creative.

The world's top direct marketing gurus wouldn't agree.

In his book *Commonsense Direct Marketing*, Drayton Bird demonstrates that, while the creative is important, it comes well down the priority ladder after the list. 'The role of the list lies at the heart of the direct marketing business,' Drayton asserts.[5] And to judge from the following quotes, most direct marketers support him.

'Selection of the correct names is probably the single most important factor in any mailing' (Arthur M. Hughes, *The Complete Direct Marketer*) Probus Publishing Co., Chicago, 1991.

'Even a good product or service with a strong offer has little chance of success if your message doesn't get through to the right prospects' (Jim Kobs, *Profitable Direct Marketing*, NTC Business Books, Lincolnwood, Illinois, USA, 1992).

'Direct mail is the world's largest advertising medium, and mailing lists are the key to its success' (Edward L. Nash, *Direct Marketing*, 2nd edn, McGraw Hill, New York, 1982).

In their book *Business to Business Direct Marketing*, Bernie Goldberg and Tracy Emerick support the gurus. They list the relative importance of a direct marketing company's four key elements as follows:

The list	50%
The offer	25%
The format	15%
The copy and graphics	10%

You need then to consider:

1. *The list in detail.* The prospects or existing customers you wish to reach. These prospects may also include key influencers who need to be an integral part of your campaign. They might not be potential users but they might be the people who give approval or sign the cheque. You must, above all, get the names and addresses of your targets correct.
2. *The offer.* This includes the offer-driven proposition you are making. It may include price or a discount or a premium. It will always include a trigger to get response and immediate positive action.

Fundraising mailings demand special skills and a unique approach. This mailing includes an appeals letter with a personalised response device attached, a brochure and a business reply envelope. The outer envelope in this instance carries not only a copy hook but evocative photographs to grab attention and boost response. A 'thank you' photo to prospective donors is also enclosed.
Courtesy The Spastic Centre of New South Wales

3. *The format.* This includes the contact strategy, which might include direct response TV, press, telephone, direct mail or even fax.
4. *The copy and graphics.* The words and pictures you use to talk to your market (which we discussed in earlier chapters) come to the fore only when the previous three elements are set.[6]

. . . up to a point

Of course, the fact that getting your list right is direct marketing's top priority is no excuse for slack creativity. There's no doubt whatsoever that an outstanding creative approach will get vastly better results from the same list than mediocrity. So when you go hunting for new leads by direct mail, make sure your creative is the best it can be.

Typically, an effective direct mail pack consists of an outer envelope, personalised letter, brochure, personalised response form and business reply envelope. The outer envelope signals the contents in an intriguing and provocative way. The personalised letter delivers the promise hinted at on the outer envelope, while the brochure details the product, the offer and the price. The personalised response form completes the communication by echoing the offer and making a strong call to action, and the business reply envelope can be used to strengthen the message and flag the closing date.

The well-designed Unisys catalogue presents the range and encourages ordering by fax or phone, as an alternative to face-to-face selling.
Courtesy Unisys Direct

The offer has to create impact and interest, and cut through directly to the person or persons in the business or the home who make the buying decision. Choosing an offer that not only reflects your product's image but gets immediate sales is one of the most critical aspects of direct marketing creativity.

By going for a large budget, you can 'stretch' the outer edge of the envelope and create dimensional mailing packages. When highly personalised, such packages can be very effective in breaking through the clutter. Time and again, the extra cost of these 'clutter busters' is more than justified by the much better-than-average results they achieve.

Apart from the creative, something else you need to watch is the co-ordination of mailings within your organisation. If another department's mailing clashes with your lead generation effort, it could affect the success of both quite dramatically. Such misadventures can easily be avoided, however, by giving each department access to a relational database, to help them plan and despatch their mailings.

Catalogues: mailed and dropped

Recent research carried out for the Australian Catalogues Association pointed to the value of catalogues as lead generators. It showed conclusively that, whether they're mailed or dropped, catalogues arriving in the letterbox are read—and read to a perhaps surprising degree.

In fact, 90% of the population will read a catalogue that looks 'right' to them. More specifically, 67% read half or more of the catalogues they receive, while 39% read most of them. On the average, 53% of all catalogues received are read—a figure that becomes all the more impressive when you consider that TV magnates are ecstatic when a programme rates in the 20s.

Catalogues are a medium you can tailor to your exact requirements. A catalogue that combines editorial content and product information can score particularly highly in readership and sales. The editorial adds interest, and gives you an ideal environment for making product-related offers.

But perhaps your biggest lead-generating opportunity with catalogues is that of using your current customer profile to target new prospects. The more information you can gather on your database about your present customers, the more accurately you can shape the merchandise and offers in your catalogue to attract others.

In the process, you'll also eliminate non-responsive products, cut your costs and get a greater return from every lead-generation dollar you invest.

American Express demonstrate their commitment to using inserts in targeted press media inserts as a method of generating sales as well as promoting American Express as the leading credit card. This dimensional insert in the shape and size of their card folds out to reveal an order form. This device increases interest and involvement with prospects which in turn leads to increased applications for membership.

If you're a mail order business, catalogues are clearly your most important medium. If you're a retailer, they're probably vital to you too. But much expertise is needed in getting them right in terms of design, message, offer/price and merchandise content. You'll find helpful guidance in the following books:

- *Direct Marketing*, Edward Nash (McGraw Hill, 2nd edn, New York, 1986);
- *Successful Direct Marketing Methods*, Bob Stone (NTC Business Books, 4th edn, 1992, Lincolnwood, Illinois, USA);
- *Profitable Direct Marketing*, Jim Kobs, (Crain Books, Chicago, 1979).

Inserts

Look in most American and European magazines and you'll see inserts—business reply cards actually stitched or glued into the publication. They're not common in Australia, largely because the majority of publishers here don't encourage them on a cost basis. But they can be extremely effective in generating extra response. Readers can't miss them. Unlike coupons, they can be removed from a magazine without mutilating the pages. And they can be put aside for further perusing, or sent away immediately.

They are expensive, however, and often include an advertisement that lifts their cost even higher. Consequently, to justify their use, they do have to attract 5 to 10 times the number of leads an average coupon or 1 800 number featured in your advertisement would get.

Loose inserts are less expensive, and enable you to cover several publications with one print run. But when you add up their printing and insertion charges, they're still a lot more costly than couponed advertisements. On the other hand, they're usually more effective in obtaining leads.

Are the extra returns worth the extra outlay? Often yes, sometimes no. In your case, I'm afraid the decision is up to you. But let me just say this.

If you don't try it and monitor your efforts through careful coding of your material by media used, you'll never know.

Trade shows and seminars

Most trade shows and seminars today are tightly targeted to key decision-makers in a particular industry. So they're an excellent opportunity for you to gather prospect names. More than that, they enable you to meet those prospects face to face—and learn in minutes the vital database information that could take you months to acquire otherwise.

To do that, of course, you have to attract prospects to your stand from wherever they are, right across the show. That means your display has to be exciting and interesting. So does your speaker or content, in a seminar situation. It may be worth adding a show special incentive to increase the impact—in which case you would probably mail and/or phone details of it to existing customers, to draw a response from them too.

Use the opportunity primarily, however, to collect as many new names as you can. But don't stop there. Make sure you qualify them in relation to your goals and future sales targets. And take the chance to get as much personal information as possible, perhaps by offering a small premium reward to prospects who provide it.

It's so easy in these situations to collect names and titles, but miss the valuable information that could lead you closer to the sale.

Trade shows and seminars, in short, can do a lot for your lead generation and general selling activities. For instance:

- You can meet prospects face to face, pre-qualify them and their interest levels, and match products and offers to their needs.
- You can arrange off-site meetings with particularly interested prospects to deepen your new relationships.

- You can often meet the top people from your potential customers, and arrange high-level meetings quickly between them and your executives. Don't waste this opportunity!
- You can compile the results of your experience into a research report at the end of the show to help you design future strategies.
- You can maintain and deepen contacts with existing customers.
- You can demonstrate new product or service innovations, and bring existing and prospective customers up to date.
- You can see what your competition is doing, and react accordingly.
- Often, peer group synergies and agreements will lead to an endorsement of your product and its benefits, and boost sales.

Watch out, then, for trade show opportunities. No other lead generation technique enables you to meet so many prospective customers face to face in such a concentrated period of time.

Card decks: share the costs

Our last lead generation technique is one of the most economical. Card deck strategies are mainly used in business-to-business marketing when knowledge of your target is sketchy. They allow you to send between five and 13 postcard-size product information and response cards in a single mailing. Each card features a different branded product, and you share the whole mailing (and hence its costs) with others.

This is an excellent opportunity for low-margin, low-budget items to come together and fund one cost-effective joint exercise. What's more, experience shows that if the mailing is well matched to your target group and includes relevant offers, it can achieve good results for you on a comparatively small outlay.

Even more widely used is a similar idea encapsulated in an insert magazine called *Business Product Review*. Like card decks, BPR gives marketers the chance to reduce the costs of promoting their products and generating leads—this time, in a targeted insert in business magazines, instead of a series of mailing cards or separate non-personalised direct mailings.

BPR is also quite an economical medium. In fact, it's almost certainly within your budget to test inserts, personalised mailings or a combination, to see which works best for you in terms of lead quality and conversion to sales.

Don't lose your lead!

Whether your business is successful or struggling, you need the new customers who are almost certainly out there in profusion, just waiting for you. And you can reach them, identify them and build a link with them—by using a lead generation technique appropriate to your product, your market and your budget.

It might be a new, technologically advanced approach, a traditional one, or a combination of both. But whatever you choose, put it to work now.

Before your competitors snatch away your lead.

Your lead generation checklist

- Have you set up a database that helps track leads and upon which you can enter your customers' records and build information? (You'll also need a back-up system or you can duplicate wrong diskettes. Keep it safe and, preferably, off-site.)
- For more simplistic applications, consider using 'Tracker for Windows', and other personal contact programmes like ACT! Also consider the many adaptable applications of Borland or Microsoft and Apple. (A more sophisticated relational database system will be required for more complicated and diverse needs. Fully integrated and relational sales and marketing databases (ISaMS) such as Transline Unitrac™ are available today. The latest client server applications working off platforms such as Informix, Oracle or Sybase will provide future database users with less expensive, flexible and expanding systems with more accessibility than many traditional mainframe applications now in use.)
- Have you surveyed your customers, analysed their expenditure and their needs, and asked for referrals? (Don't forget that American

Express recruit a worthwhile percentage of new members using 'friend get friend' techniques. They could be good for you too!)

- If you are a retailer, do you actively collect names of customers and score them as to their value to you?
- Is your advertising offer-driven? Don't ever give something for nothing, but add rewards for responding and the volunteering of quality information. Include appropriate offers in TV, radio, outdoor, press and magazines (and inserts) to help boost response and sales closure or motivate a visit to your store.
- Is your direct mail or targeted door-to-door material highly responsive? Is your outbound telephone script also offer-driven?
- Is your telephone procedure designed to gain information from casual enquiries as well as to qualify them for future prospecting?
- Do you make it easy to respond to you? Do you use 1 800 numbers (or alphanumeric), fax, mailing address and even Email address? The more ways you give to respond, the better. Remember, response devices should always be personalised and simple. They're then most likely to effect an immediate return to you.
- Does your programme include follow-up schedules such as outbound telemarketing or follow-up mailings to capitalise on your initial response?
- Have you considered all possible methods to enhance the result of your mailing or telemarketing, such as data overlays that help to target your audience more specifically and eliminate as many suspects as possible? (This will enhance the result of your campaign in terms of response. More importantly, it will also reduce wastage.)
- Have you planned your fulfilment programme to include literature that's easy to read and respond to? Have you employed sympathetic outbound telephone procedures? Have you created ways of controlling information and recording the details of prospects' and customers' reactions in your database?
- If you are in business-to-business, are your personnel actively involved in business card and qualified name collection schemes?
- Have you an internal system to monitor and prioritise prospects regularly? Does it also monitor the response and reactions to your marketing initiatives and actions?

- Finally, be sure to integrate all your offer-driven direct marketing and your lead generation activity with your response advertising, sales-force activity and direct marketing. If you do, you should enjoy ever-improving results from this synergy and interaction.

Notes

1. 'The Future of Retailing', by Timothy J. Keane, *Direct Marketing* magazine, July 1991.
2. Tom Peters, *Liberation Management*, Macmillan, London, 1992.
3. 'Leveraging the Custom Database to your Competitive Advantage', by John Goodman, VP Marketing, Helzberg Diamonds, *Direct Marketing* magazine, December 1992.
4. 'Integrated Direct Marketing: Managing the Mix' by Ernan Roman, *Marketing Magazine,* July 1992.
5. Drayton Bird, *Commonsense Direct Marketing (What is Direct Marketing?)*, p.28. Kogan Page Ltd, 1989, London.
6. *Business to Business Direct Marketing*, Bernie Goldberg & Tracy Emerick, 2nd edn, Direct Marketing Publications, Yardley, PA, USA, 1990.

20

CHAPTER

Telemarketing and Team Sales

When Alexander Graham Bell invented the telephone, people took a while to grasp the significance of his achievement. On hearing the news, the head of the British Post Office—presumably an intelligent man—said, 'Interesting, but we will never need it in Britain. We have plenty of messenger boys.' His opposite number in America, on the other hand, displayed wider vision. 'Remarkable,' he enthused. 'I foresee the day when every American city and town will have one.'

We smile. But it took those of us in marketing a very long while indeed to see the significance of Mr Bell's invention for us. For decades, it just sat on our desks, carrying out mundane communication tasks. Meanwhile, our sales teams slogged around the countryside, doing things they could have done far more quickly and effectively on the phone.

Realisation dawns

Over the last few years, however, we've started to realise just what the telephone can do as a sales force tool. But we're also realising what it can't do. Telemarketing, we're coming to see, is not a magic cure-all for every marketing ill. Rather, it's yet another marketing technique, with specific strengths and weaknesses that need to be understood. It can be extraordinarily cost-effective if used correctly—and a potential disaster if it isn't. Let me begin by making seven essential points about Mr Bell's contribution to our marketing armoury.

No database, no telemarketing

The first, and perhaps the most important, is this. You can't really do telemarketing at all unless you bring every one of your customer sales files together onto a database. I suppose you can still make phone calls without doing so, but they won't constitute telemarketing in the true sense of the word.

To use the medium properly, your telemarketer must have full details of the customer's history, particular requirements, individual foibles, current status and so on at his or her fingertips. Without them, he or she will stumble around in circles, cover old ground, display an obvious ignorance of the client's needs, and even put the relationship at risk. Nor will he or she be able to update the client data and store it cost-effectively for use on the next call. These points are all so important that I'd like to lay down a law.

If you don't have your sales files on a database, don't try telemarketing.

Part of the team

The second point is almost as important as the first one. Telemarketing is not a one-off, isolated thrust in the same way that, say, a sweepstake might be. It is—or should be—a basic, ongoing sales force activity. Consequently, your telemarketers are not a third-rate appendage to your sales team. They are key members of it. Their role in it is pivotal and central. The quality of their work will, in fact, depend largely on how thoroughly they are integrated into its operations.

More than secretaries

The third point follows naturally. When seeking a good telemarketer, companies often say, 'Jenny's great on the phone, let's give her a go—she'll do well.' Jenny may indeed be sensational, but the mind set is wrong. A telesales person won't work at peak efficiency if he or she is being treated like a secretary. Your telesales person has to be seen for what he or she is—a vital member of the sales team, on a par with the best salespeople in the territory. After all, he or she is going to replace those people in an important part of their work. Telemarketing is definitely a job for trained and talented specialists.

And they need to get the kudos their status deserves.

Non-measurable results

Point four, if not understood, is often a source of disappointment. Because telemarketing is part of the whole sales team's activities, it's normally not possible to isolate and measure its contribution to the overall sales picture. Even when telemarketing is used in a specific one-off promotion—which isn't often—attributing a precise percentage of the profits to it is extremely hard.

That frustration, however, falls into place when you look at points four and five—and the real reasons why telemarketing is used.

Long-term relationships

Point five is that telemarketing is essentially a long-term process. It's not a quick-hit sales fix. Rather, it's a relationship builder—one of the most vital aspects of the whole relationship marketing process we looked at in Chapter 18.

Telemarketing, in fact, if done properly, is perhaps the most effective way of all to develop steadily deepening one-to-one relationships with your customers. Good telemarketing can turn them into friends whose individual needs and wants are known, understood—and met—by your organisation. As Chapter 18 emphasised, the importance of that today simply can't be overstated.

'The sale merely consummates the courtship,' says leading marketing identity Theodore Levitt. 'Then the marriage begins. How good the marriage is depends on how well the relationship is managed by the seller. That determines whether there will be continued or expanded business or troubles and divorce, and whether costs or profits increase.'[1]

Sales force productivity

Point six is a crucial one in the present environment. Telemarketing can greatly increase your salespeople's productivity, by saving them huge amounts of relatively unprofitable time. It can help them to concentrate on the most lucrative accounts—and yet maintain or even increase the income from the more borderline ones.

Get help!

I want to underline the seventh and last point heavily. If you want to go into telemarketing but have no experience in it, don't go it alone. Get top professional help. Remember, telemarketing's potential for disaster equals its potential for good—because you can damage your business just as spectacularly over the phone as you can face-to-face. Don't risk it—a good telemarketing agency costs money, but it could prove one of the best long-term investments you'll ever make.

Cost-driven growth

Telemarketing really started to get off the ground when people began sitting down and calculating the true cost of a sales call. McGraw Hill in America worked out that the figure rose from $71 per call in 1975 to $257 in 1987. That was bad enough—but when you realised that it often took four or five calls to finalise a typical sale, the real cost of conversion was running around $1200–$1300 a time. This would be well over $2000 in today's money.

The figures shocked everyone who didn't run sales forces, and confirmed what they already suspected to those who did. The latter group knew their salespeople were spending thousands of hours prospecting and canvassing. They knew they weren't putting in nearly enough time with real prospects and fully qualified leads. Now they had proof of their fears—and a powerful motivation to find new ways of doing things. So the change began. And the use of the telephone for selling began to come into its own.

The $55 billion bonanza

Today, more and more sales are being conducted over the telephone. *Direct Marketing* magazine in the USA values them at around $55 billion a year. An Arthur Anderson study conducted for the US National Association for Wholesalers commented that telesales personnel—'capable inside salespeople'—would be the most important criterion for buyers in the 1990s.[2] The same study predicted that the number of field sales representatives would drop—and that about two-thirds of all sales representatives would be 'inside' by 1995. Indeed, I know of one computer software company now where two sales representatives each sell over $1 million worth of product per year—goods costing from $200 to $40 000—without ever seeing their customers.

But even with all this growth and enthusiasm, I still believe it's important to keep telemarketing and telesales in perspective. It's certainly not going to replace direct face-to-face selling. There is no substitute for a sales call. An on-the-spot salesperson can help sort out problems, give detailed advice, launch new products and keep harmony between customer and company. But a sales call can also be made at the wrong time, be a nuisance to the customer—and have totally the opposite effect to what was intended.

Preparing the way

What telemarketing can do brilliantly, as I outlined in point six, is to prepare the salespeople's way.

The technique can save them vast amounts of time-consuming legwork, by handling all the prospecting and canvassing. Telemarketing can free them from unproductive calls, by sorting real prospects from doubtful ones. It can enable them to spend most of their time on the most profitable accounts. It can ensure their call will be timely and welcomed. And it can help them give better service, by discovering in advance exactly what the customers want and need. Telemarketing can even look after many of the fringe accounts on its own. Experience shows their purchase levels can often be maintained or increased by use of the telephone alone.

In short, when linked to a database, telemarketing can greatly increase the sales force's productivity and dramatically cut their costs. That makes it a technique you can't afford not to investigate.

Qualify the inbound calls

Telemarketing can prepare the way for field salespeople in the other direction, too. When enquiries come to you through advertising, trade shows, direct mail, publicity or any other response-generating activity, start by doing what I hope you do now. Reply quickly. Get your information package out within 24 hours if possible, or 48 hours at the outside. Then, follow it up by phone. When you do, have your telemarketers probe tactfully but tellingly. Try to establish the enquirer's depth of interest, urgency of need for the product and authority to buy it. You'll soon separate the hot leads from the casual enquiries.

Once you've done all this, get the essential details onto the database

This programme was designed to get telephones ringing and quotes going out. The more quotes written, the higher the conversion to sales.
Courtesy of James Hardie Building Systems Pty Ltd

and hand them on very quickly to your people in the field. The faster they get the lead, the sooner they can follow-up—and the more often they'll close the sale before your rivals even contact the prospect.

Always mail first

One word of warning. Don't try, as some do, to phone the enquirers before you mail them your literature. Inevitably, it will be days or even weeks before you reach them all—by which time many sales will have gone elsewhere. It's much better to demonstrate your keenness by return mail first, and phone a few days after that.

The 1800 and 13 exceptions

The one exception to that rule is when the enquiry comes directly to one of your telemarketers, via a 1800 or 13 number in your marketing communication. In that case, the telesales person can proceed immediately to qualify the prospect, at a sizeable savings in time and cost.

That's another excellent reason for asking prospects to respond to a 1800 or 13 number, attended by trained people with a well-prepared script—or creating an offer that requires them to do so. It's been estimated that it costs around $50–$150 to follow-up and qualify a prospect by phone later on. That's still vastly more economical than following them all up with sales calls—but if you can get them to phone you, the qualifying costs plummet to an absolute minimum.

When you ask people to phone, incidentally, a good way to increase response is to replace the numbers with letters. For a life insurance company, the response number 13-LIFE is obviously a lot more memorable than, say, 13-3896. And the technology now exists to make the changeover possible. It's not cheap, but overseas experience shows it can be well worth doing. Seldane, an American hay fever antihistamine, puts the helpline number 800-1-4-HAYFEVER on their pack and in all their communications. American Express help to position themselves with 1800 THE CARD! Canadian Pacific Car Rentals in Canada uses dial 1-800-FOR CARS. And here in Australia, Cabcharge has started the trend with Call 13-TAXIS.

Alphanumeric, as the concept is known, could be a way to go for you.

Keep it a secret

Pre-qualifying incoming enquiries is another way to help your salespeople spend most of their time with the most likely prospects. It cuts costs and boosts sales just as much as outgoing telemarketing. And I think it's a good idea to keep the whole programme under wraps. Your competitors will wonder how you always seems to be one jump ahead of them in clinching the sale.

Anything that leaves them flat-footed and guessing has to be good for you!

Building the relationship

Besides preparing the way for sales calls, telemarketing can make an enormous contribution to the relationship-building process with each of your customers. This is another reason why your telemarketers are such key members of your sales team. How successfully those relationships are built depends to a very large extent on them. Fortunately, however, there's no great mystery about the building process. Common courtesy, a cheerful phone manner, a genuine interest in people, the ability to find answers quickly, a thorough knowledge of company procedures, and a real understanding of how your products can meet customers' needs—those are the basic qualities a telemarketer needs for relationship building. He or she has to be born with some of these qualities, while training can provide the others.

One shoe at a time

A telemarketing campaign I admire for its relationship-building dimension was one conducted by the HBA, a health fund based in Victoria, Australia. It was conceived by Simon Richards Direct. The product was stress testing and executive health care. Very large corporations were the target.

The first step was for the telemarketer to phone and find out who was the key decision-maker in the executive staff welfare area. The telemarketer would then ask for that person's secretary or assistant—and make an enquiry that usually led to instant mirth.

What was the person's shoe size?

Invariably, the secretary or assistant had to go and ask the person concerned—which spread the mirth further. So even at this early stage, a warm relationship was starting to emerge, through the repartée generated by the foot size question.

Once the size was established, the decision-maker was sent one Reebok shoe—a product with obvious links to a health care programme. If he or she agreed to a meeting to discuss the HBA proposal, the second shoe was handed over at the meeting.

This was clearly a strong motivation for the decision-maker to meet with the HBA people, free and without obligation. Reeboks aren't cheap gifts—but the promotion paid for itself after just 20 calls.

Management's role

In relationship-building and all other aspects of the technique, the telemarketer bears the brunt of the battle. But management has a very important role too. The company has to provide a quiet telemarketing environment with efficient, easy-to-use technology. And—most importantly—it has to overcome any resistance within the sales force to the introduction of telemarketing. It has to convince the salespeople that the new technique will help them make more money with less effort. And it has to let the telemarketers know that their contribution is seen as vital by those at the top of the business. If you don't really believe what they're doing is crucial, they won't either. Nothing could be more calculated to damage their effectiveness.

Good listeners

Talking, of course, is only one part of a telemarketer's job. Equally if not more important is the ability to listen. Indeed, it's by listening that you really get to know customers' individual needs and wants, and how your company can best meet them. It's by listening, too, that you hear complaints and identify areas of concern. Solving those to the customer's satisfaction is perhaps the most powerful relationship-builder of all.

Another reason for listening is that customers often have excellent

Toshiba Mobile Computers breakthrough mail pack was despatched only after determining by telephone key decision makers reluctance to embrace this technology. A FREE trial of their mobile computer arranged by further telephone follow ups, helped alter opinions and sanction the purchase of more Toshiba computers.
Courtesy of Toshiba/Australia Pty Limited

suggestions—some of which can actually be developed into product features. For instance, Pillsbury's service line once received many requests for a recipe that had appeared in a magazine advertisement. The company responded by printing the recipe on the Pillsbury pack—a reaction that increased sales and customer goodwill at the same time. Wine racks in GE refrigerators and a salt-free version of Jiffy Pop popcorn were both born of customer suggestions. So encourage your telesales people to be alert for ideas from callers, and to pass them on promptly to the appropriate people. A very saleable new product feature may well result.

The best people, the best training

By now, I hope I've made the point that telemarketing is too important to entrust to just anyone. The telesales person needs to be someone with real personality, high intelligence, quick wits, razor-sharp initiative and other superhuman qualities. He or she also needs training of the very highest order.

That will involve many things. Product knowledge, how to determine the customers' real needs by listening, and how to ask the right questions are three important ones. The telemarketer also has to learn how to read a conversation and keep it on course, when to inject a strong sales message and how to turn product features into customer benefits. In short, the telesales person needs exactly the same level of selling competence as the salespeople in the field. That's further emphasised by the following telemarketing script, kindly provided by Vicki Hogan of Hogan Marketing Services.

Notice especially how the telesales person needs deep product knowledge, plus the ability to direct the call, to listen to the customer's requirements, to respond accordingly—and to pave the way for a more productive sales call by the representative.

A slice of life

Sue Waller: Hello, is that Steve Hallam? Hi, Sue Waller from ABC Pharmaceuticals. How are you today? I'm calling you because we're setting up a new pharmacy telephone service, to operate in conjunction with our field sales force.

We've set up this new facility to give you a complete service programme. It will include regular contact from us, along with your normal rep call, plus access to us on a special direct phone number. And remember, that's in addition to seeing your rep.

Mr Hallam, I want to tell you about the new service, but firstly, can I just check that you're the person who decides what products and brands your pharmacy carries—pharmaceutical and OTC lines?

Steve Hallam: Yes, Sue, I'm the man.

Sue: Fine. Our marketing and sales manager, Peter Smith, has asked me to let you know about this additional service. We'll be working with our sales force, and we'll phone you from time to time with news of product launches and special offers. For instance, I'll tell you now about some new products in our Apollo range. Are you aware there's now an orange flavour Apollo for kids as well as the strawberry flavour?

Steve: No, but tell me more. We've done well from your original Apollo flavours.

Sue: Good. There's a couple of other things I want to mention too, but can I just check something with you first? Mr Hallam, we realise people like you are very busy, so if we were to contact you with special product deals or information, what would be the best time of the month to call?

Do you usually plan your purchases or check stock levels at a particular time each month, say the first week or the last week?

Steve: Yes, in the last week.

Sue: And which day would that normally be on?

Steve: On the Tuesday.

Sue: So if we called on Tuesday in the afternoon, would that be a good time?

Steve: Yes, I'd appreciate a call at 2.30 p.m. on the last Tuesday.

Sue: Right, I'll make a note of that. Mr Hallam, we realise some pharmacies choose to belong to buying groups—either formal agreements or informal associations of individuals. To save any confusion downstream—can I check if you're in any kind of group or do you buy directly from a wholesaler?

Steve: Yes, I'm in a group—Chemart of Bendigo.

Sue: And who do you buy in association with?

Steve: Michael Lynch Pharmacy. And I talk to Suzanne Lynch there.

Sue: What's their phone number and who's the purchasing co-ordinator?

Steve: Their phone number is 449 3099 and Suzanne usually purchases for the group.

Sue: Mr Hallam, as I mentioned earlier, we've been doing some exciting things with the Bloggo range—we've launched new Bloggo Plus for both children and adults. Firstly, for children, we've developed an analgesic so that children can now have a choice of X or Y, plus of course the chewable tablets.

You probably know that Bloggo Plus is already one of the most widely prescribed antibiotics for children. We're giving doctors X and Y stickers to add to prescriptions so it will be easy for you to see which one to dispense—you may already have seen some of these.

And the second new product we've launched is Blogocin tablets. Blogocin is an adult strength AAA antibiotic. It's based on the very successful children's strength Bloggo Plus.

Steve: Yes, I've got a good idea of those products. Charlie Watts called and gave me a lot of information but I'd like to see the range.

Sue: (Selling heavily) From the doctor's point of view, Blogocin offers some major benefits. It's a highly effective antibiotic. It has very few side effects. It has a twice daily dosage and can be taken any time regardless of meals. And finally it's a very easy prescription for the doctor to write—simply Blogocin—so you'll be seeing a lot of Blogocin prescriptions this season. Doctors are receiving details from this week.

The list price from wholesalers of each bottle is $3.82—that's 24 tablets. Because Blogocin isn't on the PBS, we don't know what the dispensed price will be—that's up to you. But to give you an example, if you added a 40% markup and your professional fees, that would be a dispensed price of $9.44—a total markup of 145%.

Of course, Bloggo Plus and Blogocin aren't our only antibiotics. Byrocin and Peakocillin are both widely prescribed products, so you'd probably always have a need for them. How are your current stocks?

Steve: We're quite low. We don't like to stock too much.

Sue: I can take an order for you now and have them delivered in the normal way.

Steve: Do you have any special deals on Byrocin or Peakocillin?

Sue: Charlie Watts, your rep, has information on bonuses and deals—I'll be happy to arrange for him to visit with all the details. And I'm sure he's told you that we're about to start a TV advertising campaign for Danfree. Our sales force is also running a display incentive programme and they have some bonus parcels for Danfree and some of the other OTC products—such as Blue-Mouth, Sweet-Tooth and the rest.

If you'd like the details of all these special programmes, I'll arrange for Charlie to tell you about them.

Steve: Yes, I'd like that very much.

Sue: Thanks for your time, Mr Hallam. We'll be in touch with you again to give you details of other special offers. And remember, we've also set up special direct access telephone lines which will be manned from 9 a.m. to 9 p.m., Monday to Friday. You'll be able to place orders and get information on special deals outside normal business hours if you need to—which might be helpful during especially busy times. The number is 02 0001111 or toll free on 1 800 2223333.

Steve: Thanks very much. I appreciate your call. Goodbye.

Sue: Thanks, Mr Hallam. Goodbye.

A very special talent

I think you'll agree that a very special talent is needed to make call after call like that, day after day. Nor are the people being called always as ready to listen as Steve Hallam. The telesales person frequently has only about 90–120 seconds to get the message over. That's about 300–400 words—each of which has to help do the job without waffle or wandering.

A top-class business-to-business telemarketer can make about 35–50 calls a day, depending on how long it takes to reach the decision-makers. That's vastly more than a sales rep can make. And it can increase the number of qualified, pre-arranged, high-priority calls your salespeople carry out by 50% or more a day.

Keep track of the data

Another essential task of the telemarketer is to record the result of every call. In fact, this is one of the most important areas of operation. As I stated earlier, you really can't have a telemarketing operation without an accurate, detailed, regularly upgraded database—and gathering customer feedback is the way you keep your database totally up to date. Here, of course, I'm assuming you have indeed embraced the concept of database marketing. There's no doubt whatsoever that switching to a database mode of operation is one of the most significant steps a modern sales force can take.

Traditionally, salespeople have kept customer data in their files and updated it themselves, as and when they could. The usual result, however, is mountains of paper in scores of different files—a widely scattered treasure of information that can never be collected and reproduced cost-effectively by the company for general sales force and marketing department use. Even in fairly large businesses, the main client history is all too often that held by the accounts department. Many other companies employ a manual system as unwieldy as it is ineffective.

But today, as we noted in Chapter 18, gathering all this information onto a database is comparatively simple. Once the information is there and regularly updated, it builds into a comprehensive profile of your company's customers. It can show you the segments where success has been found. It can perform cluster analysis, to predict where similar types of customers are likely to be. And it can be used to define purchasing patterns, their recency, frequency and monetary value, and even iron out differences in sales territories.

Moving into database marketing, in short, means putting your whole market into one marketing database, often at arm's length from your mainframe. You can then see the entire picture at a glance and do your product and customer research automatically, in the course of your normal daily selling activities.

Fighting the forces of entropy

The data-gathering aspect of telemarketing, then, has great long-term significance. But as well, it's an important part of relationship-building in its own right. Why? Because it makes you examine and re-examine all aspects of the relationship on a continuing basis. Without that discipline, apathy can so easily take over and smother the relationship's growth. The very quotable Theodore Levitt puts it this way:

'A healthy relationship requires a conscious and constant fight against the forces of entropy. It becomes important for the seller regularly and seriously to ask himself, for example, "How are we doing?" "Is the relationship improving or deteriorating?" "Are our promises being fully fulfilled?" "Are we neglecting anything?" "How do we stand vis-a-vis our competitors in the relationship?" '[3]

Breaking down the barriers

Of all its revolutionary contributions, perhaps the most productive thing database marketing can do is to break down the barriers between marketing and sales.

While certainly not intentional, those barriers have tended to grow out of the two disciplines' different functions. Marketing is concerned with the broad picture—with defining the market, ascertaining its needs, developing the selling strategy and working out the best way to communicate it. Sales, on the other hand, is concerned with the individual customer. The priority for the sales force is to get the selling message through on a one-to-one basis, and build one-to-one customer relationships.

Now, through database marketing, both activities can be linked directly together, far more cost-effectively than ever before. A database provides detailed, up-to-date information not only on individual customers but on the market as a whole. And because that information can readily be shared between sales and marketing, they can now be integrated into one unified, planned and policed selling effort.

The 3M Priority Customer Programme

This has actually happened with one of our clients, the Memory Technologies Division of 3M. Here, marketing and sales manager John Taylor has brought both disciplines into one organisational unit. He directs both marketing and sales from one central point, and guides their agreed integrated strategies right through to distribution and dealerships.

From that has come the 3M Priority Customer Programme (see also Chapter 18), a pioneering but very effective selling campaign. This trail-blazing venture combines telemarketing, database marketing and relationship marketing in a way that is still quite unusual—but that will, I believe, become more and more common in the century's closing years.

The key to it is that we hold all participating dealers' databases in trust at the agency. None is available to 3M or, of course, to the other dealers. Through telemarketing and direct mail, we target regular sales messages to all lists, usually incorporating special offers and incentives. Some of these are in the dealer's name, while others come directly from 3M.

Constant refining

With the feedback generated by every contact, the lists are constantly refined. How the end users react to each type of approach and offer is recorded. So are purchase levels and frequency. This enables us to score each customer on a points system, based on purchase history, responsiveness to offers and estimated sales potential. We can then set contact schedules for every customer, and make our sales approaches increasingly relevant and personalised. By identifying key prospects and defining their potential in this way, the whole marketing process becomes much more cost-effective.

Flexibility

According to their points score, we contact the customers monthly, bi-monthly or less often—in some extreme cases, annually—and we do it in whichever way has worked best for each one. It might be through telemarketing, direct mail or even a face-to-face sales call. Flexibility is the key—a flexibility shaped not by guesswork, but by solid selling experience.

You can see how telemarketing, database marketing and relationship marketing blend in this pioneering programme. The relationship aspect is further strengthened, as we noted in Chapter 18, by giving each priority customer a 'Priority Customer Card'—a credit-card-sized plastic affair, personalised with the customer's name and number, to recognise them as individuals, and emphasise their value to 3M and the dealer. The Priority Customer Programme has kept 3M dealers growing at a rate well above the industry average. All future planning is now based on tried and tested tactics. Every dollar involved is fully accountable.

And not a single one has been spent on traditional media advertising.

Why are the best the best?

Pitney Bowes decided to go the database route when they realised they didn't have the answer to two key questions. Why are our best salespeople outperforming the others? And why are our best customers our best customers?

What prompted the questions was the discovery that their top two salespeople were always out on the road, yet the next best performer never left the office. A little probing uncovered the difference between traditional attitudes and more modern phone-based methods. So, to even out imbalances and improve most of their sales force's success rate, Pitney Bowes put their customers into a marketing database—one that can be manipulated by marketing and actively used by the sales force in the field.

By employing a combination of telemarketing, telesales and face-to-face calls, Pitney Bowes can now manage the whole programme of capturing lead suspects and converting them to prospects. They do so by qualifying the lead and grading its worth. The process has markedly increased the percentage of leads that turn into sales.

From accounts to marketing

The switch was accomplished by taking their existing invoicing and accounts database and adding sales record card information and vital contact data. Analyses of top salespeople's experiences and known customer needs and preferences went into the mix as well. In quite a short time, a flat file was transformed into a highly effective relational marketing and sales tool. This Pitney Bowes database is transactional, too. As a result, they can monitor exactly what is going on in the field, pinpoint strengths and weaknesses and allow both sales and marketing to plan their activities very precisely. In addition, the sales and marketing efforts can be closely co-ordinated, as they are with 3M.

Furthermore, the system can be closely policed to maximise sales force productivity. By setting up times for visits through telemarketing, we are putting salespeople in front of customers who are ready to buy. That gives the sales force more chances to sell. And it's greatly improving their productive calling rates.

Billion dollar phone calls

One of the most spectacular telemarketing success stories yet is that of Dell Computers. Just eight years after Michael Dell started making and selling good, low-priced computers in his college dormitory, his corporate revenues neared $2 billion annually.

And at least half of that was being generated by telemarketing.

One reason for this staggering performance is that the company's approach is focused on customer needs rather than product features. They frequently mail customers an in-depth personalised presentation, then call to explain it in detail over the phone. Dell himself credits their success to making the customer king, instead of majoring on their own technological brilliance.

'Many companies in our industry started with a technology focus, instead of a customer focus,' he says. 'We don't build anything until we receive the order from the customer. We will do whatever it takes to satisfy the customer.'

Dell, in short, has given us a glimpse of how powerful telemarketing can be when it always puts the customer first. Now he's shown the way, some experts are predicting that one out of every three PCs will be sold direct in the USA by 1995.

Who'll do the job?

If this chapter has convinced you to set up a customer database and give telemarketing a go, I'm glad. There's just one question I'd ask you to think through very carefully. Who's going to do it for you?

You have two alternatives. You can set up your own in-house telemarketing operation. Or you can seek help from an experienced telemarketing agency. As I said in point seven, I would urge you to follow the second route. The time and cost involved in setting up your own facility—making space available, installing the equipment, recruiting top people and training them—is pretty formidable. It's far better, I think, to talk to some telemarketing agencies. Find them in the Yellow Pages. Ask to see their latest campaigns. Seek endorsements from their clients. And invite one to put together a package for you.

That way, you'll not only make the most of telemarketing's potential for boosting sales force productivity and cutting costs. You'll avoid its potential for disaster.

Notes

1. Theodore Levitt, *The Marketing Imagination*, The Free Press (a division of Macmillin, Inc.) New York, 1983, 1986.
2. Quoted by Henry 'Pete' Hoke, Jr, in an editorial in *Direct Marketing*, Hoke Communications, June 1993.
3. Theodore Levitt, op. cit.
4. 'Dell takes a megabyte of the PC manual', by Mollie Neal, *Direct Marketing,* May 1993.

21
CHAPTER

Research, Testing, Measurement and Accountability

In tough times (are there any others?), it's more important than ever to test the methodology and results of your sales promotion and direct marketing campaigns. Financial marketing authority Irwin Lowen of the USA says, 'When all the focus and discussion groups, the questions, the analyses and research have been completed, in the final analysis it is how people choose to spend their money that counts. In other words, the response, who buys what and who responds to which particular advertisement. People vote with their hip pockets.'[1]

We're after this hip pocket vote, as cost-effectively as possible. And in the new world of accountability, the experience gleaned from past campaigns is vital information when planning the next. The responses to a mailpack of one configuration versus another . . . the results of one advertisement compared to others running on different schedules ... the offer and how it appeals to various target groups—all these provide hard-won guidelines to the construction of the next promotion. The idea is to use the last campaign as a control—and to improve on it with the next one.

Following the brand image

Research in sales promotion is as important as research in advertising. The fundamental difference is that in sales promotion we follow the brand image wherever we can. We create ideas to lock into the above-the-line concept, where the creative approach has already been decided or has even been running for some time. Consequently, positioning research in sales promotion is rare. If the advertising positioning is right, it should be right for sales promotion too. If it isn't right, the sales promotion will further magnify its weaknesses.

However, research of other kinds certainly is mandatory in sales promotion. It begins with early research to get the brief right. Then it goes on to concept testing, which will most likely be done in group discussions.

An Apple for the teacher

These interviews with people in the target group can give you invaluable feedback not only on your idea but on your strategy. I well remember creating an integrated offer-driven sales promotion and direct marketing strategy for Apple. It was aimed at blocking the threat posed by IBM's new JX. We selected three groups of school teachers with knowledge of computers and their use in schools.

The results were extraordinary.

Two groups ran out of conversation on computers within 13 minutes of the start. The other group sustained conversation for only a little longer. Most teachers feared the use of computers in the classroom and the impact they would have on their jobs. We also faced petty jealousies from the staff who understood computers and those who did not.

These factors underlined the need to broaden our campaign. It still needed the big idea in the offer, to stop IBM's incursion. But it also had to provide Parents & Citizens groups and teachers with a package of communication to increase awareness of the Apple IIe and the new Macintosh. It had to educate these groups on the benefits Apples could deliver to children. And it had to help teachers to feel comfortable about the use of Apples in schools, so they could improve their computer skills and those of their pupils.

As well, we realised that the 'user friendliness' of Apples, really had to be spelled out. Using case studies and actual examples of Apples' in-school successes led to the creation of the 'Apple for the Teacher' video. With that came brochures demonstrating how children could best be helped to use Apples in the learning process. All this was in addition to the original sales promotion proposition—but it really paid off. This preliminary research lead to the creation of a campaign that put Apples on back order for 18 months.

As far as testing the offer is concerned, you can go with groups or, more normally, with concept boards. At this stage, you can compare a number of concepts, too. The concept can also be tested by techniques such as in-depth interviews, house-to-house calls and running it in mini test markets.

Get the delivery right

The most important point in sales promotion and offer-driven marketing research is in the area of deliverability. If people understand what is expected of their *actions*, these can, in theory, be judged both *quantitatively* and *qualitatively.* In my experience, however, quantitative testing is difficult in sales promotion. I know of no method that can predict the actual response rates to a sales promotion offer, only the general likelihood of success.

In the final analysis, the consumer 'votes' by buying or responding to an offer. No research I'm aware of can reproduce the precise reality of the point of sale, the opportunity to see, the competitive activity or the demands that might be made on the consumer to enter. The frame of mind of the consumers when they discover the promotion will also affect the final response.

As a result, this kind of research is best collected in hard numbers over time by the agency. Therefore, the most effective test you can do is one that replicates the normal market situation. Certain factors in sales promotion offers can be determined. Once they are, you can then build a fairly accurate assessment of the outcome of the promotion.

Above all, it is important to get the strategy right. Here you have to use experience and rely on methodology that's been tried and tested to guide you. An example of a point-of-sale audit follows. Use it!

THE POINT-OF-SALE AUDIT

Stage 1

- What roles do point-of-sale (POS) communications play:
  - — in your marketing programme?
  - — in your competitors' marketing programme?
- How do your POS programmes rate versus competitive programmes in the eyes of:
  - — consumers?
  - — trade?

Stage 2

- How important is the point of sale in influencing consumer behaviour in your product category?
- Given consumer needs at the point of purchase for:
  - — information
  - — service
  - — entertainment

How important *could* it be? How important *should* it be?

Stage 3

- What functions/tasks need to be performed to satisfy these consumer POS needs?
- Which channel members—manufacturers, retailers, consumers—are willing to perform them?
- Which channel members can perform them most cost-effectively?

Stage 4

- How should the functions/tasks be allocated?
- How should the pricing structure for the product (and for the POS programme) reflect this allocation of functions/tasks?

Databases to boost research

In the past, little research was done in sales promotion or offer-driven marketing. More will be carried out from now on, with the advent of databases that tell their own stories. They will give much of the information that quantitative research from such sources as A C Nielsen or AGB's BrandScan has provided previously.

Today's transactional databases and sophisticated profiling methodology provide marketers with true information. You can now track your audience very accurately and gain precise knowledge of them. You can profile what you have with data overlays and geodemographic information. By surveying them, you can find out much more. And as suppliers get closer to the retailer, information will be swapped between marketers and retail store groups. This database knowledge will make many of our past testing and tracking methods redundant.

'Town Hall' testing was one of these. Actually, it told us a lot about how people react to packaging and pricing. People were literally lured off the street into a convenient location and asked a barrage of questions on the product as well as the sales promotion offer. More targeted methods of testing include door-to-door and postal tests. The latter has widespread applications in direct marketing where you are testing one set of reactions to a mailing or even an outbound telephone marketing campaign. In these instances, the sales promotion offer is only one of the criteria being put to the test.

The door-to-door survey works when one set of statistically relevant people are questioned, following their trial and experience of a sample either previously dropped or demonstrated there and then. The problem with both methods is that you may be forcing the issue. In that case, you'd learn little more than you would from carefully selected groups.

Perhaps the best research in sales promotions comes only in the discovery of the appropriateness of a concept—how well it can be delivered and understood via its chosen communication media. The best promotional offer in the world will fail if it is not clearly communicated. If the promotion does not cut-through and 'scream out' above the clutter and the other offers being bombarded at the consumer, its effect will be greatly diminished.

Memory lane

Store tests were very popular way back in the early 1970s. In fact, I started my brand managership by driving a van around Manchester in England delivering and merchandising a group of new products—'Fresh Milk Concentrate', 'Top O' The Milk' and 'Flavoured Buttermilk'. In the process, Unigate Foods learned a great deal about the acceptance of these products and where to merchandise them in the cold cabinet to get best results.

As a brand manager, my work also involved the use of the RBL mini test van, a Unilever research-based service. We used this not only to test the products' acceptability but also to find more cost-effective methods of gaining the sale. From testing various product prices and value offers, we found that full value coupons offered on a new dairy product would triple the trial effect and work more cost-effectively than those of any lesser value. We also proved that, on another product, a 25p coupon would outperform a more valuable one. At the same time, we used the service to judge the acceptance of various promotions in gaining off-take.

Pitfalls to watch

A word of warning. There are difficulties in researching sales promotional offers where the emphasis is on added benefits, like a free premium, discount or cashback. People, we have learned, claim almost automatically that they'd take up the offer. In practice, of course, they don't. Very often, the most frivolous offers and those less skewed towards price would fail the test every time—but on supermarket shelves or in an advertisement, they could well perform like champions.

CSR have tested their on–pack offers and defined better performing promotions in terms of trade and consumer acceptance, state by state.
Courtesy CSR Refined Sugars

In many instances, sales promotions that attempt to reflect the above-the-line theme and support the branding effort would fare badly in research. Yet experience suggests they could be very effective in actual usage. So be guided by research—but don't accept its results too slavishly.

For instance, my colleague David Shearer tested an offer for Haywards Pickles. The TV commercial used the clever and memorable creative endorsement by Vincent Price, the ghoulish actor who starred in many horror movies. The product's theme was 'These pickles bite back'. This positioning distanced Haywards Pickles from the rest, but gave a new meaning to their extra bitter taste when Count Dracula (played by Vincent Price) sat at a dinner table devouring Haywards Pickles!

The sales promotion concept suggested somewhat 'tongue in cheek' that a steak knife for use with the cheese and cheeseboard would be a very appropriate offer. However, the consumer research disagreed, and pointed to a proposition involving a cheese brand and money discounts off complementary products. This tied in with product usage but not its unique branding. So we overruled the research and went in an extremely different—and much more exciting and memorable—direction.

A free Band-Aid was attached to the pack instead. Accompanying it were words echoing the brand's proposition, 'Ouch! These pickles bite back. Free Band-Aid'. This promotion brought the above-the-line proposition into the store, and arrested and amused purchasers as well. A secondary plus—the manufacturers gave us the Band-Aids free. They saw benefits in being associated with this highly unusual offering—a promotion that sold out, well ahead of time and budget.

The 'Gold Standard'—in-store research

Our work with Arnott's Snack Foods (now FritoLay) led to the invention of a 'Gold Standard' campaign, the culmination of much thinking on store layouts and displays.

Snack food companies mostly sell bulky space-consuming packs, full of air and product. To survive in a very competitive climate, they must get as much supermarket space as they can. That involves taking space from competitors, both on- and off-shelf. Because impulse plays a huge part in these items' purchase, you have to get maximum display space on the horizontal and vertical planes. If you can do this, you can alter your fortunes dramatically.

For this exercise, FritoLay negotiated space with every key account. The promotion had to be closely monitored and tailored for each store. Then FritoLay used 'palm top' computers to establish an ideal store layout. They literally mapped the stores. A matrix was created to show the salespeople how to lay out their stores, take command of their positioning, reduce out-of-stock situations and thwart further incursion of the brand leader, Smith's Crisps, and own-label chips.

The programme also involves Frito-Lay's sales force in doing their own 'research' into pricing, positioning and off-shelf locating, with particular emphasis on the off-shelf opportunity. Each salesperson's own research with the hand-held computer can now be transmitted back to head office and the results compiled very speedily. Where there is a problem from the competition or one of supply, the company can find out and react quickly and decisively. The information can also be extended to give a regional picture. As well, competitors' activities can be monitored extremely closely.

To use this type of system, a sales force has to be structured correctly. It has to have time both to sell and to record this vital intelligence. But once under way, the system reduces the need for outside research. And that need will be cut even further if store POS data can be fed straight to manufacturers for inventory purposes.

The FritoLay system is welcomed by retailers. It dovetails into their Apollo system, a method that helps maximise the space and shelf siting of all product categories they measure. Retailers like suppliers who help them sell products faster and more cheaply—which is just what these systems do.

The voice of experience

Over the years, most sales promotion and direct marketing agencies have built up a good knowledge of how certain types of sales promotion offers perform. We have databanks that have tracked responses to promotions, some of which were held over 15 years ago. Details change but distinct patterns emerge over time. These don't alter radically. Each promotional type performs in a typical way. However, it's important to be aware that circumstances will modify this performance. The response will change, for instance, if customers have to send in four labels instead of three. Or if they have to buy an additional product from the range. Or if the main communication medium for the offer is the pack, rather than press or TV.

Many other questions will present themselves as you plan. When is the best time to advertise a mail order offer on TV? Would press be a better medium? If so, where should you place your advertisement in the newspaper? As far as possible, let previous experience be your guide in determining the answers. Gut feelings are rarely accurate enough to provide the basis for major expenditure. Heeding past results is the best way to ensure you don't overspend the budget chasing responses, or select a sales promotion technique that fails to meet your sales expectations.

Time and money

So . . . why don't we test more often? Why isn't it our normal modus operandi? The lack of time and money seem to be the most quoted reasons. Yet, in many industries, some sort of test is always part of a new product's introduction.

Responses to a recent survey of financial clients were polarised between 'we don't test enough' or 'we test too much'. The inescapable reality is that testing does take time. Patience, discipline and control are mandatory to success. The temptation to cut corners or to test too many variables is ever present. Both have a high propensity for negating the results.

In broad principle, we should test:

- the product;
- the proposition;
- the price;
- the offer.

The answers will help us find our most fertile and lucrative prospects—the people who will buy most profitably from us, both in the short and long term. And they should also show us the most cost-effective media mix needed to reach them.

Getting started

The first step is to study your existing database and find out if can tell you *who* and *how.* One potentially fruitful way to start is to segment it along demographic lines—then divide it further according to the products the person has bought, their monetary value and the length of time he or she has been a customer. Not forgetting, of course, the customer's recent frequency and the last product purchased. If you have more than one product, this approach can also open up important opportunities for cross-selling.

Once you identify your prospects, you then have to decide how best to reach them. Avoid preconceived ideas here. Look to past experience for guidance, or be prepared to test ground-breaking new ideas. The aim is to establish your target group—those already inside your database and the hot prospects outside it. Then, grade them by primary and secondary status—and ensure your test samples are statistically valid. Otherwise, you can't hope for the representative roll-out you need.

Research checklist

1. *Pre-campaign research.* Use desk research, such as telephone interviews with previous list users. Collect as much information on your competitors as you can from publications and research-based organisations like the Direct Marketing Association of America or ADMA, here in Australia, or from successful case studies.
2. *Employ focus groups.* Delve deeply to uncover real traits and personal behaviour.
3. *Use telephone research.* This is a good alternative to street surveys.
4. *Does your agency have a history of responses to offer-driven advertising or sales promotion?* Can they demonstrate knowledge across all media? Have they been involved in testing—with and without media—various configurations of mail packs versus various test cells and varying offer values?
5. *Test the creative last.*
6. *Keep a record of test results.*
7. *Analyse everything*—the media, advertisement responses and the subsequent conversion to sales.

8. *Make the test simple.*
9. *Test, test and test again.*

My list can be supplemented. A recent article in the *Australian Direct Marketing Association Journal* by Ian Kennedy, founder and chairman of K & D Bond Direct in Australia, covers the subject admirably. Here are the key points.

13 of the most important points to remember when testing

1. *Only test one element at a time.* Don't muddy your results by introducing more than one thing in your test, as you will not know what elements produced which result.
2. *Don't be overwhelmed by the first response.* Plan and be prepared to handle all levels of response, otherwise you could ruin a good test programme.
3. *Wait for the responses to convert to sales so you understand the quality of your initial results.* All testing should be designed to measure sales, as this is the only true measure of return on investment. Measuring the 'back-end' of a test would include non-deliverables of mail, bad debts, returns, retention, etc.
4. *Always test one or two new things with every promotion.* You should always be trying to improve on your previous result. Especially with mailing, you can be continuously trying new approaches.
5. *Never change a successful test when you roll-out.* It's always appealing to add or change something when you've had a good result. If you want to, do it as a further test to confirm your ideas.
6. *The time of the test and roll-out is always different.* Always roll-out as soon as possible after the test—the longer you leave it, the greater the chance of other variations affecting the roll-out result.
7. *Make sure the test sample will yield between 150–200 responses for statistically meaningful results.* It's important to make a conservative estimate on response from your test to determine your sample and size. Much has been written on the science of testing. There are many formulas for calculating sample size of tests. (Refer *ADMA Journal* articles, 'Practical Direct Response Testing', by Vin Jenkins, 'Testing Times I', by Martin Williams and 'Testing Times II', by Martin Williams).

8. *Make sure the test size truly represents the whole market.* Many lists and databases (and even media) can be segmented into different groups or profiles. If this is the case you may need to test each segment separately as results may differ across the total base.
9. *When testing media, make sure the test audience represents a large portion of the whole.* A small test in local or regional media will only tell you the outcome in that area. If a major roll-out is required, you must test in a major market.
10. *Remember you are testing to achieve an effective cost per sale against the total campaign cost.* Testing can be seen as very costly, so make sure you project your roll-out figures against roll-out costs to see if the test is worth doing.
11. *Selection of 'nth' name does represent a good cross section of the universe.* If you decide to test 10% of a list or circulation, you can obtain a good sample by testing every tenth name or magazine produced.
12. *Testing is not just to establish cost per sale, but it is also an opportunity to review all the elements of the promotion or campaign.* During a test you will be able to measure and review the mechanics of the promotion, supply, printing, quality of product or service and reaction of your customer.
13. *Use research methods to follow-up and understand behaviour and attitudes of responders and non-responders.* Direct marketing communication is not just about response. It also impacts on your brand and image. Often because of its intrusive nature it can have a greater effect than traditional advertising methods. So it is important to use research (ie telephone) to determine the perception and attitudes of your target audience who responded and even more importantly those who did not respond.

    This will provide you with invaluable feedback on how you should proceed with your test.[2]

Notes

1. Irwin Lowen, quoted in *Insurance Direct Marketing*, p.224, Financial Marketing Limited, Pangbourne, Berks, UK. © Tony Martin 1988.

2. Ian Kennedy, Chairman, K & D Bond Direct, '13 of the Most Important Points to Remember when Testing', *ADMA Journal*, Spring 1993.

22
CHAPTER

Briefing Your Agency—And Evaluating Their Work

We're almost at the end of our interactive marketing odyssey. In the last 21 chapters, we've looked at just about every offer-driven sales promotion, advertising and direct marketing technique known for increasing your sales. Now comes the last—and perhaps the most important—question of all.

How can you help your sales promotion or direct marketing agency to make the best use of those techniques for you?

The answer is twofold. You have to give them the best possible brief. And you have to know how to evaluate the solution they create.

The four-point brief

A good brief bulges with crisp, concise, relevant information. It tells the agency all they need to know about your product, its market, its positioning, its competition and its benefits to the buyer. It tells the agency precisely what you want to achieve through this particular promotion. And it gives them a definite budget to work within.

To do all that, the brief should have four distinct components. The background to the product and its market situation. The campaign objective. The campaign strategy, including a clear definition of the target audience and the product benefits to be stressed. And the budget.

Let's look more closely at each.

Background: the planning cycle

A good way to give the agency solid background material is to present it under the first three headings of the well-known planning cycle. As you're probably aware, this consists of five probing questions. The first three are:

- where are we now?
- why are we there?
- where do we want to be?

Answer those three in some depth, and you'll give the agency very considerable food for thought.

The fourth question (how can we get there?) will be answered (hopefully) by the agency's response to your brief. And it's most important to answer the last one (are we getting there?) after the promotion, through sales analyses and research. Question five may not be part of your present brief, but what you learn from it could certainly influence your next one.

Meanwhile, how do we answer questions one to three?

Where are we now?

Where does the product stand in the market-place? What image does the customer have of it? Is it profitable or a loss line? Does it have problems—such as a reluctance by retailers to stock it? What opportunities for improvement exist? Considering points like those will give you a clear answer to question one. Don't rely on guesswork—commission some research if you're not sure of your facts. The greater accuracy of your brief will more than compensate for the cost.

Why are we there?

To answer this question, you need to think about things like the product's marketing history, its distribution, pricing and other factors that have affected its current market share and consumer image. Here again, you may need to use research to get a full and clear picture.

But as well as the quantitative data, you need qualitative information too. You have to communicate a *clear perception* of why the product is where it is. For instance, the trade and consumers may, rightly or wrongly, have developed a perception of it as an upmarket item. Admittedly, that could give you an opportunity to develop it as a premium line with a price to match. But it could also pose the risk that the trade would see the product's appeal as narrow, and hence restrict its distribution.

Such perceptions must be made very clear to the agency. In this hypothetical case, it would ensure they didn't suggest you give the retailers a night at the ballet—which could certainly confirm their impression that your product was for the elite, who didn't shop in their stores!

Where do we want to be?

Almost certainly, your product is not where you ideally want it to be. The consumer and trade perception of it may be wrong. Or it may simply not be fulfilling its sales potential. So now you have to decide exactly what you want the promotion to achieve. That could be more impulse sales. Greater brand loyalty. More retailers stocking the product. Enthusing the sales force. Or any of a dozen other goals.

The campaign objectives

At this point, our provision of background information has clearly blurred into the next section of the four-point brief—defining the campaign objective.

The short list above includes some typical objectives for an interactive marketing venture. As we've seen throughout the book, various types of sales promotion offers can achieve all those aims and many more. But remember—no single promotion can achieve them all at the same time. For the best results, your brief should set just one objective. This should be completely realistic, readily achievable within your budget and totally specific.

It might, for instance, be to increase your product's market penetration by 3% in the next 12 months. Or to raise sales by 5% in this quarter over last year. Or to achieve a 15% increase in shelf space in selected stores. Whatever it is, it must be expressed in quantifiable terms, and be fully understood by everyone involved.

The marketing strategy

Now we come to the core of the brief. The agency will use the information in this section to enlighten and inspire their creative teams, select the right interactive marketing technique and develop the whole campaign. To make the brief as effective as possible, the strategy section should be divided into the following segments.

Product positioning: this is a statement of how consumers perceive (or how you'd like them to perceive) your product in relation to its competitors. It identifies the target market, the frame of reference (competing products or services) and your product's point of difference (the specific benefit you want consumers to associate it with in their minds).

Kraft General Foods has suggested a framework for setting out a positioning statement. Their formula has become widely adopted. It works like this:

To (target market), Product X is the brand of (frame of reference) that (point of difference).

A filled-out example might be:

To drinkers of diet soda, Zippy is the brand of diet cola that has the fewest calories.

If you can position your product as clearly and concisely as that, you'll give your agency a head start.

Source of business: identify where any increased business will come from. New users? More purchases by existing customers? Or taking market share from a competitor?

Primary competition: list the main brands you are competing against, and their strengths and weaknesses. If they outperform your product at any point, be honest and say so.

Prime prospects: give a clear description of the target audience, in terms of demographics, attitudes, usage patterns and so on. Include the market's current views on your product, if they're known. What problems do your prospects have that your product can meet?

Primary consumer benefit: this is a crucial point. State the product's most important single benefit to the consumer. It may offer many, but here you name the most persuasive of them all.

It can be tangible or psychological. Whatever it is, it's the one that most clearly meets a compelling need of the target market. For example:

Force saves you money, because half a cup cleans as thoroughly as a whole cup of other detergents.

Secondary consumer benefits: list the other benefits the product offers. With our mythical Force detergent, these might be:

- leaves no detergent residue;
- especially effective on delicate fabrics;
- comes with built-in measuring pourer.

Support facts: give the reason why the consumer can trust the primary benefit promise. For example:

Force contains F3, a new concentrate that activates in water to deliver twice the cleaning power of leading detergent brands.

Offer: explain the offer you want to make in this promotion—which could be anything from a sweepstake to a price-off to a premium. Alternatively, ask the agency to suggest one as part of its creative proposal.

Tone of voice: the way the copy is written needs to reflect the personality of the brand or product. It might be hard-sell, laid back, light-hearted, tongue-in-cheek, friendly, enthusiastic or restrained. Make sure the agency understands the 'character' you seek to project.

Call to action: explain exactly what you want the prospect to do after he or she absorbs the message. Do you want them to order now and enclose a cheque? Call for more information? Visit a retail store? Or what? Be specific.

Mandatories: give the agency full details of everything that has to be in the communication, such as logos, slogans, guarantees, trade marks, legal or regulatory statements, positioning lines and so on. It's easier to tell them now than amend the layouts later on.

Other considerations: include details of anything else that could affect the promotion's creative development. Approaches that have worked in the past. Ideas on advertising media and response characteristics. Other factors like new packs, price freezes or reductions, minor product improvements and the like could all be relevant, too.

Budget

The last part of the brief provides the framework within which everything else has to happen. Set the budget—and indicate whether it is absolutely cast in stone or if some leeway exists for the production of an outstanding idea. If the latter, the agency may try just that little bit harder.

Putting such a detailed brief together sounds like a lot of effort? Yes, it is. But it's the only way to get outstanding work. A promotional programme can't rise above its brief any more than a river can rise above its source. If you want to make the most of all the insights in this book, your agency has to have a highly specific, exhaustive, factual, itemised brief.

And only you can give it to them.

Evaluating the result

Your next responsibility comes when the agency presents its campaign ideas to you. Are they right? Will they work? Should you approve them?

This can be one of the most difficult decisions you have to make. Many times, of course, you'll be excited by their concepts, and eager to run with them. On other occasions, you'll be doubtful. But if you trust your agency, and they give you excellent reasons why they've taken this tack, I'd always be inclined to go with them.

However, that doesn't mean you should blindly accept everything they give you. If you can put your finger on real reasons for concern, you should say so. If you're right, your contribution can only add to the campaign's effectiveness—which, after all, is the common goal you and the agency are striving for together.

Evaluating creative proposals demands long experience in offer-driven marketing, sales promotion and direct marketing. A thorough understanding of how consumers react to marketing approaches. A deep knowledge of your market. And a realistic appraisal of what your product offers them. You're not going to learn all that in the last page or two of this book. But there are certain things you can look for that are based on proven communication principles.

So as you evaluate the agency's work, ask yourselves these questions.

The campaign in general

Is there a big idea behind it? Are the visual concepts gripping and memorable? Does the copy highlight your primary consumer benefit? Does it make the benefit credible, by including the relevant facts? Are all your other consumer benefits stressed?

Do the pictures echo what the words are saying? Is the whole package consistent in its message—with the same ideas flowing logically through the letter, brochure and other items?

The outer envelope

If you're using one, does it have an intriguing 'hook'—a provocative line or promise that will compel people to open it? And does the message inside follow straight on from the outer envelope line?

The offer

Is the offer clear? Is it novel and imaginative? Is it a 'Big Idea'? Does it suit your market's lifestyle and known preferences? Does it offer real value? Is it appropriate to your product or service? Does it integrate with your chosen communications strategy?

The letter

Does the headline or introductory panel state the offer clearly and persuasively? Does the first sentence involve the reader at once? Does the opening paragraph promise a benefit?

Is the letter written in a friendly, conversational tone? Are the thoughts arranged in a logical sequence? Does the letter flow smoothly from point to point? Is what it says believable? Is it so benefit-oriented that it will hold the reader throughout?

Are the main benefits underlined or highlighted? Are the paragraphs no more than four sentences long? Do words of one syllable make up 70%–80% of the copy? Are the sentences short, crisp and meaningful? Has meaningless waffle been ruthlessly avoided?

Is the reader pointed to the response mechanism? Does the letter ask for the order? Does it tell the reader plainly how to go about placing it?

The order form

Does the order form or response mechanism increase the desire to buy? Does it repeat the offer and main product benefits? Does it explain clearly what you want the reader to do?

Does it help build your database by including a box with the option, 'I can't buy now, but keep me informed'? And a simple but often overlooked point—does it fit easily into the return envelope?

If your 'yes' score in all those categories is 100%, a statue of your agency's MD will be erected in the city square. But in times like these, you really need an 85%-plus score to ensure your promotional dollars will be well and profitably spent.

That's why briefing your agency and evaluating their work is so critically important. There's nothing magic about the ideas and techniques I've outlined in this book. They're all tried and proven. They work. They've achieved spectacular results for product after product and company after company, all over the world.

But just how well they work for you is ultimately in your hands.

Index

Entries in *italics* refer to the name of a book.
Entries in **bold** refer to an illustration.

InterActive Marketing Questionnaire

You've read the book. Now what?

This book may do you some good if you read it and mentally file the points it makes. But to get full benefit from it, you need to put its precepts into action.

That, of course, may be easier said than done. The case histories in the book might not closely match your situation. So the suggestions that flow from them could need a little tweaking before they will be totally relevant to your situation.

I would be delighted to assist with the tweaking process, and help you lift the book's guidelines from theory to profitable practice.

If you'd like to do that, please complete and return this questionnaire to me:

Martin Williams
c/– Prentice Hall of Aust Pty Ltd
7 Grosvenor Place
Brookvale NSW 2100

If you don't want to mutilate the book (which I hope will grace your bookshelf for many years to come), simply photostat this section and return the stats.

So let's get started!

Your name...

Position...

Company..

Address..

......................Postcode............ Phone............... Fax............

Your company's main product or service.....................................

Do your current promotional activities include:

❑ sales promotion ❑ direct marketing ❑ sales force motivation

❑ media advertising ❑ other................... ❑ none of the above?

If you do use any of these techniques, please briefly describe your present activities:

....

....

....

Which promotional areas would you particularly like to explore?

❑ point of sale ❑ sweepstakes ❑ character licensing ❑ cashbacks ❑ on-pack promotions

❑ premiums ❑ couponing ❑ sampling ❑ sponsorships ❑ cause-related marketing

❑ sales force incentives ❑ customer incentives and gifts ❑ relationship marketing

❑ telemarketing ❑ lead generation ❑ direct response advertising

❑ interactive media techniques ❑ database marketing

Does your company currently have a customer database?

❑ yes ❑ no

If you do have a customer database, please indicate how you use it:

❑ for selling to customers by ❑ direct mail ❑ telemarketing ❑ sales promotion offers

❑ for recording customer response to selling approaches

❑ for fundraising

❑ for relationship marketing—increasing customer loyalty and repeat sales

❑ for analysing, profiling and segmenting current customers

❑ for giving leads to dealers, salesforce and/or telemarketers

❑ for recording customer points or credits, in a gift or discount programme

❑ other..

If you don't have a customer database, are you ❑ planning to install one willing to consider the idea ❑ have no plans to do so?

How should I get back to you?

❑ phone ❑ fax ❑ mail

Thank you for returning this questionnaire. I look forward to talking with you soon.